BIBLICAL FORUM SERIES

VOLUME 1

BIBLICAL
AUTHORITY
AND
CONSERVATIVE
PERSPECTIVES

141150

D0112120

DOUGLAS MOO
General Editor

kregel
PUBLICATIONS

Grand Rapids, MI 49501

Biblical Authority and Conservative Perspectives

Copyright © 1997 by Trinity Evangelical Divinity School

Published by Kregel Publications, a division of Kregel, Inc., P.O. Box 2607, Grand Rapids, MI 49501. Kregel Publications provides trusted, biblical publications for Christian growth and service. Your comments and suggestions are valued.

Cover design: Alan G. Hartman
Book design: Nicholas G. Richardson

Library of Congress Cataloging-in-Publication Data
Moo, Douglas J.
    Biblical authority and conservative perspectives /
Douglas J. Moo, gen. ed.
        p.   cm. — (The trinity journal series)
    Articles reprinted from Trinity journal.
    Includes bibliographical references.
    1. Bible—Inspiratioin. 2. Bible—Inspiration—History
of doctrines. 3. Bible—Evidences, authority, etc.
4. Bible—Evidences, authority, etc.—History of doctrines
5. Evangelicalism. 6. Fundamentalism. I. Moo, Douglas J.
II. Trinity journal. III. Series.
BS480. B4752   1997   220.1'3—dc21   96-36837
                                                                  CIP
ISBN 0-8254-3349-5

Printed in the United States of America
1 2 3 4 5 / 01 00 99 98 97

CONTENTS

CONTRIBUTORS

Bruce Ellis Benson
Assistant Professor of Philosophy, Wheaton College, Wheaton, Illinois

Carl F. H. Henry
Visiting Professor at Trinity Evangelical Divinity School, Deerfield, Illinois

Daniel Hoffman
Assistant Professor of History, Lee College, Cleveland, Tennessee

Eugene Klug
Professor Emeritus of Systematic Theology, Concordia Theological Seminary, Fort Wayne, Indiana

J. P. Moreland
Professor of Philosophy, Talbot School of Theology at Biola University, LaMirada, California

Rodney L. Petersen
Executive Director, Boston Theological Institute

John D. Woodbridge
Professor of Church History at Trinity Evangelical Divinity School, Deerfield, Illinois

PREFACE

Many doctrines are vital to the Christian faith: Christology and soteriology, for instance, immediately come to mind. But no doctrine is more foundational than biblical authority. The Bible is our source for all doctrine. Believe the wrong thing about the Bible, and all other doctrines are, at least potentially, threatened. Evangelicals have long been known for their adherence to the full authority of the Bible. We at *Trinity Journal*, reflecting a core belief of Trinity Evangelical Divinity School, use the term *inerrancy* to describe this full authority of the Bible. By it we mean that the original writings of all the biblical books are without error in anything that they teach. We think this belief about the Bible is solidly based in the Bible itself and in Christian tradition and that it is vital to protect all other doctrines.

But scholars, even from within the evangelical movement, have challenged this view of the Bible. It was in response to this challenge that the chapters in this volume were written. These articles fall into two categories. The first, and largest, category is historical studies. The first editor of *Trinity Journal*, Don Carson, wanted to publish articles that would be strategic for the evangelical movement. He wisely decided that no more strategic issue had emerged than the question of what leading Christian theologians throughout history had thought about the authority of the Bible. A number of "revisionist" Christian historians were arguing that the view of the Bible that we are calling "inerrancy" was a relatively recent idea and that it had not been held by most theologians in church history. Carson commissioned a number of scholars to challenge this revisionist history; the fruit of their work is found in the first section of this volume.

In the second section, we have included two more contemporary chapters that also deal with the question of biblical authority. We trust that these chapters will provide solid reasons for Christians today to defend their confidence in the full authority of God's Word.

DOUGLAS J. MOO

5

ABOUT *TRINITY JOURNAL*

TRINITY JOURNAL is the faculty-sponsored journal of Trinity Evangelical Divinity School of Trinity International University in Deerfield, Illinois. Today Christian readers can choose from a flood of books, journals, and magazines, and we think that *Trinity Journal* has a special place in this flood of material. Our mission is to bring the very best of evangelical scholarship to the working pastor, missionary, and informed layperson. While much is written on what Christians believe, how Christians should act, how Christians should view social issues, etc., we believe that it is extremely important that Christians understand where these beliefs come from—the Word of God. We are not content with just tradition and majority opinion. We believe that the Word of God should be the solid basis and foundation for our beliefs, our teachings, and our very lives.

Trinity Journal's purpose is to present excellently researched and well-written scholarship that not only challenges one's thinking but also challenges one to a more holy walk with God. If we are to follow God more closely, we need to have a firm hold on His Word and a deep understanding of His will. If *Trinity Journal* is instrumental in serving God's people in this way, we will have met our purpose . . . to God be the glory.

If you would like to subscribe, please write to:

> *Trinity Journal*
> Attn: Business Manager
> 2065 Half Day Road
> Deerfield, IL 60015

HISTORICAL STUDIES

CHAPTER ONE

BIBLICAL AUTHORITY: TOWARD AN EVALUATION OF THE ROGERS AND McKIM PROPOSAL

John D. Woodbridge

In the last two decades a number of evangelical scholars have expended considerable energies on a renewed historical quest. They are seeking to ascertain the ancient attitudes of Christians toward biblical authority.[1] Their enterprise often has an apologetic and very personal impulsion. Some want to demonstrate a concordance between their own beliefs and the historical position of the church.

Most of the evangelicals involved in this quest acknowledge formally the principle of *sola Scriptura*. They agree that the Bible's self-attestation about its own authority should play the determinative role in formulating their beliefs. Nonetheless, they also understand that even if Protestants have not historically given authoritative weight to tradition, as have Roman Catholics, and Anglicans in a special way, Protestants have frequently attempted to bolster the case for their own position by appealing to the witness of Christians of past centuries. From the fathers in the early church, to Luther and other Reformers in the sixteenth century, to French Reformed pastors in the seventeenth, Christian theologians have tended to associate doctrinal innovation with heresy.[2] They have struggled with the problem of determining whether or not a development in doctrine is a healthy clarification of the biblical data or a dangerous departure from evangelical orthodoxy.[3] If a doctrine has a long history of acceptance by their church, or by "the church," Protestants along with Roman Catholics generally give it serious consideration.[4]

In a similar vein, some evangelicals believe that their own views on biblical authority will gain more credence in the evangelical community if they can demonstrate that these views have deep and sturdy roots in the rich soil of church history. Therein lies the motivation for their quest.

In *The Authority and Interpretation of the Bible: An Historical Approach* (New York: Harper and Row, 1979), Jack Rogers of Fuller Theological Seminary and Donald McKim, a United Presbyterian minister, challenge several well-entrenched beliefs among American evangelicals. Evangelicals have commonly assumed that the biblical writers, inspired by God the Holy Spirit, wrote infallibly. Their contention is usually based on the internal claims of the writers that what they had written came from God. It is also founded on an *a priori* premise: God cannot lie. His Word, therefore, contains no admixture of error. Evangelicals have generally affirmed that this perspective represents the

9

"historic" position of the church. Moreover evangelicals have consistently asserted that their stance reflects Christ's teaching about the Bible's authority.[5] Rogers and McKim want to disabuse evangelicals of these beliefs. One of their goals, therefore, is iconoclastic.

Another one of the authors' goals is more missionary minded. Rogers and McKim seek to persuade evangelicals of the validity of their own interpretation of the Bible's self-attestation. In this regard they argue that the biblical authors wrote infallibly on matters of faith and practice, but that they could and did err on occasion in their statements that touched upon scientific, geographical, and historical matters, as judged by modern standards of measurement. Rogers and McKim propose that it is their own analysis that reflects the authentic "historic" position of the church. They want their readers to join with them in affirming what they believe to be orthodox Reformed teaching concerning biblical authority.

Professors Rogers and McKim should be commended for their willingness to interact with many primary and secondary sources not commonly cited in previous evangelical studies on this subject. They have read widely and they adorn their argumentation with copious content footnotes. Moreover their writing style is clear and lively. Readers usually encounter little difficulty in understanding what the authors intend to say by their proposals.

The authors should also be commended for their openness to criticism of their work. In the preface to their volume, Rogers and McKim volunteer that they welcome responses and critiques.[6] In that spirit we trust that our own assessment of their interpretation will be instructive and thereby contribute to the ongoing discussion of biblical authority by evangelicals.

Indeed, analysis should proceed concerning this subject. Competent studies are quite lacking concerning large tracts of the history of biblical authority. Jacques Le Brun, Professor of Catholic History, Hautes Études (Paris), and an expert in the field, has commented about the multiple gaps in our knowledge for the seventeenth century alone.[7] Several serious studies are underway.[8] Nonetheless, a "definitive" survey of the matter seems as elusive as ever. Much of the available literature on the subject is badly dated, conceptually flawed, and thus susceptible to serious revision.[9] Evangelical scholars need to contribute technically reliable essays in this field.[10]

In our review we will first describe the central proposal that Professors Rogers and McKim set forth. Second, we will consider several methodological problems associated with their presentation and documentation. We are much interested in how Rogers and McKim do history. Third, we will propose several specific criticisms of their proposal. Our criticisms will be forthright. They are, however, designed to advance the discussion and not to inflame it. Our comments hopefully will alert the scholarly community and laypersons to several weaknesses in the approach of Rogers and McKim to writing the history of biblical authority. Our comments should also underscore some of the strengths of their proposal.

I. THE ROGERS AND McKIM PROPOSAL

For Rogers and McKim, the concept of accommodation is pivotal for any understanding of biblical authority. God accommodated Himself to our human weakness and limited capacity for understanding by communicating His thoughts to us through human words. The central purpose of God's written communication is to reveal salvation truth about Christ. God did not intend that the Scriptures should be read for technically correct information about the world. Indeed, the Hebrew authors of Scripture (for example) thought in word pictures. They did not reflect upon truth with the same categories of Western logic which are so familiar to us.[11] Consequently what we consider to be the small errors committed by the Bible's human authors do not detract from biblical authority, for the Bible's authority is not associated with its form or words but with Christ and His salvation message to which the words point.

How do we know that the Bible is God's Word? In a mysterious way the Holy Spirit witnesses to the believer that the Bible is the Word of God. Rational deductions based on external evidences for the Bible's inspiration play only a secondary if not minimal role in this process; for faith comes before reason in our apperception of biblical authority.

Rogers and McKim argue that scholars with a Platonic bent, ranging from Origen and Augustine in patristic times to Luther and Calvin in Reformation days, maintained this biblical perspective on the Scriptures. However, the seventeenth century witnessed the departure by many Protestants from this stance. Borrowing from the Aristotelian categories of their Roman Catholic opponents, a good number of Protestant theologians forged a theory of biblical authority founded more on the words of Scripture (the mere form) rather than upon Christ in the Scripture. In their rationalistic attempt to fend off Catholic apologists, these Protestants extended the concept of "infallibility" to include all the words of the biblical text. Especially among Reformed thinkers the Swiss theologian Francis Turretin (1632–1687) innovated in this regard. In the nineteenth century, Princeton Seminary professors Archibald Alexander and Charles Hodge advocated Turretin's viewpoint on Scripture in the United States. In the 1880s, the Princetonians, A. A. Hodge and B. B. Warfield, propounded the thesis that only the original autographs of the Bible are inerrant. The Princetonians were obliged to retreat to this novel ideal of inerrancy in the lost autographs because the impact of biblical criticism and certain developmental theories in science could no longer be ignored. Relying heavily upon Professor Ernest Sandeen's discussion of the Princetonians, Rogers and McKim refer to the Princetonians' position as one of Protestant scholasticism nourished philosophically by Common Sense Realism. They suggest, as does Sandeen, that the Princeton rationalistic theology shaped fundamentalism's perspectives on Scripture and ultimately those of today's conservative evangelicals.

For present-day evangelicals to recover a truly Reformed viewpoint on the Scriptures, Rogers and McKim urge them to return to the teachings about Scriptures proposed by the Westminster Confession, Calvin and Luther, and various church fathers (especially St. Augustine). They should understand that their own beliefs about biblical inerrancy are innovative and do not accord with the church's teaching. Rather they should teach that the Bible is the only infallible rule of faith and practice. Its purpose is to teach Christ and the good news about our salvation and not to present infallible data about aspects of human history, geography, science, and the like. If conservative evangelicals (and particularly a United Presbyterian readership) adopt Rogers and McKim's position, they will be able to interact more serenely with biblical criticism and modern developmental theories in science, while at the same time safeguarding a high view of biblical authority.

This, in brief, is the thrust of Rogers and McKim's argument. It is a carefully construed apologetic, attractively packaged, and apparently well documented. Much indebted to the thinking of the later Berkouwer, this apologetic is designed to justify a particular stance on Scripture from a historical point of view.

II. GENERAL CONSIDERATIONS

Before we begin our critique of several specific issues related to this apologetic, we may be well served to broach several of the larger methodological problems which affect our assessment of the book.

A. The Overly Generous Title of the Volume

A nagging discrepancy exists between the authors' title, *The Authority and Interpretation of the Bible: An Historical Approach*, and the authors' announced purpose for their book: "The intent of this study is to describe the central church tradition regarding the authority and interpretation of the Bible, especially as it has influenced the Reformed tradition of theology" (Introduction, xxiii). The broad title suggests that the book encompasses a calm and careful treatment of attitudes toward the Bible by Christians of diverse communions. The real focus of the volume is more parochial. The authors want to justify their own viewpoint on Scripture as opposed to those viewpoints that they associate with the Princeton theologians of the nineteenth century and conservative evangelicals in the twentieth.[12] They presume that the "historic position" of the church feeds into their own particular beliefs. Readers from Anabaptistic, Lutheran, Wesleyan, Roman Catholic, and Eastern Orthodox backgrounds, therefore, may find the book's title curiously misleading and presumptuous, because its expected coverage of their own histories is deficient, if not nonexistent.

B. The Apologetic Cast of the Study

The apologetic variety of history which Rogers and McKim write will make some professional historians wince. Within recent decades many church historians have attempted to salvage a modicum of objectivity for their discipline by forsaking personal briefs for their own communions. Obviously all historians write with their own biases discreetly, or not so discreetly, displayed. Because Rogers and McKim boldly announce that their goal is apologetic, professional historians, particularly European ones, may surmise that the authors' study is a throwback to past centuries of religious controversy.[13] Theoretically speaking, there is no reason why an apologetic historical piece should necessarily encompass bad historical scholarship.[14] But as we shall see, Rogers and McKim's apologetic goal on occasion overwhelms their commitment to an evenhanded treatment of the available historical sources. They have a penchant for not citing primary evidence that counters their hypothesis and for minimizing the value of scholarly works which decisively countermand their conclusions.

C. The Arbitrary Selection of Data

Rogers and McKim fail to explain to their readers how they determine who are the faithful representatives of the "central church tradition" on biblical authority. Complex though this issue may be, it is a critically important one for them if their readers are to take their pretentions with any seriousness.[15] Some historians may judge that the arbitrary character of the authors' selections constitutes a fatal wound for the study. We will note how this important methodological oversight jeopardizes the value of the authors' findings.

D. The Doubtful Documentation

Upon first glance, the footnotes which Rogers and McKim have assembled to support their contentions appear quite impressive. And yet a careful appraisal of what the footnotes actually signify reveals that they are less reliable than we might first suppose. Rogers and McKim frequently did not take great pains in their citation of sources. Unfortunately, they often trusted secondary sources too fully or misread them. On other occasions, they did not interpret primary source documents correctly. Readers should examine both their footnotes and citation of sources with a critical eye.

E. The Limiting Optic of the Authors' Concerns

Due to the fact that Rogers and McKim are so intent to prove that their own idea of limited biblical infallibility is the "historic position of the Church," the authors frequently give short shrift to the full-orbed meaning of their volume's theme: biblical authority. What "biblical authority" meant for the fathers becomes only evident in the context of what the same fathers thought about "Tradition," Christian experience, and church authority. Rogers and McKim largely bypass these concerns. The full significance of "biblical authority" for seventeenth-century Calvinists becomes only apparent when their philosophical presuppositions are carefully laid bare. Rogers and McKim do attempt to sort out some of these philosophical presuppositions, but their own categories of analysis are rigid and lack nuance (reason versus faith, Aristotelian versus Platonic, and so forth). These juxtapositions do not lend themselves to capturing the complex philosophical currents which swirled through Reformed circles during the seventeenth century. Some Dutch theologians, for example, joined Ramist and Aristotelian principles in their own thought.[16] This is an intellectual linkage which Rogers and McKim's categories of analysis cannot countenance. In fact, Rogers and McKim assume incorrectly that Ramist logic was diametrically opposed to Aristotelian categories.

F. The Propensity for Facile Labeling

As we have already noted, Rogers and McKim are given to speaking about the "historic position of the church." Another one of their habitual expressions is "scholastic," a term that both they and Professor Brian Armstrong acknowledge is difficult to define.[17] Nonetheless Aquinas, most continental Calvinist and Lutheran theologians of the seventeenth century, the nineteenth-century Princetonians, and twentieth-century conservative evangelicals are all dubbed "scholastic." Professional historians know the danger of using this expression and other ones like it (Pietist, Romantic, Enlightenment figure, Renaissance man).[18] The labels have all the trappings of "false concreteness." Rogers and McKim's consistent use of labels harks back to an outmoded method of doing intellectual history by which historians grouped individuals from different ages together without much regard for the different cultural contexts in which their subjects lived. Labeling is often a short cut for doing careful historical research. A label does not greatly aid us to understand the richness of an individual's theology, its evolution or devolution in time, or its meaning when placed against the social, intellectual, and cultural tapestry of a particular age.

G. The Inappropriate "Historical Disjunctions"

In logic, a disjunction is a proposition in which two (or more) alternatives are asserted, only one of which can be true. In their study Rogers and McKim work with a whole series of what we might coin "historical disjunctions." They assume that certain correct assertions about an individual's thought logically disallow other ones from being true.[19] Their assumption is sometimes accurate, if the thoughts being compared directly contradict each other.[20] However, in their historical disjunctions the authors create disjunctions between propositions that are not mutually exclusive. They engage in an empty form of deductive historical speculation that assumes much without sufficient proof.

A partial listing of the authors' more important historical disjunctions would include these: because a thinker believes the central purpose of Scripture is to reveal salvation history, it is assumed that he or she does not endorse complete biblical infallibility; because a thinker speaks of God accommodating Himself to us in the words of Scripture, it is assumed that he or she does not believe in complete biblical infallibility; because a thinker indicates that the Bible is the infallible rule of faith and practice, it is assumed that he or she does not believe in complete biblical infallibility; because a thinker engages in the critical study of biblical texts, it is assumed that he or she does not uphold complete biblical infallibility; because a Christian with Platonist leanings believes that reality consists of forms or ideals, it is assumed that he or she does not think that biblical revelation can be perfect even though God the Holy Spirit is its primary author;[21] because a thinker emphasizes the Christic content of Scripture, it is assumed that he or she does not also believe in complete biblical infallibility; because a thinker stresses the fact that the authority of the Scriptures is made known to an individual through the internal witness of the Holy Spirit, it is assumed that he or she does not also believe in complete biblical infallibility. Fostering a kind of history based upon deductions, these historical disjunctions cut the nerve of historical research. Only careful, open-minded historical investigation can perhaps reveal if a person adheres to limited or complete biblical infallibility. Unfortunately, historical disjunctions play too determinative a role in Rogers and McKim's analysis. Once the authors have posited a premise, they sometimes fail to demonstrate the historical accuracy of their conclusions based on the premise.

H. The Dated Models of Conceptualization

Rogers and McKim do not give much evidence of an acquaintance with recent developments in what Peter Gay of Yale University has called the social history of ideas.[22] For many decades some intellectual historians assumed that they had captured the beliefs of a movement by explicating what its founder, or its principal spokesmen, or its creeds affirmed. Rogers and McKim do the same. This form of elitist history is based on a misleading extrapolation. An example of it goes something like this: if Luther thought A, Lutherans think A. Today, scholars are much more sensitive to the disparities of belief and practice that commonly exist among clergy and laypersons from the same communion even within fifty miles of each other. European scholars like Emmanual Le Roy Ladurie have written brilliant essays in which they have examined the particularities of a religious community in a narrowly circumscribed geographical locale.[23] The bevy of books on "popular religion" has also revealed remarkable variations of religious belief and practice even in countries with a state religion.[24] Moreover, a good number of scholars have a growing appreciation for the difficulties that exist in adequately describing one person's thought. They understand the complexity of tracing their subject's changing opinions in time. To do this, they must study the individual's correspondence, printed works, and unpublished manuscripts. Moreover, they are obliged to take stock of the individual's thought with the categories of his or her age. A smaller group of historians who are experts in the book trade (Robert Darnton of Princeton University, Henri-Jean Martin of Hautes Etudes [Paris], Raymond Birn of the University of Oregon) have challenged the old-fashioned "influence histories" from another direction.[25] They want to establish roughly how many books of a given author were published, who bought or borrowed these books, and who read them, before these scholars are prepared to pronounce upon the author's influence through the printed word. Their studies are presently transforming historians' perceptions of the relative popularity of authors in a given age. Unfortunately, Rogers and McKim's awareness of these helpful new methods and models of conceptualization appears limited. As a result, their study is surprisingly dated. Writing good history is a far more difficult task than the authors imagine.[26]

I. The Bibliographical Insensitivity

Rogers and McKim demonstrate a peculiar insensitivity to the problem of doing balanced bibliographical work. In their "Selected Bibliography" concerning the Reformation (145–46), for example, they list many works supporting their interpretation. An unapprised reader would not generally surmise from this bibliography that a scholarly literature exists that challenges many of the conclusions of the authors' chosen volumes. Kenneth Kantzer's important Harvard dissertation on Calvin's theory of knowledge, for example, is strangely absent. In the footnotes the authors do interact with this other literature but sometimes at a very superficial level. The authors' insensitivity to the slanted character of their bibliographical formulations tends to subvert attempts to achieve a balanced scholarship.

Alerted to these general methodological problems, we turn to our third section where we will suggest several specific criticisms of the Rogers and McKim proposal. Due to our reluctance to comment about fields of scholarship where our own expertise is limited, our task will be a modest one. We will restrict ourselves to an assessment of several select points in their argument. Nonetheless, this third section should provide some correctives to the Rogers and McKim proposal as it relates to biblical infallibility, which is one of their foremost concerns. It should also furnish pointers to the worlds of scholarly literature which Rogers and McKim were obliged to glide by in their whirlwind passage through two thousand years of Christian thinking about the Bible. And finally, it may prompt other scholars to launch carefully delimited and technically competent studies to supplement and to revise Rogers and McKim's interpretation. For as we shall see, even our cursory study reveals that it is built upon shaky pillars.

III. SPECIFIC CONSIDERATIONS

A. The Patristic Period

Beginning church-history students learn rapidly that expressions such as the church "taught" or the church "believed" are awkward ones, especially as applied to the first four centuries. Our sources of information are painfully sparse for various Christian communities throughout the Roman world. We know little about the lives of certain men and women who followed Christ in many towns and villages scattered around the Mediterranean basin.[27] Moreover, Christians disputed with each other. Various schools of thought existed among sincere believers concerning wide-ranging theological issues.[28] And yet common traits of agreement did apparently exist among many Christians concerning biblical infallibility. Based on a survey of the extant patristic literature that bears on the subject, we know that the Fathers apparently concurred that God is the primary author of Holy Scripture.[29] They did, however, debate the way God used human authors as His instruments in the writing of the inscripturated Word. Moreover, it is fair to say the fathers generally assumed that because God is the author of truth, His Word cannot mislead or deceive in any way (whether in salvation truth, or in historical, "scientific," or geographical detail).

Professor Bruce Vawter, whose authority Rogers and McKim repeatedly invoke, frankly acknowledges the Fathers' commitment to complete biblical infallibility:

> It would be pointless to call into question that biblical inerrancy in a rather absolute form was a common persuasion from the beginning of Christian times, and from Jewish times before that. For both the Fathers and the rabbis generally, the ascription of any error to the Bible was unthinkable; . . . if the word was God's it must be true, regardless of whether it made known a mystery of divine revelation or commented on a datum of natural science, whether it derived from human observation or chronicled an event of history.[30]

Vawter's analysis appears well founded. Clement of Rome's *First Letter to the Church at Corinth* (first century) lends some support to it:

> You have studied Scripture [O.T.] which contains the truth and is inspired by the Holy Spirit. You realize that there is nothing wrong or misleading in it.[31]

In his *Dialogue with Trypho* (second century), Justin Martyr, an apologist with Platonic leanings, is more specific:

> ... but if (you have done so) because you imagined that you could throw doubt on the passage, in order that I might say the Scriptures contradicted each other, you have erred. But I shall not venture to suppose or to say such a thing; and if a Scripture which appears to be of such a kind be brought forward, and if there be a pretext (for saying) that it is contrary (to some other), since I am entirely convinced that no Scripture contradicts another I shall admit rather that I do not understand what is recorded and shall strive to persuade those who imagine that the Scriptures are contradictory, to be rather of the same opinion as myself.[32]

The great Irenaeus (second century) commented about the truthfulness of Luke's reporting:

> Now if any man set Luke aside, as one who did not know the truth, he will (by so acting), manifestly reject that Gospel of which he claims to be a disciple. It follows then, as of course, that these men must either receive the rest of his narrative, or else reject these parts also. For no person of common sense can permit them to receive some things recounted by Luke as being true, and to set others aside, as if he had not known the truth.[33]

These kind of statements and others like them should be carefully studied in their contexts. When this is accomplished, their meaning is quite clear.

Nonetheless, Rogers and McKim propound the thesis that the church fathers did not hold to complete biblical infallibility. How do they attempt to establish this perspective in the face of much evidence to the contrary and against the verdict of notable scholars such as Vawter and others, who argue that most of the church fathers did?[34] On the one hand, authors Rogers and McKim simply did not allude to Clement of Rome, Justin Martyr, Irenaeus, or other church fathers who make statements which counter their hypothesis. On the other hand, they suggest that the writings of Clement of Alexandria, Origen, Chrysostom, and Augustine support their contentions. Professor David Wells points out that the first three authors were Greek and the "fourth dallied with Greek philosophy."[35] Thus Rogers and McKim largely ignored the Roman, legal, and Western tradition among the Fathers. Their selection, therefore, is constricted and not felicitous.

Be that as it may, let us review very briefly segments of the argumentation Rogers and McKim propose for their interpretation of Origen and St. Augustine. Rogers and McKim base much of their case on the principle that God accommodated Himself to our weakness and frailty by communicating to us through the human words of Scripture. They cite an important passage of Origen (12):

> He condescends and lowers himself, accommodating himself to our weakness, like a schoolmaster talking a "little language" to his children, like a father caring for his own children and adopting their ways.

Because Origen knew that the words of Scripture were the result of God's accommodating activity, Origen "acknowledged that the New Testament evangelists and Paul expressed their own opinions, and that they could have erred when speaking on their own authority" (11).

The content of Rogers and McKim's judgment about Origen's recognition of errancy is based principally on page 26 of Bruce Vawter's *Biblical Inspiration*.[36] It is intriguing to note, however, that the authors do not cite Vawter's continuing discussion on page 27. After indicating that on occasion Origen wrote as if he did not believe in inerrancy when making a pragmatic response to an exegetical or apologetic difficulty, Vawter declares:

> It seems to be clear enough that, in company with most of the other Christian commentators of the age, he most often acted on the unexpressed assumption that the Scripture is a divine composition through and through, and for this reason infallibly true in all its parts. He could say, in fact, that the Biblical texts were not the words of men but of the Holy Spirit (*De princ.* 4.9, PG 11:360), and that from this it followed that they were filled with the wisdom and truth of God down to the very least letter.

Rogers and McKim's selective use of Vawter's scholarship is quite disappointing.

In reality, as Vawter proposes, a good case can be made for Origen the inerrantist. Origen's recognition of the principle of accommodation has no essential bearing on the subject. The principle of accommodation carries with it no logical concomitant to an errant biblical text.[37] It does not follow from the principle that God misleads us in any detail in the Scriptures because He speaks to us through human words. A father does not necessarily mislead a child because the father uses simple language that the child can grasp. A father, particularly an omnipotent and omniscient One, can speak truly though simply.

It is correct to observe that Origen, a sensitive moralist, engaged in allegorical interpretations of the Scriptures to help him smooth out the rough edges of what he thought were rather unsavory historical incidents in Holy Writ. But little evidence exists that he believed the incidents had no grounding in historical reality. In *Contra Celsum*, the Alexandrian argued point by point with Celsus, who had evidently scorned the historical reliability of many biblical accounts.[38]

Whether or not Origen was an inerrantist, albeit inconsistent on occasion in practice, is ultimately not our concern at this juncture. Open-minded scholars have differed about the matter. What concerns us more is the disconcerting discovery that Rogers and McKim do not interact evenhandedly with their documentation in sorting out Origen's attitudes on the question.

The manner in which Rogers and McKim treat St. Augustine is also instructive concerning how they do history. Upon a *prima facie* reading of several of St. Augustine's comments, we would conclude that the influential Latin believed in a complete biblical infallibility:

> It seems to me that the most disastrous consequences must follow upon our believing that anything false is found in the sacred books. . . . If you once admit

into such a high actuary or authority one false statement, there will not be left a single statement of these books.[39]

Again, he declared:

The authority of the Divine Scriptures becomes unsettled . . . if it be once admitted, that the men by whom these things have been delivered unto us, could in their writings state some things which were not true.[40]

Augustine also noted:

I have learned to yield with respect and honor only to the canonical books of Scripture: of these alone do I most firmly believe that the authors were completely free from error.[41]

Or elsewhere, Augustine wrote: "Therefore everything written in Scripture must be believed absolutely."[42] With this type of statement in mind, Professor A. D. R. Polman—whose book, *Word of God According to St. Augustine*, Rogers and McKim repeatedly cite—observes that for St. Augustine, "not even the universal council of the Church is infallible, for infallibility is the exclusive prerogative of Holy Writ."[43] And he states: "He [St. Augustine] thought it inconceivable that the Holy Spirit, the real author of Holy Scripture, should have contradicted Himself."[44]

In attempting to neutralize the import of St. Augustine's statements, which apparently teach that the Bishop of Hippo held to complete biblical infallibility, Rogers and McKim proffer this explanation (31):

Error, for Augustine, had to do with the deliberate and deceitful telling of that which the author knew to be untrue. It was in that context of ethical seriousness that he declared that the biblical authors were "completely free from error." He did not apply the concept of error to problems that arose from the human limitations of knowledge, various perspectives in reporting events, or historical or cultural conditioning of the authors.

Thus the biblical authors may have made inadvertent errors due to their limited understanding.[45]

On the contrary, St. Augustine explicitly indicated that the biblical writers knew truths about the world that they did not reveal in Holy Writ. Concerning the heavens, he wrote:

People often ask what Scripture has to say of the shape of the heavens. . . . Although our authors knew the truth about the shape of the heavens, the Spirit of God who spoke by them did not intend to teach these things, in no way profitable for salvation.[46]

For Augustine, the biblical writers did not write a scientific textbook. But when they made incidental comments about the world, they wrote infallibly and were not bound by "human limitations of knowledge" as Rogers and McKim allege.

The authors try to demonstrate that St. Augustine did not believe the Bible was infallible in matters of science, geography, and history. They cite a passage where they believe St. Augustine warned Christians "not to take their 'science'" from the Bible (26–27):

> Many non-Christians happen to be well-versed in knowledge of the earth, the heaven, of all the other elements of the world. . . . It is therefore deplorable that Christians, even though they *ostensibly* [italics mine] base their dicta on the Bible, should utter so much nonsense that they expose themselves to ridicule. While ridicule is all they deserve, they also give the impression that the Biblical authors are responsible for their mutterings, thus discrediting Christianity before the world, which is led to assume that the authors of the Scriptures were ignorant fools also. Whenever any Christian is confounded and shown to be an idle chatterer, his chatter is attributed to our Holy Books. . . .

By referring to this statement, Rogers and McKim imply that St. Augustine believed the Bible to be unreliable in scientific matters. But that is not the gist of St. Augustine's remark. He was warning poorly trained Christians who *ostensibly* base their discussions on the Bible to cease from their speculations. They were engaged in a form of chattering not biblically derived. Rogers and McKim, who borrow this quotation from Polman, fail to take note of Polman's introductory commentary on the citation:

> St. Augustine remembered vividly how many telling blows he himself had delivered during his Manichean days, against those Christians who lacking thorough instruction yet tried to defend their faith with all their might. Hence he warned the pious not to try to cover up their ignorance of fact by discussing scientific questions with an easy appeal to Scriptures.[47]

As Polman indicates, St. Augustine was arguing that the interpretations of poorly instructed Christians might be in error. He was not indicating that the Bible itself erred in its incidental teachings about the natural world.[48] Polman puts the matter this way: "Whenever, therefore, the nature of things is discovered by reliable investigation, these discoveries will always be capable of being reconciled with the Scripture."[49]

In addition, Rogers and McKim insist that St. Augustine's commitment to the principle of accommodation permitted him to be little concerned with variant readings in the biblical text (29–30):

> Augustine could take account of all the human techniques used by the writers of Scripture while affirming the divine truth of what they said. Variant readings concerning the same event were not an ultimate problem for Augustine because he saw them as the work of the Holy Spirit who permitted this pluriformity of perspectives in order to whet people's spiritual appetites for understanding

Rogers and McKim document this last statement by alluding once again to Bruce Vawter's *Biblical Authority* (38–39).[50] But their analysis does not faithfully represent Vawter's viewpoint. Vawter indicates that St. Augustine believed that on rare occasions the Holy Spirit "permitted" a biblical writer to pen what was "in apparent variance with other Scripture." But St. Augustine was embarrassed by what appeared to be a transgression of his formal principle of "no discordance in the sacred word" (38). Contrary to the impression Rogers and McKim give of his thought, Vawter writes:

> For Augustine and the Fathers in general all the "difficulties" of Scripture—and these included, besides the *cruces* of exegesis that have remained difficulties for their successors, the numerous instances where they felt the need to harmonize variant passages, to bring the Bible into accord with natural science, profane history etc. . . .—were first of all divinely intended, meant to stimulate the spiritual appetite. . . .[51]

From Vawter's perspective, Augustine and the Fathers were quite intent to harmonize the biblical data with history, natural science, and the like.

St. Augustine's commitment to harmonization and inerrancy influenced many Christian theologians during the Middle Ages. Hans Küng, himself no friendly partisan of biblical inerrancy, describes St. Augustine's impact in these terms:

> . . . it was above all St. Augustine who, under the influence of Hellenist theories of inspiration, regarded man as merely the instrument of the Holy Spirit; the Spirit alone decided the content and form of the biblical writings, with the result that the whole Bible was free of contradictions, mistakes, and errors, or had to be kept free by harmonizing, allegorizing, or mysticizing. St. Augustine's influence in regard to inspiration and inerrancy prevailed throughout the Middle Ages and right into the modern age.[52]

Küng founds this judgment on the research of the scholar H. Sasse.[53] It accords with the perspective of St. Augustine by scholars ranging from Richard Simon (1638–1712), one of the first modern biblical critics, to Polman and many other contemporary scholars of St. Augustine.

Rogers and McKim misread their secondary sources once again when they treat the thought of pre-Reformer John Wycliffe (74–75). They write:

> Wycliffe declared: "The Bible is therefore the only source of doctrine that will insure the health of the Church and the salvation of the faithful." With this understanding that the purpose of Scripture was salvation and guidance for the life of faith, Wycliffe could say "any part of Holy Scripture is true according to the excellence of the Divine Word."

This judgment is based essentially on William Mallard's article, "John Wycliffe and the Tradition of Biblical Authority," *Church History* 30 (1961): 50–51. In reality, the first quotation which they attribute to Wycliffe was made by the author Mallard (51). Moreover, just below it, Mallard wrote:

> He [Wycliffe] is thoroughly scornful of theologians who slight Holy Scripture.

> If any such persons find contradictions or errors in the Bible, their own igno-
> rance is at fault rather than the sacred text.

Then, on the next page of his essay (52), Mallard outlined what the scope of biblical authority included for Wycliffe:

> According to the most learned doctors of the tradition, Holy Scripture contained not only all Christian doctrine, but all truth generally. It was a "divine encyclopedia," a *summa* of the Wisdom of God. The Bible included mathematics, philosophy, and natural history. Although the core of Scripture could be grasped by the simplest peasant, the most learned scholar could use all his knowledge in penetrating the hidden truths. Wycliffe supported the idea of the "divine encyclopedia."

Wycliffe's use of allegory in interpretation was based on his presupposition that the words of Scripture were utterly reliable.[54] Rogers and McKim's suggestion that Wycliffe limited infallibility to salvation truths is simply unfounded, as judged by their own principal secondary source.

In our brief discussion of Rogers and McKim's handling of the church fathers and Wycliffe, we have noticed serious weaknesses in the way they manage documentation and exploit it. We could cite further illustrations of these weaknesses; but we turn now to discuss their important interpretation of Reformation attitudes toward biblical authority.

B. The Reformation

For Rogers and McKim, the testimonies of Luther and Calvin about biblical authority are critical for their interpretation: what Luther, Calvin, and to a lesser extent Zwingli believed constitutes a standard of Reformation ortho-doxy. If we would be the theological children of the Reformation, our perspectives about biblical authority should concur with those of these Reformers. The authors strangely omit any sampling from the thought of representatives of the Anabaptist movement.[55]

Rogers and McKim give a competent analysis of Luther's and Calvin's stress upon the Bible's essential function of revealing salvation truths. They correctly emphasize the role of Christ, the incarnated Word of God, in establishing the authority of the written Word, the Bible. They also understand that for Luther and Calvin doing theology should bear practical fruit in the Christian's life. Evangelical readers can benefit from these insights.

Influenced significantly by a neo-orthodox historiography, Rogers and McKim are less successful in creating an overall paradigm with which to understand the Reformers' thought. Their commitment to several of the histori-cal disjunctions to which we referred earlier throws their basic interpretation askew. Rogers and McKim assume almost mechanically that Luther and Calvin did not believe in complete biblical infallibility because they acknowledged the principle of accommodation, because they indicated that the Bible's chief func-tion is to reveal salvation truths, and because they engaged in forms of biblical criticism. Due to these assumptions about Luther and Calvin, the authors cannot adequately account for those many statements where Luther and Calvin affirm a commitment to complete biblical infallibility. The authors' either/or historical disjunctions do not easily mesh with the reality of Luther's and Calvin's both/and categories. Thus Rogers and McKim are obliged to redefine the Reformers' use of words like *error* and *infallible*.

1. The Missing Reformation Paradigm in the Rogers and McKim Proposal

When the former papists, Martin Luther and John Calvin, broke away from the Roman Catholic Church, they refused henceforth to accept the ultimate authority of councils, papal pronouncements, church traditions, and diverse ecclesiastical dicta. They would submit themselves uniquely to the authority of Holy Scripture (*sola Scriptura*).

The Reformers' emphasis upon the authority of the Bible involved no simplistic substitution of the authority of a paper pope for that of a sumptuously garbed Renaissance bishop of Rome.[56] They acknowledged a decree of a council or a tradition of the church if each had scriptural warrant. Roman Catholics shared a general commitment to biblical authority with the Reformers. And yet several differences did divide the two parties on this point. Luther and Calvin associated the essential authority of the words of Scripture with the incarnated Word, Christ. They emphasized the witness of the Holy Spirit in confirming the Bible's authority for the believer. Stressing the principle that Scripture should interpret Scripture, they affirmed that the Bible is a sufficient rule for determining faith and practice. Roman Catholics tended to emphasize the church's role in validating biblical authority. They maintained that other church authorities (papal pronouncements, tradition) should also be used in making judgments about faith and practice and in interpreting the Bible.[57]

Not only did Calvin and Luther declare that the Bible alone is their authority but they also claimed that Holy Writ is infallible. At this point Roman Catholics generally agreed with Protestants. In his debate with Luther on the subject of free will, Erasmus, a humanist who remained within the Roman Catholic camp, explained the common grounds which both he and Luther shared:

> The Holy Spirit cannot contradict himself. The canonical books of Holy Scripture originated under his inspiration. Their inviolable sublimity is acknowledged and affirmed in the dispute. Therefore one must find an interpretation which resolves the seeming contradiction.[58]

At least in principle, Erasmus followed the traditional premise that God does not contradict Himself in His Word. As a result, Erasmus argued that the differences in opinion between Luther and himself proceeded from the fact that one of them had formulated a mistaken interpretation of the text. Neither viewed the text itself as at fault. Erasmus believed that Luther erred in his interpretation because he relied on his own private judgment in determining an interpretation of the text. The sage from Rotterdam claimed that church teaching had helped him to arrive at a proper interpretation.[59]

Some genuine doubts exist as to the humanist Erasmus's own commitment to biblical infallibility.[60] But his perception of the paradigm out of which the Reformers debated Roman Catholics is sound. In the sixteenth century, Protestants and Roman Catholics did battle over principles of interpretations, both parties generally assuming that the Bible was completely infallible.

2. Luther and Biblical Infallibility

For Luther, no inconsistency existed between affirming that the Bible communicates the good news of salvation and holding the belief that the Bible is completely infallible. Nor did he distinguish between the Bible's infallibility for matters of faith and practice and its supposed capacity to err in historical, geographical, and scientific matters:

> It is impossible that Scripture should contradict itself; it only appears so to senseless and obstinate hypocrites.[61]
>
> But everyone, indeed, knows that at times they [the Fathers] have erred as men will; therefore I am ready to trust them only when they prove their opinions from Scripture, which has never erred.[62]
>
> Whoever is so bold that he ventures to accuse God of fraud and deception in a single word and does so willfully again and again after he has been warned and instructed once or twice will likewise certainly venture to accuse God of fraud and deception in all of His words. Therefore it is true, absolutely and without exception, that everything is believed or nothing is believed. The Holy Spirit does not suffer Himself to be separated or divided so that He should teach and cause to be believed one doctrine rightly and another falsely.[63]
>
> It is certain that Scripture cannot disagree with itself.[64]

The distinguished German scholar Paul Althaus gives this apt summary of Luther's statements about biblical infallibility:

> We may trust unconditionally only in the Word of God and not on the teaching of the fathers; for the teachers of the church can err and have erred. Scripture never errs. Therefore it alone has unconditional authority.[65]

Nor did Luther think it odd to search for the meaning of biblical passages in what they tell us about Christ (John 5:39) while at the same time recognizing the authority of the words of Scripture:

> One letter, even a single tittle of Scripture means more to us than heaven and earth. Therefore we cannot permit even the most minute change.[66]

Or elsewhere:

> Consequently, we must remain content with them, and cling to them [words], as the perfectly clear, certain, sure words of God, which can never deceive or allow us to err.[67]

Martin Luther's commitment to the verbal plenary inspiration and biblical infallibility of the Scriptures appears clearly documented in these statements and other ones like them.

Rogers and McKim view Luther's perspective on biblical infallibility otherwise. They write that Luther did not (87)

> hold to the theory of the scientific and historical inerrancy of the original manuscripts of Scripture that began to develop in the post Reformation period. . . . For Luther, the Bible was infallible in accomplishing its purpose of proclaiming the salvation which the Father had wrought in His Son Jesus Christ.

Upon what kind of arguments do the authors stake their claims? In the first place they do not cite many of Luther's unambiguous statements on the subject. In the second place they once again resort to historical disjunctions. They intimate, for example, that because Luther held to the principle of accommodation he obviously did not believe in complete biblical infallibility.[68] We have already noted that this type of argument building is not convincing. In the third place they present a brief listing of Luther's "critical opinions" concerning textual matters (87):

> . . . his [Luther's] statements regarding the authorship of Genesis, Ecclesiastes, and Jude; the propriety of the canonicity of Esther, Hebrews, James and Revelation; the "errors" of the prophets, the trustworthiness of Kings vis-à-vis Chronicles, and the value of the Gospel accounts.

The authors have compiled this list from one page (300) of Reinhold Seeberg's *The History of Doctrines*.[69] In his survey text, which dates from the last years of the nineteenth century, Seeberg prooftexts these "critical opinions" of Luther with little commentary. His analysis has not gone unchallenged. In 1944 the Lutheran scholar, M. Reu, published a massively documented book entitled *Luther and the Scripture*.[70] In it he evaluated Seeberg's "prooftexts" and other ones by placing Luther's suspect quotations back into their contexts. Let us consider one purported critical problem which Rogers and McKim raise following Seeberg's lead: what they call "the trustworthiness of Kings vis-à-vis Chronicles." In *Table Talk*, Luther is quoted as having said: "The Books of Kings are more trustworthy than the Books of Chronicles." Not hiding behind the possibility that this reminiscence about what Luther spoke may have been incorrectly reported, Reu comments:

> We shall only give the entire sentence from which the quotation has been taken. That will suffice to show with what little right anyone may use this as a proof for Luther's liberalism. The sentence reads: "The writer of Chronicles noted only the summary and chief stories and events. Whatever is less important and immaterial he passed by. For this reason the Books of the Kings are more credible than the Chronicles." What more does this state than that the Chronicles pass by many things and condense others which the Books of Kings include or offer in detail? In view of the different plan followed by these two Biblical books the value of Chronicles as a historical source is less than that of Kings. But there is not a word about errors in it.[71]

In more lengthy discussions Reu analyzes the context for other "critical opinions" Luther had concerning the Scriptures. He concludes that a fair assessment
of these texts reveals that the Reformer did not admit the reality of any genuine
discrepancy in the Holy Writ, although he acknowledged his own inability to
resolve some apparent problem passages.[72] This observation concurs with Luther's
statements about the complete infallibility of the Bible. Moreover, it accords with
his passion for harmonizing biblical texts.

As Reu points out, Luther assumed biblical infallibility only for the original
documents. Just as it had been the case for St. Augustine, Luther's textual
critical work was designed to remove errors in copies and versions so that the
original documents might be more closely approached. Although to our knowledge he does not speak about the original autographs as such, his practice
makes it clear that he, with humanists of his day, desired to establish better
texts (whether classical or biblical) which reflected as much as possible the
original texts of antiquity. In commenting about Acts 13:20, Luther appended
this gloss:

> Some texts have 400 (altogether 450) but the histories and reckoning of the
> years do not permit it. It is an error of a scribe, who wrote four instead of three,
> which could easily happen in Greek.[73]

Many such comments are found in Luther's glosses and in his other writings
where he deals with the harmonization of the biblical texts. They point out the
Reformer's awareness of copyists' errors and his desire to reestablish the infallible originals.

Rather than interacting evenhandedly with the arguments and evidence in
Reu's study, Rogers and McKim dismiss the work *in toto*, but do so in a most
unsatisfactory fashion. They appeal to authority. In footnote 115, page 133,
they cite a negative judgment of Otto Heick concerning Reu's study. They fail
to observe that Heick, a church historian with pronounced neo-orthodox leanings, may have quite naturally found Reu's exhaustively documented essay
disconcerting.[74] And then, in what can only be judged as an awkward attempt
to bolster the authority of Seeberg's list of "critical opinions," they cite J.
Theodore Mueller's evaluation of the quality of Seeberg's scholarship. Mueller's
assessment is found in a collection of essays, *Inspiration & Interpretation*,
written by evangelicals and edited by John Walvoord.[75] The authors misquote
Mueller in a very significant way. They have Mueller declaring that Seeberg's
History of Doctrine "represents a most scholarly and reliable treatise *on Luther's
views of Scripture*" [italics mine] (n. 114, p. 133), as if the author approved all
of Seeberg's commentary upon Luther's views of Scripture. In truth, Mueller
actually declared that Seeberg's *Dogmengeschichte* "represents a most scholarly
and reliable treatise *on this point* [italics mine] . . ." (94). What is the point to
which Mueller alludes? It is Seeberg's recognition that Luther believed in the
full authority of Scripture and that he did not associate the Reformer with any
"mechanical inspiration theory" (93–94). Mueller, however, disagreed categorically with Seeberg on other aspects of his analysis. For example, he wrote:

It is indeed very significant that Seeberg does not admit Luther's identification of God's Word with Holy Scripture, that is, his manifest teaching that the Bible, as a whole and in all its parts, is the very word of God. The claim which Seeberg here makes, is that of modern liberalism which ignores the evident historical facts [95].

Rogers and McKim's treatment of Reu and Mueller does little to enhance an open-minded reader's confidence in the reliability of their documentation, or in their manner of doing history.

3. Calvin and Biblical Infallibility

Those acquainted with the literature on Calvin's view of biblical authority know its vast dimensions. The nonspecialist finds it difficult to sort out the relative merits of a given analysis or to establish its niche in the complex Calvin historiography that exists.[76] Added difficulties emerge because Christians from many backgrounds in a spirit of triumphalism have claimed Calvin as their own. They tend to elevate one aspect of Calvin's thought which coincides with their own theological preferences, while minimizing if not denying other teachings by the Reformer.

It is fair to say that Rogers and McKim generally base their analysis concerning Calvin's attitudes to Scripture on a neo-Protestant historiography (including the studies of Ford Lewis Battles, John McNeill, T. H. L. Parker, and François Wendel and others).[77] This literature is often rich in insights about Calvin but is sometimes marred by underlying neo-orthodox presuppositions. Rogers and McKim argue that Calvin believed that the central purpose of the Bible is to communicate salvation truths about Christ and that its authority is made known to believers through the internal witness of the Holy Spirit.[78] On these points most Calvin scholars concur.

But when Rogers and McKim indicate that Calvin held a belief in limited biblical infallibility, then many Reformation scholars from diverse theological backgrounds balk. They include experts who are not themselves proponents of the Warfieldian view of Scripture. In *The Knowledge of God in Calvin's Theology* (Columbia University Press, 1952), Edward Dowey, a very knowledgeable Calvin scholar, writes:

> To Calvin the theologian an error in Scripture is unthinkable. Hence the endless harmonizing, the explaining and interpreting of passages that seem to contradict or to be inaccurate. But Calvin the critical scholar recognizes mistakes with a disarming ingeniousness. The mistake or the gloss is simply a blunder made by ignorant copyist [104].
>
> If he [Calvin] betrays his position at all, it is in apparently assuming a priori that no errors can be allowed to reflect upon the inerrancy of the original documents [105].

Or Brian Gerrish, in his 1957 *Scottish Journal of Theology* article "Biblical Authority and the Continental Reformation" notes:

Perhaps even more important is the corollary that Calvin is obliged by his view of inspiration to think of the Scriptures as inerrant, and he exercises much ingenuity in reconciling alleged contradictions, and explaining apparent errors. . . . And the other method of explanation, which he uses against errors of historical fact, is to attribute the error to a copyist, hence enabling himself to hold to the inerrancy of a hypothetical 'original document.'[79]

H. Jackson Forstman, in his *Word and Spirit: Calvin's Doctrine of Biblical Authority,* puts the matter this way:

Those who do not interpret Calvin as a literalist make much of his emphasis on Christ, the promises, and faith. Their point cannot be denied. Insofar as the knowledge of faith is concerned, Calvin does not need and does not use a theory of verbal inspiration. Neither can we deny or explain away the strong emphasis on the totality of scripture and particularly on all its individual parts. So we must also say: insofar as the wider knowledge is concerned, Calvin both needs and is forced to use scripture in such a way as to emphasize its literal inerrancy.[80]

Rogers and McKim flatly disagree with these judgments, even though they come from noted Reformation scholars whose studies they rely upon for other arguments.

4. Calvin and the Concept of Error

Rogers and McKim boldly state that Calvin "was unconcerned with normal, human inaccuracies in minor matters" in Scripture (109). They point to several comments made by Calvin in an attempt to substantiate their contention. Their list of problem passages, if slightly rearranged, bears a striking resemblance to a list found in John McNeill's influential *Church History* article of 1959, "The Significance of the Word of God for Calvin."[81] In his essay, McNeill, a distinguished Calvin scholar, attempted to demonstrate that Calvin did not believe in biblical inerrancy.[82] He sadly misconstrued his argument, however. He assumed that if he could prove that Calvin did not maintain a complete mechanical dictation theory, then the Reformer did not affirm biblical inerrancy. Obviously, Calvin does not hold such a theory in its crassest form.[83] But McNeill won only a pyrrhic victory. It does not follow that because the Bible's human authors were not automatons in their writing of Scripture, that the resultant product was errant. Such a stance limits dramatically the power of God to protect His Word. Unfortunately, Rogers and McKim tend to approve McNeill's premise, and they too assume that Calvin admitted the existence of errors in the original biblical documents.

Let us examine a few examples of the strongest evidence they muster for their case. The authors write (109):

Calvin noted that Paul misquoted Psalm 51:4 in Romans 3:4. Calvin generalized about such inaccuracies: "We know that, in quoting Scripture the apostles often used freer language than the original, since they were content if what they quoted applied to their subject, and therefore they were not over-careful in their use of words."

Rogers and McKim's suggestion that Calvin thought Paul "misquoted" Psalm 51:4 is not an appropriate evaluation. A few lines before the passage Rogers and McKim cite, Calvin declared: "And that Paul has quoted this passage according to the proper and real meaning of David is clear from the objection that is immediately added. . . ."[84] The apostles did not "misquote" Scripture, according to Calvin, because they expressed the meaning of Old Testament passages with other words. Rogers and McKim write (109):

> Similarly in Calvin's commentary on Hebrews 10:6, he affirmed that the saving purpose of the biblical message was adequately communicated through an imperfect form of words: "They (the apostles) were not overscrupulous in quoting words provided that they did not misuse Scripture for their convenience. We must always look at the purpose for which quotations are made but as far as the words are concerned, as in other things which are not relevant to the present purpose, they allow themselves some indulgence."

First, the passage which Rogers cites comes from Calvin's commentary on Hebrews 10:5, not Hebrews 10:6. Second, Calvin does not refer to the "saving purpose of the biblical message" in the passage. Third, the authors exclude an important passage from their quotation: "We must always look at the purpose to which quotations are made, *because they have careful regard for the main object so as not to turn Scripture to a false meaning.*"[85] In this deleted phrase Calvin is apparently arguing that the apostles did not intend to betray the meaning of Scripture by creating misquotations. He does not say anything about the "imperfect form of words" in this passage. Rogers and McKim claim that Calvin the scholar "discerned technical inaccuracies in the humanly written text" (110).

> In his commentary on Acts 7:16, Calvin declared that Luke had "made a manifest error" as comparison with the text of Genesis 23:9 showed.

Calvin actually wrote:

> And whereas he [Luke] saith afterward, they were laid in the sepulchre which Abraham had bought of the sons of Hemor, it is manifest that there is a fault [mistake] in the word Abraham. . . . Wherefore this place must be amended.[86]

Calvin does not tell us to whom the error should be attributed: "it is manifest that" is the language of an observation, not an attribution. It is probable the Reformer believed that a copyist had made the error. Then again, one generally "amends" a copyist's work. Further research should ensue concerning the context in which Calvin uses the word *amend*, but another "problem" text presented by Rogers and McKim tends to confirm our interpretation concerning a reference to a copyist's error. They cite Calvin's comments on Matthew 27:9 (110):

> How the name of Jeremiah crept in, I confess that I do not know, nor do I give myself much trouble to inquire. The passage itself plainly shows that the name of Jeremiah has been put down by mistake, instead of Zechariah (XI 13) for in *Jeremiah* we find nothing of this sort, not anything that even approaches it.

In this passage Calvin does not admit, as Rogers and McKim propose, that due to a human lapse the original text contained a genuine error. Rather, Calvin's observation "How the name of Jeremiah crept in" exhibits a verb which is logically associated with problems of textual transmission. Errors creep into texts during the process of copying.

Rogers and McKim write that Calvin believed that Moses "did not know any more or thought any differently about the natural order than other people of his time and culture" (112). They imply that Calvin knew that Moses had made a mistake in affirming that the moon and sun were the two great lights. For did not Calvin point out that astronomers had discovered that Saturn was larger than the moon?[87] In fact, Calvin does not acknowledge that Moses erred. According to the Reformer, Moses, in accommodating himself to his audience's perspective, used phenomenal language and thereby made an accurate observation. The moon and the sun are the largest planets in the sky as viewed by the naked eye from the earth. Calvin writes: "Had he [Moses] spoken of things generally unknown, the uneducated might have pleaded in excuse that such subjects were beyond their capacity." The next line of Calvin's quotation is very important, but Rogers and McKim omit it: "Lastly, since the Holy Spirit here opens a common school for all, it is not surprising that he should chiefly choose those subjects which would be intelligible to all."[88] To accuse Moses of making an error here would be to accuse the Holy Spirit of the same fault, according to Calvin. Rogers and McKim fail to mention this. We can learn from Calvin how important it is to try to ascertain a biblical author's intent before we interpret his words. Elsewhere in his commentary on Genesis 1 and 2, Calvin accepts at face value Moses' comments about the creation of the natural world and man. Nowhere does Calvin indicate that any of Moses' remarks about the natural world were inaccurate, when properly understood.[89] The Reformer does not hesitate to seek some form of accord between the "science" of his day and Holy Writ.[90] We will refer again to Calvin's attitudes toward this issue in a later section.

Rogers and McKim's attempt to defend the thesis that Calvin limited biblical infallibility to matters of faith and practice falters badly. It encounters the heavy opposition of Calvin's formal statements, a few of which Professor Dowey places back-to-back in this fashion:

> ". . . we see that the Spirit is not less diligent in narrating burials than the principal mysteries of faith." We "ought to embrace with mild docility, and *without any exception*, whatever is delivered in the Holy Scriptures." "For Scripture is the school of the Holy Spirit in which as *nothing useful and necessary is omitted, so nothing is taught which is not profitable to know.*"[91]

This kind of statement could be duplicated tenfold. Moreover, Calvin's extraordinary efforts at harmonizing biblical texts countermands the thesis completely. Rupert Davies, the learned Reformation scholar, who earlier notes that Doumergue's list of Calvin's "admitted" errors has questionable validity, summarizes well Calvin's attitude to Scripture:

> And the instances quoted by Doumergue of Calvin's recognition of errors in the Bible are but drops in a bucket of unquestioning reverence for the words of Holy Scripture, and indicate at most that he was very occasionally in a long career untrue to one of his most dearly-cherished ideas.[92]

5. The Reformers' Attitude Toward "Science"

Rogers and McKim propose that Luther and other Reformers did not rely on the Bible's incidental statements about the natural world in their assessment of contemporary scientific theories (87). The Reformers understood that these statements could err due to their status as accommodated language. According to the authors' interpretation, it was seventeenth-century Protestant "scholastics" (along with Roman Catholic "scholastics") who began to use the words of Scripture as the basis for establishing their viewpoints on science: "For Voetius and other Protestant scholastics the issue was clear. When the findings of science contradicted the apparent literal text of the Bible—the findings of science had to be rejected" (167). Rogers and McKim do not think Calvin and Luther reacted against scientific findings in a similar fashion.

The authors are quick to discount the implications of a passage from Luther's *Table Talk* (which they only partially cite) according to which the Reformer turned his back on Copernicus's heliocentric theory because it contradicted a biblical passage:

> There was mention of a certain new astrologer who wanted to prove that the earth moves and not the sky, the sun, and the moon . . . [Luther remarked]: "So it goes now. Whoever wants to be clever must agree with nothing that others esteem. He must do something of his own. This is what that fellow does who wishes to turn the whole of astronomy upside down. Even in these things that are thrown into disorder I believe the Holy Scriptures, for Joshua commanded the sun to stand still and not the earth (Josh. 10:12)."[93]

Rogers and McKim contend that this was "likely just a common sense remark," made "from the memory of one of his guests," "printed . . . twenty-seven years afterwards (1566)."[94] In other words, Luther did not really interact with the Copernican revolution on the basis of a passage in Joshua.

It is true that one can minimize the impact of this *Table Talk* remark by suspecting its authenticity.[95] But the criteria which Rogers and McKim use so confidently to dismiss the comment have the earmarks of special pleading. If followed, they minimize too drastically the historical value of Luther's *Table Talk*, which authors Rogers and McKim themselves used as a source of one of Luther's "admitted errors": "the trustworthiness of Kings vis-à-vis Chronicles." A more open-minded approach would lead a scholar to say that the question of the statement's authenticity and meaning remains open. It is just as probable that Luther did reject the Copernican theory with Joshua 10:12 in mind as that he made the statement as a "common sense" remark.

Rogers and McKim take some of their details about the creation of Luther's statement from John Dillenberger's *Protestant Thought and Natural Science* (Nashville: Abingdon, 1960), 37–38. Dillenberger asserts that Luther and Calvin did not defend their "scientific" views of the world based on their commitment to the biblical inerrancy of Scripture (39). But he does acknowledge that the Reformers held to a complete biblical infallibility (31):

> It is true of course that the Reformers were creatures of their day with respect to accepting the total words of the Bible as true. It would not have occurred to them to suggest that the hermeneutical principle freed them from what we today call the notion of the infallibility of the text. But it is important to note that the text free from error (except for linguistic or copy errors) was not the centre of their attention.

Rogers and McKim feel quite comfortable to use Dillenberger's comments for one phase of their analysis, but they appear quite reluctant to cite other significant statements he made.

Much debate hovers over the attitudes of Calvin toward Copernicus. In heated interchanges found in the *Journal of the History of Ideas* (1960, 1961), Professors Edward Rosen and Joseph Ratner discuss Calvin's position extensively.[96] More recently, Richard Stauffer, Hautes Etudes (Paris), has brought new materials into the debate concerning Calvin's potential references to Copernicus.[97] Then again, scholars have challenged the authenticity of a remark long ascribed to Calvin: "Who will venture to place the authority of Copernicus above that of the Holy Spirit."[98] Rogers and McKim give no hint of this long-standing debate in the text of their volume.[99] As they dismiss the import of Luther's reported remark about Copernicus out of hand, so they declare categorically that "Calvin never mentioned Copernicus . . . (166)," a remarkable supposition to be attributed to so widely read a man as Calvin.[100]

The authors contrast Calvin's openness to natural science with the stance of Melanchthon, who "stood firmly in the Aristotelian/Ptolemaic schema (p. 166)." They fail to note that in several of Calvin's commentaries, written thirteen and sixteen years after Copernicus's writings of 1543, the Reformer shows himself to be a partisan of the old cosmology: "We are indeed not ignorant that the circuit of the heavens is finite and the earth, like a little ball, is located in the middle."[101] He in fact held to the same cosmology as Melanchthon. Rogers and McKim do not mention this.

Did sixteenth-century theologians evaluate the Copernican hypothesis with an eye to its bearing upon biblical teaching? In his *Science and Change 1500–1700*, Hugh Kearney, whose authority Rogers and McKim invoke, follows the lead of Edward Rosen by citing individuals in the sixteenth century ranging from Luther (his *Table Talk* remark) and Melanchthon, to Tycho Brahe (1546–1601), who reacted against the Copernican hypothesis due in part to their interpretation of the Bible's teachings. Brahe's statement is particularly straightforward:

What need is there without any justification to imagine the earth, a dark, dense and inert mass, to be a heavenly body undergoing even more numerous revolutions than the others, that is to say, subject to a triple motion, in negation not only of all physical truth, but also of the authority of the Holy Scripture which ought to be paramount.[102]

Kearney comments about this widespread reaction against Copernicus in the sixteenth century:

The truth is that within the general range of religious opinion, Catholic, Lutheran and Calvinists alike, the Copernican view was dismissed as an absurdity. All the accepted authorities were against it. The Bible contradicted it expressly. The weight of common sense acted as an additional obstacle.[103]

Writing in the first third of the sixteenth century, Copernicus himself suspected that his theory might encounter opposition based on his contemporaries' reading of the Scriptures:

Perhaps there will be babblers who, although completely ignorant of mathematics, nevertheless take it upon themselves to pass judgment on mathematical questions and, badly distorting some passage of Scripture to their purpose, will dare to find fault with my understanding and censure it.[104]

Copernicus believed that his ideas were compatible with a proper understanding of Scripture. Many of his opponents who read their Bibles differently disagreed. Moreover, a good number of sixteenth-century thinkers forged their cosmologies with the Scriptures' words in mind as well as the teachings of Ptolemy and Aristotle. Rogers and McKim's proposal that it was the late sixteenth- and seventeenth-century scholastics who initiated the practice of looking to the Bible's words for "scientific information" is a broken reed.

C. Roman Catholics and Biblical Infallibility

Many Roman Catholics shared with sixteenth-century Protestants a commitment to complete biblical infallibility, though they stressed the infallibility in the Vulgate more than that of "the original documents."[105] One of the clearest illustrations of the Roman Catholic attitude in this regard is evidenced in a major dispute which took place in the 1580s between the Jesuit Lenhard Lessius and the Faculties of Theology of Louvain and Douay.[106] In Assertions One and Two of his 1586 Theses, Lessius proposed that the Holy Spirit did not specifically choose each word that the biblical writers employed in their texts. Rather the Holy Spirit in an undefined manner guided the writers such that they made no error even though they chose the words: "... ac simul illis specialissimo modo assistat in omnibus verbis ac sententiis, ut ne minimum quidem errorem committere possint." The theologians of Louvain and Douay censured Lessius for departing from Roman Catholic orthodoxy by not insisting that every word of the Scriptures was specifically chosen by the Holy Spirit.[107] It should be noticed that both sides in the debate acknowledged that the biblical text is infallible (with no limitations of infallibility to matters of faith and practice).

When Roman Catholics debated with Protestants, they recognized that both parties accepted the principle of an inerrant Bible. In his *Controverses* of 1595, St. François de Sales put the matter this way:

> If then the Church can err, O Calvin, O Luther, to whom will I have recourse in my difficulties? To Scripture, they say; but what will I do, poor man that I am? For it is with regard to Scripture itself that I have trouble. I do not doubt whether or not I should adjust faith to Scripture, for who does not know that it is the word of truth? What bothers me is the understanding of this Scripture.[108]

Although St. François readily granted that the Protestants held to an infallible Bible, he doubted that they had the criteria with which to interpret it correctly. How to interpret an infallible text and how to determine the canon of the Bible were two important issues debated by Roman Catholics and Protestants during the Counter Reformation, just as they had been for Luther and Erasmus.

Rogers and McKim create another misleading paradigm when they attempt to describe the apologetic arsenal which Roman Catholics allegedly used against Protestants (and from which Protestants allegedly borrowed). The authors assume gratuitously that Roman Catholic apologists with Thomistic training necessarily used Aristotelian arguments exclusively in their apologetic efforts (147):

> . . . the second generation of Reformers tried to battle Roman Catholicism by using Roman Catholics' own weapons against them. For example, Protestants tried eventually to prove the authority of the Bible, using the same Aristotelian arguments Roman Catholics had used to prove the authority of the Church.

In reality, one of the main thrusts of Roman Catholic argumentation against Protestants' claims was not based upon Aristotelian tenets at all.[109] In *The History of Scepticism from Erasmus to Descartes*, Professor Richard Popkin has carefully expounded how Roman Catholic apologists used the arguments of Pyrrhonism (skepticism) in an attempt to force Protestants to accept the tradition and authority of the Church:

> Beginning with the great Jesuit theologian, Juan Maldonat, who came to teach in Paris in the early 1560s . . . , a type of dialectic was developed, especially by the Jesuit controversialists, for undermining Calvinism on its own grounds by raising a series of sceptical difficulties.[110]

Accepting the traditions of their own communion on fideistic grounds, apologists like François Veron attempted to show Reformed spokesmen that their reliance upon the Holy Spirit's guidance or upon the guidance of regenerated reason did not afford them with the capacity to interpret Scriptures correctly.[111] Roman Catholic apologists pointed to differences of interpretations advocated by Protestant exegetes in an attempt to prove their point. From their perspective,

Protestants were doomed to fall into skepticism, despite their appeals to the authority of the Holy Spirit. François de Sales challenged Protestants boldly in this regard concerning the canon:

> Now let us see what rule they have for discerning the canonical books from all of the other ecclesiastical ones. "The witness," they say, "and inner persuasion of the Holy Spirit." Oh God, what a hiding place, what a fog, what a night. We are not in this way very enlightened on so important and grave a matter.[112]

According to Roman Catholic apologists, only the traditions of the church accepted on faith permitted Christians to determine what were the canonical books and to interpret the Scriptures with authoritative guides. Popularized by Veron, this Roman Catholic apologetic was used extensively in France and beyond. In France the French pastor Jean Daillé complained that even Catholic bakers employed it against their Huguenot neighbors.[113] The "method" was grounded not in Aristotelian arguments but in fideism. Rogers and McKim's failure to understand the linkage of the new Pyrrhonism with Roman Catholic apologetics leads them to create a misleading paradigm for understanding much Protestant thought, particularly that which emphasized regenerated reason's rights.[114]

When Protestant apologists insisted that regenerated reason (and right reason *per se*) helped them to know that the Bible was authoritative, they often did so apologetically because Roman Catholic disputants had challenged the criterion of the witness of the Holy Spirit to confirm biblical authority. These same Protestants often understood that the witness of the Holy Spirit was the primary means whereby the faithful come to a conviction of the Bible's authority. When the Roman Catholic oratorian Jean Morin highlighted difficult passages to exegete in the Scriptures, he did so with the intention of forcing Protestants to acknowledge that without church traditions, they could never arrive at a proper interpretation of the text. Protestants argued in response that the Bible is a sure, infallible Word and that Scripture interprets Scripture. These apologists did not borrow these arguments from their "Aristotelian Roman Catholic opponents," as Rogers and McKim allege. The authors have apparently not had the occasion to assess the dynamics of Roman Catholic-Protestant interchanges in the sixteenth and seventeenth centuries. The "new Pyrrhonism" was evident in Roman Catholic apologetics as late as Richard Simon's day (1638–1712).

D. The Bible As an Infallible Rule of Faith and Practice in the Sixteenth and Seventeenth Centuries

For Rogers and McKim the designation that the Bible is an infallible rule for faith and practice is pivotal for their argument. They find this expression or ones similar to it in Reformation and post-Reformation discourse. They cite these expressions as proof that the Reformers and their immediate followers limited the infallibility of the Bible to matters of faith and practice. But once again Rogers and McKim unfortunately misread the context out of which Reformation Christians made these statements. Certainly these Christians did believe the Scriptures communicate infallible truths about faith and practice.

But they did not intend to create by their expressions a limitation on the extent of infallibility of the biblical text. The issue was otherwise. As we indicated earlier, Roman Catholic apologists had argued in the sixteenth and seventeenth centuries that Protestants needed the teachings of the church (councils, tradition, papal pronouncements) in addition to biblical data, in order to apprehend correct instruction about salvation. For example, in his 1609 Catechism the famous Roman Catholic Guillaume Baile presented this question and answer for lay persons:

> Are all things necessary for our salvation found expressly in Scripture? No. It is for this reason that Scripture sends us back to Traditions some of which being divine have as much authority as if they were written.[115]

To this kind of Roman Catholic claim, Protestants frequently responded that the Bible alone is the sufficient and infallible rule of faith and practice. That is, Christians did not need other sources of information (councils, tradition, etc.) in order to formulate their soteriology. It did not cross the minds of these Protestants to use this expression as a phrase circumscribing the extent of biblical infallibility.

Article V of the French Confession of Faith (A.D. 1559) establishes well the context for the expression "rule of faith":

> . . . And inasmuch as it [the Bible] is the rule of all truth, containing all that is necessary for the service of God and for our salvation, it is not lawful for men, nor even angels, to add to it, to take away from, or to change it. . . .[116]

The Bible alone is sufficient to inform us about our salvation and how we should serve God; we do not need any other source of information, as Roman Catholics constantly stipulated. The Bible is also "the rule of all truth."

Frequently Protestant churches and individual writers proposed in one section of a creed or theological treatise that the Bible is an infallible rule of faith and practice and elsewhere in the same creed or treatise that all the words of the biblical text are without any error whatsoever. In that Rogers and McKim do not fully acknowledge the context into which many Protestants placed the expression "the only infallible rule of faith and practice," they tend to ignore passages which counter their interpretation. For example, in treating the Belgic Confession of Faith (1561), they cite the seventh article, "The Sufficiency of Holy Scriptures to be the Only Rule of Faith."[117] They point out a reference in it to the Bible as an "infallible rule," but they pass over a clause of Article 5 of the same confession which indicates that "all things contained within them [the Scriptures]" are to be believed:

> We receive all these books, and these only, as holy and canonical, for the regulation, foundation, and confirmation of our faith, believing, without any doubt, all things contained in them, not so much because the Church receives them. . . .[118]

Or, in considering the Scots Confession of 1560, Rogers and McKim note

Article XX's discussion of councils, but do not make explicit the reason why the Scots were to refuse the authority of councils:

> For plaine it is, as they wer men, so have some of them manifeslie erred, and that in matters of great importance.[119]

The teachings of councils could be accepted to the extent that they reflected the Word of God, which by implication did not err as did the participants at councils.[120]

In his *Sur les Conciles et les Commandements. . .* , Pierre Viret (1511–1571), an associate of Calvin, declared that he accepted the Scriptures' authority on the basis of the Holy Spirit's witness.[121] Citing St. Augustine as his mentor, he noted that books of the Bible contained no errors and thus serve as "infallible rules" for judging doctrine:

> [The Holy Spirit] did not permit any error to be mixed in their books, because He wanted to leave them for us as infallible rules with which to examine doctrines.[122]

Viret contrasted the supreme authority of a completely infallible Bible with that of popes, councils, and other Roman Catholic authorities.

Pierre Du Moulin's *Du juge des controverses traitte auquel est defendu l'autorite & la perfection de la Saincte Escritures* (1630) represents an important Reformed apologetic of the early seventeenth century.[123] In it the author indicates that French Reformed Christians believed the Bible to be a sovereign judge and "regle infaillible de nostre foy" and that all Christian churches of the world agreed that it was "divine, sacred" and "the word of God" (64–65). He noted that the apostles were infallibly inspired by the Holy Spirit (211). He proposed that the "originaux" of the Bible were uncorrupted whereas the Roman Catholic Vulgate was error marked (18):

> But if the truth of the *originaux* of the Bible had been put in doubt then the rule of faith would not have been assured [322].[124]

But the Jews kept the *originaux* "en leur purete" (322). And then, even though his philosophical propensities were Aristotelian, as Rogers and McKim argue, Pierre du Moulin in good Reformed fashion argued that Scripture should interpret Scripture (412), that our reason is well founded only when it conforms to the Word of God (261), and that it is by the witness of the Holy Spirit that the "fideles" come to accept the authority of the Holy Scriptures (321–22).[125]

The English apologist, William Whitaker (1547–1595), helps us to understand to what part of the Scripture Protestants referred in using the expression the "rule of faith." Whitaker was Regius Professor of Divinity at Cambridge University for a good number of years.[126] The famous Catholic disputant Bellarmine recognized him as one of Protestantism's most able defenders. [127] Whitaker identified the rule of faith with the contents of the entire Bible in his *A Disputation on Holy Scripture Against the Papists especially Bellarmine and Stapleton* (1588), the most extensive book on Scripture written by an Englishman in Elizabeth's day.[128] In response to a Bellarmine charge, Whitaker makes it clear that the rule of faith included everything written in the Scriptures— histories and the like, not "salvation truths" only:

> Is it not necessary for us to know the commencement of the church, its propagation, and continual conservation and government, and the promises made to the patriarchs concerning the Messiah? Surely he blasphemes who denies this . . . although it may be ceded that all the histories are not equally useful and necessary, because many may be saved without the knowledge of many histories; yet in reality they are all not only useful, but necessary also. For although they are not all requisite to the being of faith, yet they contribute greatly to its better being . . . although perhaps more things than can be styled simply necessary are delivered in scripture, yet it does not therefore follow that the scripture is not a rule. For although the scripture contains some things which are not simply and absolutely necessary; nevertheless, it is a rule to which all doctrine ought to be conformed. We say that the Scriptures are a rule, because they contain all things necessary to faith and salvation, and more things may be found in them than absolute necessity requires. We do not attach so strict and precise a notion to the term 'rule,' as to make it contain nothing but what is necessary . . . [660–61].[129]

Whitaker also affirmed that the Bible never errs:

> But, say they, the church never errs; the pope never errs. We shall show both assertions to be false in the proper place. We say that scripture never errs, and therefore judge that interpretation to be the truest which agrees with scripture [476].

Moreover, as we shall see, he believed that the original autographs were infallible. Whitaker, then, joined the concept of inerrancy to the expression "the infallible rule of faith and practice."

Was Whitaker himself an early Protestant "rationalist," emphasizing reason's powers to establish biblical authority? No, he saw himself differently. He reviewed Calvin's discussion of the external testimonies to biblical authority but, like Calvin, he stressed the Holy Spirit's role in this regard:

> These topics may prove that these books are divine, yet will never be sufficient to bring conviction to our souls so as to make us assent, unless the testimony of the Holy Spirit be added. When this is added, it fills our minds with a wonderful plentitude of assurance, confirms them, and causes us most gladly to embrace the scriptures, giving force to the preceding arguments. Those previous arguments may indeed urge and constrain us; but this (I mean the internal testimony of the Holy Spirit) is the only argument which can persuade us.[130]

Or, he wrote: "But in like manner as no man can certainly assent to the doctrine of faith except by the Spirit, so can none assent to the scriptures but by the same Spirit."[131] Whitaker wrote as a good Calvinist.

We could refer to other spokesmen drawn from Puritan and Continental

Reformed and Lutheran ranks to demonstrate our contention that Protestants did not intend to limit the extent of infallibility by describing the Bible as an "infallible rule of faith and practice." Such an idea was foreign to their mindset. Rogers and McKim do not faithfully represent their perspectives in this regard.

E. The Post-Reformation Period and Biblical Infallibility

Rogers and McKim should be applauded for their conversance with recent scholarship concerning what some have called post-Reformation orthodoxy and that others have labeled Protestant scholasticism. Studies by Jill Raitt, Brian Armstrong, John P. Donnelly, and others have broken new ground in our understanding of the thought of late sixteenth- and seventeenth-century theologians.[132] Much work remains to be accomplished in this field where some new hypotheses are more exciting than reliable.[133]

Rogers and McKim are less helpful, however, when they attempt to relate these studies to one of their paramount interests: biblical infallibility.[134] They portray many of the Continental Protestant theologians of the seventeenth century as uncritical disciples of Aristotle and therefore as "scholastics." These theologians were the ones who introduced complete biblical infallibility to Protestant communions and began to treat the Bible's words as conveyers of technically correct information about the world. Whereas the Reformers accented the saving function of the Bible's message, the "scholastics" emphasized its literary form. In brief, they departed significantly from the teachings of Luther and Calvin

For Rogers and McKim, Melanchthon launched what became the scholastic movement for the Lutherans, while Theodore Beza (1519–1605), influenced by several Italian Aristotelians, did the same for the Reformed communities.[135] In England, Puritans were largely spared from falling under scholasticism's sway. Their philosophical premises, frequently drawn from Ramist sources, acted as effective antidotes.[136] Unfortunately, John Owen (1616–1683) eventually turned some of his fellow Englishmen toward scholasticism later in the seventeenth century.[137]

Rogers and McKim's analysis stumbles at several points. First, despite much discussion about the place of predestination in seventeenth-century Reformed thought, the divines' penchant for metaphysics, and other matters, the authors never elucidate persuasively why the usage of "Aristotelian" logic or categories led so-called scholastics to formulate a belief in complete biblical infallibility.[138] Perhaps it is for this reason they do not tell us who was the first theologian to make the doctrinal innovation. If no Protestant theologian had previously entertained the idea, it is strange that contemporaries did not signal the name of this influential innovator, so concerned were they about doctrinal innovations. Second, and on a contrary note, Rogers and McKim do not adequately explain why the Ramist philosophical dispositions of certain English Puritans should have kept them from affirming biblical inerrancy. Perhaps their silence on this point stems from the disconcerting reality that there were Ramists who affirmed complete biblical infallibility. Third, the authors' categories for understanding the philosophical options of the seventeenth century are quite restricted. They do not capture the complex philosophical combinations sometimes found in the thought of an individual theologian. We should explain the nature of our reservations in greater detail.

After commenting upon the careers of Melanchthon, Peter Martyr, G. Zanchi, and Theodore Beza, among others whom they describe as "transitional figures," Rogers and McKim wisely observe, "It remains difficult to give a clear, and comprehensive definition of Reformed scholasticism" (185).[139] And they note, "We need to speak of shifts of emphasis rather than drastically different doctrines when we contrast Calvin with his scholastic followers" (185). And yet two pages later (187), the authors abandon their former caution:

> In theological method and especially in their view of the authority and interpretation of Scripture, post-Reformation scholastics were more like Thomas Aquinas and his medieval approach than they were like Calvin and his Reformation position.

This latter charge is a remarkable one, given their previous statements.

Absent from Rogers and McKim's study is any sustained interaction with Robert Preus's detailed studies of Lutheran divines in the late sixteenth and seventeenth centuries.[140] Preus, who has examined the primary sources of these Lutheran theologians more than any other present-day scholar, does not find that they engaged in any essential distortion of Luther's thought about biblical authority.[141] Also absent from the authors' discussion are the conclusions of John Robinson, who has studied the primary sources of Continental Reformed theologians with remarkable care. His doctoral dissertation, "The Doctrine of Holy Scripture in Seventeenth-Century Reformed Theology" (1971) was directed by François Wendel, the renowned Calvin scholar from the Protestant Faculty, the University of Strasbourg.[142] A reading of this thesis would have well served the authors, who, beginning with the seventeenth century, focus their attention almost exclusively upon Reformed traditions, despite the title they gave to their volume.

Based upon his reading of the writings of the principal Reformed theologians of France, the United Provinces, and Switzerland, Robinson makes these general observations which have a bearing upon Rogers and McKim's proposals:

1) The use of scholastic terminology (*essence, accidents, materia* . . .):

> This scholastic terminology regarding Scripture was used in a standing controversy with the Roman Catholics concerning the chronological precedence of the Scripture versus that of the Church. . . . Perhaps the most significant thing about the use of these scholastic terms in defining the nature of Scripture is that the majority of the seventeenth century Reformed theologians made relatively little use of them [28–29, 188].

2) The commitment to biblical infallibility *before* the writings of John Owen and Francis Turretin:[143]

[Johannes Hoornbeeck (1617–1666) offered excerpts from a number of prominent Dutch theologians of the late sixteenth and early seventeenth centuries in support of the following statement.]

All the Scriptures are divinely inspired; nothing at all was written except what the Holy Spirit himself included; thus nothing whatsoever was in fact able to be in error (41).

3) The role of the Holy Spirit in confirming the authority of Scripture:

Regardless of how the Scriptures were related to the work of the Spirit in the heart, it is this interior action of the Holy Spirit which was considered to be decisive [55, 185].

[Robinson cites a passage from Polanus (1561–1620) in this regard. Polanus was twice rector of the University of Basel, philosophically sympathetic to Ramus, and a believer in complete biblical infallibility]:

So that one may be persuaded by the certainty of faith that Scripture is from God, and that he accepts it not as the word of men but, as it is in truth, as the word of God which acts in you who believe, it needs the internal witness of the Holy Spirit [56].

According to Robinson, the seventeenth-century Reformed divines molded their thought about the Scripture in the context of polemics with Roman Catholics, in contact with Aristotelian philosophy, and under the influence of John Calvin. He concludes, however, with a pivotal remark: "Their efforts to present a theology of the Scriptures consisted above all in an attempt to determine the teaching of the Bible about itself" (195). Against the panoply of Robinson's sturdy analysis of the primary sources, Rogers and McKim's analysis appears less than strong.

The authors reveal one of the weaker interfaces of their interpretation when they link different philosophical preferences with inerrancy or errancy. Their paradigm that "Aristotelians" were generally deductivists, rationalistic, and inerrantists whereas Platonists-Ramists were generally inductivists, fideistically inclined, and believers in limited infallibility is simplistic and reductionistic.[144] And yet they use a form of this paradigm throughout their volume. It is particularly inappropriate for any analysis of seventeenth-century theologians. In that century one can find individuals with sympathies for either Aristotle, or Plato, or Descartes, or Ramus, who affirmed biblical inerrancy. The philosophical presuppositions of a thinker did not fashion in a deterministic way his attitudes toward the Scripture.

The authors' presentation wavers at another point as well. Paul Dibon, Hautes Etudes, Paris, has analyzed painstakingly the relationship between philosophical currents and theological discourse in the United Provinces in the seventeenth century. He finds that there were theologians who combined in one person an appreciation for Ramus and Aristotle.[145] In his study *Scripture in the Westminster Confession*, Rogers himself notes that the Westminster Divines had been influenced by both Aristotle and Ramus.[146] Then again, some

Reformed theologians attempted to discover the teachings of the real Aristotle, whom they opposed to the Aristotle of the "scholastic" Roman Catholics.[147] Moreover, in the works of these theologians praise for Aristotle can fall upon one page and praise for Plato on another.[148] Or, a theologian could appreciate Aristotle's emphasis upon syllogistic logic while being disconcerted about other aspects of the Greek's teachings.[149] Rogers and McKim's interpretative grid does not fit very well over the multiformed contours of theological and philosophical discourse in the seventeenth century. Interestingly enough, Rogers presents a more refined interpretation in his *Scripture in the Westminster Confession* (1967) than in the present volume.

In the present volume the authors' blanket charges are overdrawn. Many of the seventeenth-century divines were pious Christians, sincere in following their Lord.[150] It is quite unfair to infer that for them, "reason had at least equal standing with faith in religious matters . . ." or to suggest that they had "substituted philosophical speculation for growth in the Christian life as the goal of theological work . . ." (186).

Geoffrey Bromiley, for many years Professor of Church History at Fuller Theological Seminary, warns us about digging a chasm between Luther and Calvin and the Continental Protestant theologians of the late sixteenth and seventeenth centuries:

> In these writers the doctrine of scripture is no doubt entering on a new phase. Tendencies may be discerned in the presentation which give evidence of some movement away from the Reformation emphases. The movement, however, has not yet proceeded very far. The tendencies are only tendencies. What change there has been is more in style, or, materially, in elaboration. The substance of the Reformation doctrine of scripture has not yet been altered, let alone abandoned.[151]

Unfortunately, Rogers and McKim, who cite Professor Bromiley extensively concerning the "tendencies" of post-Reformation theologians, did not take the church historian's warning to heart, as judged by their more extreme statements.[152]

F. The English Puritans, the Westminster Confession of Faith, and Biblical Infallibility

One of the most prominent pillars which Rogers and McKim hoist into place to support their proposal concerns the attitudes of the English Puritans (particularly the Divines at the Westminster Assembly, 1643–1649) toward Holy Writ. Much of their discussion (200–218) is based on Rogers's study, *Scripture in the Westminster Confession: A Problem of Historical Interpretation for American Presbyterianism.*[153] That work, therefore, should come under our purview in an evaluation of Rogers and McKim's argument.

According to Rogers and McKim, the English Puritans affirmed limited biblical infallibility but did not adhere to a belief in biblical inerrancy. Remarkably enough, in his brief discussion of inerrancy, Rogers does not offer a single illustration of a Westminster Divine who indicated that the Bible did err in any way (Rogers, *Scripture*, 305–6). This silence can be explained in several ways.

Rogers would have us believe that "the question of the errancy or inerrancy of Scriptures is one which is strange to the Westminster Divines," in that they drew up their Confession in an age (pre-scientific) when the problem had not yet emerged (Rogers, *Scripture*, 305–6). Thus, the silence. On the contrary, Professor John Gerstner, against whom Rogers and McKim frequently spar in their joint book, argues that Rogers cannot find Westminster Divines who affirmed that the Bible did err in matters of history, science, geography, and the like.[154] Thus, the silence. For Gerstner, the Westminster Divines' concept of infallibility should be equated with a full-blown inerrancy. The Rogers-Gerstner discussion bears some striking resemblances to the Briggs-Warfield debate which took place nearly one hundred years ago.[155] Moreover, Rogers does appreciate Briggs's scholarship, whereas Gerstner prefers Warfield's historical research on the matter.

It would be fruitless for us to enter into a detailed analysis of this debate which has exercised these scholars and others for many years. Nonetheless several general remarks might prove helpful. First, the burden of Rogers and McKim's demonstration tends to rest upon historical disjunctions: because the Westminster Divines believed that the principal purpose of the Bible is to teach salvation truths, because they indicated that the internal witness of the Holy Spirit confirms the authority of the Scripture to the faithful, they did not believe in complete biblical infallibility (or inerrancy).[156] And once again, we suggest that adherence to those particular beliefs does not preclude a belief in the latter doctrine.

Second, if we are to understand what the word *infallible* meant for the Divines, it might be valuable to consider the connotative freight their Puritan forebears gave to that term. Rogers and McKim argue that the Puritans were preserved from "scholasticism" because their philosophical premises were generally Ramist in orientation. In setting the stage for the Westminster Confession of Faith, Rogers in his thesis speaks about the theological influence of the Ramists: William Temple (1555–1627), William Perkins (1558–1602), and William Ames (1576–1633).[157] In that Ames is the last Ramist before Westminster whom Rogers approvingly discusses, the theologian's use of the word *infallible*, given Rogers' perspective, should help us to understand well what the Westminster Divines meant by the expression. Rogers writes: "Ames represents the Puritanism of which Miller [Perry] speaks when he says that 'the dialectic of Ramus was blended perfectly with the theology of Augustine and Calvin'" (95).

Ames presents his views on Scripture in a popular text, *The Marrow of Sacred Divinity* (1623, 1627, 1629), a work used for many years at Harvard College in North America and on the Continent.[158] We cite his statement on Scripture *in extenso*, given its significance (I.34):

> 2. Only those could set down the rule of faith and conduct in writing who in that matter were free from all error because of the direct and infallible direction they had from God.

> 4. They also wrote by the inspiration and guidance of the Holy Spirit so that the men themselves were at that point, so to speak, instruments of the Spirit.

5. But divine inspiration was present among those writers in different ways. Some things were altogether unknown to the writer in advance, as appears in the history of past creation, or in the foretelling of things to come. But some things were previously known to the writer, as appears in the history of Christ written by the apostles. Some things were known by a natural knowledge and some by a supernatural. In those things that were hidden and unknown, divine inspiration was at work by itself. In those things which were known, or where the knowledge was obtained by ordinary means, there was added the writers' devout zeal so that (God assisting them) they might not err in writing.

6. In all those things made known by supernatural inspiration whether matters of right or fact, God inspired not only the subjects to be written about but dictated and suggested the very words in which they should be set forth. But this was done with a subtle tempering so that every writer might use the manner of speaking which most suited his person and condition.[159]

Like other Protestants, Ames declares the Bible is an infallible rule of faith and practice. But he goes on to claim that the words of Scripture are inerrant. He notes that the authors of the rule of faith and conduct were "free from all error" because God infallibly directed them (2). The authors could not err in writing about creation, history, and so forth (5). In matters of right and *fact* (italics mine) God inspired not only the subject matter but suggested the words, while he yet preserved the authors' integrity (6). In brief, Ames apparently equated biblical infallibility with inerrancy.[160] Moreover, in articles 27–31 he appears to associate biblical infallibility with the original autographs:

27. The Scriptures are not so tied to these first languages that they cannot and ought not to be translated into other languages for common use in the church.

28. But, among interpreters, neither the seventy who turned them into Greek, not Jerome, nor any other such held the office of a prophet, they were not free from errors in interpretation.

29. Hence no versions are fully authentic except as they express the sources, by which they are also to be weighed.

31. God's providence in preserving the sources is notable and glorious, for neither have they wholly perished nor have they been injured by the loss of any book or blemished by any serious defect—though today not one of the earlier versions remains intact.[161]

If the Ramist Ames does set the categories for interpreting the Westminster Confession, then Rogers and McKim have seriously misread that document concerning what the word *infallible* means (I.4) and how it relates to the original autograph's hypothesis (I.7).[162]

Obviously more research should ensue concerning the thought of other pre-Westminster theologians such as Temple, Perkins, and others. But it is clear from the Ames example that Ramism did not deter Puritans from embracing with other Protestants (whom Rogers labels scholastics) the idea that the Bible is "completely" infallible. Moreover, our research reveals that Ames's position was in full accord with that of the Cambridge professor William Whitaker (1547–1595), whom the Roman Catholic apologist Bellarmine admired as one of the best English Protestant disputants.[163]

Rogers, who cites exclusively secondary sources about Ames, evidently did not become acquainted with the actual writings of the theologian. Due to this kind of methodological lapse, Rogers's *Scripture in the Westminster Confession* and Rogers and McKim's joint study apparently do not give us the last word on the English Puritans and the Westminster Confession.[164] Even our brief comments allow us to affirm this.

The interpretation of I.8 of the Westminster Confession has long troubled Reformed theologians:

> The Old Testament in Hebrew (which was the native language of the people of God of old), and the New Testament in Greek (which at the time of the writing of it, was most generally known to the nations), being immediately inspired by God, and by His singular care and providence, kept pure in all ages, are therefore authentical; so as, in all controversies of religion, the Church is finally to appeal unto them.

Rogers and McKim give this commentary about the authenticity of the originals: "The authors of the Westminster Confession apparently meant by the word authentical that the text of Scripture in the original language was to be considered the final source of reference for understanding" (212). In *Scripture in the Westminster Confession*, Rogers is more specific: "Orr is right in denying that the authors of the Confession of Faith separated the autographs from the working copies of the Hebrew and Greek Scripture" (398). In making this observation, Rogers challenges the interpretation of B. B. Warfield and John Gerstner that the Westminster Divines were alluding to the "original autographs" as authentical in this passage.[165] Rather than reviewing the details of their long-standing debate, let us seek to throw some light on it from a vantage point not usually considered.

In his debate (1588) with Bellarmine, the English apologist Whitaker, whom we mentioned earlier, discussed in detail the meaning of the word *authentic* as it relates to the "originals."[166] In consonance with the Council of Trent, Bellarmine and other Roman Catholic apologists had claimed that Jerome's Latin Vulgate was authentic. Whitaker, and other Protestants with him, responded by saying that only the Hebrew and Greek originals were the authentic ones:

> We, on the contrary side, say that the authentic and divinely-inspired scripture is not this Latin, but the Hebrew edition of the Old Testament, and the Greek of the New [135].[167]

Translations are not authentic (144–45):

> . . . we do not say that one should stand by these translations as of themselves authentic, but appeal to the originals alone as truly authentic.

Like the Westminster Confession after him, Whitaker indicated that the Holy Spirit was the source of truly authentic Scripture:

> For authentic scripture must proceed immediately from the Holy Ghost himself . . . (2 Tim. 3:16); now Jerome's translation is not divinely inspired; therefore it is not authentic Scripture [148].

But what specifically did the Englishman mean by the *originals*? Was he referring to the "original autographs" or to the Greek and Hebrew texts which he had in hand? He used the expression *originals* for both. Wrote Whitaker about the original autographs:

> That Scripture only, which the prophets, apostles, and evangelists wrote by inspiration of God, is *in every way* (italics mine) credible in its own account and authentic [138].

But he assumed that the Hebrew and Greek texts of his own day (save the Septuagint) so closely reflected the autographs that they too, in one sense, could be justly called the "originals."[168] God had protected His Word as it passed from copyist to copyist throughout the ages.

When Bellarmine claimed that there were errors in the "originals" as represented by the Hebrew and Greek texts, Whitaker responded sharply:

> These then are the passages which Bellarmine was able to find fault with in the originals; and yet in these there is really nothing to require either blame or correction. But, even though we should allow (which we are so far from doing, that we have proved the contrary), that these were faulty in the original, what could our adversaries conclude from such an admission? Would it follow that the Hebrew fountain was more corrupt than the Latin streamlets, or that the Latin edition was authentic? Not, surely, unless it were previously assumed, either that canonical books of Scripture cannot be erroneously copied sometimes by transcribers, or . . . [160].

Whitaker, then, blamed any conceivable error on transcribers' mistakes.[169] No error existed in the autographs. On the contrary, the Vulgate possessed very real errors in the autograph itself which were not due to the negligence of copyists:

> The Latin Vulgate edition is most certainly and most plainly corrupt. And the corruptions I speak of are not casual, or slight, or common errors, such as the carelessness of copyists often produces in books; but errors deeply rooted in the text itself, important and intolerable. Hence is drawn the weightiest arguments against the authority of this edition [162].

Whitaker had recourse to St. Augustine's writings to justify his analysis of the "originals" question.

The discussion of the Ramist William Ames resembles Whitaker's analysis, although it is much more brief. It is quite probable that the Divines at Westminster thought about the "originals" in much the same fashion as their English predecessors: that is, the truly "authentic originals" were the autographs which the Hebrew and Greek so closely mirrored that they too could justly be called the "originals."

These scholars, who suggest the idea that "inerrancy in the original autographs" is a late nineteenth-century innovation, would do well to review more closely Roman Catholic and Protestant controversies in the sixteenth century. In those controversies the question of the originals was explored in depth. Moreover, they should reconsider the writings of Tertullian, St. Augustine, and other church fathers on the subject. In his *Histoire critique du Vieux Testament* (1678), Richard Simon summarized St. Augustine's position on this matter with these words (1):

> But because men were the depositories of the Sacred Books, as well as all other books, and because the first originals (*originaux*) have been lost, it was in some regards impossible to avoid several changes, more by the passage of the time, than by the negligence of copyists. It is for this reason that St. Augustine above all recommends to those who wish to study the Scripture, to apply themselves to the Criticism of the Bible, and to correct the mistakes in their copies.[170]

The idea of inerrancy in the original autographs has a long history.

G. Challenges to Biblical Infallibility in the Sixteenth and Seventeenth Centuries

If Luther, Calvin, and other Reformers held to biblical infallibility extended to all the words of the canonical Scriptures, and if, as Professor Bromiley indicates, the post-Reformation "orthodox" did no more than elaborate or emphasize too heavily certain aspects of Reformation doctrine on Scripture, an important question comes to mind. What was the nature of the first significant attacks against complete biblical infallibility? Rogers and McKim do not treat this subject as such. Nowhere do we find in their essay sustained discussion dedicated to continental thinkers such as Hugo Grotius[171] (who influenced greatly Jean LeClerc), La Peyrère (who influenced Spinoza and Richard Simon),[172] William Holden (who influenced Simon),[173] Spinoza[174] (who particularly set the stage for biblical criticism in the Enlightenment), and Richard Simon (another important biblical critic for Enlightenment authors), or to Jewish writers, whose works on occasion caused consternation among Christians. Because the story they tell possesses elements which are misleading, it calls for a careful exposition of the attacks *against* complete biblical infallibility in the late sixteenth and seventeenth centuries.

In a forthcoming study we shall treat the origins of modern biblical criticism in some detail. Here we will briefly sketch the general configurations of some of the diverse challenges to complete biblical infallibility.

Already in the sixteenth century Erasmus, who appreciated Lorenzo Valla's philological studies, and other Christian humanists had raised questions about certain texts in the Scriptures. Then again, Michel Servetus and followers of Faustus Socinus challenged directly the concept of the Bible's reliability in all details.[175]

Another challenge emerged from a loosely knit group of thinkers variously called *libertines* (both theological and moral).[176] Calvin himself wrote against them. Their common beliefs have been well surveyed by Rene Pintard in his massive study, *Le libertinage érudit dans la première moitié due XVIIë siècle* (Paris: Boivin, 1943). Including in their numbers Pomponazzi, Pierre Charron, Gabriel Naudé, Gui-Patin, and others, these individuals borrowed many of their arguments from the pyrrhonical arsenal in their veiled swipes at Christian authorities (the Bible, church traditions and leaders, and so forth). Perhaps a few were atheists; others were bare-boned deists who had shucked off Christian revelation and ecclesiastical authority. The sophisticated Roman Catholic priest, Mersenne, claimed in 1625 that there were twenty-five-thousand atheists in Paris.[177] Undoubtedly Mersenne's figures are bloated, but they do point to a current of outright skepticism about the Christian religion in early modern France. Descartes hoped to provide a counter stroke to this form of skepticism in his own work.[178]

Some Roman Catholic writers such as Father Jean Morin so pushed the pyrrhonical argumentation against Scriptures that they inadvertently contributed to the undermining of biblical authority. Richard Simon complained about this unexpected result coming from Morin's writing.[179] Morin, a fellow oratorian, had tried to force Protestants into the Roman Catholic camp by citing the difficulty of exegeting certain biblical passages without the help of Roman Catholic traditions. In this regard he followed the lead of Bellarmine and Stapleton, whose arguments were more nuanced.

Another source of unease for defenders of biblical infallibility stemmed from Jewish sources. Of particular importance in the late sixteenth and seventeenth centuries were the writings of Elijah Levita (1468–1549), who wrote *Massoret ha-Massoret* (Venice, 1548).

Levita raised questions about the Massoretic pointing of the Hebrew text. He suggested that the vowel points and accents were appended to the Hebrew text by Tiberian Jews centuries after Christ's life.[180] The Jesuits Genebrard and Guillaume Baile used this observation in an attempt to shake Protestants' confidence in the certainty of their Hebrew texts.[181] Could not unpointed Hebrew words be interpreted in many different ways? How could Protestants know that they interpreted the Old Testament correctly without the church's help? Also of great import for Christian theologians were the writings of Aben Ezra (1089–1164).[182] This rabbi "wondered" how a complete Mosaic authorship of the Pentateuch could be defended, given various texts which militated against it (such as the account of Moses' death).[183] In his influential *Tractatus theologico-politicus* (1670), Baruch Spinoza specifically exploited Aben Ezra's list of problem texts and pointed out other ones from other books in the Old Testament in his epochal attempt to destroy complete biblical infallibility. Wrote Spinoza about the beliefs of his opponents:

> I grant that they [contemporary theologians] are never tired of professing their wonder at the profound mysteries of Holy Writ; still I cannot discover that they

teach anything but speculations of Platonists and Aristotelians to which . . . they have made Holy Writ conform; . . . The very vehemence of their admiration for the mysteries plainly attests, that their belief in the Bible is a formal assent rather than a living faith; and the fact is made still more apparent by their laying down beforehand, as a foundation for the study and true interpretation of Scripture, the principle that it is in every passage true and divine.[184]

It should be noted that Spinoza assumed that Christians, whether Platonists or Aristotelians, viewed all the contents of the Bible as infallible. Thus, he thought that if he could find only minor contradictions in the Pentateuch and elsewhere, he could claim that he had accomplished his task. Richard Simon, who developed his famous "public scribes hypothesis" in part to fend off the brunt of Spinoza's argumentation, interacted vigorously with Aben Ezra's list of problem passages as well.[185] Thus, Jewish authors provided some of the data that both Roman Catholics and skeptics employed in their duels with Protestants.[186]

Some prominent Protestant divines argued that the Massoretic pointing was inspired by the Holy Spirit. The Buxdorfs of Basel, John Owen, Francis Turretin, and others in the United Provinces and elsewhere, did so. Eventually this retrograde stance was given creedal status for several cantons of Switzerland in the *Helvetic Consensus Formula* (1675). In arguing in this fashion, the divines wanted to guarantee the certainty of the biblical text.[187] They were worried about the apologetic gambits of Roman Catholics and skeptics. Some of them suspected the intentions of the Reformed theologian Louis Cappel, who had published studies (*Arcanum punctuationes*, 1624; and *Critica sacra*, 1650) where he argued against the inspiration of the Massoretic pointing. Cappel was able to publish one of these works only with the help of the Roman Catholic apologist, Jean Morin.[188]

Rogers and McKim observe correctly that those Protestant theologians who accepted the divine inspiration of the Massoretic pointing stepped beyond the teachings of the Reformers. But as we saw earlier, they assume incorrectly that these theologians' commitment to the principle of complete biblical infallibility was itself novel. This unbelief was well in line with the best Reformed and Lutheran traditions.

In his article, "Scepticism, Theology, and the Scientific Revolution in the Seventeenth Century," Richard Popkin has convincingly argued that the Christian world faced one of its most severe "scientific" challenges concerning biblical authority, not from Galileo and other Copernicans, who in the face of opposition maintained that their scientific hypothesis accorded with a proper interpretation of an infallible Bible, but from the attempts by Christian thinkers to reconcile biblical history with the new science

The flood, and the descendance of all mankind from Noah and his family provided serious difficulties when examined in the light of new geographical, anthropological, meteorological data, and mechanistic physics. Mersenne and Pascal, among others, had tried to explain how 40 days and 40 nights of rain could provide enough water to inundate the entire Earth so that even the highest mountain could be covered. . . . Archbishop Ussher (who calculated the date of

Creation as 4004 B.C.) made valiant efforts to reconcile with the Bible the data obtained by the explorers.[189]

The problems of reconciling Scripture with "new findings" began to reach a crisis point. Enter Isaac La Peyrère. Writes Popkin:

> . . . the whole enterprise of reconciling Scripture and the new science was blown apart by a mad genius, Isaac La Peyrère (Pereira), who, I believe, really set off the warfare between theology and science.[190]

In his far-fetched study, "Men before Adam, or A discourse upon the twelfth, thirteenth, and fourteenth verses of the Fifth Chapter of the Apostle Paul to the Romans, By which are prov'd that the first Men were created before Adam" (Latin ed., 1655; English, 1658), La Peyrère developed his remarkable pre-Adamite theory.[191] He argued that recent data from America, China, and Greenland revealed that human beings existed as far back as 50,000 B.C., thus throwing into jeopardy the 4,004 B.C. date for creation supposedly derived from the historical materials in the Bible.[192] Popkin notes that La Peyrère proposed a "theory of the independent origin of different cultures, the local occurrence of the Flood, the derivation only of Judeo-Christians from Noah, etc."[193] He challenged a commitment to biblical infallibility by spinning hypotheses which directly countered biblical teachings. What's more, he did so as a Roman Catholic.

Reaction was swift. La Peyrère was hauled into prison in Brussels. He eventually recanted his novel ideas before the pope in Rome, blaming his "errors" on his Protestant upbringing.[194]

The oratorian's influence was selective but immense. The principal founders of modern biblical criticism, Baruch Spinoza (1632–1677) and Richard Simon (1638–1712), were both intellectual debtors to La Peyrère's studies. Simon, for example, had long discussions with La Peyrère when the latter was an aged man in the late 1660s.[195]

Built upon misleading premises, Rogers and McKim's analysis does not adequately explain the efforts of early "scientists" to reconcile their investigations with biblical teachings. Many of these thinkers believed that all the words of Scripture are infallible.[196] Edward Brerewood, the first astronomer at Gresham College in the 1590s, wrote a lengthy piece, *Enquiries touching the Diversity of Languages and Religions through the cheife parts of the world* (London, 1614), where he tried to adjust new data coming from travel literature, the reports of mariners, the writings of antiquity, and his own primitive observations with what the Bible taught about the origins of languages and peoples.[197] Brerewood and other early "scientists" demonstrated remarkable dexterity in attempting to come to grips with all the words of Scripture, not just those thats bear on salvation truths. In introducing his uncle's posthumous "scientific" book (1614) Robert Brerewood affirmed that all European Protestants believed in "the infallible verity and full sufficiency of the Scriptures."

In many regards the vitriolic four-volume debate (1685–1687) between Richard Simon and Jean Le Clerc was one of the culminating points in a multifaceted movement away from complete biblical infallibility.[198] Taking place in what Paul Hazard has called "The Crisis of the European Mind (1680–1715)," this debate shook the confidence of leading members of the Republic of Letters (ranging from John Locke to Pierre Bayle) in the complete infallibility of Holy Writ.[199]

Even with its helpful comments about Bacon, Descartes, Cappel, the "deists," and the "Socinians," Rogers and McKim's study does not afford us with the makings of a comprehensive paradigm for understanding the forces which drove some Europeans to consider abandoning their commitment to complete biblical infallibility.[200] In the late sixteenth and seventeenth centuries, complete biblical infallibility was not being created; rather, some Europeans experienced the trauma of trying to uphold the position in the face of criticism sweeping in from many different directions.

H. The Old Princetonians and Biblical Infallibility

Curiously enough, Rogers and McKim do not discuss the struggles over biblical authority during the French *Siècle des lumieres* and the German *Aufklärung*, or elsewhere on the Continent.[201] They limit themselves to comments about John Locke, Thomas Reid, David Hume, and a few other English thinkers. How members of the Church of the Desert in southern France (Reformed Christians, incidentally), how Wesleyans in England and "Pietists" in Germany thought about Scripture are missing chapters in their story.[202] For that matter the authors generally give but scattered coverage to the attitudes of nineteenth-century European Christians toward Scripture. They do consider Scottish and English theologians, however.

Rogers and McKim fix concerted attention on what they call "Reformed scholasticism" in the United States. They identify its flowering with the instruction dispensed at Princeton seminary (founded in 1812). They propose that the influence of Francis Turretin's "scholastic" beliefs about Scripture determined to a large extent those of the Old Princetonians, particularly concerning biblical inerrancy.[203] For example, they explain Professor Archibald Alexander's commitment to that stance with these words (273):

> Because of his roots in Turretin, however, Alexander held fast to the postulate of the Bible's inerrancy in all things. He wrote: "And could it be shown that the evangelists had fallen into palpable mistakes in facts of minor importance, it would be impossible to demonstrate that they wrote anything by inspiration."

This explanation has a marked reductionistic quality when we recall that Christians from various communions had held complete biblical infallibility throughout the centuries and had assumed that this belief accorded with the Bible's teaching about itself.

The authors bring to their study insights drawn from the burgeoning literature about Old School Presbyterians in the United States (including the Princetonians). The studies of Sydney Ahlstrom, Theodore Bozeman, and others have informed scholars about the impact of Common Sense Realism/ "Baconianism" upon Presbyterians as well as upon American culture in general during the nineteenth century.[204] Rogers and McKim suggest that the Princetonians joined "Baconianism" to their "Protestant scholasticism." Earlier in their analysis they note the impact of Scottish Common Sense Realism upon John Witherspoon (1723–1794). Witherspoon was destined to play a major role in Princeton's history (246):

> Thus Witherspoon brought from Scotland to America the apologetic approach to Scripture that had led to conflicts between Scripture and emerging science in Switzerland and England. He prepared the groundwork on which the nineteenth-century Princeton theology would be built.

"Reformed scholasticism," Princeton style, married Common Sense Realism. According to the authors, this union spelled trouble ahead for American Protestants: ". . . the later fundamentalist-modernist controversy over the inerrancy of Scripture in the twentieth century was, in principle, already set in motion [by Witherspoon]" (246). The Princetonians were the culprits in preparing its denouement. Once again we encounter a strangely reductionistic hypothesis for so knowledgeable scholars as are Rogers and McKim.

Rogers and McKim's general analysis of the Old Princetonians contains some valuable insights. Yet it is ultimately disappointing. Several considerations lead us to make this unwelcome judgment.

First, the authors do not set the historical stage well for understanding the nineteenth century Princetonians. They do not comment upon Reformed traditions in the thirteen colonies. If they had done so, they might have noted William Ames's *Marrow of Christian Divinity* (1623, 1627, 1629) which served as an important textbook at Harvard during the seventeenth century. We recall that Ames advocated biblical inerrancy in that volume. They might have discovered that Jonathan Edwards, one of the most brilliant intellects of the eighteenth century, maintained a belief in complete biblical infallibility.[205] They might have observed that some Americans had questions concerning the concept of biblical infallibility in the early eighteenth century: that is, more than one hundred years before the idea of establishing Princeton Seminary was more than a twinkle in the eyes of Archibald Alexander or Ashbel Green.[206]

Second, Rogers and McKim paint the Princetonians into a corner as if they were the doughty lone defenders of an outmoded doctrine. In point of fact many contemporary Europeans and Americans from non-Presbyterian communions affirmed the same belief. Samuel Taylor Coleridge caused an uproar in the British Isles and North America by challenging the concept of complete biblical infallibility in his *Confessions of an Inquiring Spirit* (1841).[207] Coleridge acknowledged that he was attacking a belief which many English Christians from diverse ecclesiastical backgrounds cherished. He cited the remark of a "well disposed" skeptic about this point:

> I have frequently attended meetings of the British and Foreign Bible Society, where I have heard speakers of every denomination, Calvinist and Arminian, Quaker and Methodist, Dissenting Ministers and Clergymen, nay, dignitaries of the Established Church,—and still have I heard the same doctrine,—that the

Bible was not to be regarded or reasoned about in the way that other good books are or may be; . . . What is more, their principal arguments were grounded on the position, that the Bible throughout was dictated by Omniscience, and therefore in all its parts infallibly true and obligatory, and that the men, whose names are prefixed to the several books or chapters, were in fact but as different pens in the hand of one and the same Writer, and the words the words of God himself; . . .[208]

Coleridge responded:

What could I reply to this?—I could neither deny the fact, nor evade the conclusion,—namely that such is at present the popular belief.[209]

According to Coleridge (writing at the same time as the early Princetonians), many of his fellow Englishmen believed in complete biblical infallibility; Charles Hodge felt constrained to respond to Coleridge's theory of "gracious inspiration" in his *Systematic Theology* (1871).[210]

In *Lectures on the Evidences of the Revealed Religion* (multiple editions, 1838), the clergy of the Church of Scotland in Glasgow gave a detailed analysis of their commitment to complete biblical infallibility in the original documents.[211] Reverend Andrew King argued that should contradictions be proved in Holy Writ, ". . . they would indeed form a conclusive argument not only against the *inspiration* of Scripture, but against its character generally as a revelation from God" (125). Then King, representing the other pastors, proposed that any alleged contradictions are due to copyists' errors:

Some contradictions are owing to incorrect readings in the manuscripts from which our present text has been formed. You may remember that, in the argument which was so ably stated in the preceding lecture, proving the genuineness of the books of the Old and New Testaments, the thing maintained was not that we have these books *absolutely* but that we have them *substantially* as they were written [127].

On the Continent theologians like the Swiss Beck, whose essay, "Monogramata Hermeneutics N.T.," Charles Hodge published as the first article in the first volume of the *Biblical Repertory* (1825), pointed out the distinction between original autographs and translations, and the role of copyists' errors:

The scrupulous care taken of the Sacred Writings, and the custom of using them constantly in the church, is sufficient to convince us that they have been preserved from any serious alterations, yet they could not be entirely defended from the fate of all other ancient writings. The autographs appear to have perished early, and the copies which were taken, became more or less subject to those errors, which arise from the mistakes of transcribers, the false corrections of commentators and critics, from marginal notes, and from other sources. These errors may have been extensively propagated, and in some instances they may have had an origin anterior to any MS. or means of correcting the text now extant [27].[212]

Moreover, in his review of William Lee's influential volume, *The Inspiration of Holy Scripture* (see *The Biblical Repertory* 29 [1857]: 660–98), Charles Hodge indicated his belief in the complete infallibility of the Bible and attributed "difficulties" in the text to copyists' errors and "our ignorance." In his *Theopneustia* (1841), Louis Gaussen, Professor of Systematic Theology (Oratoire, Geneva), argued for complete biblical infallibility.[213] Then again, John Henry Newman, converted to Roman Catholicism, commented in 1861 about his adopted church's long-standing commitment to complete biblical infallibility:

> I suppose I am not wrong in saying that there has been in the last three hundred years a growing tendency in divines to abandon the doctrine of the verbal inspiration, and to acquiesce in an inspiration quoad res et sententias without any tendency whatever to allow the errability of the sacred writers in any of the most minute facts of physics, history and other human sciences. What is the universal sentiment has ever a claim upon our reverence and submission; and I for one am not bold enough against such authority, and against that intrinsic difficulty of the hypotheses on which I have already dwelt, to hold that any error whatever, however slight, is admissible in the sacred writers.[214]

The inference that European theologians in the first half of the nineteenth century had *en masse* abandoned a commitment to complete biblical infallibility is not well considered.[215]

In the United States Christians other than Old School Presbyterians held to complete biblical infallibility.[216] The important New Hampshire Confession (1833), which summarized Baptist credal beliefs, reads:

> We believe that the Holy Bible was written by men divinely inspired, and is a perfect treasure of heavenly instruction; that it has God for its author, salvation for its end, and truth, without any mixture of error, for its matter. . . . [217]

In his well crafted essay, "Baptists and Changing Views of the Bible, 1865–1918," Norman H. Maring observes:

> In the 1860's Baptists shared a predominant belief in the inerrancy of the Bible.[218]

The famous evangelist, Charles Finney, criticized an author who denied the inerrancy of historical sections of the Bible:

> The ground taken by the writer is that the historical parts, especially, of the New Testament are not inspired, not even with the inspiration of such a degree of divine superintendence as to exclude error and contradiction from them. He takes the ground that there are palpable inconsistencies and flat contradictions between the writers of the Gospels, and points out several instances, it appears to me, very much with the art and spirit of infidelity, which he affirms to be irreconcilable contradictions. The ground taken by him is that the *doctrinal* parts of the New Testament are inspired, but that the *historical* parts, or the mere narrative, are uninspired.

> Who will not see at first blush that, if the writers were mistaken in recording the acts of Christ, there is equal reason to believe they were mistaken in recording the doctrines of Christ?[219]

Certainly no friend of the Old School Presbyterians, Finney affirmed complete biblical inerrancy:

> . . . there is a real substantial agreement among all the writers, and that when rightly understood, they do not in anything contradict each other. It implies, that the several writers always wrote under such a degree of divine illumination and guidance, whether of suggestion, elevation, or superintendence as to be INFAL-LIBLY SECURED FROM ALL ERROR.[220]

Like John Wesley, leading Methodist theologians such as Samuel Wakefield (1799–1895) believed in complete biblical infallibility.[221] Many of the Continental Lutherans who came to America brought high views of Scripture with them. C. F. W. Walther, an early leader among nineteenth-century Lutherans, understood that if one finds errors in Scripture he establishes his reason above God's Word. Walther declared in 1858:

> He who imagines that he finds in the Holy Scripture even only one error, believes not in Scripture, but in himself; for even if he accepted everything else as truth, he would believe it not because Scripture says so, but because it agrees with his reason or with his heart. "Dear fellow," writes Luther. "God's Word is God's Word, and won't tolerate much doctoring."[222]

The attempts of Rogers and McKim and others to isolate Princetonians as reactionary defenders of biblical infallibility becomes less than convincing when placed against the broad sweep of European and American Christianity in the nineteenth century. Many volumes were published in which authors defended the complete biblical infallibility of the original autographs without making a reference to the Old Princetonians as authorities.[223]

Third, Rogers and McKim rely too heavily upon Ernest Sandeen's analysis of the Old School Princetonians as it relates to the question of biblical infallibility.[224] In another study we present a critical evaluation of Ernest Sandeen's interpretation.[225] Here we can make but a few comments to indicate why such a reliance is hazardous.

In a word,

> Sandeen argues that Archibald Alexander (1772–1851), one of Princeton Seminary's first theologians, was not dogmatic about verbal inspiration and complete biblical infallibility. His student, Charles Hodge (1797–1878) began to stress verbal inspiration, but still remained reticent to affirm biblical inerrancy dogmatically. Buffeted by the findings of Higher Criticism and developmental science, A. A. Hodge (1823–1886) and B. B. Warfield (1851–1921) advocated the doctrine of inerrancy in the original autographs (1881) as a dodge to escape mounting attacks on Scripture. Sandeen boldly affirms that this doctrine "did

not exist in either Europe or America prior to its formulation in the last half of the nineteenth century."[226]

Happily, Rogers and McKim dismiss Sandeen's judgment that Archibald Alexander, one of the early teachers at Princeton seminary, was not dogmatic about his commitment to verbal inspiration. In an article which Rogers and McKim cite, Sandeen declares: "First, the Princeton theologians agreed that the 'inspiration of the Scriptures extends to the words'. Archibald Alexander did not feel obliged to be dogmatic about the point, but after Charles Hodge adopted the position, no change occurred at Princeton regarding verbal inspiration."[227] On the contrary, Alexander was quite dogmatic on the point. He defined inspiration as

> such a divine influence upon the minds of the sacred writers as rendered them exempt from error, both in regard to the ideas and words.
> This is properly called plenary inspiration. Nothing can be conceived more satisfactory. Certainty, infallible certainty, is the utmost that can be desired in any narrative and if we have this in the sacred Scriptures, there is nothing more to be wished in regard to this matter.[228]

As we saw, Rogers and McKim acknowledge that Archibald Alexander held to complete biblical infallibility, attributing this commitment to the influence of Francis Turretin upon his thought.

But the authors follow Sandeen too closely in his interpretation of Charles Hodge's famous "flecks in the Parthenon" comment. In his *Systematic Theology* (1.170), Hodge speaks about "errors" in the Bible:

> The errors in matters of fact which skeptics search out bear no proportion to the whole. No sane man would deny that the Parthenon was built of marble, even if here and there a speck of sandstone should be detected in its structure. Not less unreasonable is it to deny the inspiration of such a book as the Bible, because one sacred writer says that on a given occasion twenty-four thousand, and another says twenty-three thousand, men were slain. Surely a Christian may be allowed to tread such objections under his feet.

Sandeen uses this statement as his principal evidence to demonstrate a new shift at Princeton between Charles Hodge and his son A. A. Hodge. According to Sandeen, A. A. Hodge and B. B. Warfield were obliged to create the doctrine of inerrancy in the original autographs due to mounting pressures of higher biblical criticism and science.[229] A. A. Hodge and B. B. Warfield articulated this new doctrine in their joint article of 1881, "Inspiration."[230] Writes Sandeen: "One could no longer dismiss them (errors) as had Charles Hodge—as flecks of sandstone in the Parthenon marble. Hodge and Warfield retreated."[231]

Sandeen, unfortunately, fails to cite Charles Hodge's next lines following the Parthenon illustration:

> Admitting that the Scriptures do contain, in a few instances, discrepancies

which without our present means of knowledge, we are unable satisfactorily to explain, they furnish no rational ground for denying their infallibility [1:170].

Elsewhere in his theology text, Charles Hodge declares:

> The whole Bible was written under such an influence as preserved its human authors from all error, and makes it for the Church the infallible rule of faith and practice [1:182].

In other words, Charles Hodge did not accept the possibility that the "errors" were genuine ones.[232]

Already in the 1880s some critics had claimed that Charles Hodge had not believed in inerrancy. They, too, cited the Parthenon illustration. To this charge, B. B. Warfield replied:

> Dr. Charles Hodge justly characterizes those (alleged errors) that have been adduced by disbelievers in the plenary inspiration of the Scriptures, as "for the most part trivial," "only apparent," and marvelously few "of any real importance." They bear, he adds, about the same relation to the whole that a speck of sandstone detected here and there in the marble of the Parthenon would bear to the building.[60] ([Footnote 60 reads]: We have purposely adduced this passage here to enable us to protest against the misuse of it, which in the exigencies of the present controversy, has been made, as if Dr. Hodge was in this passage admitting the reality of the alleged errors. . . . How far Dr. Hodge was from admitting the reality of error in the original Biblical text may be estimated from the frequency with which he asserts its freedom from error in the immediately preceding context. [152, 155, 163 . . . 165, 166, 169. . . .])[233]

Rogers and McKim do not misread Charles Hodge's Parthenon illustration as badly as Sandeen. They write (286):

> Hodge the teacher was able to dismiss such problems as minor. Hodge the theorist, however, was unable to admit that the problem might reside in his understanding of the issue.

They do intimate, however, that the teacher in Hodge did not take the possibility of real errors in the text as a serious affair.[234] To this sort of interpretation, Warfield's rejoinder still stands.

Rogers and McKim draw even closer to Professor Sandeen's interpretation when they discuss what they believe were innovating traits in the theology of Archibald Alexander Hodge. They argue that A. A. Hodge's *The Confession of Faith: A Handbook of Christian Doctrine Expounding the Westminster Confession* (1869) represented marked departures from the teachings of the Westminster Confession. Concerning the role of the Holy Spirit in confirming biblical authority, for example, the authors declare (300):

> Hodge could not accept the authority of the Scripture as the Westminster Di-
> vines had because of the internal testimony of the Holy Spirit.

They evidently overlooked Hodge's emphatic discussion about the Holy Spirit's
role in his *The Confession of Faith*:

> Yet the highest and most influential faith in the truth and authority of the Scrip-
> tures is the direct work of the Holy Spirit in our hearts.
> The Scriptures to the unregenerate man are like light to the blind. They may
> be felt as the rays of the sun are felt by the blind, but they cannot be fully seen.
> The Holy Spirit opens the blinded eyes and gives due sensibility to the diseased
> heart, and thus assurance comes with the evidence of spiritual experience.[235]

Or, the authors propose that A. A. Hodge changed the content "of the Princeton
defense of Scripture."[236] Like Sandeen, they suggest that the Princetonian introduced the hypothesis of inerrancy in the original autographs in the 1879 revised
edition of his *Outlines of Theology*, whereas he made no allusion to it in the 1860
edition of the same work.[237] This new stress on inerrancy in the original autographs was necessary due to the increased number of "scientific" and "higher
critical" problems opponents of complete biblical infallibility were raising.

Rogers and McKim do not indicate that this belief was a common one, widely
shared by contemporaries. The authors tend to ignore the fact that the Baptist
Alvah Hovey had claimed infallibility for the original autographs in his *Manual
of Systematic Theology and Christian Ethics*, published in 1877, or two years
before the revised edition of Hodge's *Outlines for Theology* appeared;[238] or the
fact that in his 1869 commentary on the Westminster Confession, A. A. Hodge
(like the divines at Westminster) designated the "authentical" Scripture as the
Old Testament "written in Hebrew and the New Testament in Greek, which were
the common languages of the large body of the Church in their respective periods;"
and he noted that ". . . the Scriptures in those languages are the absolute rule of
faith, and ultimate appeal in all controversies";[239] or the fact that in 1825 Charles
Hodge had published Beck's essay where the Swiss distinguished clearly between
lost original autographs and copies;[240] or the fact that Archibald Alexander had
claimed biblical infallibility for the writings which were available in Christ's
day: "We have the best evidence that the Scriptures which were in use when
Christ was upon the earth, were entire and uncorrupted, and were an infallible
rule."[241] Rogers and McKim fail to recall the multitude of tomes from the first
half of the nineteenth century where infallibility was claimed solely for the
original autographs. They do not remember the detailed debates over the "originals"
in the sixteenth century between Roman Catholic and Protestant apologists. In
charging A. A. Hodge with doctrinal innovation in this matter, the authors reveal
the extent to which they have been swayed by Ernest Sandeen's highly touted
but remarkably fragile thesis. We recall that Sandeen boldly declared: "This
doctrine [inerrancy in the original autographs] did not exist in either Europe or
America prior to its formulation in the last half of the nineteenth century." If
anything, A. A. Hodge gave added emphasis to a doctrine with a long history in
the Christian church.

We shall leave to others the analysis of Rogers and McKim's controversial interpretation of B. B. Warfield's apologetic for biblical authority. We should, however, comment about their reference to Warfield and the original autographs hypothesis. Rogers and McKim write:

> Warfield, with Hodge, thereby shifted the arena of discussion away from what the actual Bible said and was. They based their entire apologetic case on the inability of anyone to bring forth evidence from the nonexistent autographs. With such an unassailable, though artificial position Warfield felt secure. Individual facts that arose from critical study could never topple the Princeton theory of inerrancy. Warfield affirmed: "We cannot set aside the presumption arising from the general trustworthiness of Scripture, that its doctrine of inspiration is true, by any array of contradictory facts, each one of which is fairly disputable."

Rogers and McKim follow Sandeen's suggestion that Warfield and Hodge conspired together to create an unassailable apologetic for Holy Writ's inerrancy.[242] The critic of the doctrine could prove the errancy of Scripture only by locating errors in the original autographs. Since the autographs were lost, the critic could never gain access to them in order to prove his case.

In reality, Warfield and Hodge were emphasizing a position long honored by many Christians throughout the ages. The Bible gives no indication that copyists of Scripture were inspired; only the biblical authors were. As Augustine, the English apologist Whitaker, and the Roman Catholic critic Richard Simon pointed out, copies in fact do have errors in them. Then again William Ames observed that God providentially protected the biblical writings as they passed through time such that no gross distortions ruined them. For many Protestants, versions were "authentical" to the extent that they reflected the "originals." The autographs could be approached through the use of what we today would call textual criticism. Rogers and McKim's analysis reveals a perplexing unfamiliarity with the Reformation tradition on this point.

Ongoing research in the correspondence of A. A. Hodge and B. B. Warfield for the late 1870s and early 1880s gives no hint of a conspiratorial mentality shared by these two men.[243] What they said privately to each other, neither Sandeen nor any other scholar knows. As a result, the conspiratorial thesis can only be based on a psychological reconstruction, which is methodologically illegitimate in historical studies. In his bibliography for the *Roots of Fundamentalism*, Sandeen acknowledges that he did not consult the B. B. Warfield papers because at the time of the writing of his study they were not available to scholars.[244] Nor is there any indication in his bibliography that he surveyed the A. A. Hodge papers. Rogers and McKim would have been well apprised to weigh the evidence for their bold assertions with more care.

Fourth, the authors limit the major formative factors concerning the Old Princetonians' view of Scripture to the impact of Francis Turretin's thought and Baconianism. Undeniably, these two sources of influence were important ones. But those acquainted with the Old Princetonians' reading fare know that they poured over many works on Scripture other than those of Francis Turretin.[245] They read the studies of Germans, Englishmen, and fellow Americans on biblical inspiration. For that matter, as Rogers and McKim observe, the Princetonians specifically rejected Turretin's belief concerning the inspiration of the Massoretic pointing, whereas Charles Hodge indicated that he disliked the "tincture of scholasticism which pervades his work" (280). Turretin's teachings were greatly appreciated, but only within limits.

Moreover, scholars have not yet fully clarified what the significance of "Baconianism" might have been for the old Princetonians.[246] Did the Princetonians view "truth" differently than the Reformers? We propose that in the main they did not. Did not Calvin and Luther, despite their great concern to understand the meaning of God's mighty acts in history, treat the Bible atomistically on occasions in their sustained efforts to harmonize the words of Scripture? Did not Luther and Calvin use the "law of noncontradiction" in their harmonization studies while at the same time they grasped the "saving truth" that Jesus Christ is the way, the truth, and the life? The Princetonians' Baconianism did not quarantine them in another cultural paradigm such that they could not share with the Reformers some common grounds for understanding religious and epistemological issues.[247] As we have seen, the Princetonians' stress on complete biblical infallibility was not an innovation in the Reformation tradition.

It is true, however, that the Old Princetonians (influenced by Common Sense Realism) may have overestimated mankind's ability to understand an apologetic case for Christianity based on external evidences, and this despite their Reformed anthropology. They may have underemphasized the role of the Holy Spirit in persuading the faithful of the authority of Scripture. But even on these points we should speak with great caution. We noted A. A. Hodge's 1869 statement concerning the decisive role of the Holy Spirit in this regard, though he did accent the value of external evidences.[248] Then again, Professor Theodore Bozeman warns us that

> Ernest R. Sandeen's comment that "it is with the external not the internal" that Princetonian Old Schoolers dealt is a substantial exaggeration, as applied to the ante-bellum development.[249]

Rogers and McKim's interpretation, which tends to neglect the Princetonians' discussions of the "internal evidences" for the Bible's authority, their references to God's accommodation in human language, and their affirmations that the Bible is not a scientific textbook *per se*, bears the marked imprint of Sandeen's intriguing but ultimately misleading hypotheses.[250]

Much more could be said about Rogers and McKim's attempt to isolate the Old Princetonians from the central church tradition on biblical authority and to place them in a "stagnant tributary."[251] But we should press on to the authors' discussion of "Recent Efforts to Recover the Reformed Tradition."

I. The Rogers and McKim Proposal: Its Debt to Karl Barth and the Later Berkouwer

After reviewing what they call "Evangelical Reactions to Reformed Scholasticism" (380–405), Rogers and McKim proceed to a pivotal study of Karl

Barth, G. C. Berkouwer, and the United Presbyterian Church in the U.S.A. They give their discussion the title, "Recent Efforts to Recover the Reformed Tradition" (406–56). The authors praise both Barth and Berkouwer for setting the record straight concerning what the Reformers really taught. Concerning Barth, they write (426):

> Barth's "theological exegesis" allowed him to affirm much of Reformed confessional doctrine. . . . Barth's theology was a theology for preachers. Those who followed him were helped to proclaim God's Word with confidence in a world that wanted certainty. And yet they were allowed to be modern persons, not confined to philosophical obscurantisms or constricting systems of the past.

A propos Berkouwer, they declare (437):

> Berkouwer thus offered twentieth-century evangelicals the Reformation stance as an alternative between scholastic rationalism and liberal subjectivism. He proposed a Reformed doctrine of Scripture that was neither rationalistic nor subjectivistic. It was rather a view that correlated the divine message of Scripture with human faith in it. It was not a philosophical fideism, but a Reformation focus on the Bible's saving function.

Evangelicals acquainted with Karl Barth's neo-orthodox views concerning biblical inspiration at first may be surprised that the authors esteem the Swiss theologian's perspectives so highly. Their surprise might be less intense concerning the authors' encomium for Berkouwer if they recall that Professor Rogers translated the Dutch professor's *Heilige Schrift* into English under the title *Holy Scripture* (1975).[252]

Once we understand Rogers and McKim's great debt to the neo-orthodox categories of Barth and those of Berkouwer, then a possible answer to a haunting question begins to emerge.[253] Why does their volume falter as judged by the standards of careful historical craftsmanship? The answer to that question may be this. Rather than trying to interact evenhandedly with the data with which they were acquainted (even if it went against their favorite ideas), Rogers and McKim attempted to do history using the categories of the later Berkouwer as the lenses through which they viewed their material. By this we mean that the later Berkouwer's "historical disjunctions" may have become Rogers and McKim's working premises. Since Berkouwer does not believe in complete biblical infallibility and argues that the Bible's chief function is to reveal salvation truths (428–29), then those figures of the past who declared that the Bible reveals salvation truths also did not believe in complete biblical infallibility. Since Berkouwer thinks that God's accommodation to us in human language necessitates an errant Bible (431–33), then those individuals who spoke of accommodation denied complete biblical infallibility. Since Berkouwer argues that according to the Bible "error" relates solely to "sin and deception" (431), then Augustine, Calvin, and Luther only describe error in that way. Since Berkouwer does not believe that the Bible's incidental comments about history and "science" are reliable (431), then Augustine, Wycliffe, Calvin,

Luther, and others did not believe this either. Evidently, Rogers and McKim took the later Berkouwer's premises, and to a certain extent those of Barth, and crushed them down hard on whatever data they considered.

It is quite probable, then, that the Berkouwer lenses blurred Rogers and McKim's historical vision.[254] How else can we explain the repeated historical disjunctions, the unfortunate misquotations, the selective use of evidence, the wringing of secondary sources such that their authors' own analyses become misshapen? We examined only a relatively small number of the footnotes in this chapter. We fear that a more thorough analysis will reveal methodological infelicities of remarkable proportion.[255] The authors' categories of analysis lent themselves to a patchwork form of documentation where secondary sources were sometimes surveyed for statements that, taken in isolation, would support the authors' interpretation. In brief, the authors' apologetic concern along with their failure to consider the conceptual problems in doing good history overwhelmed their obviously well-intentioned desire to "set the record straight" concerning biblical infallibility. They wrote more as theologians doing apologetics than as historians.

Our hypothesis concerning Rogers and McKim's reliance upon the categories of the later Berkouwer, is just that, a hypothesis. Other influences may have been at work to create their systematic use of historical disjunction and their method of doing history.[256] Nonetheless the very high marks they give the neo-orthodox theologian Karl Barth and the later Berkouwer tend to give some weight to our suggestion.

IV. SOME CONCLUDING REMARKS

In our review we first set forth Professors Rogers and McKim's central proposal. Then we noted several methodological problems associated with it. And finally, we evaluated several specific portions of their argumentation. We followed the authors down segments of their own chosen pathway through nearly two thousand years of Christian history.[257] We interacted with them on their own grounds, using essentially their own trusted sources.[258] Where our own expertise was limited, we did not venture to evaluate their findings. Other specialists may want to do so.

What conclusions can we draw from our survey, which, though lengthy, is paradoxically so brief? Although Rogers and McKim's volume bears the title *The Authority and Interpretation of the Bible: An Historical Approach*, we discovered that their real interests were actually quite narrow and apologetic. They wanted to baptize as evangelical the hypothesis that the Bible is infallible for matters of faith and practice but errant in matters of science, history, and the like. Modern-day evangelicals have usually associated this designation with the teachings of neo-orthodoxy.

If Christians are to accept Rogers and McKim's proposal, they should know what they are buying. They should understand the nature of the scholarship which underlies it, the kind of Bible that results from it, and the problem of discerning what that latter Bible's real authority might be.

We have already presented our estimation of the scholarship which upholds it. Rogers and McKim give their own description of the Bible that results from it. They distinguish between the "central saving message of Scripture and all of the difficult surrounding material that supports that message" (461). It taxes the imagination to think that St. Augustine, Calvin, or Luther, whose authority Rogers and McKim repeatedly invoke, would have ever characterized Holy Scripture in this sharply dichotomized fashion.[259] Rogers and McKim's claim upon these past Christians is indeed tenuous.

The authors' description of the Bible creates for them the same kind of dilemma that neo-orthodox scholars before them faced: how to distinguish the infallible "central saving message" from the errant "difficult surrounding material." This is a critical problem because Christianity is grounded in the dirt and dust of human history. Salvation truths are planted in the Bible's historical discourse about things that happened. In his 1861 essay on inspiration, John Henry Newman clearly exposed the difficulty of sifting out "salvation truths" from the biblical materials:

> The practical difficulty in the latter solution is that of drawing those facts which are in materia fidei et morum, and those which are not so. Where are we to stop, if once we grant that a sacred writer is not protected from error in any one of his statements? . . . [Now] since Scripture contains a multitude of facts which in their substance belong to human history, but which it viewed in a religious light and in one way or other connects with the miraculous and providential operations of the Almighty God, how is it possible that we can allow the possibility of error in statements concerning them without infringing the inspired teaching, weakening the argument for its doctrines, its interpretations of human affairs, and its vehicle of divine appointments (operations)?[260]

Rogers and McKim do not give us answers to Newman's questions. Nor do they afford us with much explicit guidance concerning the criteria by which we may sort out "salvation truths" from the Scriptures.[261] They do say, however, that "Ancient principles must be applied using all that we can learn about language and cultures from the human and social sciences of the twentieth century" (461). What this means in practicality is that the infallible salvation material can shrink or expand in accordance with the latest givens in higher biblical criticism, cultural anthropology, or findings from other disciplines. As the changing "givens of modernity" set standards for understanding Scripture for Bultmann, so they do for Rogers and McKim. In a word, the believer is obliged to give up the doctrine of *sola Scriptura* as the Reformers perceived it because his or her reason influenced by shifting "givens" becomes another authority. Our reason helps us to determine an infallible canon within the Scripture. Ironically, then, Rogers and McKim's proposal which they package as one of "faith" before "reason," cracks the door open to the radical criticism of the Bible. Their unqualified fideism concerning the role of the Holy Spirit in confirming the authority of Scripture to believers is matched by an apparent unqualified confidence in reason's rights to superintend biblical studies. They offer to evangelicals a proposal that, like Karl Barth's, is subject to unraveling. The findings of "higher criticism" can continually reduce the core of "faith and practice" truths to a smaller and smaller epicenter.

What will become of their book? In several regards Rogers and McKim's survey is a disappointing piece. The authors obviously labored long hours upon it, carefully forging their proposal. But despite their sincere Christian motivations for composing it, their efforts will probably be less than satisfying to them. Because they so desperately wanted to plead a certain case, they generally sacrificed their claims to evenhanded scholarship by discounting out-of-hand contrary evidence, by neglecting worlds of technical scholarship bearing on their broad subject, by fixing too uncritically upon a neo-orthodox historiography, and by relying too heavily upon secondary literature rather than examining primary sources for themselves. As a result, their volume lacks that quality of reliability which gives good historical surveys their endurance. For this reason and others, professional historians will probably tend to bypass their study in years to come. Much like Will and Ariel Durant's *The Story of Civilization*, their volume may grace library shelves. But, in a similar fashion, it too may seldom be noted in bibliographies of first-class monographs. Unless the authors are prepared to revise their work thoroughly, their volume's future is cloudy, at least from the point of view of its acceptance by competent specialists. And eventually, scholars' reviews will probably percolate down to lay readers who may have been initially impressed by the daring proposals, the simple prose, and the footnotes which appear impressive until they are scrutinized.[262] It would be regrettable, therefore, if many evangelical pastors and lay people take the book's central proposal too seriously because they are unaware of its deficiencies.

Regrettably, the words of one of Dorothy Sayers's characters capture the dynamics of Rogers and McKim's apologetic efforts: "There's nothing you can't prove if your outlook is only sufficiently limited."

In a way which the authors probably did not envision, their study creates a call for those historians engaged in the current quest to discover the ancient attitudes of Christians toward Holy Writ. These historians should do their research in an evenhanded manner, consider well the conceptual problems associated with their undertaking, and write technically competent analyses on delimited subjects before attempting the grand synthesis. Evangelicals who emphasize with St. Augustine, Calvin, and Luther that the Bible's chief function is to reveal salvation truths about Christ, who acknowledge the Holy Spirit's role in confirming biblical authority to believers, and who rest confidently in the complete infallibility of God's Word, have no reason to resent their quest, let alone fear their findings.[263] The Bible is God's sure Word to humankind. It was for yesterday; it is for today; and it will be for tomorrow.

CHAPTER TWO

TO BEHOLD AND INHABIT THE BLESSED COUNTRY: INSPIRATION, SCRIPTURE, AND INFALLIBILITY – AN INTRODUCTORY GUIDE TO AUGUSTINE STUDIES, 1945–1980[1]

Rodney L. Petersen

The purpose of this chapter is to provide an introductory guide to reflections between the years 1945–80 upon Augustine's thought as it pertains to the areas of revelation, inspiration, Scripture, and infallibility. No apology is needed for the value of this study upon the work of the church's chief theologian with respect to the sources of its theological reflection. Not only is Augustine's own work the subject of a great deal of debate as to its systematic formulation and development,[2] but also there has been a veritable explosion of Augustinian studies in the years since the Second World War. This chapter cannot begin to survey all of the literature in the areas outlined above, but perhaps it can provide a guide to some of its chief elements.

In addition to the many fine studies which will be noted throughout its context, this chapter is guided by the following bibliographic sources and journals. First, a useful and easily accessible introduction to work on Augustine may be found in *The Oxford Dictionary of the Christian Church*, 2nd edition, ed. by F. L. Cross and E. A. Livingstone (New York: Oxford University Press, 1974). Four of the more complete guides to work on Augustine are (1) "Bibliographia Augustiniana," by Carl Andersen, published as a supplement to the book he entitled *Augustinus-Gespräch der Gegenwart* (Köln: Wienand Verlag, 1962): 459–583, and later separately; (2) *Repertoire Bibliographique de Saint Augustin 1950–1960,* by T. Van Bavel (The Hague: Instrumenta Patristica, iii, 1963); (3) *Augustine Bibliography* (Boston: G. K. Hall, 1972), produced by the Institut des Études Augustiniennes, Paris, which publishes special Augustinian studies, the *Revue des études augustiniennes* with its annual *Bulletin Augustinien*; and (4) Terry L. Miethe, ed., *Augustinian Bibliography, 1970–1980. With Essays on the Fundamentals of Augustinian Scholarship* (Westport, Conn.: Greenwood Press, 1982).

Of the several journals dedicated in whole or in part to studies in Augustine, the following should be cited: *Augustiana; Revue des études augustiniennes; Zeitschrift Augustinus; Augustinum* (since 1961); *Augustinian Studies* (since 1970); *Recherches augustiniennes* (since 1958), as well as the various publications of the Oxford Patristics Congress as published through *Studia*

Patristica (edited by K. Aland and F. L. Cross). Particular note should be made of the series of articles by Rudolf Lorenz: "Zwölf Jahre Augustinusforschung (1959–1970)," which appeared in *Theologische Rundschau* 38 (1974): 292–333; 39 (1975): 95–138, 253–86, 331–64; 40 (1975): 1–41, 97–149, 227–61. I have been guided in places by this effort which treats several of our items more extensively.

This chapter will be divided into four areas: (1) Revelation, (2) Inspiration, (3) Scripture, and (4) Infallibility. In each of these areas we will look at representative work by Augustine[3] and then consider some of the critical evaluative literature. Revelation deals with the possibility of knowing divine things, wisdom, or knowledge not immediately apparent from the world of sensation and reason. In the Judeo-Christian tradition the emphasis has been more upon disclosure than discovery.[4] Inspiration deals with the action of God in guiding the minds of His prophets, apostles, and their disciples to an understanding of those things pertaining to true wisdom and to activity which may lead toward virtue and charity.[5] Scripture, as traditionally conceived in the Christian churches, is the result of that process of inspiration as it bears indirectly, through prophets, upon their written documents or directly upon those works in their own right.[6] Infallibility is a property posited of inspired writings in connection with another agency or in their own right.[7]

I. REVELATION

It is quite evident that the question of the possibility of revelation and belief in its bestowal runs throughout Augustine's life's work.[8] This quest for a transcendent meaning on Augustine's part has led some scholars, notably Aimé Solignac, to consider Augustine in light of current existentialist thinking.[9] According to Solignac, it is not anachronistic to think in this way with respect to Augustine. For, it is argued, Augustine began with the problem of his self and attempted to find transcendent meaning.[10] Such an approach has helped to make Augustine more understandable in terms of modern sensibilities. In following out this line of thought Franz Körner has sought to understand the problem of why Augustine may have taken up the ideas and beliefs which became so central to his later self-identity. By delineating Augustine's use of Platonic and then Plotinian ideas of illumination, Körner believed it possible to understand Augustine's conception of meaning, a theocentric anthropology given to contemplation and love.[11] Only in such a way, Körner argued, can one study the personhood of Augustine (not oblivious to his context) in his own right. While such an existentialist point of view is useful in explaining the way in which the young Augustine works toward the idea of revelation, it remains to be seen whether it does full justice to his later conception of it.[12]

Gerald Verbeke, who also finds in existentialism a useful tool to understand Augustine's personal quest for knowledge of God, notes that in Augustine's ascent by an interior return and through Neoplatonic inspiration there are introduced important Christian corrections. While such an existential approach may be useful in understanding some of the dynamics in Augustine's life that from a certain point of view compelled him to adopt either a Neoplatonic or more scriptural Christian perspective, in the end such an approach cannot deal adequately with the presumed content of revelation (however interpreted) that drew Augustine's attention toward it (for whatever reason).[13] Throughout most of the history of Christendom revelation has been conceived as a kind of divine truth or mode of understanding which exceeds the natural human intellect.[14] For Augustine there are certain conceptions (e.g., the Incarnation) that cannot be derived from sensation or from reason, i.e., from corporeal or spiritual vision.[15] These he attributed to divine revelation which might be disclosed in the visible form of a theophany or invisible forms of memory and divine illumination. In asking about the nature of Augustine's conception of revelation in our period, then, we will begin by looking at the question of theophany and then move on to consider the equally complex, but more discussed issue of memory (*memoria dei*) and its relation to neoplatonism.

First, we may turn to the work of Jean-Louis Maier.[16] Maier emphasizes the point that, beginning as part of the orthodox anti-Arian movement in the fourth century seen in various Eastern fathers and in Ambrose, one finds a distinction developed between the missions and consequent revelation of the various persons of the Trinity. These distinctions are expanded by Augustine in whom one can find a differing emphasis placed upon the "visible" revelation of the Father, as in theophanies (which may also be temporal disclosures of the full Godhead), and the "invisible" revelation of the Son and Holy Spirit, particularly as they provide a present witness in the soul. The question of the visibility of God as it may pertain to the problem of theophany was taken up at various points by Augustine, but particularly in letters 147 and 148. Letter 147 is called "The Book of the Vision of God."[17] Here Augustine asks about the nature of our future spiritual bodies and their ability to see God. He writes that God cannot be localized, and therefore cannot be seen with bodily eyes. The vision of God is granted to those with a "clean heart."[18] In letter 148 he argues against all forms of anthropomorphism.[19] The eyes of this body cannot see God and never will. Such a statement was a part of Augustine's contention that not only is God invisible, but He cannot be divided into any one aspect of His creation.[20] However, the invisible God can be seen in an invisible manner by the eye of the mind with the requisite moral purity.[21] Still, Augustine admits, God did upon occasion make it possible for Himself to be seen by assuming a discernible form.[22] To see such a theophany was made possible by the will of God. Basil Studer discusses the nature of such theophanies as raised in Letter 147 in light of the current Arian controversy and the distinctions made by Ambrose between a natural and willed form of divine revelation as such pertains to the nature of God.[23] Whether or not this distinction goes back to Origen's idea of the logos extending itself as it chooses has been a matter of some debate, the significance of which is discussed by Studer.

A related question at this point is that of the bestowal of the grace required to see God as He wills to make Himself known or even visible. Theophanies are not necessarily seen or understood by all. A question such as this takes us quickly into the Pelagian controversy and understanding of the relationship between grace and revelation. C. Kannengiesser raises this question in connection with Augustine's commentary on Psalm 118 (= 119), a theological question taken up at Augustine's insistence by the Council of Carthage in 418.[24]

According to Augustine, as demonstrated by Kannengiesser, the discernment or knowledge of God's will is a gift of His grace as is the necessary virtue for its fulfillment. To see is to receive strength, to receive strength is to see.[25]

To return to Maier, as one understands the question of revelation, so one will perceive the manner of the eternal procession of the Son and Spirit. In other words, one finds in the Augustinian dynamism of revelation a picture of the Trinity as *memoria dei, intelligentia dei,* and *amor dei.* Augustine's idea of *memoria dei,* so Maier argues, ties his conception of the revelation of the Father to particular acts in history. This underscores the value of the biblical record for Augustine and, together with the internal witness of the Son and Spirit, helps to delineate a Trinitarian conception of revelation.[26] One can well imagine the significance of this in the midst of the Arian crisis. Citing *On the Freedom of the Will* (3.21.59–62) and *On True Religion* (25.46), TeSelle underscores the importance of the historical dimension of this Trinitarian revelation. He writes: "But the biblical revelation offers . . . divinely revealed narratives and prophecies, reaching backward to the creation and forward to the eschaton."[27] The importance of this is seen in the context: challenged by Prophyry's argument that credible mediation between the divine and human worlds must have "historical" validation, Augustine went ahead and argued this point for Christianity in his work *On True Religion.*[28] An interlocking relationship appears to be established between an external or visible form of revelation (theophany) made possible by the will of God, and an internal, divine witness, a gift of God's grace.

Having followed Maier to underscore the imperative value of the historical and contingent in Augustine's view of revelation, one must add that the picture is not always quite so clear. About the same time as Augustine wrote *On True Religion* he was also carrying on a correspondence with his friend Nebridius. In 389 Nebridius brought a question to Augustine with respect to memory and imagination: Can memories or fantasies arise of themselves or do they require images received through the senses?[29] In his reply to Nebridius, Augustine writes that the things "which we remember are not always things which are passing away, but are for the most part things that are permanent."[30] The memory can function without there having been past sense experience. As such it would seem that certain religious truth can be known apart from theophany or historical contingency. Again Nebridius writes, now pointedly with respect to revelation: How do the heavenly powers reveal things to us through dreams? Do their thoughts compel our thoughts? Do they show us things accomplished, if not bodily then through the imaginative faculty? How do such dreams relate to our own bodily stimulus?[31] Augustine replies by writing that the body affects the mind and the mind the body.[32] He then calls to Nebridius's attention what he had written (in Letter 7) that memory may be utilized apart from sense images. For the mind to form images of material things, however, sense experience is necessary. He then divides such images into three classes: corporal, rational, and intellective.[33]

This discussion continues to raise the problem of that internal witness, the *memoria dei,* in Augustine's thought. According to Goulvan Madec, Augustine used the idea of the memory as it pertained to God not in the sense of natural reason or a natural inclination toward divine things but more in connection with a special activity of the Spirit prompting and leading our minds. Apart from the prompting of God's grace such truth as might be discerned is held captive in unrighteousness.[34] Such a conception of memory is quite different from that of Cilleruelo, who views Augustine's idea of *memoria dei* as similar to a kind of natural reason or inclination (e.g., *Conf.* 7.17.23: "Yet was there a remembrance of thee with me").[35]

In connection with this discussion we might remember Maier's suggestion that not only do we encounter the *memoria dei* through the work of the Spirit in the individual's soul, but also in creation. Ragnar Holte also emphasizes a confluence of natural and divine knowledge by appealing to Paul's development of the implicit knowledge of God available to all in Romans 1. The voice that speaks within the individual is met by a natural revelation of God in the created world.[36] According to Madec, although one can discern in Romans 1:20 an ascent to divine knowledge from the created world, as in Platonism, this does not implicitly lead to a recognition of God. As we noted in Letter 148, the vision of (ascent to) the invisible God comes only with purity of heart, which occurs in connection with belief in Christ. Both creation and history bear traces of divinity but this divinity will never be understood apart from the gift of purity. With this we are brought back to Kannengiesser's connection in Augustine between revelation and spiritual development. The one cannot be separated from the other. Quoting Ambrose approvingly, Augustine writes:

> God is not seen in space, but in the pure heart; nor is He sought out by the eyes of the body; nor is He defined in form by our faculty of sight; nor grasped by the touch; His voice does not fall on the ear; nor are his goings perceived by the senses.[37]

DeVeer argues that Augustine took his concept of "revelare" and "revelatio" from Paul and the Synoptics.[38] Two types of revelation were conceived by Augustine: that of contingent events often revealed through dreams, and the revelation of doctrine or the divine truth of Christian teaching. Revelation is a quality which belongs both to Christian teaching and to inner illumination. In the context of his analysis of several church fathers from the apostolic period to that of Augustine, Rene Latourelle argues that Augustine borrows from John the evangelist the language by which he expresses the idea of revelation.[39] The center of his thought is tied to Christ conceived of as the mediator and way to God.[40] This idea does not have to be seen as set over and against that of de Veer. Rather, both views offer complementary perspectives on the operation of revelation in Augustine's thought. While deVeer's concentration can be said to be more in the direction of man's perception and of openness to the possibility of natural revelation, Latourelle's focus remains directed toward the agency of the mediator who makes possible as well as clarifies the qualified nature of natural revelation since the fall.

Making something of a further distinction in Augustine's conception of the way in which dreams may be used of God in the context of internal revelation, Dulaey argues that Augustine does not consider dreams to be revelatory as in

Platonism.[41] While dreams are not sources of higher knowledge in themselves, God can use dreams to make His will known. So, it is argued, Augustine used Porphyry's understanding of dreams in the development of his own theory of psychology and knowledge. We shall take up this point again when we turn to Augustine's understanding of inspiration.

A discussion of internal witness and revelation raises the question of the extent to which Augustine appropriated Neoplatonic philosophy. This is a subject for which we can provide only a provisional guide. It is raised for us in a pointed way by Augustine's friend Nebridius, who writes to Augustine expressing his pleasure in receiving Augustine's letters; for, he says, "They shall bring to my ear the voice of Christ, and the teaching of Plato and Plotinus."[42] The earlier discussion of this topic goes back to Adolf Harnack[43] but it received a certain summary form in the work of Prosper Alfaric.[44] Alfaric contended that only long after his "conversion" did Augustine accept the Christian faith in opposition to Neoplatonism. By the 1920s, however, there grew a counterattack which pushed Augustine's acceptance of the Christian faith and his criticism of Neoplatonism back to an earlier period in his life. This was led by the work of Charles Boyer,[45] who stressed the importance of Ambrose's preaching in developing a receptive attitude in Augustine for Neoplatonism.

A new dimension of the problem was raised after the Second World War in the work of Pierre Courcelle.[46] Courcelle developed the idea that Augustine received both Christianity and Neoplatonism through the teachings of Ambrose.[47] This Neoplatonism was primarily the thought of Plotinus[48] mediated by Ambrose, together with that of Origen, Philo, and the Cappadocians. Working within Courcelle's general thesis, as he maintains all must do since its articulation, F. E. Van Fleteren has analyzed Book 7 of the *Confessions*.[49] He maintains that one is able to find examples of "ascent" language in the *Confessions* which have parallels in Augustine's Cassiciacum period.[50] Many have focused on the question of "participation in the divine truth," a kind of "surmounting of the sensual world, as the place where both the Christian life and Neoplatonism meet,"[51] the differences being in how that participation is effected. This is not to deny the value of the material world, as in Gnosticism or Manichaeism, but it is to see it as relative when compared with God and the spiritual world.[52]

A. H. Armstrong argues that with respect to the body and material world, Augustine is closer to Plato and the later Neoplatonists than he is to Plotinus.[53] Plotinus held to the existence of a naturally immortal soul, hence to a kind of natural divinity. Such was not the case for Augustine. Pursuing the complex traditions of Christian and Neoplatonic thought as they had developed by this point, Armstrong delineates areas of agreement and disagreement in Augustine with this philosophical context. John J. O'Meara also looks elsewhere for further influence on Augustine, and with the older work of W. Theiler (1933), O'Meara emphasizes the importance of Plotinus's disciple, Porphyry.[54] Plotinus influenced Augustine's "conversion syndrom," according to O'Meara, whereas Porphyry was more influential with regard to the nature of salvation (despite his hostility to Christianity).[55]

Robert J. O'Connell argues that Neoplatonism exercised a major influence on Augustine's thought, specifically a strong Plotinian influence.[56] He writes,

"It was Plotinus who helped most in clarifying what Augustine said, and what he meant by what he said. As a result I have been led to underline Plotinus' influence on Augustine to an extent unknown since Bouillet, Grandgeorge, Alfaric and Nörregaard were apparently discountenanced by the work of later Scholars—Theiler, Henry, O'Meara among them."[57] O'Connell attempts to establish his case by comparing Plotinian and Augustinian texts. In line with Courcelle, O'Connell argues that Ambrose's preaching created a receptive attitude in Augustine's mind for a Neoplatonic version of Christianity, but Ambrose contributed less than Plotinus to the eventual structure of Augustine's Christianity. Regarding the distinctively *Christian* nature of Augustine's thought and commitment, O'Connell writes, "The question of Augustine's sincerity as a Christian, then, seems more than ever a false problem, one that serves only to mask the real question at issue: how adequate, objectively, was the Neo-Platonic *intellectus* which Augustine—sincerely, though at points mistakenly—believed to correspond to the content of the *fides catholica?*"[58] According to O'Connell, the only way to answer this question is through a close study of Augustine's work from his conversion onward.

Much of the preceding discussion underscores the importance of Courcelle's study early in our period.[59] Peter Brown even contends that Courcelle's work "has laid the foundations of all modern views of Augustine's evolution in Milan."[60] The relationship between what one could refer to as Augustine's "scriptural Christianity" and Neoplatonism is complex. While O'Connell is correct in saying that a proper assessment of the relation between the two contributing intellectual traditions of Augustine's conception of revelation needs to be based upon a thorough study of Augustine's particular works, it is striking that Augustine himself, in decisions made between the two, acknowledges that Scripture is always to take precedence.[61] In defining the content and dynamics of revelation in Augustine's thought, this admission needs to be taken seriously.

Following a line that is somewhat more negative in its assessment of Augustine's appropriation of Neoplatonism, we may begin by citing the work of R. A. Markus. He contends that Augustine's use of philosophy is "technical" in nature.[62] The central facts of Christianity are seen by Augustine to be historical and therefore somewhat at variance from the sphere of philosophy, which is an intellectual, analytical, and clarifying activity.[63] Yet, as Markus recognizes, the situation is not completely clear. Augustine also calls Christianity "the one true philosophy."[64] "In practice," Markus writes, "Augustine overcame the dilemma by confining his interest in what we would recognize as philosophy to the level he distinguished—as 'technical.' He subordinated it rigidly to the study of the scriptures which contained the truths necessary for a Christian."[65]

In continuing this somewhat more negative assessment of Augustine's Neoplatonism, one may cite the earlier work by Mary Patricia Garvey.[66] In this now dated thesis she examines the development of Augustine's thought from the time of his conversion to his ordination (A.D. 386–391). A number of studies have been written more recently that either illustrate Augustine's critique of Neoplatonism in particular works or attempt to chart his movement away from Neoplatonism to a faith more systematically defined by biblical revelation. For example, John A. Mourant argues that the degree of Neoplatonism in Augustine has been overemphasized in recent years.[67] On the basis of his study of the dialogues written at Cassiciacum, considered by some to be the *most* Neoplatonic of Augustine's works, Mourant sees Christianity superseding and subordinating Neoplatonism. Agreeing with what we have previously noted in Markus, Mourant contends that the function of philosophy in Augustine's thought is limited to the "explication of the truths of faith."[68] It should be noted, however, that it is at this juncture that Harnack's point needs to be raised once again: To what extent is the faith altered by the terms given for understanding?

Mourant's fine study of the dialogues written early in Augustine's career is matched by others concerned with different treatises. For example, William A. Christian argued with regard to *The City of God*, written during the later end of the spectrum in Augustine's literary career, that the purpose of Book 11 in that work was the refutation of Neoplatonism.[69] Later in our period Robert Russell continued this line of thought with additional nuances.[70] While Augustine's enthusiasm for Neoplatonism diminished over the years, it never completely vanished. It simply became more critical. The cosmology of Neoplatonism was refuted in *The City of God* but not its doctrine of illumination, important for our interest in revelation as well as inspiration. He continued to insist that here there is no conflict with Christianity.[71] But if Augustine continues to be generally positive toward Platonic natural philosophy, he is, according to Russell, pointedly critical of its moral philosophy. So, for Russell, "Any critical assessment of Augustine's relationship to Neoplatonism would seem to require a distinction between the respective roles of Augustine as Christian philosopher and apologist."[72] Whether such a distinction can hold at the place where ethics and philosophy meet is to be questioned.

Alfred W. Matthews argues that the relationship between Augustine's Christianity and Neoplatonism is to some extent determined by when one believes he became a Christian: (1) Some contend his conversion took place in the garden as described in Book 8 of the *Confessions*, certainly during his time at Cassiciacum (W. J. Sparrow Simpson, Gibb and Montgomery, P. M. Löhrer, P. de Labriolle, J. Burleigh) when Christ is accepted by Augustine as the ultimate authority (*Against the Academics* 3.2.43). (2) Others maintain that this occurred at the time of his baptism in Milan (Capanaga, W. Thimme). (3) Still others hold that Augustine only became a Christian at some later point as he grew in his understanding of the faith (Marrou, E. Hendricks, again, W. Thimme).[73] In other words, it is argued that (1) Neoplatonism led Augustine to Christianity, (2) Augustine was a Christian prior to becoming a Neoplatonist, or (3) Augustine received Neoplatonism and Christianity together.[74] In his fine study of the five-year period between Augustine's "conversion" and ordination (A.D. 386–391), Matthews sees an important and gradual shift in Augustine's thinking that included moral and occupational changes, a new attitude toward the Catholic church, and a shift in intellectual priorities in favor of a scriptural Christianity.[75]

It is this scriptural Christianity which increasingly worked its leaven in Augustine's life, progressively dominating his religious quest and giving structure to his understanding of revelation.[76] Certainly by the time of the writing of *On the Trinity* Augustine had come to believe clearly that there is no final knowledge of God apart from Christ.[77] He appears to have also concluded that, since the Fall, prophets' words were needed, as "rain from dark clouds," to convey adequately an understanding of God.[78] If he had entertained some possibility for the Platonic theory of reminiscence earlier in his life, that was now rejected.[79] If there is any revelation outside of the canonical Scriptures, it is only sufficient to condemn us.[80] The love of temporal things, the foulness of our sins holds us back from eternal things.[81] It would seem, as maintained by Gilson, O'Meara, and others, that Augustine promoted an increasingly scriptural understanding of revelation at the expense of Neoplatonism; his work seems to have had at least an "inhibiting" impact upon Neoplatonism in the West.[82]

II. INSPIRATION

Granting the reality of revelation for Augustine, to discuss our second topic, inspiration, is to discuss how God bestows His wisdom or skill on particular individuals,[83] or again, how the Holy Spirit so operates as to guide the minds of prophets and stimulate the faithful in understanding and in the performance of acts of virtue or charity. The manifold dimensions of the problem confronting us here may be seen in the questions of whether inspiration is something given only to persons or to persons and books and how it may be related to various members of the Trinity, to religious knowledge, and to knowledge in general. The question of inspiration is one that touches upon a variety of disciplines: e.g., perception and epistemology, linguistics and symbolic logic, ontology and human cooperation or operation in time. To make the question even more difficult, our problem is set out by the following two positions: For Portalié, inspiration in the Western church "owes to Augustine its exact formulation in the sense of a 'strict biblicism' (Harnack, *History of Dogma*, 5:98). . . ."[84] By contrast, Markus writes, "A 'theory of inspiration,' in our modern sense, he never took the trouble to work out. The nearest he comes to formulating anything of this kind is in his remarks on the nature of prophetic insight."[85] J. N. D. Kelly confirms the latter viewpoint by noting that to the extent a doctrine of inspiration exists in Augustine it is in his treatise *The Literal Meaning of Genesis*, Book 12.[86] It is here that Augustine delineates his vision.[87] Corporeal vision "is perceived through the body and presented to the senses of the body."[88] Spiritual vision pertains to the cognitive or rational powers of the mind.[89] Intellectual or intelligible vision is the gift of discernment or judgment.[90] These three kinds of vision are scaled in such a way so that intellectual vision is higher than spiritual vision, which is more excellent than corporeal vision.[91] Corporeal vision may err because it is dependent upon the senses. Spiritual vision may be led astray through some desire or incorrect understanding. Intellectual vision, however, never errs. If it understands, it possesses the truth; if it fails to understand then, implicitly, it does not possess the truth.[92]

Building on his thinking as it pertains to the three kinds of vision or perception, Augustine continues by arguing that there are two kinds of rapture: spiritual and intellectual. The former is a kind of "divine guidance and assistance . . . it realizes it is seeing in a spiritual way not bodies but the likeness of bodies." This is a state that is more than sleep, whereby even future events are recognized and divine assistance given for understanding, as happened to John with the Apocalypse.[93] The second form of rapture or type of inspiration occurs when one has been carried out of the body, "where transparent truth is seen without any bodily likeness . . . vision . . . darkened by no cloud of false opinion. . . ." Augustine summarizes intellective rapture by noting:

> There the brightness of the Lord is seen, not through a symbolic or corporeal vision, as it was seen at Mount Sinai, nor through a spiritual vision such as Isaiah saw and John in the Apocalypse, but through a direct vision and not through a dark image, as far as the human mind elevated by the grace of God can receive it. In such a vision God speaks face to face to him whom He has made worthy of this communion.[94]

On the basis of the twofold form of rapture delineated above, it is of interest to ask whether there exists a mantic form of inspiration in Augustine's conception of prophetic utterance. The case is not immediately clear. However, there are other questions which we shall consider before this one. First, we must ask how anything is known according to Augustine. There will be no attempt to enter fully into an Augustinian epistemology here. Still, something needs to be said, since the question of perception is closely related to that of inspiration as already noted in Augustine's commentary, *The Literal Meaning of Genesis*. Second, if something can be known, how is it learned? Who or what teaches us? Only after these considerations will we return to the question of the extent to which natural means, especially the rational mind, can be overcome by the supernatural and what the implications of this might be for Augustine's conception of the nature of the canonical Scriptures.

The three classes of vision or perception (corporeal, spiritual, and intellectual) are central to Augustine's theory of knowledge. Before developing these ideas and the context of faith that undergirds them, Augustine had become influenced by the skepticism of the Academy. The degree of this dependence is uncertain. In the *Confessions* it appears that the same Ambrose who pointed the way toward Christian belief was the one who first provoked in Augustine a more intensive Ciceronian or skeptical attitude.[95] Testard illustrates this dependence in his definitive study of the relationship between Cicero's philosophy and its influence upon Augustine,[96] a philosophy representative of the New Academy but tempered by the need for ethical duty in the world. Whether Augustine actually became a skeptic in a more formal sense or was merely attracted to the position has been a matter for discussion in our period.[97]

In any case, what was probably Augustine's first work as a Christian, *Against the Academics,* was written as a criticism of a position to which he was at least attracted. Skepticism could show up philosophical inconsistencies, the insufficiencies and compromises made by reason. Skepticism, as an attitude of mind, could free one for immediate ethical activity. But now the Augustine of Cassiciacum and the skeptic clearly part company. For skepticism finally leads to rational chaos, personal self-sufficiency, and detachment. According to Heil, whom I am following here, for Augustine, "The skeptic's mental quietude is replaced in Augustine's Christian theology by the Beatific Vision, the quasi-mystical ecstasy which awaits the soul in its ultimate confrontation with God."[98] Heil argues that in *Against the Academics* Augustine attacks the aims of skepticism, rather than the position itself, attempting to show that certain knowledge is at least intelligible, if not inevitable. The problem of skepticism becomes, then, not a rational question but a moral one, one in which the will is directly involved. Heil's work is a fresh approach at what has usually been interpreted as more of a direct confrontation in the arguments of Augustine with Trygetius and Licentius.[99] It is clear here and elsewhere that Augustine was quite familiar with the competing philosophical schools of his day. TeSelle has offered perhaps the best recent summary of these in English and concludes that while it is no longer possible to view Augustine as "a solitary genius," the one who "changed the subsequent history of Western thought," nevertheless he did bring many of the older insights "into the different contexts of Christian belief and obedience.[100]

As we have already noted, central to Augustine's attack upon skepticism is the belief that certain knowledge is possible. Charles Cochrane, in his classic study, discusses the effect of Augustine's transmutation of the older intellectual heritage for Western consciousness.[101] According to Cochrane, *scientia* (science), knowledge that is the result of corporal and spiritual vision, can only lead toward better "adjustment" in the world. It cannot satisfy the deep longing which every person has, the longing for *felicitas* (happiness).[102] As we have noted, Heil brings this point out. This line of thought has led Frederic Copleston to acknowledge that there is a certain eudaemonistic element to Augustine's philosophy.[103] This longing reveals our dependence upon *sapientia* (wisdom) for the categories of order needed to govern our being.[104] As Ronald Nash has noted, the mind has two functions: it can seek both wisdom and knowledge.[105]

In work beginning with his refutation of skepticism and carrying through the Pelagian controversy, Augustine not only drew a distinct connection between truth and happiness but also argued that certitude is possible, that one did not have to be content merely with probability.[106] Several different though generally similar attempts were made in the course of his treatises to delineate different classes of objects and perception.[107] Augustine acknowledges that two sources of truth present themselves when dealing with the world as it impinges upon us: reason and authority. The relationship between these concepts and the knowledge toward which they contribute at different levels of perception are tremendously complex.[108] The purpose of including them here is limited by our aim to understand more clearly what Augustine meant by inspiration.

To begin with reason, Augustine argues that man is not committed to a state of mere probability or agnosticism. His own doubt posits his self-existence.[109] In distinction from the skeptics, then, Augustine argues that man can know something—that he exists, lives, and understands. Beginning with faith, which we shall consider momentarily, Gilson delineates the steps in Augustine's epistemology that include rational evidence, the existence of the soul, possibility of sense knowledge, and finally of rational knowledge.[110] Through these developmental stages one is led toward the necessary supposition of divine ideas and of divinity.[111] Gilson sees a bond between this kind of trusting and Descartes's *cogito.*[112] Gerard Verbeke argues that while a parallel exists, Augustine's affirmation operates primarily in drawing potential knowledge (the ideal world) into actual understanding.[113] As Copleston puts it, "Augustine's attitude to sense knowledge is much more Platonic than Cartesian."[114] Whichever may be the case, many recent interpreters of Augustine's epistemology have cautioned against making his theory of knowledge more systematic than it actually is.[115] Augustine clearly posits certain knowledge; however, it is knowledge apart from the operation of the senses, derived from the soul's certainty of itself, along with the existence of the irrefutable laws of mathematics and logic, and standards of judgment.[116]

In terms of the three levels of knowledge schematized earlier, corporeal vision or sensual knowledge is the lowest form of knowledge.[117] By it one is made aware of external objects. Augustine was conscious of the relativity of sensation. While the senses themselves do not lie, they may be misinterpreted through an erroneous opinion, a lack of understanding, or other confusion. Spiritual vision, or cognition, may also be deceived through misinterpretation, imagination, or other such falsehood because the rational mind may not take all things properly into consideration.[118] But even sense knowledge may be used as a path toward acknowledging God and the ideal world.[119] We observe the senses even as we observe the testimony of others. The objects of sense are judged in terms of standards appealed to by the human intellect. At one place, these standards may simply be the laws of logic and mathematics or, further, natural laws or standards. Interestingly, Augustine defends sense experience despite his recognition of its liability to error and his perceived Neoplatonism. Nash suggests two reasons for this: (1) Augustine's religious authority, the Bible, depends to some extent on sensual testimony; (2) Augustine, in his concern for discovering truth, recognizes that while occasionally in error the senses generally report the truth.[120]

Faith is a necessary element in Augustine's epistemology. It relates both to ideal speculation and knowledge as derived from the world of sensation. Gilson writes: "In its final form the Augustinian doctrine concerning the relations between reason and faith comprises three steps: preparation for faith by reason, acts of faith, understanding the content of faith."[121] To believe is not a step which is taken apart from thought. Augustine writes that to believe is "to think with assent."[122] In *On the Usefulness of Believing*, Augustine writes to his friend Honoratus, whom he had earlier convinced to join the Manichees, that belief is necessary in every area of life.[123] We have no hope of recovering the past, so must believe. We have no certainty with respect to the future, so must believe. With respect to the present we cannot learn everything ourselves on a first-hand basis. We must believe the evidence of others.[124] It is of note that one of the places where Augustine develops these ideas with respect to the ineluctable nature of time and its bearing upon faith and epistemology is in the account of his own progress toward faith, *The Confessions*.[125]

According to Harry A. Wolfson, Augustine's definition of belief belongs to the tradition of Clement of Alexandria. It united the stoic idea of συψδκατυεσιω with belief,[126] thus involving an assent of the will.[127] Faith directs the will, leading reason to recognize and articulate what it sees.[128] This operation of the will toward faith is still related to man's rational nature: "Neither may be given priority exclusive of the other."[129] In his treatise *On the Morals of the Catholic Church*, Augustine seems to connect faith and reason through love or desire.[130]

Faith, a precondition for knowing,[131] always acknowledges some authority.[132] P. Magnus Löhrer sees a development in Augustine's conception of belief as it is associated with the idea of authority that must always stand behind the act of faith.[133] As Löhrer writes, in the dialogues written at Cassiciacum the main idea comprising Augustine's understanding of authority was the *auctoritas divini intellectus*. Augustine writes of God in *Against the Academics* as a divine teacher and example who "in His mercy toward mankind" abased and degraded

> The greatness of His divine Mind by assuming a body in order that souls, enkindled not only by His words but also by His example, might be able to return to themselves and without the wrangling of arguments to have a taste of their true country.[134]

But in the writings that follow the dialogues Augustine's conception of authority becomes more identified with his understanding of Scripture.[135] There develops a "growing submission of his mind to the *auctoritas divinarum scripturarum unde mens nostra deviare non debet.*"[136] This, for some interpreters, is closely united to Augustine's growing recognition of the authority of the community of the church.[137] The relationship between the authority of Scripture and that of the church is a matter which will be briefly considered later in this paper.

The idea that the assent of belief is consent to an authority has been analyzed by R. Heinze and R. H. Lütcke in terms of Augustine's context.[138] On the basis of the work of F. Dvornik, Bonner writes that this idea of "authority" must be carefully understood in Augustine with respect to political terminology of the day. Rather than implying coercive power (*potestas*), authority (*auctoritas*) is better conceived as the noncoercive power of tradition or moral suasion.[139] This understanding of authority highlights the tension in Augustine's conception of the idea as it moves from the *auctorites divini intellectus* to *auctoritas divinarum scripturarum*. For Augustine Christ is at the same time divine authority and the inner teacher. Whereas Augustine had early revolted against the idea of authority, he had come to understand its proper association with authenticity. According to TeSelle:

> Now he came to recognize that there may be a place for authority, understood as "authentic" and "authoritative" testimony on the part of others, and for belief in that testimony when one does not have direct experience or rational proof of a matter.[140]

However, while this newly understood idea of authority may reside in Christ, the question for inspiration is to what extent Christ remains a kind of inner teacher or may only be known on the basis of past inspired witnesses or texts telling of Him.

The tension in Augustine's concept of authority as it may relate to perception and understanding raises the question of how one learns, of symbols and their value. This is central to Augustine's dialogue with his son Adeodatus in *On the Teacher*. After a lengthy discussion of words as signs of things signified,[141] Augustine spends the balance of the treatise discussing the nature of things. He argues, finally, that knowledge is possible because Christ, the Truth, is the Inner Teacher. We learn nothing from words themselves. One is taught not by words but "by means of the things themselves which God reveals within the soul."[142] Man remembers by means of outward signs, by words. It is God who teaches within. So he writes:

> Now we may not only believe, but also begin to understand that it has truly been written on divine authority that we are not to call anyone on earth our master because there is only one Master of all who is in heaven. But what *in heaven* means He Himself will advertise to us by means of men, through signs and outwardly, so that we may by turning inwardly to Him be made wise. . . .[143]

As noted by Ann Clark, this text, which begins with a discussion about speech and words, ends by discussing the aim of speech and of teaching.[144] It is clear that "the significations of words are somehow distinct from them and yet revealed by them." When this idea is applied to our interest in inspiration, the question must arise as to the plausibility (to say the least) of a kind of propositional inspiration in Augustine. This is a very complex topic, one which will be handled somewhat more fully in our next division. Suffice it to say here that many, and clearly those who would stress the primacy of the Inner Teacher in Augustine (quite evident in his early writing), would argue quite strongly against such a possibility. For example, Alan Richardson, in arguing against the equation of religious faith with propositions, writes with respect to Augustine:

> Faith for Augustine is not intellectual assent to certain scriptural propositions; it is the awakening of the mind to Truth, a new way of seeing things, a means of understanding what before did not make sense, the acquiring of categories of interpretation by means of which our whole experience and thought become rational and coherent.[145]

On the other hand, Nash writes that this ignores much of what Augustine says about faith. According to Nash inward faith is guided by the statements of Scripture.[146] These are statements, we might add, that may imply a kind of propositional revelation, an accommodation of the ineffable word to our corporeal, sensual natures.[147]

Understanding is the reward of faith. True understanding is wisdom (*sapientia*), which found is happiness.[148] Understanding cannot be had apart from the purification of faith. While this wisdom is similar to the Plotinian *nous*, as Cochrane notes, it takes on an added significance from Augustine's Christian belief, which is important for our understanding of inspiration.[149] For Plotinus, the function of the *nous* was to communicate through a series of emanations or through ecstasy with that which is proper to the Divine Mind.[150]

For Augustine, such separation as existed was the result of will, not of being.[151] The ideas in the mind of God could be known directly (precisely *how* directly becomes part of the debate over illumination in Augustine) without recourse to a theory of emanation or unconscious ecstasy.[152] Independent of corporeal and spiritual perception, exemplary ideas as they are a part of the larger *sapientia* of God could be perceived, at least intuited, at the level of intellectual vision, given the necessary attitude of mind and heart. According to Aimé Solignac, behind Augustine's understanding of divine ideas lay not only Christian revelation but also the influence of Plotinus, Celsus, and Albinus.[153] But as Theodore Kondoleon points out, Augustine cannot accept the Platonic view that ideas could have an independent existence apart from God.[154]

While the rational mind (spiritual vision) operates within the matrix provided by the intellectual vision, knowledge of exemplary truths or divine ideas are received from God through illumination. In a perceptive study by Viktor Warnach the essential identity of Augustine's theory of illumination and inspiration is established through Augustine's emphasis upon the Inner Witness.[155] There are various theories as to how this illumination of the intellectual vision operates.[156] The intuitionist or ontologist position argues for a direct vision of divine truth. Defended prior to our period by Johannes Hessen,[157] it has been taken up in a new way by Ronald Nash. Nash argues that when one discusses the question of the Divine Light (knowledge of the immutable ideas in the mind of God) one really needs to discuss not one but two lights—the uncreated light of God and a corresponding although mutable light which is man's intellect. "God has endowed man with a structure of rationality patterned after the Divine ideas in His own mind. Man can know truth because God has made man like Himself."[158] This modification of a strict ontologist position would seem to meet some of the objections posed against an ontologist reading of Augustine, who, at any rate, stresses the need for moral purity for whatever kind of participation in the Divine Light occurs. A second, "abstractionist" view identifies the "light" of the mind with a Thomistic sense of intellect.[159] A third position argues that Augustine's doctrine of illumination does not deal as much with the origin of ideas as with the conveyance of a quality of certitude in judgment or perception.[160]

In light of Augustine's conception of *sapientia*, the world in which man lives, even the basis of his ability to judge or think with certitude, is a world of one divine activity. All truth is finally a form of revelation, though it may reach us at different levels of perception.[161] Man is a part of a beneficent creation. Truth which brings wholeness is readily available to man.[162] Separation from the world, from God, comes at the level of self-will which always leads toward alienation or, finally, nonbeing.[163] Knowledge of that creation is possible. Knowledge is real, not mere illusion, as at its highest level it participates in the Divine Mind itself. According to Cochrane, whom I am following here, this places Augustine's understanding of the self between the ontological dualism of the Manichees and the false antithesis of body and soul characteristic of Platonism.[164]

In light of the preceding discussion we can return to the question of inspiration in Augustine's thought as it has been interpreted since WWII. Central to the discussion is the extent to which natural means, the mind, is overcome or directed by the supernatural, bearing in mind the question of whether or not this is the proper way to phrase our concern. First, however different interpreters have understood the nature of inspiration in Augustine, all agree with the fact that Augustine was convinced of the divine inspiration of Scripture.[165] It was something he seems to have almost taken for granted, although there are places where, if not proven, he at least indicates that such an idea is attested to by Scripture itself.[166] In the period immediately prior to ours Charles J. Costello was so impressed by the fact of inspiration in Augustine's thought that he wrote: "St. Augustine's belief in the inspired character of the Scriptures stands out so prominently in his writings that one almost hesitates to make it a special topic of treatment."[167]

Debate begins with the nature of this inspiration. It is divided largely between those who stress divine agency and others who attempt to carve out some ground which, while holding to a process begun by divine initiative, nevertheless is open, in varying degrees, to human operation or cooperation. Before turning to several representative opinions on the question in our period, some of the texts and vocabulary for discussion should be set out.[168] Augustine's treatise, *The Harmony of the Gospels*, is important to consider. It was written against those (e.g., the Manichaeans, Porphyry) who argued against the Christian faith because, it was alleged, Christ left no writing of His own and what was written by the several Evangelists had apparent discrepancies. In reply to these attacks Augustine emphasized the divine inspiration of Scripture. The Evangelists wrote "by divine authority" emphasizing different dimensions of Christ's ministry.[169] Furthermore, ". . . it is by the disciples of Christ . . . [that] the works and the words of Christ have been made known, on which this Christian religion is established. . . ."[170] Finally, while the disciples have written this, it should be conceived of as His having written:

> . . . since the truth is, that His members have accomplished only what they became acquainted with by the repeated statement of the Head. For all that He was mindful to give for our perusal on the subject of His own doings and sayings, He commanded to be written by the disciples, whom He thus used as if they were His hands.[171]

As Augustine turns his attention to the narratives of the Evangelists in Book 2 of *The Harmony of the Gospels* he lays more stress on the human dimension in the authorship of Scripture. For example, he writes that each Evangelist delineated his own account of Christ's life and, while apparent differences exist, they stand in harmony with each other when conceived properly.[172] Despite apparent differences in the narrative, varied verbal usage, or other additions or omissions, "the truth of the Gospel, conveyed in that word of God," is fully reliable. Furthermore, he adds, one should be less concerned with the "temporal symbols" or words by which something is said and "rather in the truth of the facts themselves. . . ."[173]

There are a great number of other texts which could be cited; they will be as the discussion requires it.[174] The treatise, *The Harmony of the Gospels*, is an important place to begin as it deals so centrally with the issue of the authorship of the Christian faith and the manner by which it is conveyed. When we turn our attention to the words which Augustine uses for what has been rendered into English as "inspire," our attempt to understand what Augustine meant by inspiration is not furthered significantly.[175] According to Polman, the word *inspirare* occurs most frequently with respect to the activity of various members of the Trinity in the authorship of Scripture. Other words like *dictare, suggerere*, and *gubernare* are also used.[176] Polman adds, significantly, that *inspirare* is particularly used in Augustine's debate with the Pelagians. It is the Spirit who inspires faith, goodwill, and love.[177] Yet, indicative of the fact that the word *inspirare* may not have received a very precise meaning by this point, Augustine can write that he is able to refute under the inspiration of the Spirit those who blaspheme the Gospels.[178] In writing this he nevertheless distinguishes between the inspiration of the authors of Scripture and his own or that of other Christians in his day.[179] This apparent double usage has led Polman to conclude that "he probably used the word in two senses: one broad and the other narrow."[180] The same duality of interest may be seen in Augustine's use of *dictare*.[181] The words *suggerere* and *gubernare* are also used by Augustine but with less frequency, *gubernare* with respect to God's guidance and *suggerere* with respect to recall.[182] On the basis of his study of the terminology for inspiration and its usage, Polman concludes:

> St. Augustine obviously wished to maintain both attitudes at once. The Bible was both the exclusive work of the Holy Spirit alone and at the same time the exclusive work of the Biblical writers. Beyond that St. Augustine did not theorize.[183]

While it is not possible for us to theorize much beyond this point, I would like to return to the similarity Warnach underscores between inspiration and illumination in Augustine before moving any further into some of the representative theories of inspiration in our period.[184] The reason for this is that I believe we can gain some insight into Augustine's thinking with respect to inspiration through his thoughts on illumination. Progress must be limited; for in a letter to Evodius, Augustine tells us that the essential nature of intellectual vision is mysterious.[185] He writes that his best thinking on the subject can be found in his "literal" commentary on Genesis, Book 12, the portions which we cited in part at the beginning of this section.[186] While what he states in his letter is essentially "mystery,"[187] what he writes in *The Literal Meaning of Genesis* has been grounds for considerable speculation. In his discussion of intellectual knowledge and illumination (as Augustine uses the terms), Portalié writes of the centrality of this idea to the entire structure of Augustine's thought. "For Augustine," Portalié writes, "the understanding has need of the light of God, its sun, to attain truth just as the will needs the grace of God, the supreme good, to attain virtue."[188] In summarizing a chronological listing of Augustine's discussion of illumination, Portalié concludes that the problem of illumination or intellectual vision revolves around what Augustine meant by "We see the unchangeable truth" and "We see it in the divine light." We have already noted the three major interpretations of this idea in Augustine. Applying them to the question of inspiration, we might deduce the following.

If Augustine's idea of intellectual vision is best interpreted from an ontologist or intuitionist perspective, perhaps the way is open for a mantic or ecstatic understanding of inspiration. Might this be merely an extension of the "natural" operation of direct vision into the divine ideas? On the other hand, if Augustine is best interpreted by the scholastic or abstractionist view of intellectual vision, whereby his understanding is conceived as the God-given ability of the intellect to produce on its own the ideas germane to intellectual vision, then perhaps there is little room for divine agency in inspiration itself. Finally, if the function of intellectual vision is primarily the gift of making certain judgments, then perhaps inspiration in Augustine is best seen as a kind of clarity given to natural understanding.

These three options with respect to intellectual vision seem to bear upon the options taken with regard to the question of inspiration. For example, Hermann Sasse has argued that the church under the leadership of the apologists took over uncritically from Hellenistic Judaism and paganism "the disastrous opposition of revelation and philosophy, of prophecy and ecstatic enthusiasm. . . ."[189] According to Sasse, Augustine in his defense of Christianity appealed to the prophets of the Old Testament and to the Sibyls of Hellenism to aver the truth of the faith. "Prediction is still prediction whether it is proclaimed by prophet or sibyl."[190] Such a focus upon inspiration and prophecy as the foretelling of future events misses the point of prophecy in the Bible. Augustine adopted too readily the pagan idea of ecstasy which made the authors of the biblical books only instruments of the Godhead, inspiration as "a suggestion of thought, words and phrases."[191]

Yet Sasse recognizes that the picture is not completely clear. He willingly acknowledges elsewhere that Augustine allows for the personal contributions of the human author.[192] In such places Sasse emphasizes the role of the Spirit in aiding the memory and guiding judgment in terms of what should be related, but ultimately Augustine is leaving room for the free operation of the human consciousness. In conclusion, Sasse writes that Augustine does not have a uniform teaching on inspiration; rather it is one that oscillates "between *dictare*, which makes man a mere tool, and *suggerere*, which does not exclude human cooperation." Augustine's mistake, according to Sasse, was that rather than start where the Bible does (2 Tim 3:16; 2 Peter 1:19ff.) he began with Hellenistic Jewish and pagan theories of ecstatic possession.[193]

Similarly, Bruce Vawter believes that Augustine is open to the charge of sharing in a "one-sided and disproportionate emphasis on divine responsibility for Scripture" which was characteristic of the patristic period.[194] For Vawter this is illustrative of a confusion of biblical concepts with a nonbiblical theory of inspiration inherited from the world of philosophy. In addition to this philosophical confusion, the idea of God as the primary *auctor* of Scripture—a term in process of development in the fourth and fifth centuries—is worked out in the context of ecclesiastical controversy in North Africa. Desirous of defending the idea of the essential unity of the Old and New Testaments against Manichaean criticism, Catholic Christians referred to their common authorship by God.[195] While Vawter and the others he cites (K. Rahner, D. Stanley, R. F. Smith) are critical of this view of authorship and the concomitant development of biblical inerrancy, A. Bea is seen as one who follows along with it.[196]

Like Polman, Sasse and Vawter see both the human and the divine dimensions in Augustine's theory of authorship. Unlike Polman, however, they believe that Augustine's view of inspiration is either mantic or borders on being so and is hopelessly compromised by the nonbiblical spirit of Hellenism as forged, perhaps, by a defensive posture. Polman, however, is not nearly so negative. As we have seen, he recognizes the human and divine emphases in Augustine[197] and ends by drawing some helpful qualifications of one's reading of Scripture which belong as well to Augustine. These seem to underscore Augustine's desire to see in Scripture a book which is divine without sacrificing its humanity.[198]

Geoffrey Bromiley looks at the same material cited by Polman, Sasse, and Vawter.[199] Noting what Augustine wrote with regard to Christ using the evangelists "as if they were his own hands" (*De consensu evangelistarum* 1.35, 54), he adds that there existed an "impulse" in the patristic period to adopt pagan and Hellenistic Jewish theories of ecstatic inspiration. Bromiley adds, however, that perhaps the church's experience with the "excesses of Montanism served as a check" upon such developments. He warns that one should not take dictation theories too far as they may pertain to Augustine's idea of inspiration.[200]

Indeed, Heinrich Vogels went further in the period prior to our study.[201] He wrote that in the illustration of Christ as "the dictating Head" and the Evangelists as his "writing hands," Augustine was less interested in developing a theory of *how* the evangelists were inspired than he was in affirming the unity of the Evangelists' message with each other and with Christ. To serve this latter purpose, he appealed to the Pauline idea of the mystical body. Indeed, when one reads the passage in question without referring to the context, one can find a theory of inspiration by dictation; but if it is in context, it seems that Vogels reads the passage more accurately.[202]

It would appear that Vogels's opinion is strengthened by J. N. D. Kelly's attitude toward Augustine in these matters.[203] Kelly begins by observing, as others have, that Christianity inherited the concept of the divine inspiration of Scripture from Judaism. He notes that when Jesus and the apostles quoted the "Old Testament" it is clear that they regard it as the word of God (2 Tim. 3:16; 2 Peter 1:21). He continues by asking what was understood by "inspiration" in the patristic period; Kelly answers by elaborating upon two traditions of interpretation. First, in Hellenistic Judaism, inspiration implied a kind of possession by the Spirit, who seized the now unconscious prophet. This mantic theory of inspiration can be found in Philo of Alexandria, Athenagoras, and some of the other church fathers, but particularly among the Montanists. Second, there is the position of the greater part of the orthodox church. While willing to use the illustration of the writers of Scripture operating as instruments of the Spirit, "the orthodox tradition was careful to avoid the implication that their role was purely passive."[204] Cochrane agrees in stressing the breaking activity of Montanism, holding the orthodox tradition back from a mantic interpretation of inspiration.[205] Writing specifically with regard to Augustine, Kelly adds:

So Augustine, discussing the activity of the evangelists, admits [*Ser.* 246, 1] that they used their own personal reminiscences in compiling the gospels, the function of the Spirit being to stimulate their memories and preserve them from error. It was not a case of His imparting a fresh revelation to them; rather did He regulate and control their mental powers [*De consensu evangelistarum* 3.30].[206]

TeSelle seems to echo Kelly's understanding by writing that in his defense of the Bible Augustine is inclined "to refrain from too hasty an assertion of the power of God and instead to acknowledge the problems and wrestle with them philosophically. . . ."[207] Kelly concludes by adding that few if any of the Fathers probed anymore deeply into the question of inspiration.

There are further issues which could be drawn in here but will be considered elsewhere: the problem of profane or pagan inspiration as with the Delphic sibyls and the question of inspiration and the Septuagint. Some tentative conclusions are now in order as they were for the first section of this paper. I wish to make three points. First, I follow Markus, who argues that the nearest Augustine came to working out a theory of inspiration comes in Book 12 of *The Literal Meaning of Genesis*. Augustine himself says as much. Here Augustine discusses prophetic insight as part of a larger discussion on the nature of perception. The highest form of perception is that illumination which comes together with intellectual vision. The prophet is the one who not only has visions but also has the insight to interpret them. Some prophets merely have insight into public events; others are able to discern hidden things. But, as Markus writes, "What constitutes a 'prophet' is a special quality of judgment or of understanding."[208] Second, the illumination of the intellectual vision that one receives is for the objects of the mind as the rays of the sun are for the objects of corporeal vision.[209] The mind is clarified, eternal truth is made visible by illumination just as the will requires grace. Finally, the emphasis in Augustine's conception of inspiration, while variously interpreted, seems to this writer to be more illuminative or intellective than mantic, particularly in light of Augustine's wider thinking with respect to perception. Augustine does use at times terminology which is more consistently employed by an ecstatic or mantic tradition of inspiration. This, unfortunately, may have yielded "unwholesome fruit" in the Middle Ages when for some Christians the Scriptures became the text for all knowledge. Although for Augustine everything in Scripture is inspired and of God, he was extremely careful in the conclusions of his exegesis.

III. SCRIPTURE

According to Augustine all of reality can serve as a sign or world of signs of the divine reality. The meaning of such signs becomes apparent to us through the illumination of memory or reason. Signs guide us to higher realities. As the cosmos is a vast plethora of signs, so are words.[210] In both cases the letter kills, but the spirit—the internal meaning—engenders life. But how to progress to that meaning? In his commentary on Psalm 119:105 ("Thy word is a lantern unto my feet, and a light unto my paths"), Augustine asks whether this verse is making reference to Christ, "He who was in the beginning God with God. . . ?"[211]

Interestingly enough, his answer is no. The reference here is to Scripture, the word sent to prophets and preached by apostles,[212] the word which is efficacious for our salvation. This word works both according to its outward form as well as with respect to its inner signification under the guidance of the Spirit or inner light.[213]

It is clear from the insight given us in the *Confessions* that the awakening of Augustine's interest in philosophy stimulated his greater interest in and eventual respect for Scripture. At this early period Scripture had "a personal authority" (Meagher's expression) for Augustine. Increasingly it came to dominate his thinking (as was noted in the first section of this paper),[214] delineating the lines that his more systematic speculation and spirituality would take. Augustine's increasing respect for Scripture came at both a personal level and in terms of his capacity as apologist and bishop of the church. In fact, it remains a moot question as to what extent this doctrine of Scripture (if we can even use that phrase) was dependent upon his apologetical needs. TeSelle writes that Augustine's life was so busy that "he wrote little that was not called forth by some challenge. . . ." And where there was no specific challenge, Augustine often wrote in terms of a chosen work or person with whom he could react.[215] Oswald Loretz even argues that Augustine adopted a position of "biblical inerrancy" with respect to Scripture largely as a "defensive reaction" against his detractors.[216] In developing a view that does not directly challenge either of these positions, Frederick van der Meer writes that Scripture seemed to keep Augustine from floating away into a "neo-Platonist world of imperishable ideas." The Scriptures kept Augustine thinking about the things of this world and their ultimate significance. Furthermore, not only did Scripture anchor Augustine's theory, as it were, it also guided his thinking and reasoning in a sea of "ceaseless Hellenistic chatter."[217]

In order to understand how Augustine's view of Scripture has been perceived since WWII it will be important for us to ask, first, about some of the chief factors which led to Augustine's increasing respect for Scripture—polemics, intellectual growth, and service to the church. Second, the question of the significatory value of language, here biblical language, needs to be broached: of what value is the "lantern" with respect to the "light" (Ps. 119:105)? Finally, how Augustine interpreted Scripture will be handled.

In dealing with Augustine's growing appreciation of revelation as defined by Christian sources, we noted in the first part of this paper his increasing use of and recourse to Scripture for authority. In the fifteen-year period between his first stay in Milan as a rhetorician to his eventual elevation as bishop in Hippo, Augustine makes some dramatic moves in biblical understanding that would mark the future course of Latin Christendom even down to the present. Different scholars have attempted to divide up this period variously in order to understand Augustine's transition from Manichaean auditor to Catholic apologist, noting the influence of Ambrose, Plotinus (Porphyry, etc.), and Paul along the way. As we noted, aspects of this transition with regard to the question of Augustine's conversion and consequent moral, occupational, attitudinal, and intellectual changes in the first division of this paper,[218] so we can add to this list Augustine's changing understanding of Scripture.

Some have seen the time of the formation of Augustine's monastic community at Thagaste (A.D. 389) as the place to begin to mark an important shift in his attitude. Others have pointed to the time when he became a priest (A.D. 391) and requested leave of Valarius to study Scripture. Still others have argued for the time of his elevation as bishop and the authorship of *The Harmony of the Gospels* (A.D. 397). In one of the most thorough studies in our period marking such a transition, A. D. R. Polman argues that taking such movement into account is basic to an understanding of Augustine's theology.[219] In the first period, under the influence of Neoplatonism, Christ is seen as the eternal word. Scripture is no more than a starting point. And the preaching of God's Word is but a call to follow the glorious example of Christ.[220] But a shift occurs, according to Polman, whereby the authority of Christ is retained yet Scripture is given increasing recognition during a time of radical change for Augustine between his ordination (A.D. 391) and elevation as bishop (A.D. 397).[221] Polman writes:

> On the pilgrimage to the heavenly city, the Scriptures or the Word of Christ become a sure guide and a strong support, and in the preaching of His Word, we find the cause and the soil of the new life of the children of God.[222]

In the *Confessions* Augustine tells us that his new attitude toward the Scriptures began with Ambrose's teaching: "The letter kills but the spirit gives life."[223] In reflecting upon some of the recent literature which has attempted to analyze Augustine's growing respect for Scripture during this anti-Manichaean and developing Catholic phase of his career we need to begin with the year 1930, the fifteen-hundredth centenary of Augustine's death.[224] This year and that of the anniversary of his birth, 1954, were marked not only by a fresh interest in Augustine but also by a number of helpful guides to the older literature of his life and work.[225]

As Augustine moved from lay apologist to priest to bishop, his relationship toward Scripture was affected directly by the Manichaean question.[226] Furthermore, it has been argued that the precise nature of Augustine's criticism was directed toward Faustus of Milevis, whose work provided the foil against which Augustine developed much of his thinking about the nature of Scripture.[227] The question of the nature and limits of authority for Christians was an important one in North Africa in the late fourth and early fifth centuries. A church council in Hippo in 393, one in Carthage in 397 and again in 419 dealt with the nature of the canon of Scripture. The opinions of the Manichaeans, particularly of Faustus and his disciples, helped to force the question of the text of the Bible. Aware of his own limits in this growing hermeneutical and exegetical clash, Augustine began a correspondence with Jerome on the nature of Scripture, seeking Jerome's aid, correspondence that ran from circa A.D. 394–419.

Many of these issues, as summarized by Ries, were touched upon in a significant way in 1930. H. J. Vogels worked on the way in which Augustine's doctrine grew out of Scripture;[228] P. Lagrange drew further attention to the connection between exegesis and Catholic authority;[229] Katharina Staritz and others pointed to important differences between Manichaean and Augustinian cosmology with respect to the book of Genesis;[230] Paul Monceaux's work on Manichaeanism and other expressions of North African sectarianism continues to be of immense value.[231] The work of Alberto Pincherle carries these older studies into our period.[232] Even as Alfaric can be seen as the older authority on the question of Augustine's thought from the time of his adherence to Manichaeanism until he became a convert to Neoplatonism, so Pincherle is the authority for Augustine's theological evolution through the anti-Manichaean period, the time of the formation of Augustine's doctrine of Scripture.[233] According to Pincherle's work, next to the influence of Ambrose and Cyprian upon Augustine there stands that of Tyconius. If Ambrose was influential in guiding Augustine toward the importance of allegorical exegesis, so Tyconius delineated certain rules for interpreting the Scriptures that would guide Augustine's theology into the period ahead, undergirding his growing understanding of the place of the church and its authority through Scripture in distinction from the claims of the Manichees.

The importance of the exegetical guidelines of Tyconius upon Augustine's thinking bears not only upon the immediate question of exegesis, as can be seen in Augustine's treatise *On Christian Doctrine*,[234] but also upon that of the structure of the canon itself in Augustine's thinking. When Augustine considers why certain books and prophets are included in the canon while others are excluded as not specifically bearing the "authority of religion,"[235] he seems to use as criterion that which pertains directly to the appearance and destiny of the "City of God" and its head, Jesus Christ.[236] This appears to be an application of Tyconius's first exegetical rule concerning the Lord and His body.[237]

If Tyconius's thought as presented by Pincherle and others is helpful in delineating some of the structural and exegetical developments in Augustine's thinking as it pertains to Scripture in the early fifth century, the work of R. A. Markus offers useful insight on the way in which the idea of prophetic inspiration becomes attached to the entire canon.[238] Markus argues that in Augustine's earliest treatises prophecy and history are conceived as distinctly different conceptual categories in Scripture. Building his thinking on Augustine's work, *On True Religion*, Markus writes that prophecies are believed to be revealed to individuals *quasi privatim* and to all *per historiam* and *per prophetam* (regarding the past and future respectively).[239] In the context of his anti-Manichaean works Augustine's thought will increasingly emphasize not the duality of content in the Bible, history and prophecy, but the idea that the whole Bible is at the same time history and prophecy.[240] Finally, by the writing of *The City of God*, history and prophecy "are almost synonymous." Scripture has developed into a monolithic, prophetic entity in its own right. In this way, Markus adds, "inspiration" becomes coextensive with "canonicity" and canonicity the criterion of prophetic inspiration.[241] The universal church, the body of Christ in which Augustine now serves as bishop and pastor, is the bearer of this text now conceived of as "a single communication, a single message in an intricate code, and not as an exceedingly heterogeneous collection of separate books."[242]

The growing confidence which Augustine places in Scripture has been noted throughout this paper. In addition to the works of Matthews, Polman, and others that have been cited we should also mention the study by Ulrich

Duchrow.[243] Duchrow traces what he believes is a transition from the Greek epistemological idea of "seeing" in Augustine's thinking to the more Semitic concept of "hearing" as tied closely to his idea of the significance and function of Scripture. For Augustine the Pauline theologian, the pastor seeking to interpret the world for himself and his congregation with the gifts of grace and illumination, the Bible takes on the added value of being the authoritative sign of God's attitude toward humanity.[244] In his treatise *On Catechizing the Unlearned*, Augustine makes it clear that the advent of Christ is the event that lends authenticity to those signs that prefigured his incarnation as well as to those subsequent to his work.[245]

If we can learn something of God in the natural world by viewing God's creation as a vast network of signs pertaining to his reality, lifting our minds to reflect upon His divinity, so also may Scripture be viewed.[246] At this point in our discussion of the way in which Augustine's understanding of Scripture has been perceived in the last thirty-five years we need to look briefly at the significance Augustine places upon language. The most important texts will be found in his works *On the Teacher* (A.D. 389), *On Christian Doctrine* (A.D. 396), and *On the Trinity* (A.D. 399–419), each written during different periods of his life.[247] Whatever contradictions may exist in Augustine's argument, the general conclusion Augustine reaches in *On the Teacher* is that human teachers can teach us only the meaning of words or signs. For more than this,

> Only the Internal Teacher, which is Christ dwelling in the mind, can teach by at once displaying to the mind the reality to be known and providing the language for its understanding. He is the source of both the objects encountered and the light which illuminates them for our understanding.[248]

If Augustine in *On the Teacher* appears to stress an interior truth that may to some degree denigrate the use of signs or written words, by the time he has begun his work as a bishop one finds a fresh evaluation of the use of signs. In *On Christian Doctrine*, they are said to carry us to divine things. Following the preface, Augustine divides this treatise into four sections: the first deals with the discovery of the meaning of Scripture, the last three sections deal with its expression.[249] His discussion of signs and what they signify continues from where he left it in *On the Teacher*.[250] According to Markus, Augustine stresses the triadic nature of signification: there is the object for which a sign stands, the sign itself, and the interpreter.[251] There are, Augustine tells us, two classes of signs: natural and conventional. Conventional signs are those that humans use to disclose their minds to others.[252] The only reason we have for making and giving signs is to indicate to another what is going on in the mind of the sign-maker. Words are the most important of all signs.[253] Scripture was at first given in one language, then many. Scripture "signs" to us what is the will of God as revealed to those who received prophetic inspiration.

> And in reading it, seek nothing more than to find out the thought and will of those by whom it was written, and through these to find out the will of God, in accordance with which they believe these men to have spoken.[254]

But precisely because Scripture has been written by men living in different circumstances, signifying things differently, there is the need for an interpreter of Scripture.[255]

Moving to our third text, *On the Trinity*, it is here we find an extensive treatment of a theory of signs in relation to Augustine's attempt to understand the Trinity.[256] Books 1–7 demonstrate this doctrine out of Scripture, books 8–15 illustrate it from nature, book 15 is written for those who wish to understand these things more deeply. Here Augustine argues that there is a difference between the external spoken word and an internal word, the former being a sign of the one within.[257] But the focus of *On the Trinity* is not on a theory of language but upon the question of how we can know God properly. Here the function of Scripture as authority is delineated. Augustine argues that there are three kinds of error one ends up with when speculating about the nature of God: (1) Anthropomorphists try to give God the qualities they discern through experiences and reason. (2) Philosophers end by giving God the qualities which they originate in their own minds. (3) Mystics somehow think that they can rise above the material world but cannot and are weighed down by their own humanity.[258] Not only do we hear echoes here of various different religious or philosophical groups of which Augustine had once been a part or against which he fought, but also we discern an ability to understand God as based on the various levels of perception or vision that Augustine delineates elsewhere as well as here.[259] Augustine's conclusion, however, is that only through Scripture—the canon of religious authority written by those who received the gift of prophetic inspiration, an aspect of intellective vision or illumination—through these signs is the mind lifted unambiguously to God.

> In order, therefore, that the human mind might be purged from falsities of this kind, Holy Scripture, which suits itself to babes, has not avoided words drawn from any class of things really existing, through which, as by nourishment, our understanding might rise gradually to things divine and transcendent.[260]

For Augustine all the world and all of Scripture is a sign attesting to the divine reality.[261] At least in *On the Trinity* Scripture, as a reflection of the interior word given the prophet, may be called the word of God in this external sense.

Reference should now be made to some of the various interpretations of how Augustine may have conceived of language, and particularly the language of the Bible.[262] Early in our period Ludwig Wittgenstein criticized what was felt to be a simplistic referential notion of language on Augustine's part.[263] In fact, Augustine's view seems somewhat more complex, at least as analyzed by Markus. Darrell Jackson argues further. Illustrating how Augustine's use of signs develops out of the Stoic tradition, Jackson argues that Augustine's originality comes in applying this theory of the function of signs to Scripture and its interpretation as he is concerned with the hermeneutics of moving from sign to signification.[264]

In Duchrow's study of the progression of Augustine's epistemology toward Semitic "hearing" the early tension in Augustine between perception and language is highlighted. He confirms the work of Rudolf Lorenz with respect to a somewhat deprecatory early attitude toward language to convey deep meaning.[265] Language, like other aspects of the sensual world, forms shadows and traces of the ideal world. Duchrow's conclusions with regard to the temporal value of language in Augustine's later evaluation of Scripture are similar to and confirm the work of Gerhard Strauss.[266] Strauss's focus on Augustine's use of signs in *On Christian Doctrine* drew out what appears there as an apparent parallelism between the word as speech and the incarnation.[267] Duchrow moves the discussion of the epistemological function of language by showing that with *On Christian Doctrine* Augustine begins to emphasize the wholly verbal structure of man's understanding, attempting, perhaps, as Lorenz puts it, to ward off the radicalism of his teaching on grace and illumination.[268] In the prologue to this work Augustine clearly condemns those who believe that they can responsibly read Scripture in a kind of immediate or charismatic sense. While Duchrow's point needs to be carefully considered, the idea of an Inner Teacher, as raised in *On the Teacher*, seems to continue somewhat in Augustine's tension between the interior and exterior word.[269] Furthermore, even in the preface of *On Christian Doctrine* God remains the teacher.

While Augustine as bishop and guardian of the faith may be attempting to depart even further from the earlier Neoplatonic "radicalism" that characterized his own faith and perhaps that of others in his diocese, what is said in the preface to *On Christian Doctrine* cannot dampen the deep metaphysical connection between what is signified in Scripture and the language or expression of the Bible.[270] This association runs deeper than any verbal restriction.[271] Augustine retains a deep ideality of meaning which, as Cochrane had earlier illustrated, finds itself mediated, not totally rejected in Christian thinking.[272]

Douglas Johnson illustrates the way in which he feels Augustine overcomes the dualism of classical thought.[273] Through a careful statistical study Johnson shows that Augustine's use of the term *verbum* is not out of a Neoplatonic context and cannot be equated with the Greek *nous* but rather conveys the idea of an involved God.[274] Johnson thus seeks to revalue Augustine's understanding of the spoken word, arguing that he avoids using the term *verbum* for the second person of the Trinity, uniting it instead to Scripture and to preaching.

What stands out clearly in this discussion is the close connection both Strauss and Duchrow highlight between Augustine's theory of signs or linguistic philosophy, if we may call it that, and what we must next consider: his interpretation of Scripture.[275] To understand the words or signs of Scripture there needs to be not only some deep level of identity or empathy between the author(s) and interpreter but also a knowledge of language, number, music, and history—a knowledge of that which is to be interpreted as well as the means of interpretation.[276]

This, of course, is the point of *On Christian Doctrine*, in the preface of which Augustine argues pointedly against a purely self-taught and charismatic interpretation of Scripture.[277] In full agreement with Brunner, Eugene Kevane has taken this further and has argued that a plea for a Christian *paideia* or educational program may be found in the preface which is then sketched out in the balance of the treatise.[278] One finds here "a program of education for the new People of God arising in the era of the New Testament. It possesses its own body of Sacred Literature, the Divine Scripture . . . even as the natural peoples of the past had their literature that formed the core of their educational systems . . . Homer . . . Vergil. . . ."[279] Both Brunner and Kevane are accurate in their assessment. In his *Confessions* and elsewhere Augustine is not reticent in noting the value of his wide educational background, albeit its subsidiary worth when set next to Scripture.[280] Yet, as mentioned earlier, Hill's emphasis on the practical value of this work for preachers in the Latin West, as opposed to a consciously predetermined program of education, is probably accurate.[281]

Given Augustine's qualified appreciation of classicism, combined with his clear "abandonment of secular literature in favor of the Bible as the repository of historical truth," recourse to the tools of his rhetorical and classical background were used to deal with the frequent enigma of Scripture.[282] These mysteries for Augustine, as Cochrane summarizes them, have already been alluded to throughout this paper. They are basically two: (1) the problem of verbal differences in the text, which, as we have seen, are handled by Augustine through the use of his understanding of words as symbols; (2) the more substantial apparent differences in narrative, morality, and teaching.[283] These, of course, were the precise issues which had earlier led Augustine to the camp of the Manichees. They are the issues dealt with, among other places, in the treatise *On Christian Doctrine*.[284]

It is from Ambrose that Augustine caught a glimpse of how what appeared as dead words and a deadening tradition could be made alive. The nature of the allegorical tradition which Augustine learned from Ambrose as well as others in the Christian East has been the subject of several important studies in our period. In addition to the works already cited we must first mention that of Wolfson. Wolfson illustrates the way in which Augustine extended Paul's use of the term allegory to include all nonliteral senses of the text.[285] This is not to be construed as a neglect for the literal sense of Scripture, for this is the foundation for any further spiritual understanding or application.[286] While for Paul the term seems limited to a nonliteral interpretation of certain salvation events—historical phenomena in the Old Testament, primarily as they prefigure Christ's advent—the broadening of this method by Augustine and others was in part (aside from any internal hermeneutical reasoning which may have occurred) to deal with a series of controversies faced by the church. Wolfson, citing Origen, specifically mentions the Gnostics, who denied historicity, the Jews, who denied the prophetic value of certain Old Testament passages, and simple Christians, who tended toward anthropomorphism in their faith.[287]

In his penetrating study of the function of allegory in Augustine's writing, Jean Pépin argues for the primacy of typological thinking in Augustine as opposed to a stricter definition of allegory better represented by Origen. This is an important point to stress. For example, Augustine always proceeds from the literal event without denigrating it, whereas Origen begins with the allegorical event in such occurrences as the Exodus story.[288] James Preus has helpfully pointed to the distinction Augustine makes between "spiritual" and figurative interpretation.[289] The difficulties Augustine had in rectifying the allegorical interpretation of Scripture in light of the conception of the verbal inspiration of

Scripture allegedly held by him are drawn out by J. Barton Payne.[290] It was in light of these difficulties of rectification, according to Payne, that Augustine developed his fourfold method of exegesis. Not only did Augustine face the problem of inspiration at this level, but closely related is the question of a plurality of literal meanings that may inhere in a particular text. It seems clear that Augustine held to such plurality, although not firmly.[291] The intent of the biblical author, however, could never be wholly incorrect even though he might not have understood the full intent of his prophecy. Portalié notes that had Augustine's idea of the plurality of literal meanings not been generally abandoned by most, havoc would have resulted for any kind of scientific exegesis.[292]

While Scripture finds a primary place in Augustine's thinking, he nevertheless relies upon the metaphysical system he is delineating in order to understand Holy Writ; and in this effort at understanding he makes recourse to the wider church tradition as it had developed by his day. The nature of this tradition has been brought out by Altaner.[293] Clearly Augustine makes wide use of Origen, Clement of Alexandria, Gregory of Nazianzus, and Gregory of Nyssa. An interesting facet of this ecclesial heritage is the degree to which it was influenced by Platonic philosophy. Cornelius Petrus Mayer has argued that Augustine was able to overcome Manichaean dualism only by making recourse to a Platonic ontology. Such Platonism had a decisive effect upon Augustine's hermeneutics as well as ontology and understanding of salvation history.[294]

In addition to this church tradition, however "Platonically" cast, Augustine reached into the camp of the Donatists, to the work of Tyconius, to find needed guidelines for the interpretation of Scripture that he failed to find through Ambrose and others. The full effect of Tyconius upon Augustine has yet to be measured. Tyconius's influence upon Augustine's understanding of history and eschatology is raised by Edwin Fromm;[295] and in particular the recent and careful study of Tyconius by Paula Landes should be consulted.[296] Consideration too should be made of James Preus's illustration of the interpretation Augustine places upon Tyconius's third rule: "Of Promises and the Law."[297] In the context of the Pelagian controversy this guideline for interpretation is dealt with more fully under the rubric "spirit" and "letter."[298] The result is the derivation in Augustine of a two-value literal sense which finally leads to a reading of the Old Testament never in its own right but always in light of the New Testament. This, of course, would have significant ramifications for medieval exegesis.[299]

While allegorical interpretation with its vital typological emphasis remains key to Augustine's hermeneutics,[300] he is never wholly at ease, as perhaps was the case with Origen, with such a development. This is clear in his repeated efforts to exegete properly the first several chapters of the book of Genesis. In the context of this work two general rules for his exegetical work became prominent. The first is Augustine's attempt to find the proper literal meaning of the text. When this fails, as it often does, then recourse is made to allegory to draw out the spiritual significance of the text.[301] Obscure things, Augustine writes, are written to stimulate thought. Where one fails to understand the text, one is to give glory to God.[302] Nevertheless Augustine held that all necessary truths for our salvation and for pious lives are abundantly clear in Scripture.[303] The second is Augustine's "extreme prudence," as Portalié puts it, in the determination of the meaning of Scripture. That is, while the Scriptures are of divine origin and absolutely inerrant for Augustine, in Portalié's opinion, he is quite reticent about offering an interpretation of the biblical text that appears to be at variance with the results of science.[304] Non-Christians clearly know true things about nature. In light of this Augustine fears that Christians will talk nonsense, thinking they are defending the faith while making themselves appear foolish before the "infidel."[305]

Augustine's work in his commentaries on various books of the Old Testament was often done against the background of the Manichaean challenge to Catholic Christianity.[306] But the rules he formulated there and in his more systematic treatises were brought to bear upon the New Testament as well.[307] Both Testaments were clearly the work of one author, the same God at work before the Incarnation as after.[308] The same God who created the universe inspired the Scriptures.[309] The end of both is a hermeneutic of love. "Scripture teaches nothing but charity," Augustine writes.[310] On this point few disagree. This is the goal of all exegesis.[311]

In a penetrating study of Books 1–3 of Augustine's *On Christian Doctrine*, Hermann-Josef Sieben disagrees with Mayer's understanding of Augustine's hermeneutic. Sieben argues quite persuasively that Mayer misunderstands certain tendencies in Augustine's work, that love is preeminently identified with *res* or the thing of faith far more than with the quest of faith, which has certain Platonic affinities. Because of this Sieben believes that there is less Platonism in Augustine's exegesis than Mayer finds.[312]

While love is the aim of Augustine's exegesis one important question which continues to surface in Augustinian scholarship is the question of when *caritas* becomes *coercitio*. This has been brought out in terms at Augustine's social policy by numerous commentators. As TeSelle notes, the study of Dideberg on Augustine's commentary on 1 John is strangely silent on this.[313] Dideberg's work is helpful, however, in delineating the relationship between love and the Holy Spirit. While the Scripture does not state that the Holy Spirit is love, Augustine often implies an identity between the Spirit and *caritas*.[314]

Before concluding this section mention must be made of two further problems as they touch on Augustine's concern for Scripture. The first pertains to Augustine's views on translations of the Bible and the second to extracanonical literature. Augustine generally favors the Old Latin and Septuagint versions, although he also has recourse to the old African texts of North Africa.[315] In the context of his epistolary debate with Jerome, Augustine's appreciation of Jerome's translations, which were to become the Latin Vulgate, would be increasingly valued. Augustine's use of the Septuagint provides helpful insight into how Augustine viewed both inspiration and the canonical Scriptures and illustrates as well the difficulty of coming to sure conclusions on Augustine's thought in these matters.

Augustine insisted on the inspiration of the Septuagint.[316] In *On Christian Doctrine* he acknowledges it as the preeminent authority with respect to the Old Testament. He follows the legend of the seventy translators, arguing that the miraculous consensus in their separate translations is a manifestation of the power of the Holy Spirit in their work. If differences are found from the Hebrew original, then it is to be assumed that they were willed by the Spirit under "the dispensation of Providence." The Holy Spirit worked through these authors as was most suitable to bring the Gentiles to a knowledge of the truth. God had said something through Hebrew to the Hebrews and through Greek to the Gentiles. Augustine's use of the Septuagint is complicated not only by the legend of its origin but also by the fact that both the apostles and Christian community through the fourth century were using it authoritatively.[317] The differences between the Hebrew Old Testament and Septuagint were known. Origen used the former for scholarship and the latter in his sermons. By 391 Jerome had turned his attention fully to his Latin version, basing his Old Testament work upon the Hebrew rather than Septuagint version.

These efforts on Jerome's part became a problem for Augustine, and shortly after Augustine had become a priest or presbyter in the church, he wrote to Jerome and raised the matter with him. Augustine felt that Jerome should accord greater authoritative recognition to the Septuagint.[318] Augustine again raised the matter with Jerome in a letter dated after he had become bishop.[319] He was disturbed by the tumult that had occurred in the city of Oea after the public reading of Jerome's new translation and was critical of Jerome for raising such problems. The wording was unfamiliar, and the Greeks especially denounced the new translation as false.[320] In reply Jerome tells Augustine that he doesn't know what he is talking about.[321] We find a classic encounter here between the scholar, Jerome, and the ecclesiastical defender, Augustine. Augustine does not drop the matter here but again writes Jerome, now confesses the usefulness he sees in Jerome's work, and requests further information and a copy of Jerome's translation.[322]

The position which Augustine takes toward the Septuagint following his correspondence with Jerome has similarities but is not identical to that which he held before the debate. This may be seen in several passages in *The City of God* where he now lauds the work of Jerome.[323] Augustine continues to insist upon the inspiration and authority of the Septuagint and Hebrew Old Testament.[324] However, when problems arise between the two it is the job of the interpreter to find the deeper, mystical identity of intent in the divergent passages. Furthermore, Augustine now acknowledges that when it comes to factual detail, genealogies, dates, etc., the original (in this case the Hebrew Old Testament) is to be preferred above the later translations. While later translations, like the Septuagint, may be inspired with the same Spirit as fired the inspiration of the first prophet,[325] copyists' errors may creep into later translations.[326] One can see the way in which Augustine the bishop now works out such discrepancies in his exegesis of the divergent account of Jonah's prophecy to the city of Nineveh.[327] According to the Hebrew, Nineveh is given forty days to repent, whereas in the Septuagint only three days. Augustine concludes that according to what Jonah actually said, the Hebrew is to be believed. Yet the Holy Spirit still inspired the translation of the Septuagint to speak the truth but "under a different signification," in order that the reader might "raise himself above the history, and search for those things which the history itself was written to set forth." Augustine continues to draw forth the spiritual point behind the signs: Nineveh is a prophetic representation of the church of the Gentiles brought to penitence by Christ, who is signified by the forty and the three days. He was with His disciples for forty days following His resurrection, prior to His ascension, and He arose from the grave on the third day.[328] Following in the footsteps of the apostles, who used both translations, Augustine seeks to do the same, granting authority to both, primacy in factuality to the Hebrew, and harmony at the level of spiritual meaning.

If one can see in the preceding the strong dimension of ecclesial authority which enters into Augustine's use of the Septuagint, one may also find a strong sociological identification in his attitude toward extracanonical literature no matter how inspired it may claim to be.[329] Turning once again to *The City of God*, we find Augustine asking the question why certain prophecies of the patriarchs or books mentioned in the Old Testament are not in the canon.[330] His answer is that there is a certain logic to what is there: it is material which pertains directly to Christ and his church, *The City of God*, either by way of prefiguration or by those of immediate intimacy with the Lord.[331] Other material of greater antiquity was not included because its age would only raise suspicions about it. Augustine admits he is not sure why certain books mentioned in the Old Testament are not in the canon, but he goes on to make a distinction between that which by divine inspiration pertains to the "authority of religion" and that which by historical diligence remains a part of the "abundance of knowledge."[332] Further on in the text Augustine points out that one may find truth among the philosophers.[333] There may even be prophets among them. However, Augustine argues, things known by conjecture, instinct, or given by demons, which their prophecies are, are different from that which is announced by God's angels or given by His Spirit.[334] Whatever truth the philosophers have, it is God-given but lacks the stamp of religious authenticity, hence authority.[335]

In concluding this portion of our brief study into perceptions on Augustine's understanding of Scripture, one may note with TeSelle that "Augustine's use of Scripture is structured by a heritage of interpretation." He "strives for intelligibility within the framework of faith."[336] As Bonner has argued, Augustine maintains Scripture as the first rule of authority for the church, yet Scripture is not the only "rule of faith."[337] Recourse to the Rule of Faith is needed for accuracy in understanding Scripture. This is to be found in the baptismal creeds and in the custom and apostolic tradition of the universal church.[338] As Augustine strives for understanding his concern is not with a multiplicity of passages of Scripture as much as for their underlying significance for the life of faith as it pertains to charity. How and in what way Augustine cites Scripture is of more importance than its mere recitation. For this reason the work of Anne-Marie La Bonnardiere, as she attempts to isolate the clusters of biblical texts that Augustine uses at various points in his career, is so important.[339] Augustine's use of Scripture and his understanding of what constitutes the canonical Scriptures are both inextricably related to his theology.[340] In this sense, and without forgetting its inestimable importance for our present pilgrimage, Scripture as such is not as important as its end, which is charity.[341]

IV. INFALLIBILITY

"The Bible has been acknowledged as authoritative by Christians in every century, including the first."[342] This statement by Alan Richardson could be echoed by almost if not every name cited in this paper, not only for the early church in general but also for Augustine in particular.[343] Yet immediately a further question arises: in what sense "authoritative"? From the premise of divine inspiration accorded to the canonical Scriptures, B. B. Warfield deduced the inerrancy of Scripture.[344] One researcher in our period has even argued that Augustine has only two primary exegetical principles: charity as the end of the Bible, inerrancy as its primary characteristic.[345] One may say that Augustine held to the infallibility, even inerrancy of Scripture, and yet as we have seen that hardly ends the matter. It is, rather, the door to further inquiry. There is the question of reality itself and its mediation (*res-signum*) through the canonical Scriptures. There is the problem of perception, of illumination and the intellective vision, of how this is related to inspiration and the gift of prophecy. Finally, revelation in Augustine can hardly be discussed apart from ontology, especially since Alfaric's contention at the beginning of this century that Augustine turned first to Neoplatonism and only then to Christianity.

Infallibility for Augustine is the door to critical analysis, not the last word in the question of truth. If *On Christian Doctrine* shows us anything, it teaches the absolute necessity both of taking Scripture as seriously as we take the natural world and of the importance of critical analysis.[346] Both the created order and prophetic signs of God's love are designed to lead us to Him who is love and to our neighbor.[347] This concern for the ideal and created realms, a concern on God's part that called forth His self-disclosure in the Incarnation, seems to imply at least some form of a correspondence theory of truth in Augustine, albeit with a significant degree of accommodation in Scripture. Augustine's *Confessions*, as premeditated as they are, have helped us trace his attitude toward Scripture through the time of his elevation as bishop. We can continue to follow his reflections in this regard by taking note once again of his correspondence with Jerome. Having considered this epistolary exchange, we shall then briefly take up the question of infallibility with respect to the language of the Bible.

Augustine began his correspondence with Jerome over the question of the truth of the Bible. In Letter 28 Augustine is critical of what he perceives to be Jerome's interpretation of Galatians 2.[348] Peter, having eaten (the Lord's Supper?) with Gentiles while visiting Antioch (2:12), withdraws his association following the arrival of a delegation of Jewish legalists. In light of this, Paul criticizes Peter for his fear of the Jews and the implications arising from his behavior, that the Jewish law and customs are still applicable.[349] Jerome, following the tradition of Origen, suggests that the entire incident was a tactical maneuver contrived by Peter and Paul in order to rebuke the Judaizers more effectively. Augustine, however, will permit no discrepancies in Scripture.[350] He is deeply concerned about the problem of falsehood. If we can't trust Paul here, why, Augustine asks, trust him in the areas of marriage, promise, and worship or in the matter of resurrection? Augustine draws attention then to the precarious nature of the truth once aspersions have been cast upon it. The implications are significant both for the soul and for society.

The context for this concern is particularly revealing. Augustine has, of course, been preoccupied with the Manichaean challenge to the church. Central to their critique was the alleged immorality, lack of harmony, and unreliability of the Bible.[351] In the following year he will write *On the Harmony of the Gospels,* which through its cultural perception and rules for interpretation attempts to deal with apparent deficiencies in the gospel narratives, verbal discrepancies, and other Bible difficulties. We have already noted similar concerns as they pertain to the Septuagint. Furthermore, in 395 Augustine wrote his treatise *On Lying,* which deals in a focused way with the problem of truth and falsehood.[352]

The question of the truth of the Bible, then, is one with which Augustine is preoccupied in the years following his elevation as Bishop of Hippo. He raises it in other letters with Jerome,[353] then in a significant way once again in Letter 82. Here Augustine's concern is not only in contrasting truth with falsehood but with error as well.[354] Again Augustine contrasts his position with that of the Manichaeans.[355] The context for this concern continues to be the controversy between Peter and Paul in Galatians 2. Here it arises even more centrally in relation to the need to create an understandable scheme of salvation through eras of law and grace. The question of relative truth and commendation or condemnation of behavior emerges: to what extent are truth and ethics accommodated to particular historical-cultural periods? What can be said to have happened (perhaps with commendation under a particular dispensation of God's grace) that would be condemned as false or viewed as immoral today?[356] What, we may say with Augustine, is the difference between *mendacium* and *honesta dispensatio?*[357] Augustine's concern is to defend the complete reliability of Scripture, grounding its infallibility or inerrancy upon the fidelity of God. His interests are clearly pastoral; his desire is for the edification of the body in doing this. This moves the question of verbal discrepancies, differences in the narrative, and other problems into the realm of interpretation, away from questioning the truth of the Bible, as was the case with the Manichaeans.[358] For Augustine, as we noted earlier in *On Christian Doctrine* and now in *On Lying,* signs, properly interpreted, must communicate clearly, if not always completely, that which they are designed to signify.[359]

Augustine's understanding of the truth of the canonical Scriptures has been of fundamental significance for the attitude toward the Bible held in Latin Christendom. Wolfson writes that faith for Augustine means believing, first, all that is written in Scripture, understood together with the teaching of the tradition. Wolfson cites Augustine's work *On the Spirit and the Letter,* "'What is believing (*credere*),' he exclaims, 'but consenting (*consentire*) to the truth of what is said,' [*De spir. et litt.* 31.54] for to believe in God, he further says, means nothing but 'to yield our consent (*consentire*), indeed, to God's words' [ibid., 34.60] and 'to believe (*credere*) is itself nothing else than to think with assent (*assensione*)' [*De Praed. Sanc.* 2.5]"[360] In all of these statements, Wolfson concludes, it is implied that faith is closely associated with "consent" and "assent" to Scripture.[361] Wolfson's assertion, then, is that there is an association in Augustine between the words of the Bible and faith. They cannot properly be set at odds with each other. The question of *how* those words are to be believed is, of course, another matter, dealt with in part in *On Christian Doctrine*. Does Augustine locate truth in the words of the Bible even in a kind of propositional way? Our answer seems to be both yes and no. Words as signs point to a deeper reality. Yet there remains Augustine's concern that signs communicate clearly and be properly interpreted when they seem to convey falsehood or disharmony.[362] In other words, there appears to be a relative identity between the "material" principle of revelation in Augustine (the Inner Teacher) and the "formal" principle (the canonical Scriptures).

Despite the contradictory movements that have been spawned from Augustine's work in Western intellectual history, he appears to have contributed markedly to the idea of the infallibility of the canonical text of Scripture.[363] His influence continued for many in this respect well into the nineteenth century when, according to James Burtchaell, the idea of the inerrancy of Scripture was first systematically challenged.[364] This developed as a result of the Enlightenment and new empirical disciplines for all and in a focused way among Roman Catholics largely through the Tübingen School of interpretation.[365] Without touching upon various Protestant or Roman Catholic efforts at theological retrenchment in the face of modernity, we may move rapidly into our period and survey several of the ways in which Augustine has been viewed with respect to the question of infallibility.

When the question of the nature of biblical truth came up before Vatican II, various scholars turned to Augustine in an effort to understand both how the Bible should be properly viewed and, by some, where the church may have begun to misunderstand the nature of biblical truth.[366] In this context P. Zerafa wrote that biblical inerrancy "is one of those truths which needed no impact of special historical circumstances to come to full light: it was the preferred doctrine of the Church from the very beginning,"[367] In defending this statement Zerafa cites Augustine's Letter 82. He then criticizes the position of Pierre Benoit, who had maintained that the limits of inerrancy could be established by a predetermined "formal object" of inspired writing.[368] In an earlier work Benoit had distinguished between the inspiration of the prophet and that of the scriptural writer, inerrancy being primarily the property of the inspired message rather than that of the resulting written page.[369] Part of the difficulty with this position develops, of course, when one begins to posit multiple authorship for various books of Scripture.[370]

Interestingly, Zerafa believes that Augustine not only stands opposed to "a predetermined biblical object," but he also cites Augustine as one who first recognized the problem of the truth of the Bible becoming bound to a given culture or certain literary forms. Hence the usefulness of the human sciences and need for rules of interpretation in order to understand Scripture, as presented in *On Christian Doctrine*. According to Zerafa, Augustine clearly felt that some placed too much weight upon the idea of an inerrant text, others too little. The former used Scripture to defend their own opinions of the world, the latter "despaired of locating their scientific knowledge in the holy books."[371] Augustine was apparently aware of the fact, then, that an actual understanding of the limits of inerrancy would only be found through a hard, critical study of the text.[372]

Sasse agrees with Zerafa in believing that Augustine held a position of biblical inerrancy that, for Sasse, may be characterized by his attitude toward the Septuagint.[373] But for Sasse this infallibility was compromised by its derivation from pagan or Hellenistic theories of mantic or ecstatic possession. Furthermore, the effort on Augustine's part to adopt a concomitant position of inerrancy toward Scripture in order to harmonize the difficulties of the Bible was clearly, according to Sasse, a failing enterprise; Augustine's error came, in part, because of his polemical and apologetic concerns.[374] Sasse's position has been influential in our period. For example, the prolific Catholic theologian Hans Küng cites his work in discussing the influence of Augustine upon the development at an ill-conceived idea of the infallibility of Scripture.[375]

In attempting to rescue the "truth of the Bible," Oswald Loretz has sought to redefine the locus of the Bible's infallibility, not an infallibility associated with the words of the text as much as with the Hebrew idea of God's faithfulness, a Semitic rather than a Greek conception of truth. Loretz as well cites Sasse's study in arguing that the patristic church's and Augustine's adoption of "biblical inerrancy" was a "defensive reaction" against the church's detractors conditioned by pagan theories of instrumentality.[376] Similarly, Loretz fears the promulgation of a kind of "double truth" that may result here.[377] He writes, "Because of holding this theory Augustine had to explain away the difficulties which the real facts presented him with. He could do this only by having recourse to the idea of a 'deeper sense' which he presumed to be present."[378] There is much that commends Loretz's concern as it has developed in the wake of Vatican II. Indeed, it seems Augustine's position in Letter 28, where he contrasts truth with falsehood, is similar in many ways to what Loretz has articulated. Still, as we have noted, and in all probability a part of his concern that signs adequately communicate that which they signify, Augustine appears to have adopted a more all-inclusive view of infallibility by Letter 82. In light of this apparent understanding of the infallibility of the text, the question has arisen as to whether or not there is an exaggeration of the "divine" element in Scripture at the expense of the "human" element. Such is alleged by Loretz and becomes the concern of others like Gerhard Strauss and Bruce Vawter. Earlier in our period Strauss delineated his fear that just as Augustine's Christology was susceptible to a kind of "subtle Docetism" so too was his doctrine of Scripture.[379]

Bruce Vawter agrees. In an initial study he argues that while the church has always held to the inspiration of Scripture, it has never defined the "how" of this inspiration. He contends that a view of inspiration other than that of instrumentality may lead to a different understanding of the truth of the Bible.[380] In *Biblical Inspiration*, Vawter considers the idea of instrumentality more fully.[381] Citing Pannenberg, Vawter argues that there was an undue emphasis placed upon Hellenistic rather than Semitic modes of thought in the patristic period.[382] The fathers are said to have conceived of revelation as "propositions directly inspired by God." Exploited through allegorism, such an idea of inspiration led to a biblical infallibility that could only be defended by a diminished concern for literary and historical criticism, a "Docetic" Bible.[383]

The idea that the truth of the Bible is best upheld through a doctrine of its infallibility or inerrancy is one that in the eyes of some has been increasingly untenable for the past two centuries. Recently Jack Rogers and Donald McKim have argued that there exists a Platonic division in Augustine's thought between the knowledge that is possible of this world (*scientia*) and the realities of God and eternal principles (*sapientia*). Through illumination (Augustine's Inner Teacher) the mind can come to know eternal verities. According to Rogers and McKim, the doctrine of biblical inerrancy is unnecessary and never was the true doctrine of the church. They posit a distinction between infallibility and inerrancy, the former applying to matters of faith and practice, the latter to scientific detail and technical errors.[384] While this distinction may be helpful in its own right, it seems not to do justice to Augustine's understanding of signs. These may not communicate fully, but they do nevertheless communicate truly. Augustine's concern for the accuracy of Scripture seems to come instead at the level of interpretation, the text itself being patently without error as well as without falsehood.[385] Earlier Dewey Beegle argued that while Augustine approximates a doctrine of inerrancy in theory, this is "vitiated in practice" by his allegorical interpretation of Scripture.[386] In responding to Rogers and McKim, John D. Woodbridge has continued to identify inerrancy with Augustine. Woodbridge writes, "Even if we are not happy with St. Augustine's projected solutions to the textual problem, we can gain an appreciation from them for his concern that not one word should create a real contradiction in Holy Writ."[387]

Johannes Beumer is only one of several who argues that Augustine approaches the question of the authority of the Bible as both a defender of the church[388] and as pastor to the faithful, in distinction from the roles of the exegete and philologist Jerome.[389] According to Beumer, the Bible increasingly replaced purely philosophical speculation in Augustine's mind. He is able to state categorically: "The authority of Scripture is greater than that of the greatest genius of men."[390] Such authority extended beyond the individual prophets to the canon itself,[391] a canon that bore a full sense of inerrancy.[392] Yet, Beumer adds, a more limited view of inerrancy may also be found in Augustine, where the emphasis is laid upon an affirmation of the veracity of religious truth more than scientific truth (*sapientia* more than *scientia*).[393] In fact, according to Beumer, Augustine may be the first to attempt to make a distinction in Scripture between the truth of salvation and "profane" truth. In some ways Beumer argues similarly to Rogers and McKim, but perhaps with the greater caution called for by Woodbridge: Augustine's distinction between *sapientia* and *scientia* does not so much restrict the truthfulness of Scripture to the former as determine Scripture's focal concerns. Beumer's own provisional conclusion seems balanced: Augustine attempted to stress the divine intention without denying the human agent.[394]

CHAPTER THREE

ERASMUS AND THE CORRESPONDENCE WITH JOHANN ECK: A SIXTEENTH-CENTURY DEBATE OVER SCRIPTURAL AUTHORITY

Bruce Ellis Benson

While the correspondence between Erasmus and Eck has received but scant attention, one might argue that their debate approaches the importance of another more famous one with which the name of Johann Eck is usually associated. Although the exchange consists of only two epistles, Erasmus's reply provides probably his most candid views on Scripture. Moreover, Eck claims to speak on behalf of the whole Christian tradition. Interestingly enough, this aspect may account for the lack of attention previously accorded this correspondence: it seems that Eck's view is a classic statement of the position held by virtually all of Christendom at that time and more specifically, of the Roman Catholic Church until recently. What makes these documents so fascinating today is their almost uncanny resemblance to current discussion.

With the appearance of Erasmus's *Novum Instrumentum* in 1516 came both a wellspring of approbation and a barrage of opprobrium. One of his friends reassured him that many at Cambridge were "great supporters of [his] edition of the New Testament; what a book it is!—So elegant, so clear, so delightful and so highly necessary in the opinion of all men of sound judgment."[1] Yet such was not the tone of all his commentators. Much of the reaction was critical and forced Erasmus to hone his apologetic abilities throughout the remainder of his life. Even prior to its release, disapproval of the project came from the Louvain humanist-turned-theologian Maarten van Dorp, with other of his colleagues later following suit. Further, criticism came from Jacques Lefevre in France and from certain quarters in Spain and Italy. Possibly the most caustic dispute centered upon the critique by the Englishman Edward Lee.[2]

When the German theologian Johann Maier von Eck addressed his letter to Erasmus in 1518, his confrontation with the rising monk Martin Luther was still a year and a half away. Eck held the post of professor of theology at the University of Ingolstadt and, on the whole, was highly favorable toward the humanist agenda and the work of Erasmus in particular. As to the fundamental value of this project, there can be no question that Eck supported it enthusiastically. Nevertheless, this did not deter him from taking issue with certain of Erasmus's comments in the *Annotationes* to the *Novum Instrumentum*.

In publishing the *Novum Instrumentum* Erasmus intended to accomplish a variety of objectives. It was, first and foremost, a complete edition of the

Greek New Testament. One of the recurring themes in the Erasmian corpus is the necessity of a command of Greek in order to permit a scholar to study the New Testament in the original tongue. Yet, even if theologians of the day knew the language, they still faced the problem of procuring a text. Because printed copies were unavailable, manuscripts predominated. Minimizing this difficulty, Erasmus also wished to offer a new Latin translation to supplement or even replace the Vulgate. He believed that it had suffered from various interpolations and corruptions, aside from certain passages he considered to be less than adequate translations. Further, he deemed the work of his predecessors, such as Lorenzo Valla and Jacques Lefevre, praiseworthy but inadequate. Such arguments as these are well elaborated in his reply to the objections of Maarten van Dorp.[3]

In attempting to justify his editorial alterations and, at places, radically different Latin translation, Erasmus included a collection of specific explanations for particular readings. By these explanations, known as the *Annotationes*, he hoped to "explain to the reader's satisfaction why each change was made, or at least . . . pacify him if he has found something he does not like."[4] Although Erasmus could rightfully be considered a master at walking a fine line, either these notes failed to elucidate his positions adequately or else they revealed entirely too much; for many of Erasmus's disputants found fault with them.

It was in regard to certain of these explanations that Eck presented his critique. While one might doubt his sincerity, he opens his letter with a friendly greeting and a curious comment concerning Erasmus's good nature, claiming his character to be such "that even uneducated folk may send you quite barbarous letters and be sure of your lively attention."[5] Certainly this was true, though Eck could hardly have been said to have fallen into either of these categories, for his criticism was incisive and respectfully delivered.

Eck's first contention concerns the lengthy notation on Matthew 2:6, specifically that

> many people are offended at your having written in your notes on the second chapter of Matthew the words "or because the evangelists themselves did not draw evidence of this kind from books, but trusted as men will to memory and made a mistake."[6]

As we shall see, Eck's apprehensive response stems from his judgment that such an assertion may be inimical to the faith.

Throughout the *Annotationes* much of Erasmus's concern is with the determination of correct textual readings. Though he might not be properly labeled a textual critic in the modern sense of the term, he does attempt to sift variants and is reasonably able thoughtfully to apply certain critical principles.[7] For example, he grasps the principle of the harder reading and utilizes this in various passages, such as Matthew 2:6. Erasmus does find refuge from seeming contradictions or errors on occasion via tropological or allegorical interpretation, though he is reluctant to resort to this in other instances. In the note on Matthew 2:6 he seems to conclude that, due to a memory lapse, the Evangelist has erred.

Matthew 2:6 consists of a citation of the messianic prophecy found in Micah 5:2, yet with a significant disparity. Whereas the Old Testament passage emphasizes the insignificance of Bethlehem, that in the New speaks of it as not the least of Judah. The Hebrew and Greek terms in each translate into Latin as *parvulus* and *minima*, respectively. In discussing this discrepancy, Erasmus cites the possible explanations considered by Jerome.[8] First, Matthew may have quoted the answer of the Pharisees, making the error a result of their inaccuracy. Or second, Matthew, like the other Evangelists, may have trusted his memory, rather than referring directly to the text. As Erasmus acknowledges, these possibilities placed Jerome in somewhat of a dilemma.

In the first edition of the *Annotationes*, Erasmus limits his comments to the above, along with a technical discussion of the textual problem itself. Yet in later editions, for example that of 1522, he expands these remarks in an attempt to come to terms with this ostensible contradiction. Erasmus dismisses the first option as far-fetched: the Pharisees were known for hypocrisy, not for ignorance. Although Erasmus says that Jerome presents the other possibility as impious, he himself considers it more probable, especially since he maintains that there is a higher standard of accuracy for the prophet than for the Evangelist. His conclusion is that, while falsity would be intolerable in Scripture, slips of the memory are perfectly admissible. It seems Jerome was unwilling to decide on this matter, though he chooses the reading of Micah in that it is similar to one cited by the apostle Paul. What Jerome wishes is that the freedom granted the Evangelists to render passages in other words would also be extended to the translator.[9] Such liberty Erasmus also desires.

Yet Erasmus pushes for a far more daring objective: the acknowledgment that the Evangelists and other writers of Scripture could have erred, albeit in matters of little import. Moreover, in regard to this particular instance, he conjectures that the Holy Spirit may have intentionally allowed this error or even that Christ wished to incorporate a more human element in Scripture allowing himself alone to be the one unique Truth. However, Erasmus insists that, whatever the case, the gist of Scripture is unassailable truth.[10]

Judging from his comments, Eck appears to perceive Erasmus as at once proposing several different theses. Of course, Eck is responding not to the more extended and somewhat bolder comments of later editions but to those of the first. In light of the perspicacity of Eck's evaluation this is all the more interesting. Certainly the more obvious of Erasmus's claims is that in this instance the biblical passage is simply inaccurate. From this Eck reasons that if one writer can err, the door is opened to the contingency that others might not be immune from errors. Eck is unwilling to follow such a path, and he believes that he is not alone.

> Listen, dear Erasmus: do you suppose any Christian will patiently endure to be told that the evangelists in their Gospels made mistakes? If the authority of Holy Scripture at this point is shaky, can any other passage be free from the suspicion of error? A conclusion drawn by St. Augustine from an elegant chain of reasoning.[11]

The misquotation itself is comparatively minor and touches on nothing essential to the faith, but to allow the possibility of an insignificant inaccuracy is tacitly to brook the contingency of others.

Were Eck's objection merely an isolated case that could be ignored as obstinate niggling, one might discount his argument. What disallows that course is that one of Erasmus's earlier disputants, Maarten van Dorp, takes a strikingly similar tack. While the publication of the *Instrumentum* was still nearly two years away, Dorp wrote to caution Erasmus concerning the advisability of the project. It must be mentioned that Dorp had various interests in addressing Erasmus concerning this matter, not least of which is the prompting he was receiving from his colleagues at Louvain. Be that as it may, Dorp appears genuinely disturbed to hear Erasmus claiming that the Vulgate contained numerous corruptions which he intended to remedy. Dorp argues that were Erasmus to demonstrate that Scripture contains errors, he would jeopardize its trustworthiness and in so doing refers to the same authority cited by Eck.

> For a great many people will discuss the integrity of the Scriptures, and many will have doubts about it, if the presence of the least scrap of falsehood in them becomes known. . . . Then we shall see what Augustine writes in a letter to Jerome: "If falsehoods were admitted into Holy Scripture even to serve a useful purpose, what authority can they still retain?"[12]

What Eck and Dorp may not have in common is that the latter does not appear to have made any disjunction between the Vulgate text and the original autographs. One may contend that Dorp is here specifically defending the Vulgate, though by virtue of such a confusion of the two he is implicitly defending both. Eck cannot be charged in this manner for he is responding to the suggestion of an original error, not one of transmission.

From this same notation, Eck further surmises that Erasmus has a differing model of inspiration. In using phrases like "trusted to memory" and "draw evidence of this kind" it would seem that the writers acted as scholars compiling information. Eck's view of inspiration is that they were directed as to content through being "taught all truth by the Holy Spirit." Moreover, "the Spirit chose men of no schooling, who could neither read nor write and made great scholars of them."[13] Eck's second point of disagreement sheds further light on his idea of inspiration. In Erasmus's explanation of Acts 10 he claimed that the Greek of the apostles was a different idiom than that of Demosthenes and had been learned from ordinary conversation. Eck cautions Erasmus that such a statement is unwise, for "it was not from the Greeks but from the Holy Spirit that they learnt their Greek."[14] He also refers to a similar instance in the commentary on Matthew 4 where Erasmus says, "I wonder that the evangelists misused this word [θεραπεύων], which would seem rather one to be avoided."[15] From Eck's perspective it appears that Erasmus is, in effect, attempting to correct the Holy Spirit.

Erasmus's response of May 1518 contains what may well be the most revealing of his comments on Scripture. When he replied to Dorp, for instance, he claimed that "no one asserts that there is any falsehood in Holy Scripture."[16]

While appearing fairly definite, this statement does not necessarily disclose his actual opinion but merely maintains that in calling for revisions in the Vulgate he is not therefore implying that Scripture itself is in error. Though his statements in this epistle are still guarded, they are indicative of his understanding of Scripture's truthfulness.

With regard to Matthew 2, Erasmus reminds Eck that he (Eck) had only cited the second option of a disjunctive statement, that following the "or." How does Eck know for certain that Erasmus sides with this opinion? Erasmus claims to be merely "quoting other men's opinions,"[17] some of which come from the pen of no less a scholar than Jerome himself. Erasmus claims to be doing the same, presenting the alternatives for the reader without resolving the dilemma; he is not actually saying that the apostle did, in fact, err.

Although Erasmus maintains that he has not passed judgment, he does believe that were an error found it would not cast aspersion on Scripture's integrity.

> Nor, in my view, would the authority of the whole of Scripture be instantly imperiled, as you suggest, if an evangelist by a slip of the memory did put one name for another, Isaiah for instance instead of Jeremiah, for this is not a point on which anything turns.[18]

He illustrates this by pointing to Peter, whom (he says) Augustine and Ambrose consider as having had "a few lapses" after the Spirit came upon him. Merely because of this, one does not discount all that Peter said and did. Further, even such authorities as Augustine and Jerome were mistaken at points, though nonetheless highly respected. Evidently Erasmus does not have the same idea of the Holy Spirit's inspiration as Eck has in mind. Whereas Eck seems to hold that Scripture was written under complete supervision of the Spirit so that none of its content would be allowed to err or even be grammatically inferior, Erasmus limited inspiration such that the Spirit "was present in them so far as pertained to the business of the Gospel, but with this limitation, that in other respects he allowed them to be human none the less."[19] As to Eck's related objection that Erasmus appears to say that the authors used sources and worked as scholars, he responds by referring to 2 Timothy 4:13, where Paul asks Timothy to bring his books and parchments. Then, in that inimitable Erasmian fashion, he promises to comment fully on this in a later edition.

Erasmus has no intention of denying that the Holy Spirit gave the gift of tongues, but it seems far more likely to him that the biblical writers learned Greek from their environment rather than through the Spirit. He reasons that if the Old Testament writers learned Syriac (what modern scholars would call "Aramaic") through conversation, it is not unnatural to assume the same source for those of the New. As Jerome said, because of the political situation the whole area knew Greek. The difficulty Erasmus foresees with asserting that the Holy Spirit tutored the apostles in Greek is that their Greek is manifestly inferior in style and filled with "clumsiness of language, not to say barbarism, which we cannot attempt to conceal."[20] One cannot escape the conclusion that the Spirit taught an inferior Greek, according to the precise grammatical standards which Erasmus, as a humanist, maintains. Unfortunately, Erasmus apparently does not realize that the Greek of the apostles' age was not classical, but *Koine*. Moreover, he considers Pentecost to have little bearing on the New Testament writers' abilities in Greek, for Scripture does not state that they wrote the Scriptures in Greek through supernatural power. He distinguishes between the gifts of tongues and prophecy on the one hand and the guidance of the Spirit provided in the composition of Scripture on the other.

In support of his criticism of the apostles' use of Greek, Erasmus once again cites Jerome as his precedent, for this church father did not hesitate to critique Paul in this respect. With regard to the use of θεραπεύεων, it must have been used by the translator. Further, in asserting that it was "misused" he is saying not that the word had been abused but utilized differently than might be expected and a cause of surprise, though not necessarily criticism.

Though far more could be said concerning this aspect of the dispute, let us turn now to a brief consideration of the second facet, that of Erasmus's preference for Jerome over Augustine. In commenting on John 21:22 Erasmus mentions that he values Jerome's opinion over that of Augustine. Eck takes issue with this judgment for he deems Augustine's expertise in philosophy and theology to excel Jerome's and he quotes the humanist Francesco Filelfo in agreement. He fails to mention that in the same text Filelfo went on to say that Jerome's knowledge of Greek was superior to that of Augustine, who moreover had no acquaintance with Hebrew.[21] Eck admonishes Erasmus to

> cease therefore . . . to darken by your criticisms a leading light of the church, than which none has been more illustrious since its first pillars. Admit rather that Augustine was a great scholar, steep yourself in his works and turn his pages with all diligence, and you will regard as quite shameless the man who dares prefer any of the Fathers to Augustine as scholar.[22]

To consider the influence of Jerome upon Erasmus is a formidable agenda that extends beyond the scope of this chapter. Though there can be no doubt that Jerome's impact upon Erasmus was significant, there appears to be no complete treatment of their relationship.[23] As early as 1500 he wished to produce an edition of Jerome's works, for he was impressed by "the goodness of the saintly man who of all Christians was by common consent the best scholar and best writer . . . the supreme champion and expositor and ornament of our faith."[24] This reverence may have been inculcated in Erasmus through the influence of the Brethren of the Common Life.[25] From Jerome's writings Erasmus derived at least two principles that became foundational to his endeavor. First, Erasmus considered Jerome's insistence on basing theology upon Scripture to be the antidote to the disease of scholastic theology.[26] Second, he recognized in Jerome's distinction between prophet and translator a defense for his own function as grammarian.[27]

When Erasmus attempts to answer Eck he first distinguishes that his preference for Jerome is in no way a slight of Augustine, for he regards both as exemplary. Yet he cannot "allow Jerome's reputation to be put in the shade; and would clearly suffer injury if he were placed second to a man whom he far outdistances."[28] He first diminishes the importance of the quotation of Filelfo by saying that he carries little weight to be cited as authoritative and that the remark was a "casual" one made to a friend. Though many scholars hold Augustine in high esteem, Erasmus thinks Eck is incorrect in saying that all consider him the pinnacle of Christian theology. The explanation as to why some place him

> above Jerome or Ambrose is partly that he is more frequently quoted by those authors who have acquired a despotic position in our universities, either because they found him easier to understand than them or because his pronouncements are more definite than theirs.[29]

At this juncture Erasmus addresses Eck's charge that he has neglected to read the works of Augustine. Whereas his discourse is fairly calm to this point, Erasmus demonstrates a modicum of irritability that Eck could suggest such a thing. He claims to have quoted from almost all of Augustine's works "in more than thirty score places"[30] and suggests that it may be Eck who is negligent in reading Jerome. Erasmus does not exaggerate in claiming frequent citation of Augustine, in some cases even in preference to Jerome.[31]

However, Erasmus clearly considers Jerome the better of the two scholars and contrasts their training. Whereas Jerome was born near Italy and educated in Rome, Augustine was born in "barbarous" Africa, "where literary studies were at an amazingly low ebb."[32] Jerome was raised in a Christian home; Augustine did not study the Scriptures until later in life. Moreover, Jerome had more time to devote to studies than Augustine, who was preoccupied in his position as bishop, and therefore outshone Augustine in his knowledge of Greek and his familiarity with the works of philosophers and theologians and even in the use of dialectic. "And yet Augustine calls Cicero a mock philosopher, being of course the genuine article himself, though Cicero, if I am not mistaken, had read somewhat more widely in Greek philosophy than Augustine had in Holy Scripture."[33] Erasmus claims that in one page of Origen he could gain more concerning "Christian philosophy" than he could in ten times that of Augustine. However, he maintains that he wishes not to diminish the reputation of Augustine, whom he now respects even more than in his youth; rather he desires both Jerome and Augustine to be exalted.

While Erasmus thought highly of all the Fathers and considered their writings "true" theology in contrast to that of the scholastics, as a humanist who placed a high premium on education, knowledge of languages, and an exemplary literary style, he cannot help but favor Jerome. Moreover, Jerome served as a philological model for Erasmus, being at once a source of technical information and providing a precedent for Erasmus's work as biblical translator. Jerome had delineated a distinction between prophet and translator, considering himself in the latter capacity. According to Jerome, such a role requires not inspiration, as Augustine maintained, but scholarship. Over this issue Jerome and Augustine were in clear disagreement; regarding this same sort of distinction Erasmus and Luther were also to spar.[34] Hence, what could be interpreted as an equivocating attitude toward Augustine may be explained by Erasmus's acceptance, to a certain degree, of Augustine's theology while being yet critical of his understanding of translation.

What emerges from our analysis of this correspondence is that Eck and Erasmus are fundamentally at odds over what are ostensibly unrelated concerns. Yet, they appear somehow interconnected, even if neither Eck nor Erasmus recognized this fully.[35] Erasmus here provides, first, an indication of his stance concerning the infallibility of Scripture. Again, it is difficult to define precisely whether he specifically says that Scripture does err, even though it appears impossible to escape this implication. Certainly William Whitaker, among others, reached the tentative conclusion that Erasmus did not hold to Scripture's infallibility.[36] That Erasmus received sufficient pressure to force him to recant his statements concerning Matthew 2:6 in the 1527 edition appears to justify Eck's interpretation of Erasmus's comments as well as to demonstrate the astuteness of his prediction that no Christian would endure such allegations.[37] What may be even more significant is that Erasmus distinguishes between the realms of faith and practice and what might be termed peripheral matters, such as historical detail. This is particularly manifest in his closing remarks on the subject to Eck.

> Christ allowed his chosen to make mistakes even after they had received the Paraclete, but not to the extent of imperilling the faith, just as we admit that the church can err in places, but short of any risk to faith and religion. In any case, how do you know whether Christ did not wish to reserve the credit of being right without exception for himself alone?[38]

Such a limitation on inspiration is unacceptable to Eck, and it is clear from his wording that he understands the mass of Christians to agree with him.

Yet, how does Erasmus's limitation on inspiration relate to his preference for Jerome? Most obviously, Erasmus is indebted to Jerome for the idea of explaining Matthew 2:6 as a slip of memory, though he is reluctant to depict Jerome as actually opting for such a possibility. Augustine, however, did not share this reluctance; in several of his epistles to Jerome he rebukes him in no uncertain terms.[39] It is from one of these that Eck and Dorp take their citations. Augustine responds to Jerome's assertation that Paul's rebuke of Peter in Galatians merely had been feigned. He contends that if falsehood or deception was utilized even with good intent it would yet tarnish the integrity of Scripture. Though Jerome appears eventually to have changed his mind on this issue, Erasmus may well have been influenced by his suggestion that Scripture may contain falsehood. As plausible as this deduction may be, however, it is more a supposition than a confirmed interpretation.

While Erasmus's reflection on these and other related matters was undoubtedly not the only precedent for the biblical criticism of Spinoza (d. 1677) and Richard Simon (d. 1712), certainly the latter acknowledged his indebtedness to Erasmus. What is interesting to note is that this controversy with Eck in many respects anticipates certain of their conclusions, as well as some of the objections voiced in response by their contemporaries. Even more significant, however, is the striking resemblance to recent discussion.[40] One of the most remarkable characteristics of Erasmian thought is that it is so often a distant mirror of our time. And this instance seems no exception.

CHAPTER FOUR

S. T. COLERIDGE AND THE ATTACK ON INERRANCY

Daniel Hoffman

Samuel Taylor Coleridge (1772–1834) is often recognized today only as a great English romantic poet, but in the nineteenth century he was better known as a theologian.[1] Indeed, he was a philosopher, literary critic, scholar, writer, and "talker," and several recent works have examined his influence on English thought in these areas.[2] He earned his income largely as a lecturer: he was not an ordained minister (although he had considered becoming a Unitarian minister while a student at Cambridge), and his religious writings therefore reflect the views of an educated layman who did not have to fear that his opinions would offend his congregation or a religious superior. Nevertheless, after flirting with pantheism, Unitarianism, and German rationalistic philosophies, he became a champion of traditional Christian beliefs after about 1810.[3] This is not meant to imply that he was ever thoroughly orthodox: his extensive borrowing from other writers,[4] including people like Spinoza and Lessing,[5] would never have made him popular with ecclesiastical authorities.[6] However, his effect on English thought should not be minimized: J. S. Mill, who was not in sympathy with Coleridge on many points, still called him one of "the two great seminal minds of England" (the other was Jeremy Bentham) and added that "there is hardly to be found in England an individual of any importance . . . who did not first learn to think from one of these two."[7]

This chapter will demonstrate that Coleridge helped develop and popularize in the English-speaking world the notion that the Bible is infallible only in religious matters. By studying Coleridge, those who influenced him, and those whom he influenced, we can add historical context to the debate among evangelicals on biblical inerrancy.[8] Indeed, the history of Christian thought about Scripture has become an important area of study (even beyond its significance for Western religious and cultural development) because of the modern attempt by those who deny the complete accuracy and truth of the Bible (and by those who uphold it) to claim that their own position is the view that has predominated throughout the history of Christianity.[9] The writings of Coleridge on this subject provide a valuable reference point in the historical controversy, illustrating as they do that he was one of the earliest and most important English authors to argue for what today is known as limited infallibility.

A number of the terms used above should be explained and defined before an analysis of the primary sources begins. "Inerrancy" as used in this chapter will indicate the doctrine which holds that the Scriptures in their original autographs, properly interpreted, are wholly true in everything that they affirm, whether that has to do with doctrine or morality, or the social, physical, or life sciences.[10] The word *inerrancy* is not derived from any particular text of Scripture and historically this doctrine, with modifications that will be noted where appropriate, was designated by the term *infallibility*. Thus, these two words will be used interchangeably despite recent attempts to claim "infallibility" by those who would hold that only certain portions of Scripture are without error (usually those portions that deal with matters of "faith and practice").[11]

Another important term, which is directly attributed to Scripture (2 Tim. 3:16), is "inspiration." It will refer to the work of the Holy Spirit in guiding human authors to compose and record God's selected message in the words of the original documents.[12] Next, "revelation" will designate the disclosure from God to man of that which otherwise would not be known of God's person, purpose, or work.[13] Finally, higher criticism, which made its impact in the nineteenth century in literary and historical criticism of Scripture,[14] generally describes a tendency to treat the Bible in the same way as other pieces of ancient literature.[15] But because higher critics often assumed that there really was no difference between the Bible and other books, they frequently held notions about inspiration and infallibility which contrasted with the common beliefs of Coleridge's era.[16]

From the time of the Reformation through the eighteenth century in Europe, the authority of Scripture had been under discussion as an issue in Catholic/ Protestant debates about the proper source for religious faith and practice.[17] But there was usually agreement regarding its inspiration and infallibility, as James Burtchaell points out:

> Despite a radical disagreement on these issues both groups persevered in receiving the Bible as a compendium of inerrant oracles dictated by the Spirit. Only in the 19th century did a succession of empirical disciplines newly come of age begin to put a succession of inconvenient queries to the exegetes.[18]

Such a consensus on biblical inerrancy existed in England in the early nineteenth century among both clergy and laymen.[19] However, only in the later nineteenth century, in response to several clear denials of biblical infallibility, did English theologians feel the need explicitly to affirm their beliefs. For example, the Anglican divine, William Lee, in his work on *The Inspiration of Scripture*, published in 1857, gives a clear statement of the orthodox belief in the full inspiration and infallibility of Scripture.[20] J. Robert Barth summarizes Lee's teaching:

> In his view, the Bible is protected from all possible error or inaccuracy not only in conveying matters supernaturally revealed by God but also in conveying matters learned by natural means: details of history, geography, chronology, etc.[21]

Coleridge had earlier acknowledged that complete biblical infallibility was the popular belief in his day in England:

I have frequently attended meetings of the British and Foreign Bible Society, where I have heard speakers of every denomination, Calvinist and Arminian, Quaker and Methodist, Dissenting Ministers and Clergymen, nay, dignitaries of the Established Church,—and still have I heard the same doctrine,—that the Bible was not to be regarded or reasoned about in the way that other good books are or may be;—that the Bible was different in kind, and stood by itself. . . . their principal arguments were grounded on the position, that the Bible throughout was dictated by Omniscience, and therefore *in all its parts infallibly true* and obligatory, . . . how often you yourself must have heard the same language from the pulpit! . . . What could I reply to this?—I could neither deny the fact, nor evade the conclusion,—namely, that *such is the present popular belief.* [ital. mine][22]

Since nearly all Englishmen believed in an inerrant Bible during Coleridge's lifetime, it is surprising at first to see that Coleridge's view, as presented in his *Confessions of an Inquiring Spirit,*[23] does not reflect this belief. However, a small minority of philosophers and theologians, mainly in Germany, had developed views in connection with their critical studies of Scripture that denied biblical infallibility in the years before Coleridge developed his theory. It was at least partially due to the influence of these men that Coleridge was unable to accept inerrancy. Notable examples of writers who had directly or indirectly denied complete biblical infallibility from the late sixteenth century through the early nineteenth include Socinus (Fausto Sozzini, 1539–1604),[24] Benedict (or Baruch) Spinoza (1632–1677),[25] Richard Simon (1638–1712),[26] Matthew Tindal (1655–1733),[27] Jean Le Clerc (1657–1736),[28] Hermann Reimarus (1694–1768),[29] Johann Semler (1725–1791),[30] Thomas Paine (1737–1809),[31] and Johann Herder (1744–1803).[32] Coleridge was aware of many of the theories being taught in Germany, having studied there in his youth, and unlike many of his fellow Englishmen, he continued to monitor with interest the thinking coming from the Continent.[33] He was familiar with several of the men mentioned above and shared their methodological concern for handling the Bible as another work of great literature.[34] Yet, it was the work of Gotthold Lessing (1729–1781) and Johann G. Eichhorn (1752–1827) that made the greatest impact on the development of Coleridge's particular contribution to the inspiration and inerrancy question.

Lessing's critical views on the Bible were similar to those of Reimarus, whose works he edited and published as the notorious *Wolfenbüttel Fragments* (1774–78). As an "Editor's Counter-proposition" appended to the fifth fragment (which was soundly condemned because of its denial of the historicity of the resurrection), he said: "For the Bible obviously contains more than is essential to religion, and it is a mere hypothesis to assert that it must be equally infallible in this excess of matter."[35] Lessing intended to read the Bible just as he would Livy and in so doing saw contradictions among the eyewitness accounts of the Gospels similar to the differences found among eyewitnesses to events in any era.[36] To those who would respond that the Gospel accounts were *inspired* history, rendering them immune from any error, Lessing replied: "But, unfortunately, that is only *historically certain*" [ital. mine].[37] Lessing had previously stated "historical truths cannot be demonstrated," and "If no historical truth can be demonstrated, then nothing can be demonstrated by means of historical truths."[38] He concluded that "accidental truths of history can never become the proof of necessary truths of reason."[39] Thus, the historical certainty of inspiration (and its assurance of biblical infallibility) was really no proof at all.[40] This does not imply that Lessing doubted the resurrection, as did Reimarus. Lessing based its validity, however, not on any supposed historical truthfulness in the scriptural accounts but upon its own intrinsic truth recognized subjectively.[41] Lessing divorced "religion from the history of religion" in order to avoid having to defend the "illogical historical record."[42]

Basil Willey describes well the important effect Lessing had on Coleridge:

> Coleridge certainly absorbed these views and made them his own, and they entered so closely into his developing thought that much later, when he came to write the *Confessions*, he seems to have incorporated some material from his Lessing transcripts.[43]

Green's attempt to vindicate the originality of Coleridge in his introduction to the second edition (1849) of the *Confessions* serves rather to highlight certain aspects of Coleridge's dependence on Lessing. Green admitted: (1) "Coleridge was a student of Lessing's writings"; (2) ". . . the recollections of those writings would blend with his own thoughts and lead him to adopt similar arguments, and even in some instances the same expressions"; (3) for both Lessing and Coleridge, evidence for the "truths of Christianity" was not to be sought in the historical documents but was "of an internal character."[44] More important for the inerrancy issue was Green's concession that

> Lessing might indeed have suggested to him the fallacy of considering the Scriptures as the revelation itself and the sole criterion of truth, to which the human reason is to bow as to an infallible oracle forbidding further questioning.[45]

Green proposed that instead of having plagiarized from Lessing, Coleridge was so immersed in Lessing's work that "the salient points of the German author, whom he confessedly studied and admired, became so impropriated by, and amalgamated with, his own mind, that they were no longer remembered."[46] Certainly it is no exaggeration to conclude that the writings of Lessing played a role in the formation of Coleridge's view on biblical infallibility.[47]

Eichhorn was also instrumental in shaping later thinking on issues relating to the accuracy of Scripture. He first used the term *higher criticism* in distinction from "lower" or textual criticism. He is often regarded as the "father of modern Old Testament criticism" for his contributions to what later became the widely accepted documentary hypothesis relating to the formation of the Pentateuch.[48] Eichhorn viewed the Old Testament prophets as artists who consciously produced their "visions."[49] He also studied the Gospels and theorized they were derived from a single Aramatic source. Overall, the effect of his views encouraged critical study of the biblical text but brought into question the reliability of the narratives by emphasizing the human element in their composition.

Coleridge was very familiar with the work of Eichhorn. As a student at the

University of Göttingen in 1799, he attended a New Testament course taught by Professor Eichhorn[50] and had also read Eichhorn's *Introduction to the Old Testament*.[51] In later years, he referred to him more often than any other German theologian.[52] In fact, Coleridge wrote to his son Derwent in 1819:

> . . . Eichhorn's introductions to the O. & N. Testament, and to the Apocrypha, and his Comment on the Apocalypse . . . will suffice for your *Biblical* Learning, and teach you to attach no more than the supportable weight to these and such like outward evidences of our holy and spiritual Religion.[53]

Eichhorn was probably the greatest single source for the exegetical methods used by Coleridge.[54] However, Coleridge was never a great technical historian or higher critical scholar. Attempts to capture the thinking behind the methods used by those who were such critics were more in line with his interests.[55] It is important to note his ties with Eichhorn and Lessing exactly because of the negative assumptions regarding the accuracy of the biblical text presented in their works. How could this be incorporated with a belief in the divine inspiration of Scripture?

Coleridge attempted to resolve this question for his own satisfaction and to aid those who might be perplexed by similar concerns in his *Confessions of an Inquiring Spirit*. This work gives in a more systematic fashion than is usually to be found in Coleridge's writings his theory on the inspiration and infallibility of the Bible. It was written in the form of seven letters addressed to a friend concerning "the bounds between the right, and the superstitious, use and estimation of the Sacred Canon."[56] Coleridge sought to approach this subject in a neutral manner, "above the contagious blastments of prejudice."[57] He would not assume that discrepancies existed in the Bible but neither would he "lie for God" if they did exist.[58] In this manner he studied the Scripture and set down this principle: "whatever *finds* me, bears witness for itself that it has proceeded from a Holy Spirit."[59] He recognized this was in sharp contrast to the current belief in verbal inspiration extending to all of Scripture:

> the doctrine in question requires me to believe, that not only what finds me, but all that exists in the sacred volume . . . was—not alone inspired by, that is composed by men under the actuating influence of the Holy Spirit, but likewise—dictated by an Infallible Intelligence;—that the writers, each and all, were divinely informed as well as inspired.[60]

This would seem to involve a definition of inspiration that was not different in kind from that of other prominent writers but different only in degree. According to his explanation, the human authors of Scripture would not be specially informed on matters of history, science, etc., and so (as men will) they might err in these areas. Coleridge did *not* doubt their accuracy as recorders,[61] but, as Lessing had before argued, such accuracy did not insure complete infallibility or constitute useful proof to a skeptic.[62] Coleridge did not accept "revelation" in Scripture as completely true, but all things in the Bible were not revelation: only such matters as had been stated directly by the authors as the actual words or commands of

God (recorded as such) were unquestionably true.[63] Thus, he divorced inspiration from revelation and more important, inerrancy from inspiration.[64]

Coleridge's prime concern in formulating the revised view of inspiration given in the *Confessions* was to uplift the human quality of each book as the work of individuals with different backgrounds and interests, writing over the course of more than a thousand years.[65] The current understanding of inspiration (which preserved inerrancy) sometimes affirmed a dictation theory which denied the personality of the authors.[66] For Coleridge, this was an unnecessary stumbling block to an honest inquirer examining Christianity and an untenable position for any enlightened scholar.[67] His own theory was that "the spirit of the Bible" and not the "detached words or sentences" should be considered "infallible and absolute."[68] In other words:

> The Bible considered in reference to its declared ends and purposes, is true and holy, for all who seek truth with humble spirits and an unquestionable guide, and therefore it is the Word of God.[69]

However, apart from those "ends and purposes" there could be incidental errors:

> And if in that small portion of the Bible which stands in no necessary connection with the known and especial ends and purposes of the Scriptures, there should be a few apparent errors resulting from the state of knowledge then existing— errors which the best and holiest men might entertain uninjured, and which without a miracle those men must have entertained; if I find no such miraculous prevention asserted, and see no reason for supporting it—may I not, to ease the scruples of a perplexed inquirer, venture to say to him: "Be it so. What then? The *absolute infallibility* even of the inspired writers in matters altogether incidental and foreign to the objectives and purposes of their inspiration is *no part of my Creed*." [ital. mine][70]

Coleridge minimized the importance of the errors his system allowed. He even argued that problems encountered due to discrepancies between authors of different books of Scripture, and various other types of mistakes, benefited Christians by preventing "us from sinking into a habit of slothful, undiscriminating acquiescence!"[71]

When the *Confessions* were finally published, the views expressed caused a considerable stir in England, and Coleridge was both praised and condemned. For those who were aware of the critical studies on Scripture, his theory that it was the "spirit" of the Bible that was infallible left room for them to affirm the plenary inspiration and other articles of faith and still incorporate the new information coming from Germany (and elsewhere). However, for many others his acknowledgment of even "incidental" errors was a denial of the Word of God.[72] The real struggles over the issues being raised by the higher critics and the questions soon to be introduced by the theory of Darwin were not fought in England until the latter half of the nineteenth century.[73] But Coleridge had already provided an answer to one part of the problem by allowing theologians to determine subjectively whether any particular verse or passage was vital to the "ends and purposes" of Scripture as a whole.[74] Many of the leaders in the Broad Church movement especially followed his lead in denying complete biblical infallibility while at the same time stressing the value of Scripture to meet the spiritual needs of individuals. The most prominent of these were Thomas Arnold (1795–1842) and Frederick Denison Maurice (1805–72).[75]

Arnold was one of the few scholars or clergymen in England in the first half of the nineteenth century who was well acquainted with higher critical thinking and what it might mean for traditional Protestant beliefs on Scripture. This was due to his study of both the German higher critics and to his reading of Coleridge.[76] Like Coleridge, he affirmed the human character of the biblical books while placing the truth of Christianity outside the realm of historical or scientific evidences to its validity.[77] He also separated inspiration from revelation and implied that the human authors of Scripture only had some truths revealed to them. In regard to the Old Testament he said: "in a great many points . . . the patriarchs may have been no better informed than the Heathens around them."[78] Thomas Arnold's son Matthew commented on the impact his father and Coleridge had in getting a revised notion of inspiration accepted, to some degree, in England:

> In papa's time the exploding of the old notions of literal inspiration in Scripture, and the introducing of a truer method of interpretation, were the changes for which, here in England, the moment had come. Stiff people could not receive this change, and my dear old Methodist friend, Mr. Scott, used to say to the day of his death that papa and Coleridge might be excellent men, but that they had found and shown the rat-hole in the temple.[79]

Maurice also took notice of the new theories about inspiration and infallibility of several earlier writers. He knew and appreciated some features of Lessing, placing him among those he considered the "wisest and greatest" of their age.[80] His approach to the Bible was practically the same as Coleridge's.[81] He approved of biblical criticism but always maintained a high personal reverence for Scripture.[82] He felt a strong concern for the young Christian who was told to believe the Bible on the basis of "external evidences" which might be good enough in themselves but would certainly cause a thoughtful person to raise some questions. The course that attempted to *prove* the infallibility of Scripture would "infallibly make the doubter what you accuse him of being."[83] Maurice instead proposed that readers view the Bible as a book which meets human needs[84] and then for them, as for himself, it would not cause perplexities but would resolve them.[85] To those critics who felt he was hiding some secret doubt about the Bible and the doctrine of inspiration he said:

> I am conscious of just as much unbelief about the books of the Bible, as I am about the facts of nature and of my own existence. I *am* conscious of unbelief about those facts; oftentimes they seem to me quite incredible. I overcome this unbelief . . .[86]

If this did not reassure the skeptics, Maurice would probably not have been too worried, as the question of whether he believed there were errors of fact in Scripture did not concern him.[87] Regarding the writers of the biblical books, he said: "I most assuredly should *not* give up the faith in God which they cherished in me, if I found they had made mistakes."[88] On the meaning of inspiration, Maurice is easier to pin down. Biblical inspiration was not "generically unlike that which God bestows on His children in this day."[89] Thus, he held to an inspiration which did not insure inerrancy in a manner reminiscent of Coleridge.

Several other men in nineteenth-century England were affected by the modified theory of inspiration proposed by Coleridge. Willey summarizes,

> of those who did learn from Coleridge, it is enough to mention Sterling, Carlyle, J. S. Mill, J. C. Hare, Thomas Arnold, J. H. Newman, James Martineau, F. A. J. Hort, F. D. Maurice, Charles Kingsley, Matthew Arnold, Walter Pater and many others.[90]

Of course this was a general influence that did not necessarily extend to the views on inerrancy all these men held. Yet even concerning the narrower question of Coleridge's work on Scripture, Dean Farrar in 1884 was able to say:

> To it were due the sermons of Arnold and of Robertson, of Whately and Thirwall, of Hare and Kingsley. . . . It was in this spirit that . . . Frederick Denison Maurice laboured for years amid obloquy and opposition.[91]

If the effect of the *Confessions* cannot be directly traced to all those who ultimately formed similar views, it still seems fair to conclude there was a general diffusion of influence that, together with other factors, led Christians away from a belief in complete biblical infallibility in the last half of the nineteenth century. Indeed, the similarity of the position developed by Coleridge with the modern one of limited infallibility is striking. Coleridge certainly anticipated current statements that the Bible is infallible on matters of "faith and practice" and that it is inerrant when teaching of "salvation" but could still include "technical mistakes." His recognition of the human personalities of the scriptural writers and his concern to study the Bible as one does other books, while relatively novel in his own day, are almost universally recognized as valid today. His belief that much of what they produced was not divine revelation but merely human, and possibly errant, literature foreshadows in particular the position of those modern historians and theologians who believe that the human character of Scripture necessitates an errant Bible.[92] His work on the inerrancy question is important therefore because it both influenced the thinking of certain theologians after him and is a representative of modern attempts to reconcile higher critical assumptions with a belief in an inspired Bible.

CHAPTER FIVE

WORD AND SCRIPTURE IN LUTHER STUDIES SINCE WORLD WAR II

Eugene F. Klug

I. INTRODUCTION

Luther came to the world's attention with his posting of the Ninety-five Theses, October 31, 1517. The issue had to do with the sale of indulgences and the significance or role they played in the sacrament of penance. Could they be bought without repentance? As a priest with a dedicated pastoral heart Luther agonized deeply over this question. He sought to debate the matter, not in order to trouble the church, but to clarify a very important point in the spiritual life of the people he served at Wittenberg. Once he saw the great stir caused by his challenge to the current practice in the church, he responded immediately in his *Explanations to the Theses,* early in 1518, defending his right on the basis of Holy Scripture to question what was going on in the name of Christ's church. The Gospel itself was at stake. In his introductory statement to the *Explanations* he made it very plain that he took his stance on Scripture's authority. Already he was indicating that there was no higher authority in the church than God's Word, specifically on doctrines and teaching.

The oath of fealty to the Sacred Scriptures that Luther took on October 4, 1512, when he was made a doctor of theology by the authority of the church itself, was for him a very serious responsibility and charge. He lived by it faithfully all his life, a sworn Doctor of Sacred Scriptures. To proclaim its truth was a duty entrusted to him by the church itself. It was a commission from God. It was this high trust in God's expectations of him to be a loyal teacher of the Holy Scripture which finally led him into open conflict with the church under the papal hierarchy. Luther never saw his actions as those of a willful rebel against the church but only as dutiful obedience before God and to His Word. From this *Knechtsgestalt* ("servant stance") before God's Holy Word Luther never wavered.

In comparison, contemporary theology is a troubled and troubling arena of conflicting opinions about the Holy Scriptures. To what extent and in what way are they to be viewed as the Word of God? In what way and to what extent are they to be looked upon as a human product? In spite of all confusion and debate on these questions, the fact remains that the Bible is the great unifying mooring point—for all that passes as Christianity. Insistence that the *kerygma* must be redesigned to meet the demands of modern man's thought-forms has left the Bible's content a largely time-bound and out-of-touch medium:

117

and much biblical criticism has shredded the Bible's authority and integrity as the Word of God.

Luther's theology, on the other hand, was grounded upon implicit confidence and trust of the text of Scripture as the inviolable Word of God. Nothing could be true in theology, nor demand of faith, that went beyond Scripture or that Scripture did not plainly teach. It was throughout God's incontrovertible truth, authoritative in itself, by its very nature.

II. LUTHER AND THE BIBLE—FIVE HUNDRED YEARS LATER

The giant figure has lost no luster nor paled in its gravitational pull. Luther studies and research, if anything, have mounted new drive and magnetism. The Sixth International Congress for Luther Research meeting at Erfurt, August 14–20, 1983, in the German Democratic Republic on the occasion of the 500th anniversary of the Reformer's birth is a case in point. That year, 1983, was also the centennial of Karl Marx's death. The ubiquitous posters of Communist propaganda blazoned this fact before every visitor's eye. Yet it was not Marx's death that drew the crowds to East Germany but Luther's anniversary. Luther's greatness, however, is intrinsically tied up with his commitment to follow the Bible, and the Bible alone, even in the face of incredible ecclesiastical opposition.

In the early part of this century Karl Holl offered a similar evaluation of Luther's ongoing relevance to Christian theology. Often thought of as the dean and teacher of a whole new breed of Luther scholars, Holl's influence extended widely among Protestants and Catholics alike. "In remembering Luther," stated Holl, "we do not memorialize the dead but deal with one who is very much alive and with us."[1] Much of contemporary Luther research still owes its impetus to the original work of Holl, who showed that Luther's lasting significance was traceable not only to the fact that "Protestantism has not produced Luther's superior or even his equal" but also and especially to the fact that "he far excels our present generation in original creative power."[2] "The meaning of his Reformation is not exhausted in the fact that he changed certain doctrines and institutions of the Catholic church" but in that "he rebuilt from the ground up" man's conception of God and God's purposes toward man, and thus "eventually touched all the questions that beset us today."[3]

Holl minimizes the idea that the generation before Luther was passionately yearning for religious reform, or that it was deeply depressed with all sorts of political, economic, and social problems. He does not discount their presence nor the "immense amount of sighing and complaining about the church," but he discerningly adds, "what was lacking was the holy wrath that gives vent to an outraged consciousness" and refuses to settle and live comfortably with the *status quo*.[4] When Luther, therefore, decided to enter the monastery, it was not simply as a result of the lightening bolt on the outskirts of the village of Stotternheim but because he took seriously all "the ingredients of Catholic piety," "churchly morality, monastic discipline, sense of personal unworthiness, strictest self-examination, deep contrition in the practice of penance, cultivating love of God"—indeed "Luther engulfed himself with them."[5]

When Luther finally broke through to the pure Gospel, from all this clutter of manmade piety, to see and understand that righteousness before God was freely imputed to the sinner for Christ's sake and by faith, it was as though the heavens opened to him. This "new view of God came to him as a surprise, as a sudden enlightenment." But this was not of his own making: it was closely tied to the scriptural base. "It came to him through Paul, who opened Luther's eyes to the fact that all of his striving was a mistake."[6] It was a theology of glory, man's glory, versus a genuine *theologia crucis*, that found its hope and salvation in the bloody wounds of Jesus through whom alone there was forgiveness for the troubled conscience. At that point "the unmitigated impulses of primitive Christianity came alive again with triumphant power."[7]

By so uncovering the Gospel of forgiveness for himself and for the ailing church in his day, Luther "reaffirmed the powerful motives that distinguish Christianity from all other religions." It was the neuralgic point. "Relentlessly he emphasized that the concern of religion is not whether I want to have anything to do with God but whether God wants to have anything to do with me."[8]

It was the word that the world needed most and still needs now. That is why Luther still has an abiding, worldwide appeal, says Holl, for Luther was not only for Germans but for the world. "He belongs to humanity," and "we are confident that his attainments will continue to be cherished."[9] A visit to Germany today, particularly to the heartland Luther sites, will confirm that the historian Leopold von Ranke was right when he wrote more than a century ago: "Das deutsche Volk hat einmal geliebt, und der Mann war Luther" ("The German people have ever loved only one man, and that man was Luther.") It was not his person, however, as much as it was the cause which he so courageously and devotedly championed.

On the Wartburg, during his unwelcome exile after the Diet of Worms had denounced him and placed him under the imperial ban as an enemy of the church and state, Luther was often troubled by the incredible size of the storm that had brewed around him. One question popped up again and again as he viewed the deep chasm that had opened between him and the official church: "Are you alone wise?" He spoke of the difficulty he had living with a conscience that had been taught to bend before manmade ordinances as though they came from God, to dare oppose the pope and brand him as the very Antichrist, a lowly monk against the so-called vicar of Christ on earth. "How often did my heart quail, punish me, and reproach me with its single strongest argument: Are you the only wise man? Can it be that all the others are in error and have erred for so long a time? What if you are mistaken and lead so many people into error who might be eternally damned?" When such black moods and doubts overtook him, Luther turned again and again to the Sacred Scripture, where "Christ with his clear, unmistakable Word strengthened and confirmed me, so that my heart no longer quails, but resists the arguments of the papists, as a stony shore resists the waves, and laughs at their threats and storms."[10] Karl Holl took note of Luther's sensitivity on the issue of his growing cleavage with the church:

> As is generally known Luther's judgment on himself was rather severe, and he
> moved between moments of great confidence in what he was doing and grave

doubts, wondering: "Do you think that all previous teachers have known nothing? In your opinion, must all our fathers have been fools? Are you the only favorite child of the Holy Spirit left in these latter days? Would God have allowed his people to err so long?"[11]

All his life Luther contended with such *Anfechtungen* from within and from without. The only recourse he had for comfort and guidance was the Holy Scripture. Nothing surpassed Scripture in schooling one's theology, in finding one's bearing point; and as Luther looked expectantly and with unquestioning trust into the deep, clear pool of Holy Writ, he found in its depths the lucid, uncomplicated answer of God for sinners' salvation.

Nothing else explains Luther's avid, assiduous study, memorizing, pondering of the Bible throughout his life. "He never lost his capacity for astonishment," states Holl, "and he retained throughout life those childlike eyes that the miraculous is the commonplace; for him the great remained great." While he downgraded himself, he elevated others but none so much as God and His Word. "The church itself," Holl reminds us, "had granted him his doctor's title," but Luther never gloried in it, humbly explaining that "in his renewal of the gospel he had only exercised his office as a doctor of Holy Scripture." As a servant of the church, Luther believed that he first of all was a servant of God and His Word. This awareness "gave him a new and decisive criterion for evaluating himself," and so "when Luther called himself God's unworthy instrument, this was more than the usual pious phrase."[12] Luther was convinced that he was not indispensable to God's purposes, for "God can create many Doctor Martins," and "if He will not finish the task through me, He will through someone else."[13] What Pauck cites is reminiscent of Luther's sobering words in one of his treatises against the Antinomians, chiefly Agricola, in the 1539:

A thousand years ago you and I were nothing, and yet the church was preserved at that time without us. He who is called "who was" and "yesterday" had to accomplish this. Even during our lifetime we are not the church's guardians. It is not preserved by us. . . . It is another Man who obviously preserves both the church and us. It is a tragic thing that there are so many examples before us of those who thought they had to preserve the church, as though it were built on them.[14]

Even Joseph Lortz, a Roman Catholic scholar, sings Luther's praises as one who "belongs in the highest gallery of creative geniuses, a genius in the highest sense of the word"; and when one assesses how the Reformation came to be, there is no quandary, "for Luther is the Reformation."[15] "Luther," Lortz continues, "is a spiritual giant, or, as Althaus puts it, an ocean; the danger of drowning in him, the danger of inadequate mastering, simply appends itself to the great mass of materials."[16]

Lortz goes on to admit that his earlier thesis, "that Luther was no theologian," was an obviously mistaken, prejudicial view. But he does not back down from his labeling of Luther as a "subjectivist." It helps his cause little to assert that the word *subjectivist* can have either a pejorative sense or simply be a factual statement of the case, because he then adds lamely that "the important thing to note is that the Bible is not given or entrusted to the individual but to the Church!"[17] Precisely here is where Luther parted company with Roman Catholics.

One of the finest biographical sketches of Luther to have appeared in recent times, when there have been so many, is that of Daniel Olivier, a French Roman Catholic. His assessment of Luther runs much more sympathetically than that of Lortz, not to say much more objectively true. His concentration is the crucial period of Luther's trial culminating at Worms, April 18, 1521. Olivier points out that it was not Luther who put himself forward but his opponents; that Luther never claimed a prophetic sort of posture; that there was no ground to the accusation that Luther was the propounder of any new doctrines which, in tune with the Scriptures, the fathers of the ancient church had not safely taught. Luther's only court of appeal was the Sacred Scriptures, and who could fault him for that? True, "the official authority of the Church did not see in Scripture what he saw," but Luther never closed the book on "the possibility that there was an interpretation other than his and truer than his" as regards Scripture's meaning.[18] "But Scripture could not be taken lightly," says Olivier of Luther's attitude.

> To ask him to retract his Scriptural theses without offering him in return the true interpretation of the Word of God was to invite him to close up the Bible for good. He had asked the Church to help him move forward in his knowledge of Scripture and the answer had been that he must stop trying to understand it.[19]

Luther was convinced that Scripture was on his side—no one arose to disprove it!—and he was equally convinced, says Olivier, that "only Scripture has not erred."[20] Compromise was out of the question, with the integrity of God's Word at stake. This was the issue at Worms. There had not been a word too much, not a word out of place," says Olivier in reflection on Luther's heroic refusal to recant. "It had contained the whole Luther case in a nutshell. The wonder was not his obstinacy, nor his persistence, but that, without having sought it, he had from the very beginning put his finger on a linchpin of Christianity, of the human spirit and of history."[21] John Todd, a lay scholar and also a Roman Catholic, in a biography of Luther, expresses what so many others have, amazement at the incredible phenomenon of Luther's extraordinary corpus of writings. Books by and about Luther occupy more space in major libraries than those concerned with any other human being except Jesus of Nazareth. Todd deplores the fact that in some quarters people "make a caricature of Luther, as though he might be some kind of foul-mouthed Billy Graham."[22] Here was the man who "ushered in a whole new way of life in Europe, a genius," not "some kind of fanatic," and yet few people other than theologians and historians have ever read his story, laments Todd.[23] Like most others Todd recognizes Luther's total commitment to the Bible, but toward the end of his book he manages to transform this into a sort of Barthian notion, according to which Luther conceived of the Word only as "the message of Jesus of Nazareth, Christ, speaking through the Bible."[24]

Ernest Schwiebert has produced one of the acknowledged classics on Luther's life in our time. Rightly he too pinpoints Luther's appearance at Worms as one of history's most crucial moments. The stakes were not only "the right of individual liberty of thought and conscience, the very cornerstone of modern Protestantism and of democracy," but rather "whether the teachings of Scripture would stand or the traditional Roman hierarchical system which ruled in all matters of faith." Here was the continental divide of modern history: "Luther spoke but a single sentence, but its reverberations still resound throughout Christendom."[25]

Herman Schuster takes note of the fact that few people in Luther's day could read or write and therefore argues that Luther's Bible translation could have meant very little to most. Thomas Münzer ran with this in one direction, exploiting the credulous, naive nature of people, claiming for himself inner enlightenment by the Spirit rather than through the written Word. To Luther's credit it must be said that he was bound by the text and was preeminently a faithful preacher of the Word, unwilling to exploit his eloquence to mislead tender minds. Accordingly, "the chief thing is not, that Luther once again restored the Bible, but that he understood it correctly," resisting the allegorizing of its contents, binding himself to "the natural meaning in accord with its historical sense."[26]

Much has been made of the fact that Luther was not a systematic theologian in the usual sense of that word today. Paul Althaus, acknowledged giant among Luther interpreters in this century, takes issue with that easy criticism, asserting that in all that Luther wrote, his lectures, sermons, treatises, he is constantly the teacher of doctrine. It is a commitment he draws from Scripture's authority in all theological matters. "Luther," states Althaus, "thinks theologically in constant intercourse with the Scripture as exegete and preacher." He adds: "The longer my study of Luther, the stronger is the impression that Luther makes hardly a theological step without grounding and direction through or on a verse of Scripture."[27] Everything Luther touches, including his references to the early Christian fathers, is always with a regard toward the authority of the biblical text. The fundamental question, *quid Deus nobiscum agat* ("what God has to do with us"), Luther seeks to answer from the Word of God, which speaks clearly concerning God's wrath against sin on the one hand and of God's loving mercy in Christ on the other hand, of Law and Gospel in other words. Here, Althaus observes, the great significance of *sola fide* over against *ex operibus* ("by works") is laid bare.

More and more scholars have come to appreciate the consistency of Luther's theological expression. Among these is Friedrich Kantzenbach, longtime head of the famed Löhe eleemosynary institutions at Neuendettelsau. "Luther," states Kantzenbach, "was far in advance of his opponents in the understanding of the structure of dogmatic statements."[28] Kantzenbach also questions Lortz's charge that Luther was "subjectivistic" and not "fully Catholic" in his doing of theology. In the same context he points out the flaws in Brandenburg's (a Roman Catholic) book on the pre-Reformation Luther, which he (Kantzenbach) asserts was "greatly influenced by Gerhard Ebeling's work in Luther research." Ebeling, charges Kantzenbach, sought to justify his own hermeneutical views by quoting

Luther to try to buttress his own notions, all of which show their kinship and dependence upon Bultmann's existentialist theologizing. It is Kantzenbach's considered judgment that "an understanding of the Bible based on any particular sort of historical criticism makes it difficult to come to a full understanding of Luther's theological concern in his interpretation of the Scriptures."[29] Yet he is not ready to sack so-called "accepted standards of historical criticism." Somewhat ambivalently he warns, however (and here he is quite correct):

> As long as we apply only the principles of historical criticism to the words of Holy Scripture, we might well find in the end that all we have is a heap of theological statements which, in the last analysis, contradict each other. Only when we really listen to what the Scriptures say shall we be free from the danger of wanting to force individual statements into some over-all system. An involvement in the exposition of the Scriptures enables us to perceive a unity beneath the apparent contradictions. The internal structure of the Scripture is quite clear.[30]

Luther could not have agreed more. Likewise Luther would have concurred with Kantzenbach's call for a forthright articulation of the differences dividing the churches to this day rather than attempting to single out individual pieces, as Hans Küng has done on the article of the sinner's justification before God, claiming that Barth and the Roman Catholic Church taught and thought alike in concert with the Reformation. The facts are that Küng has not understood either Luther or the Reformation, or for that matter Barth, and perhaps even Catholicism. "We have to confront Catholic theology with Luther's total concern," admonishes Kantzenbach, "and not with isolated statements," torn out of context.[31]

James Nestingen has assembled some of the wilder and "way-out" views on Luther found in contemporary assessments. Luther, he states, has been variously described as "petty," "outrageously maddening," responsible for "absolutizing the state, " "authoritarian," an "embarrassment" to the church in an ecumenical age, "indefensibly vile" in his position against the Jews and supportive of "modern acquisitive capitalism."[32]

Narrowing the focus on Luther's devotion to Holy Writ, Nestingen reflects the manner in which some contemporary thinking runs: "Having kicked the pope out of bed with the Bible, has Luther now crawled into the same bed, insisting that the Bible is his own book and that it has to be read his way?" Nestingen clearly distances himself from that sort of critique of Luther as well as from the following all-too-familiar thought pattern in our day: "Do not Lutherans open themselves to the same charges that Luther himself leveled—that is, placing Luther or selected Lutheran writings between themselves and Jesus?" It is Luther's *attitude* toward the Scriptures that is to be respected and emulated, as well as that of other faithful heirs of the Reformation. Apotheosis of man, or of his writings, is the last thing that genuine heirs of the Reformation intend!

James Atkinson, a British scholar, contributes the valuable insight that Luther is in no way to be seen as a mere restorationist after the manner of various nineteenth-century leaders of revival movements. "Luther never made the error," avers Atkinson, "of trying to foist on to the Church some idealized external primitive pattern of life from the early Church, as the Independents and Radicals were to do later." In marked contrast to these groups, says Atkinson, "Luther's soul was saved in his study, by hard, costly work on the text of the Bible. He had found the theology offered by the Church true neither to the Bible, experience, nor common sense."[33]

An important listing of sources is that of Ernst-Wilhelm Kohls in his chapter on Luther studies since 1970.[34] Kohls's listing limits itself to German works. He is of the opinion that in research on Luther the key is not merely in Luther's rediscovery of the central Christian teaching concerning the justification of the sinner *sola gratia/fide propter Christum* but in Luther's absolute dependence upon the scriptural Word. Thus the canons of reason and philosophy played no role in theology, states Kohls of Luther. He also credits Wilhelm Maurer with directing Luther studies toward this insight and in lesser measure also Gerhard Gloege, Lennart Pinomaa, and Heinrich Bornkamm,[35] among others, with having brought this emphasis back into the foreground. Luther knew no other Gospel or Christ than the one revealed in Scripture. The Scriptures remained forever his point of departure (and return!) in theology. In contrast, the so-called new hermeneutic—Kohls points the finger at Ebeling, among others—has cluttered the picture with its hypotheses and constructions, actually reconstructions, of the text of Scripture, all of which tend to obliterate rather than explicate the text. "In the years since Helsinki (1963)," states Kohls, "it has become clear that the issue is not on the teaching concerning justification but the primary fact of God's personal revelation of Himself in the Holy Scriptures, as our Lutheran Confessions have also summarized it."[36]

In the same commemorative volume Steffen Kjedgaard-Pedersen traces developments in Scandinavian countries on Luther research. Among these are Regin Prenter's study on the hermeneutical question and Inge Lonning's on the "Canon within the Canon."[37] Jos. E. Vercruysse sketches developments in the Netherlands,[38] and this is followed by a review of happenings in France, Italy, and Spain.[39] Lowell Green of America summarizes developments in English-speaking lands since 1971,[40] discussing biographies of Luther, his theology (but little on the Word!), his work as Reformer, and then finally his relation with others, such as Chemnitz, the seventeenth-century orthodox theologians, and also Roman Catholic scholars of recent vintage.

In other surveys of recent work on Luther, few mention Luther's attitude to Scripture.[41]

III. LUTHER'S TOWER EXPERIENCE

The "tower experience" in Luther's life refers to the time when he broke through to a scriptural understanding of the righteousness of God as pertaining not to God's own sublime, inherent holiness and righteousness but to the imputed righteousness that is ours, without our merit, freely, for Christ's sake through faith. For years, indeed centuries, it has generally been agreed that Luther's conviction on this point was reached sometime during the period after he had begun to lecture on the Bible at Wittenberg, 1512–13. In recent decades, however, this assumption has been challenged by several distinguished Luther researchers; and we must briefly treat the question here, because it bears on the question of when Luther came to rest his case supremely on the authority of Scripture.

A leader in this new approach to Luther's *Turmerlebnis* has been Ernst Bizer.[42] It is Bizer's thesis that Luther's comment in the Latin edition of his works, 1545, is the key. There Luther states:

> I had indeed been captivated with an extraordinary ardor for understanding Paul in the Epistle to the Romans. But up till then a single word in Chapter 1 (17) had stood in my way. For I hated that word "righteousness of God," which, according to the use and custom of all the teachers, I had been taught to understand philosophically regarding the formal or active righteousness.[43]

The "up till then" Bizer construes as the second lecture series on the Psalms, which occurred in 1518 and followed after Luther's encounter with the learned papal legate, Cardinal Cajetan. It was at this meeting through the theological interchange occurring there, according to Bizer, that Luther finally nailed down in his own mind and thinking the conception of justification of the sinner before God as coming about through faith alone, faith laying hold of the Gospel, the promise of imputed righteousness in Christ.

Bizer is joined by quite a number of scholars in his view, among them Ernst Kinder, Albrecht Peters, Peter Meinhold, Uuras Saarnivaara, Lowell Green, to mention a few. The latter devotes a large part of his recent book[44] trying to prove that he came to his view as early as 1955 and quite independently of Saarnivaara, who first published his thesis in 1951. Green's position grounds itself on the notion that it was Melanchthon, not Luther, who first taught that "justification does not depend upon righteousness within the individual, but on the alien righteousness of Christ," and that up until the time of 1518–19 Luther did not know how to distinguish Law and Gospel.[45] Thus to Melanchthon Luther owed not only his excellent knowledge of Greek and Hebrew but also his forensic sense of justification.[46] In addition, it was Melanchthon, according to Green, who stressed justification *sola fide*.[47] Green also contends that Luther's teaching on justification was thus influenced more by the Johannine than by the Pauline texts.[48] To these very debatable points of view Green adds one more controversial point when he takes exception to the assertion that Luther and the (early) Melanchthon spoke with united voice in the Lutheran Confessions, labeling those who support this view "obscurantist."[49]

Saarnivaara's argument is hardly as involved, especially not on the score of elevating Melanchthon as Luther's teacher on the subject of justification. He traces this to Luther's own discovery in the epistles of Paul, but late, 1518–19. "The entire content of his discovery in the tower," states Saarnivaara, "was the insight that, according to the simple and literal meaning of this written Word of God, man is justified by the gracious imputation of God when by faith he appropriates the Gospel promise of forgiveness of sins in the blood of Christ."[50]

Arrayed against the supporters of a late *Turmerlebnis* is an equally impressive band of notable scholars, including Ernest Schwiebert, Leif Grane, Heinrich Bornkamm, Heiko Oberman, James Atkinson, A. Skevington Wood, Ian Siggins, and Kurt Aland. This is not to mention the dean of Luther scholars, Julius Koestlin, who though active in the nineteenth century taught many Luther scholars of our century where to look for and how to conceive a proper understanding of Luther's theology. The argument for an early "tower experience" is very strong in Koestlin's thinking. Both sides readily grant that extant writings, lecture notes, letters, sermons of Luther from the period 1513–18 are far fewer in number than those that follow after that time. But what is available demonstrates beyond a shadow of a doubt that Luther has come to an understanding for himself personally, and is sharing it with his students and hearers from the pulpit and with various correspondents, of the theology of the Cross, which is at the heart of his new understanding of righteousness *coram Deo*. So quite apart from the somewhat cryptic reference in the 1545 edition to Luther's writings is the fact that the new insight of the Gospel is there already, says Schwiebert, soon after the summer of 1513. This can be established from Luther's first lectures on the Psalms, 1513, which had been preceded by his lectures on Genesis.[51] Atkinson joins Schwiebert in this timetable of events, pointing to Luther's preparation for his Psalm lectures of 1513 and stating that "it was his work on the Bible that saved him."[52]

Leif Grane underscores convincingly the fact that already in this early period, 1513–18, Luther is grappling with the truth of the Gospel for the sake of his hearers, thus showing his abiding pastoral heart, and that he was left far behind other theological opinions, not to mention the canons of pagan philosophy, including Aristotle.[53] Skevington Wood argues cogently for the earlier date, too, against Saarnivaara, simply because Luther himself explains that the turning point in his life and theology came shortly after his doctorate and the lectures which followed, 1513–14.[54] Ian Siggins alludes to the struggle over the "tower experience" prompted by the work chiefly of Saarnivaara and Bizer, but contents himself with the fact that most scholars leave it at the traditional point, around 1512–13.[55] He pays special kudos in regard to this early dating of Luther's commitment to the *theologia crucis* to the work of von Loewenich.[56] It is Siggins's thesis that "Luther's doctrine of Christ has suffered from the common but erroneous assumption" that Luther is a Paulinist rather than a Johanninist, whereas the facts are rather that Luther saw a full harmony between these writers, as well as the rest of Holy Scripture, in behalf of its *theologia crucis* and the justification of the sinner by God's grace for Christ's sake through faith.[57]

In a review of Bizer's position as set out in *Fides Ex Auditu*, Roland Bainton somewhat guardedly states that he would not "venture a critical comment without first working through the whole body of material afresh."[58] But it is obvious that he finds Bizer's position, as well as Kinder's, who defends the former, hard to swallow.

In final assessment of this problem, which is mentioned here because it portrays vividly Luther's handling of the text of Scripture as the trustworthy Word of God, one need not venture far actually to note that already in his Romans lectures of 1515–16, specifically on the verse most in dispute, Romans

1:17, Luther has advanced beyond medieval theology to generally clear utterance, when he states:

> For the righteousness by which a person is worthy of such salvation, of God, by which alone there are righteous people before God, is revealed in it (in the Promise, or Word), because formerly it was considered hidden and to consist in a person's own works. But now it is "revealed," because no one is righteous unless he believes, as it is written in the last chapter of Mark (16:16): "He who believes," from faith to faith, as is written, Hab. 2:4: "The righteous, namely, in the eyes of God shall live by faith," that is, only through complete faith in God will he be saved. This is the eternal life of the Spirit.[59]

Accordingly, the point at which Luther could declare for himself that "I felt that I was altogether born again and had entered paradise itself through open gates," occurred well before 1518. This is borne out by his lectures on the Bible which had preceded, including *scholia* on Romans, Hebrews, the Psalms, and others. "The totally other face of the entire Scripture [which] showed itself to me" had been an open book for Luther soon after he began his lectures on the Bible at Wittenberg, 1512–13. In the period that follows, his letters, sermons, and also his *Explanations on the Ninety-five Theses*, all indicate that a "radical reformation" has already gone on in him and that it is from this base, firmly grounded on the scriptural Word, that he ventures to share his newly found Gospel with the world against whatever foe. He could no longer be dissuaded, least of all recant a position so vital to his own spiritual peace before God. It was this Gospel, lucidly proclaimed, which was drawing students by the thousands to Wittenberg, soon making it the largest university in Europe; and the populace in general flocked to here Luther preach the Word at Wittenberg's *Stadtkirche*.

IV. OTHER TANGENTIAL ISSUES

One is almost inclined to term some of the issues exciting contemporary Luther studies "peripheral piffle." They very often have no bearing on the central points at the nub, or eye, of the Reformation storm. Someone has observed that it is in the nature of German university life that a professor's claim to fame, the ability to excite and to attract students to his lecture hall, often lies in his capacity to spin the web of awe and mystique over his audience or to strike new lode by coming up with some novel, unique, controversial, often "way-out" position. This appears to have been the case with Erwin Iserloh's widely read and disputed *The Theses Were Not Posted*. It immediately stirred the desired result of widespread debate, though many just shrugged it off as bizarre, in view of the overwhelming evidence to the contrary. In a way it was unfortunate that Iserloh's fame came to rest on a matter of so little significance, since his competence in the field of Reformation studies is deserving of more note than that. A few individuals lent a sympathetic ear; most did not. Gert Haendler apparently agreed to give some credence to the idea but then added, almost casually, that "the posting of the theses proved to have much less historical foundation than had been supposed; in any case, the image of a hammer-swinging Luther was problematical to begin with."[60]

Kurt Aland is one of the redoubtable antagonists who entered the fray from his citadel at Münster to challenge the groundless notion of his colleague, Iserloh. Aland shows that there is no solid evidence to throw into doubt Luther's own rehearsal of the event as occurring on October 31, 1517, with the posting on the Castle Church doors. Luther may well have sent copies to reigning ecclesiastical principals like the Archbishop Albrecht of Mainz and especially his immediate superior, the Bishop of Brandenburg. But the notion that only several weeks later he then publicly circulated the theses fails for lack of evidence. As a matter of fact in a fortnight, with incredible speed, their content was known virtually all over Europe. There is every reason, therefore, to agree with Aland that "the problems in the limelight today, will not have lasting validity [and] will undergo a change in a foreseeable future."[61]

There is something symptomatic and telltale about the nature and direction that Luther research has taken in recent years. Side questions often seem to have come on center stage, much like sideshows at a carnival. The central issues which Luther isolated in his call for Reformation, all of which were doctrinal, seem to have been forced to the side, or if they are raised at all for discussion, end up quite distorted from Luther's straightforward, uncomplicated statement of the case. The recent Sixth International Congress for Luther Research at Erfurt was no exception. The opening day's central theme was the topic *causa Lutheri* ("Luther's cause"). All manner of responses were voiced, first by the principal essayists and their respondents and then by speakers from the floor. Luther would undoubtedly have been surprised, especially perhaps by the often involved and convoluted efforts at stating his *causa*. For him, throughout his life, the matter was, and always remained, the answer to the question, "Wie bekomm ich einen gnaedigen Gott?" ("How do I know that God is gracious to me?"). The answer lay in his soteriological discovery of the true nature of the Gospel, the forgiveness of sins *sola gratia/fide* for Christ's sake. That was the central point always for him whose pastoral heart reached out for the assuaging of spiritual torments in troubled consciences, including his own.

Moreover, the second of the important *causa Lutheri* had to do with the source of revelation, Holy Scripture, where this precious truth of the comforting Gospel lay cradled for sinners's sakes. Luther knew no other, nor would he be diverted by any other, authority than God's own precious Word, Holy Writ. *Haec regina debet dominari:* "This queen must rule; all must obey and be subject to her," Luther states in commenting on Paul's exhortation to the Galatians that they ought to turn deaf ears to any other Gospel than that which the apostle had first brought them (Gal. 1:9). "No other doctrine should be put forth in the church than the pure Word of God, that is, the Holy Scriptures; otherwise every teacher and hearer with their teaching deserves to be cursed."[62]

Another question that has recently appeared on the horizon of Luther studies, exciting a certain amount of debate, is the thought and utterance of the older Luther. Partial reason for this can be found in the very sharp, often coarse, outbursts of Luther against protagonists like the pope, on the one hand, and some of his supporters, like Henry of Braunschweig, on the other. It is also in these twilight years that Luther seems to have turned violently against the

Jews, while early in life he had spoken hopefully and positively about them in his treatise *That Christ Was Born a Jew* (1521). Scholars are quick to point out the sharp difference between this treatise and the one of 1543, *Of the Jews and Their Lies*. In fact, present-day evaluators are often quick to assure their Jewish friends that Luther was an angry old man, perhaps even senile and maybe ill, not only in body but also in mind.

What is the answer? Among scholars who have devoted time and energy to unraveling the puzzle of what appears to be a marked altering of Luther's personality is Mark Edwards.[63] Edwards by and large dismisses the notion that Luther was no longer mentally sharp and in command of his senses as old age and increasing bouts with illness enveloped him. Luther "remained involved and productive to his death."[64] He retained his strong faith, his robust sense of humor, and he let loose with his blasts of anger only when first of all attacked unfairly and viciously.

Moreover, says Edwards, "Luther could never just attack [but] he always had to profess and confess as well."[65] This meant that Luther was never primarily moved by arguments of history or logic but chiefly by theological implications grounded in Scripture. He fought by Scripture's authority. He would tolerate no attack on God's Word and the Gospel which it proclaimed. Hence his tirades against the papacy and then in later years the Jews are not to be traced to irascible old age or racism.[66] Edwards apparently agrees with Heiko Oberman's assessment that "Luther's anti-Jewish polemics cannot be understood properly apart from his apocalyptic beliefs," that he felt "that he was living on the eve of the Last Judgment, that with the establishment of the Reformation and exposure of the papal antichrist within the church, the devil had unleashed his last, most violent attack on the true church," and that moreover, "the devil's servants in this final assault were the papists, the fanatics, the Turks, and the Jews."[67]

Edwards appears to be more on target with his evaluation of Luther in this volume than he was in his earlier work.[68] Here he stated that "Luther was incredibly abusive to all his opponents" and that he often used *ad hominem* blasts against their person, for example, against Karlstadt, Zwingli, the peasants, the Schwaermer, the sacramentarians, and the like.[69] Luther seemed to think of himself as a kind of latter-day prophet, says Edwards. This notion, however, is quite unsubstantiated in Luther's view of himself and his role in history. Edwards is more on target when he explains that Luther viewed such adversaries as instruments of Satan, diverting his minions away from the truth and from the authoritative Scriptures, the ground on which Luther always fought his battles.

Moreover, as far as Luther's "incredibly abusive" language is concerned, it has been my personal discovery that the Reformer is hardly ever, if at all, coarse and outspokenly virulent when he preaches, in his lectures, in his letters, or even in his table talk when he has a live audience in front of him. His heated blasts are reserved for the written responses, in almost every case previously provoked, often viciously and unjustifiably, by his opponents. This does not excuse Luther for the sharpness of his rhetoric; but in writing a response to such opponents he felt he needed, in the pattern of the day, to make his points sharply and in kind, for in Luther's mind the attack was not so much against his person but against the Word of God, and this was satanic, he was quite convinced.

Recent attention to Luther's older years and "last battles" was not entirely beyond what might have been expected. Luther's youth and the crisis years between 1517 to 1530 had been pretty well explored. Saarnivaara refers to Otto Wolff's forecast in 1938 that the meaning of the Gospel for Luther was just coming into its own in Luther studies, and Saarnivaara closes his book by posing the question: "Is it too much to hope that as World War I was followed by a 'revival' of the 'young Luther,' World War II will be followed by a 'revival' of the full Reformation Gospel of Luther—and of Scripture?"[70] Saarnivaara's expressed hope and forecast were correct on at least one score: the attention of scholars was no longer riveted, as it had been, on the life and times of the younger Luther after the Second World War. But his prophetic hope that there might be more attention paid to Luther's concern for the Word and the Gospel has largely fallen by the way.

Grabbing the center of the stage rather has been the concentration on Luther's older years and the violent temper he displayed in his late writings. For instance, H. G. Haile more or less assumes that Luther's illnesses and the increasing weight of his years explain the changes in mood and the outbursts.[71] Siggins, on the other hand, takes issue with those who point to Luther's later years as a time monopolized by irascible anger and limited productive power, pointing out that "the real impress of Luther's life and thought was stamped upon Protestantism in these later, maturer years."[72] These, after all, were the years when Luther's great influence extended over countless thousands through his writings and ceaseless production, like the completion of the Bible translation and the production of the prodigious *Genesis Commentary*. Moreover, these were the years when literally thousands of pastors and theologians were trained and prepared for their work under his watchful eye at Wittenberg. Scott Hendrix chimes in on this chord, noting that from the beginning of Luther's life as Reformer of the church to the end it was always his "intention to exercise the duty of a good pastor."[73] Thus when Luther leveled his big guns at the papacy, as he continued to do ever more powerfully to the end of his life, he was always moved to do so because of the "satanic lies with which it (the Roman church) deceives souls and draws them away from Christ."[74] What Hendrix perhaps fails to do with Luther-like punch is to account for the fact that the pole star around which Luther always moved was Holy Writ. By it he fought his battles, early and late.

One of the few modern scholars who has most sensitively analyzed Luther's tirades against the Jews, the papacy, and others is Gordon Rupp, the esteemed English Luther scholar. Thus in writing for *Face to Face*, a publication of the Anti-Defamation League of B'nai B'rith, Rupp takes note of the fact that in all of his treatises Luther was writing responses, having been provoked or incited by others. Rupp speaks of Luther's inclination to rough speech under duress. He has in mind a passage from Osborne's dramatic play, *Luther*, particularly where Luther at the burning of the papal bull blurts out, in Osborne's version: "You see the signature? Signed under the seal of the Fisherman's ring, by one certain midden cock called Leo, an overindulged jakes' attendant to Satan himself, a glittering worm in excrement known to you as his holiness the Pope." Agreed, says Rupp, Luther handles the pope and speaks of him in terms like Captain Ahab of the hated white whale; but, urges Rupp:

> Do not misunderstand. There are many thousands of pages of Luther which you may read without ever meeting anything offensive. In his polemical garden there is a large compost heap; but it is a garden, not a sewage farm.[75]

He suggests that some of Luther's sharpness against the Jews was prompted by the activities of the Jews in that day which caused sects to spring up among the Christians with sectarian notions based on various practices of Jewish laws and customs. This relapse into Judaism, states Rupp, "confirmed for Luther fears he had already expressed about other radical reformers."[76] For Luther this issue was a theological one, not racial, political, or economic. Luther was no racist. Nor did he resort to "compromise and accommodations" when it suited his purposes, as Edwards holds.[77] This was never true for Luther. He was always ready to negotiate, if peace and harmony might prevail, but never at the expense of God's Word of truth, Holy Scripture. On this point Luther would never, could never, have compromised himself and his conscience. He wore his faith on his sleeve for all to see, and this involved unquestioning commitment to the ultimate court of appeal in matters theological, the Bible, the "Holy Spirit's book."

V. SCRIPTURE – THE WORD OF GOD

If one question is to be singled out as having stirred theological debate in the nineteenth and twentieth centuries, it is the question of whether the Scriptures are to be identified with the Word of God. Should the Bible be termed the Word of God? If so, in what sense? Is it in itself, by virtue of its self-proclaimed inspiration, the Word of God throughout? Or is it the Word of God in view of the saving *kerygma* which it contains and thus not in a plenary sort of way but because it witnesses to the Gospel? Is it the Word because it may become God's instrument through which the sinner is brought into confrontation with Him who is the true and only Word, Christ?

These and other questions swirl around no less in Luther studies. We will attempt to show that for Luther the identification of Scripture as the Word of God was an accepted axiom.[78] Luther, of course, regularly spoke of the Word of God with reference to the oral, proclaimed Word, and therefore in simple identification with the Gospel, and also frequently with Christ, the Word. But at the same time, throughout his writings and throughout his life, he very frequently identified the written word of Holy Scripture as God's own Word.[79]

The unity of this Word, Old and New Testament, was a fundamental reality for Luther. In spite of various Bible difficulties and apparent contradictions, with which he was amazingly familiar, he never wavered from his conviction that the Holy Spirit was the principal author of the Bible, even though the various books in it had been written at sundry times and by sundry writers, prophets, and apostles. Thus one can rightly claim, without fear of serious challenge, that for Luther the inspiration by God of Holy Writ was the ground for its place in his heart and mind as the inviolable, indisputable Word of God.

With the advent of a more skeptical handling of the biblical text this stance of Luther has been seriously accosted and every effort made to claim him in support of a freer, more elastic view. This would allow for a denial of Scripture's actual inspiration, the simple identification with the Word of God, and the handling of the text as a primarily human document of ancient pedigree. But the question is whether Luther can be made to fit this dimension in modern critical treatment of the biblical text. The advocates and supporters of the modern stance are not hard to find. In fact, since the canons and decrees of a skeptical, higher critical methodology have pretty well prevailed in all quarters, it is more difficult to find those who will acknowledge Luther's principal adherence to the truthfulness of the text of Scripture.

Wilhelm Maurer correctly remarks that "between Luther's understanding of Scripture and ours stands the historical-critical inquiry of the past 200 years" but implies that this alters the situation as regards previously held views on Luther's theology of the Word, even though he assures his readers that it need not entirely negate the significance of Luther's thought for us.[80] In Maurer's view the "ancient church took over from Judaism the representation concerning the inspiration of the Biblical writings and inclusion in the canon"[81] and moreover "Luther's understanding of the inspiration of the apostolic witnesses had to do not with the recording of the Biblical text, but with the oral witness concerning it."[82] Maurer, as is generally known, was a pious Christian believer who wanted the church to fulfill its God-given task of proclaiming "the self-authenticating Word of God" to the world and was convinced in his heart that the Word was able to create anew and "conquer the world," in spite of the weaknesses, foolishness, and sinfulness of those proclaiming it.[83]

A similar hope and mandate for the church in our day was also in the heart of Saarnivaara. Luther's "tower experience," which he placed late in the Reformer's development, contained "both of the principles of the Reformation": 1) that Scripture is the revealed and inspired Word of God and as such the highest and only standard and norm of Christian faith and life; 2) that according to Scripture the sinner is justified by grace alone, through faith in Christ. "The former was not the new element in the discovery, but rather its prerequisite. The latter was the new insight that Luther discovered or rediscovered."[84] Evidently Saarnivaara refuses to let modern critical judgments govern his understanding of Luther.

Peter Meinhold takes the same stance, namely, that when Luther speaks of the Word, he first of all has in mind the historical, written, external Word which is the scriptural text, a position which Luther set in cement through his encounter with Enthusiasts. "For Luther there is no working of the inner Word," states Meinhold, "if the outer, external Word has not first of all *preceded*."[85] "Vocable and Spirit together build a tight unity for Luther."[86] Meinhold at the same time lets it be known that he does not concur in this view of the Word; Meinhold's stance is to be understood more in the nature of a Barthian confrontation of the sinner by the Word of God, Christ through the witness of the biblical word.

Skevington Wood, on the other hand, opts for a more conservative position, stating that when Luther promoted Scripture's authority against that of the church, he "was not just ventilating a theory [but] trying to reflect the pattern of Scripture itself."[87] Luther realized "the significance of the minutiae in Scripture," but this did not deter him, "since he believed each single word to be inspired."[88] It was that Word that gave birth to the church, not vice versa; it was the Word which was parent and the church its offspring, for the Scripture bore its own "self-authenticating character of the inspired writers."[89] Of course, a reading of Luther will show that "by the Word, he did not invariably mean Holy Writ," for besides referring to the text of Scripture, he sometimes used Word "with reference to Christ Himself, and sometimes with references to the content, or act of preaching."[90] This view of Luther, Wood sums up by stating that "all that Luther taught about the authority of the Bible and the nature of revelation found its climax and corollary in his doctrine of inspiration," for which "a miracle of the Spirit was required [a miracle], parallel between the written Word and the incarnate Word."[91]

Obviously the position taken by Wood is unacceptable in most theological quarters today. But even the redoubtable Paul Althaus, whose preeminence in Luther studies is generally acknowledged, is frank to admit that this is correct. "Although Luther criticized the Bible in specific details," says Althaus, the Reformer was nevertheless committed to viewing Scripture "as inspired in its entire content by the Holy Spirit," for which reason "it is therefore the Word of God", or "the book written by the Holy Spirit."[92] Althaus does not agree with Luther but he concedes that it was the text itself that was inspired and, therefore, was the Word of God in its very ontological being by virtue of this inspiration.[93]

James Nestingen acknowledges that in the *Smalcald Articles* (1537) Luther has the "external Word" in mind when he says that "God will not deal with us" in any other way as regards his revelation of himself and his purposes[94] (*SA* 3.8). Thereupon, however, Nestigen erodes Luther's dependence upon the scriptural text by his discussion on the difference between "significative talk" and "effective words" as regards Luther's theology of the Word, with focus on the latter.[95] What Hestingen has to say sounds little like Luther but more like Ebeling's "word-event" thinking, which is not dissimilar from Barth's notion of the Word coming through from outside when and where God wills, the Bible being witness or record of the early Christian community's faith. It is a far cry from Luther's forthright, uncomplicated reliance upon the text. Little wonder that Nestingen's analysis leads him to claim that "there is something elusive about the Word."[96]

Closely parallel to Nestingen is John Loeschen, who, while grappling knowledgably with some of the main themes in Luther's theology, ends up by calling Luther "a functional theologian" on the doctrine of the Word. "The Word to which God has bound Himself is found in Scripture," says Loeschen, and "apart from that Word the highest piety is idolatry, opinion in the guise of truth; unless we keep to the Word of Scripture like a hare to its hole, as Luther put it so quaintly in a sermon of 1522, all is lost."[97] But to identify the Bible with the Word of God is to misunderstand Luther and become guilty of "legalistic theology, barren exegesis, and a denial of the Spirit," says this supporter of "functional theology." "As important as the appeal to the objectivity of

God's Word is in Luther's theology, he *never* identifies that Word with the written text," claims Loeschen, "and even differentiates, within what he considers God's Word, what is and is not relevant, and under interpretation, to his existential situation" (emphasis added).[98] Indeed in such a view the Word becomes elusive, a moving sort of thing. Eric Gritsch agrees with Loeschen, stating that "Luther rediscovered the now *so self-evident* truth that the Word of God, embodied in the word of man, *changes* in time and therefore becomes a *debatable item* in church history" (emphasis added)[99]

By every rule of measurement the most significant and acclaimed essay at the fifth Luther Congress, held in Lund in 1977, was delivered by Regin Prenter. "No one will quibble over Luther being a theologian of the Scriptures," states Prenter, and that "the Scripture was for Luther the Scripture of God."[100] But Prenter does not mean that the Scripture is the Word as such. Rather it is a creative Word, as much for the authors as for the readers, in that God allows his voice to come through it, the hidden God thus breaking through the written Word in a creative sort of way.[101] In the final analysis Prenter opts for a definition of the Word in Luther akin to that of Karl Barth's. Respondents to Prenter, Wilhelm Dantine and Samuel Preus, did not challenge substantively his notion of Luther's theology of the Word. Preus spoke for a view of revelation which conceived of God's acting apart from and "outside the correlation of Scripture and justifying faith."[102] Against Scripture's clarity and authority Preus asks, "Do we really want to argue that Luther's conclusions are a binding exegesis of Scripture for all Christians for all time?" He (Preus) answers: "The answer might be 'yes.' But the question should not be avoided simply by arguing [as Luther did] that Scripture is unambiguously clear."[103] On that wave length Preus would find himself, as Erasmus did, to be Luther's target, in *De servo arbitrio*.

Prenter's view of Luther's theology of the Word had been previously stated in his *The Word and the Spirit*. [104] Acknowledging that "men do not dream or speculate their way to God," and that "no one can meet the God of the Word who is indifferent to the written Word of the Bible," Prenter ambivalently contends that it is "biblicism" to speak of the Bible itself as the Word of God and therefore only correct to say that it may become the Word through its witness of the living God in Jesus Christ, who alone is the Word.[105] Thus he is very critical of orthodoxy for its being locked in a "fixed point" sort of theology on the Word and for its support for the "theory" of "verbal inspiration," both of which are "no longer tenable, since the advent of historical criticism."[106] Yet Prenter is sharp in his rejection of Bultmann's existentialist theologizing, for the reason that the *kerygma* itself is lost.

Heinrich Bornkamm takes a similar line.[107] He, too, rejects any identification of the Scriptures with the Word of God, because of the so-called assured results of higher criticism, and labels "Word of God" that which in Scripture portrays Christ and faith, the Gospel. In Bornkamm's thinking "only then is it correct to speak of *sola Scriptura* when it is equated with *solus Christus*."[108] In a statement that is somewhat reminiscent of the renowned Dutch scholar, G. C. Berkouwer, Bornkamm avers that "the Bible is something organic, something with limbs or branches, which has a central meaning, from which alone it must be viewed: Christ and the Gospel."[109] Yet Bornkamm was a good historian and in his *Luther's World of Thought* he acknowledges that in the Leipzig Debate Luther fought against the evils of an authoritarian ecclesiastical system with the Holy Scriptures alone. "In the end Holy Writ remained the one and only source of truth to him," writes Bornkamm, "and the road to truth was open, not to an especially favored class but to every believer," by which doctrine on the "priesthood of believers the difference between clergy and congregation ceased to exist for him."[110] When it comes to identifying *where* this Word of God is, the most Bornkamm will admit is that we are to "look for His footprints in the Bible."[111]

True to Luther, Gerhard Ebeling cautions that Scripture ought not be "handled as a wax nose."[112] He quotes Luther approvingly when the Reformer states: "Whenever I have a text which is a nut whose shell is too hard to crack, I throw it at once against the rock (Christ), and find the sweetest kernel."[113] Without question Christ, as the central theme of the Scriptures, was for Luther an interpretive key. But Ebeling misreads Luther when he cites 2 Corinthians 3:6 on the "letter and the spirit" and interprets this as distinguishing between the text or letter of the Scripture and the spirit or evangelical core. For Luther, this passage refers to the apostle Paul's exhortation to distinguish carefully between law and Gospel. The same error is made by Regin Prenter, Paul Althaus, and Lennart Pinomaa. For all the excellence of his work on Luther's theology, Philip Watson comes off at the same point with figures like Prenter and Bornkamm. "For Luther, all authority belongs ultimately to Christ, the Word of God, alone," Watson says, "and even the authority of the Scriptures is secondary and derivative, pertaining to them only inasmuch as they bear witness of Christ and are the vehicle of the Word."[114] On Scriptures as "secondary" to Christ there can be no argument. But that the Scriptures are merely to be relegated to "bearing witness" or being a "vehicle of the Word" immediately show that a Barthian view is being offered, not Luther's. On the opposite side, favoring the interpretation above, stand Friedrich Beisser and Hermann Sasse, among many others. Sasse shows that this tendency to think of the "letter" as referring to the written text is an "aversion that goes back to Schleiermacher."[115]

Fred Meuser and Stanley Schneider have edited a volume in which the various writers echo the same uneasy pair of refrains.[116] On the one hand, we are told that for Luther the Bible was "the Holy Spirit's own peculiar book, writing and word, [and] in every syllable."[117] But side by side comes the lament over "stereotyping and distorting" Luther's view of the Bible as being in fact the Word of God.[118] Remarkably, this contributor, Theodore Liefeld, also agrees with what Yves Congar has to say about Aquinas and Roman Catholic theology being virtually of one mind on "the absolute primacy of Scripture over all other authority," a position in which "he [Luther] was completely Catholic." "I believe," says Liefeld ingenuously, "we have no serious quarrel with Congar, or Rome, at this point"[119]— Liefeld shows not only his skirts but also a misunderstanding of both Luther and the Romanist position as set at Trent. By contrast, in a commemorative essay in honor of Paul Althaus's seventy-fifth birthday,[120] Franz Lau takes note of the impassable gulf existing between Luther's view of Scripture's supreme authority and that of Rome with its commitment to tradition under the authoritarian teaching voice of the petrine office.

We have mentioned Hermann Sasse above. Partially in protest against the demythologizing of the biblical text and the erosion of its authority, he left his post at Erlangen and affiliated with the conservative Lutheran Free Church of Germany, eventually moving to Australia via America, where he taught for a short time at Concordia Theological Seminary, Springfield, Illinois. Sasse upheld the position that "Luther believed the Bible in its totality, in the Old and New Testaments, in the Law and Gospel, to be the Word of God itself in writing."[121] He was also critical of the kind of exegesis that dug around in Scripture for the so-called *sensus plenior*, the fuller sense, in the manner especially of Roman Catholic exegetes. But then strangely, as though red flags were waved before his eyes at the sound of the words "orthodox," or "verbal inspiration," or "biblical inerrancy," he disowned these concepts as being entirely foreign in Luther's thought.[122] Here Sasse does not follow Luther's very simple and servant-like bowing before the queen.

Gordon Rupp, in the 1947 Cambridge lecture series that brought him to world attention, is considerably more guarded in reflecting Luther's mind and theology on the subject of the Word.[123] As Rupp points out, Luther's view of the Bible as the "Holy Spirit's book" is an emphasis exemplified by the famous phrase on a coin of Joachim II (1564):

God's Word and Luther's Teaching
will never pass away.[124]

Rupp goes on to say a positive word in behalf of Lutheran orthodoxy, which has so often been accused of building a stilted image of Luther particularly on the Word:

> When all is said and done, there is very much to be said for the modern verdict that "this view of Luther is one-sided." But it is also profound and religious, and perhaps with all its one-sidedness, it comes fundamentally closer to the real Luther than all the modern "Luther Renaissance" with its many-sided source criticism, and refined historical and psychological methods. For the orthodox view of Luther in the seventeenth century did remain in an unbroken tradition of faith, with the age of the Reformation.[125]

William Landeen likewise insists that Luther did not hesitate to identify the Scriptures with the Word of God.[126] If and when Luther spoke critically of any book of the Bible, observes Landeen correctly, he usually did so in comparison with other biblical books that he found more doctrinally productive. The primary fact, therefore, in Luther's theology of the Word is that "Luther clearly held to the inspiration of all the Bible."[127]

VI. SCRIPTURE'S AUTHORITY

"The Word, the Word must do it," Luther parried against the Enthusiasts, who were claiming inward, direct revelation from the Spirit.[128] It was a conviction born of deep personal struggle and that for Luther had reached the continental divide at the Diet of Worms with his cry, "My reason is captive to the Word of God." *Sola Scriptura* in the purest sense was the working principle in his whole theological pursuit, preaching, teaching, writing. His was a genuine obedience under the Word.

In his inimitable way, he pointed out that even as Abraham had his Sarah, and as Balaam was required to listen to the ass through which God spoke to him, so we must learn to bow before Holy Scripture. Its authority is normative for the church: there can be no other, simply because God has so ordered or arranged things. It is to be the touchstone for all teaching in the church.

Here is where the Roman church became a sectarian partner with the "fantastical spirits," as Luther termed the Schwärmer, simply because both parties chose to set another voice, a human authority, over that of God. Only the Scripture could be the source for the *fides quae creditur* ("the faith which is to be believed") if one is to be Christian: anything else was pseudo-religion. Luther felt a similar fury toward those who dared to "depotentiate" the divine authority of the Scripture as he felt toward those who willfully denied Christ's true deity. "What would finally remain certain and clear in Holy Writ, yes, in any language," he asks, if such license went unchecked?[129] His trust of Scripture's truth and accuracy on all matters was implicit, particularly the articles of faith, because Scripture "is too clear, too powerful, and maintains itself against anything men may bring against it."[130] Luther would quite agree that one can pretty well determine a person's attitude toward all of Christian doctrine from his attitude toward the Holy Scriptures.

Concern for purity of teaching is tied up with his concern and respect for the Sacred Scriptures. His last sermon, preached at Eisleben, February 16, 1546, includes a sharp rejoinder against those who substitute "Joseph's pants or the pope's juggling tricks," in other words some ecclesiastical relic or ceremony, in place of God's Holy Word, baptism, or the Lord's Supper.[131] It was the same wave length on which he preached so eloquently at Wittenberg during Invocavit week in 1522, quelling the riots in early March. With the same authority, that is, Scripture's, and even greater finesse, he refuted Erasmus in his Scripture-laden, Scripture-grounded treatise on the *Bondage of the Will.*

In his attitude toward the Scriptures, Luther stood squarely in the tradition of the church fathers, e.g., Augustine. Hermann Dorries shows that like Augustine Luther would subject himself to no human authority, including the fathers, in the way he subjected himself before and under Scripture's authority.[132] For both men, Luther and Augustine, it was the apostolic posture that "we must obey God rather than men" (Acts 5:29). Luther, states Dorries, found the thought totally objectionable, in fact revolting, that the Holy Scripture should in any way have derived its authority from men, be that ecclesiastical or secular prince, or any other kind of worldly authority, even the pope.[133]

It would not be possible to cite all the many places in Luther's works where this attitude toward Scripture can be shown to give structure to his theology like a spinal cord. But most students of Luther's writings will immediately think of his *magnum opus* against Erasmus. It is no mistake to do so. Luther's appeal to Scripture's authority is at its very best and most compelling here against the cosmopolitan and widely respected scholar of Rotterdam. Henry Atherton, in his preface to the 1931 edition of the *Bondage of the Will,* writes:

> This book is most needful at the present day. The teachings of many so-called Protestants are more in accordance with the Dogmas of the Papists, or the ideas of Erasmus, than with the Principles of the Reformers: they are more in harmony with the Canons and Decrees of the Council of Trent than with any Protestant or Reformed Confessions of Faith.[134]

Friedrich Beisser has written what is probably the most respected book in recent times on Luther's attitude toward the Scriptures.[135] Beisser addresses three primary questions: On what does Luther ground Scripture's clarity? What in fact does clarity of Scripture mean or include? How does Scripture itself evidence or validate its clarity? In answer to the first question, Beisser shows at length that Luther's position stems from Scripture's own assertion that it is God's authoritative revelation to us, which we must trust unwaveringly.[136] For Luther the Bible is the bearer, in external, objective fashion, of the full Word of God; we should look for and expect no other.[137] For himself Beisser tends toward the neo-orthodox position; but in treating Luther he does not sway from the latter's commitment to the text, and he counts as nonsense the notion that Luther is somehow the father of the higher critical methodology.[138] Moreover, Bible difficulties posed no particular problem for Luther as to its absolute authority in the church.[139]

In answering the second question Beisser refers to the familiar point on *claritas externa* and *claritas interna*: Scripture's external, outer clarity, which makes its meaning clear even to the eyes and minds of an unbeliever, though he refuses to accept or believe what is said; and the internal clarity, which the Scripture opens up for the eyes of faith, the eyes that have seen the Savior, Christ, and received him into the heart. Luther grounds this on the evident purpose of God not to confound further the darkness in which men are by nature but to reveal clearly his gracious intents and purposes for sinners' reception and salvation.[140] For Luther this results from God's inspiration of the biblical text, so that it is not only reliable but also clear. The eyes of faith do not first of all validate it or constitute its clarity, meaning, or efficacy; rather, faith is the evidence of the Scripture's authority and of all its attributes, which are a part of its divine character.

The answer to the third question, how Scripture gives evidence of its clarity, impinges on the second. The Holy Scriptures as God's Word are self-validating, confirmed by the Holy Spirit's decision to act and build his church through them, through their witness. God is at work, and this He Himself shows us in mighty fashion through the Scriptures. Thus the Word tells us not merely that God is merciful, but it also proclaims the very acts through which God's mercy is made ours, through Christ. God accomplishes His purposes, Luther held, through despised and lowly veiled means, *larvae Dei.* These "veils of God" are the Word itself, Holy Scripture, as well as first of all and in a preeminent way His own Son who, though incarnate in the sinful flesh, was holy and without sin. So, too, the Word, though given through human witnesses and authors, carries divine aegis and infallibility.

These earthly forms are not swept aside, but God chooses to act through them, through what men despise as lowly and unworthy. We must not look elsewhere, cautions Luther, for God is a God close at hand and has chosen to come to us through these veils, the Word, baptism, the Lord's Supper. To try to *ascend* to Him by self-chosen ladders is madness when He has chosen to *descend* to us through His own instruments or means of grace, particularly through His Word.[141] Luther is not ambivalent: he finds no problem between the clarity of the Word and the hiddenness of God or the mysteries that reason can not fathom. Only modern, skeptical theology had fancied for itself a problem here, a problem which results from its prior rejection of the authority, clarity, and inviolability of the biblical text. For Luther, when the Spirit leads to understanding through the preached Word, or the written, this is no illusory phenomenon, but the promised fulfillment of God's own intended purpose.

The encounter with Erasmus was important for Luther, states Meinhold, not only because of the central article on justification *sola gratia* and the corresponding doctrine of man and his sin but also because it sharpened for Luther the whole matter of scriptural authority vis-à-vis humanism.[142] The same holds true for Luther in his encounter with Zwingli at Marburg, though Meinhold does not seem to catch the full power of Luther's scriptural commitment in this context.[143] As Meinhold treats *Deus absconditus* ("the hidden God"), he seems to miss the emphasis Luther makes on the basis of the *larvae Dei*. Luther grounds what we know of God, hence *Deus revelatus*, on the God-given veils, as opposed to God's *Verborgenheit* (or "hiddenness"), where we must put a finger on our lips and refrain from speaking of things about which we do not know. Luther believes that, by God's revelation of Himself through His chosen "veils," He placed Himself within our reach, as for the shepherds at Bethlehem; but the closer God is to us in this way, the more the believer recognizes the distance that stands between him and his Lord, and in no way does he think that he can take his God into his own hands and shape Him as he will.[144]

Siggins likewise points to Luther's *Bondage of the Will*, which the Reformer "composed faster than most people can read it," not merely as the nub of his encounter with Erasmus but as his clearest defense of Scripture's authority, grounded on its inspiration and clarity on all articles of faith, especially the Gospel and justification *sola gratia/fide*.[145] Siggins rightly observes that Luther scholars must not confine their studies merely to that famous treatise, for to "savour the power and eloquence of Luther's mature theology, there is simply no alternative to extensive reading in his voluminous biblical lectures and sermons."[146] This corresponds closely to my own arguments, which I have sought to demonstrate with many citations from Luther's exegetical works.[147]

Leif Grane's cogent argument is worth hearing: "If the clarity of Scripture is the same as its authority, then this means that this is also the same as the content of the Scripture."[148] Grane goes on to show that this is precisely the reason why Luther always cites the Scriptures first and then the Fathers. "If the Scripture is clear, then it is also understandable," is the way Luther approached his task as exegete; and "if it is understood, then it is also brought to bear, or is efficacious, precisely through its content."[149] This more or less conforms to the fundamental rule in biblical interpretation, that the task of the exegete is essentially that of *enarratio*, simply unfolding what is so evidently there.

Friedrich Gogarten likewise attests that for Luther the scriptural Word must always rule, for it is clear, it tells God's revelation of himself, it is efficacious, authoritative, and without error.[150] It was Luther's working principle that for every believing Christian equipped with the ordinary tools of language and grammar, "the Scriptures had a single, fast and firm meaning."[151]

Siggins in his earlier work underscores the same truth regarding Luther's *modus operandi* in scriptural exegesis. Scripture is not equally important in all places; there are shades of light as regards given doctrines. But Luther stands firm on this platform that Scripture is without question consistent in its teaching, specifically in its focus on Christ. Thus Luther works with a commitment to the text, Siggins observes, and this is coupled with his remarkable agility and at-homeness with the whole of Scripture.[152] This commitment and agility is a hallmark of his exegesis. "The firmness of the exegetical base upon which Luther's exposition is built is revealed at all points by his consistent use of biblical words and phrases in the manner and intention in which Scripture uses them."[153]

Siggins is right to observe that, as far as Luther is concerned, Christ is the true center of both Old and New Testaments, the central hub of Luther's biblical exegesis. It is also true that for Luther *sola Scriptura* was in perfect harmony with *solus Christus*. But what also needs to be said, but is not often admitted nor noted by Siggins, is that Luther held a companion principle very dear and close to his heart: If my opponents quote Christ or what they imagine Christ to have said or thought or done, *against the Scripture*, I will quote the Scriptures against their "Christ."[154] There was, in other words, no other tribunal, if Scripture was gone. Therefore, Luther's earnest exhortation at all times remained: "Stick to the Word of God. Ignore every other—whether it is devoid of Christ, in the name of Christ, or whether it is issued in any other way."[155] The incarnate Word was in perfect, full harmony with the inscripturated Word, and vice versa, for the Eternal Word was its Lord.

Against the sects, the "fantastical spirits" as he termed them, Luther held the fort with Holy Scripture as his only weapon. We have previously referred to Edwards's recent study on *Luther and the False Brethren* and his viewpoint that Luther stood opposed to them because of his "conviction that they all shared the satanic spirit."[156] Hans-Martin Barth, writing a few years earlier than Edwards, joins him in this judgment, namely, that Luther viewed his work and himself as the target of Satan's frontal attack against the Reformation, chiefly because of the Word, the external Word of Scripture.[157] Luther never doubted that there were genuine Christians among them, in spite of their aberrations, a thing which needs to be repeated along with Edwards's tendency to paint Luther as a somewhat abusive opponent of these sectarian spirits. Were he to be asked what was needed to stymie this sort of theologizing, his answer would be to encourage "recourse to the authoritative Scriptures," for one need only "refute their position with the Scripture and help them out of their error."[158]

This accords exactly with Atkinson's judgment that as far as the "spirits" in Rome were concerned, Luther detected that the same process was and had been at work; accordingly "it was the authority of the Bible that modified the authority of the Church and her tradition."[159] Luther never lost his regard for tradition, history, or ecclesiastical structure as such, but on the authority of the text of Scripture which he was probing, all institutions and "all terms that he vouched underwent a transformation."[160] When Luther demolished the famous three walls behind which the Church of Rome had shielded itself against all threats from within and without—power over all temporal rulers, supreme authority for interpreting the Word or Scripture, and sole authority to call a church council—it was with Scripture's authority that Luther rammed down the gates of the heretofore impregnable fortress.

That blast was sounded in the opening part of his 1520 treatise *On the Babylonian Captivity of the Church*. In the same year, in his *Open Letter to the Christian Nobility*, as Atkinson cites it, Luther had asked: "If what they claim were true, why have Holy Scripture at all? Of what use is Scripture?" And then with sharpest satire, the Reformer says: "Let us burn the Scripture and be satisfied with the unlearned gentlemen at Rome who possess the Holy Spirit."[161] A year later at the Diet of Worms, he was put to the severest test; but as Atkinson observes, he did not go into this confrontation with closed eyes, for "he knew he had God's Word, and he knew equally clearly that his opponents had only their own."[162]

Hermann Schuster also refers to Luther's *Babylonian Captivity of the Church* to emphasize Luther's commitment to scriptural authority. Luther, he notes, was aware that in matters that pertain to God and His revealed purposes, one dare not even trust one's own thought, however pious and however piously motivated. Human words and thoughts are just no match for God's words, and "no violence is to be done to the words of God, whether by man or angel."[163] This required that the words of Scripture be taken "in their simplest meaning," never "apart from their grammatical and proper sense, unless the context manifestly compels it," for to do otherwise is to "make a mockery of all the Scriptures," and to turn everything "into allegories," a practice that had been going on in the church from the time of Origen; as a result, his views had long ago been sharply repudiated.[164]

Schuster also takes note of Luther's increasing horror over the crowding of Christ out of the church and out of its theology by the intrusion of supposedly pious practices, usages, ceremonies, masses, pilgrimages, relics, monastic life as a higher form of holiness, worship of countless saints, including Mary, and even her mother, St. Anne, all of them constituting a veritable train of sacred focal points but all of them detracting from the central saving message of the Gospel itself.[165]

But Schuster, too, shows that he is looking at Luther's biblical commitment with the colored glasses of modern skepticism. "The Reformer," he states, "viewed the Bible with a freedom unheard of before this; he was not tied to the letter or word, [but] looked upon the Bible as a human document and practised a freewheeling sort of critique over it."[166] Schuster claims further that Luther's method of textual study "frees us from slavery to the letters of the text" and the doctrine of verbal inspiration, thus allowing us today to present people with the New Testament's message "in the thought-forms of our day."[167] He ventures to put Bultmannian existentialistic thoughts into Luther's mouth by asserting that it would be in harmony with Luther's pattern of thinking to say that "the criterion by which it becomes the Word of God for me" rests ultimately on "the daring personal faith" by which I come into "the living tension of Christian existence."[168] The fact, of course, is that Luther never thought or taught this. He repudiated any position in which faith takes any authority away from the Word of God as a dangerous turning inward upon oneself, *incurvatus in se*. Citing German philosophers and even Schweitzer as examples, Schuster closes with the pious hortatory thought: "Let us finally begin the process of becoming real Christians."[169] Luther would have difficulty recognizing himself in the portrait Schuster paints of him and of his theology of the Word.

Bernhard Lohse[170] is much closer to the truth when he asserts that Luther's *modus operandi* in dealing with any and all of his opponents was to "set pointed Scripture passages in the center" of the dispute. Scripture's authority, its clarity, and its self-interpreting capacity were all tied together. Walter Mostert observes wryly that if Luther were to be admitted to the theological faculty today it most certainly would be as exegete, undoubtedly in the Old Testament; but there would be little or no respect for the Reformer in contemporary exegesis.[171]

Scripture was viewed by Luther as having an evident meaning in its external form, a meaning that was to be understood, to enter the mind and heart with its content, and to be received in faith. Luther would have opposed the notion of a *sensus proprius*, a more proper or a deeper sense known only to man's inner spirit in pursuit of self-understanding in modern existentialist terms. Whatever ontological happening there is in the Christian experience must be tied, so Luther held, to the authoritative, efficacious Word itself, Holy Scripture, from which a person comes to know his Lord and Savior. The task that modern interpreters of Scripture therefore have is not merely to ape and repeat Luther's slogan that the Scripture interprets itself but, like Luther, to bring their *Anfechtungen* and doubts always and again under Scripture's light, states Mostert. Moreover, ours is never the task of trying to understand the author better than he understood himself; but since we are dealing with God's Holy Word, to let the Bible speak with its unique authority and power and application.

For Luther the core theme of Holy Scripture was God's justification of the sinner through Christ: our sin is laid upon Him, His righteousness is made ours, in the wondrous double exchange of which Isaiah spoke (40:2). Nothing dare militate against this central truth as theologians and average Bible readers go about their interpreting of the Scriptures. Mostert closes with the appropriate question, drawn from Luther: "Had Christ been crucified a hundred thousand times and had nothing been said about it, what profit would the act of His being brought to the cross have been?"[172] Mostert might have gone on in concluding his article to add Luther's own answer: "Therefore to the act also the use of the act must be added, that it may be declared through the Word and that one may hold it by faith and, thus believing, may be saved. Wherever the Word of God is, there is forgiveness of sin."[173]

What Luther stated in his meeting with Cardinal Cajetan at Augsburg, 1518, that "no believing Christian can be forced to recognize any authority beyond the Sacred Scripture, which is exclusively invested with Divine right," was a principle by which he lived and operated all his life to the very end. Skevington Wood is quite right in quoting these words from that encounter.[174] Cajetan stood for the position that the church, or the papal office, was the only official interpreter of Holy Writ. Luther repudiated that position and reversed it. He was committed to the rule that *Scriptura Scripturam interpretatur* ("Scripture is his own interpreter") and needs no other, assuming and granting that knowledge of the language, grammar, the context, the analogy of faith have all gone before and are all operative. Luther was convinced that God did not reveal Himself and His gracious purposes in a biblical text that shrouded us in further darkness beyond that which we already have by nature. This was Luther's retort to Erasmus when the later expressed preference for an open mind and skepticism as regards some of Scripture's pronouncements. Which Christian, Luther roars, would dare to talk like that? Brian Gerrish is among those who acknowledge that Luther never departed from a "strict view of verbal inspiration."[175]

Closely tied to Luther's basic principle that *Scriptura sui ipsius interpres* is the ministerial use of reason, not the abnegation of it. Reason can never be a free agent but must be answerable to Scripture's authority. Joined to this authority were the remarkable attributes of God's Holy Word to deliver its message clearly to the questing mind, a message that was not this, today, and that, tomorrow; or this in one man's thinking and that in another's; but it has one intended, literal sense, as God purposed to give it for our hearing, understanding, reception in faith. *Sensus literalis unus est* ("the Scriptures have one literal sense"), and it is the very devil, Luther opines with Erasmus, to conceive of it having different meanings in any passage. For Luther the whole idea of "double exegesis" as regards Scripture's meaning, as Bornkamm acknowledges, was absolutely excluded.[176]

Moreover, the Bible's message is harmonious, one that bespeaks Scripture's unity. Kurt Aland has stated very appropriately of Luther's stance on this point that "to conceive of the New Testament in such a way (as though not in harmony) and to split it up into different sections of unequal worth would be fundamentally to misunderstand it."[177] Wood, quoting Francis Pieper, closes his brief in behalf of Luther affirming that Luther would be "horrified at people who dare assert that Scripture is not entirely and in all its parts the Word of God."[178] Luther's own statement in behalf of Scripture's unassailable authority is beyond cavil in clarity:

> Therefore if people refuse to believe, you should keep silence; for you have no obligation to force them to regard Scripture as God's Book or Word. It is sufficient for you to base your proof on Scripture. This you must do when they take it upon themselves to say: "You preach that one should not hold to the teaching of men, even though Peter and Paul, yes, even though Christ, were men, too." If you hear people who are so completely blinded and hardened that they deny that this is God's Word or are in doubt about it, just keep silence, do not say a word to them, and let them go their way.[179]

Skevington Wood takes note not only of Luther's commitment to the divine inspiration of Scripture but also of the fact that this doctrine "is inseparably linked with that of inerrancy" in the mind of Luther, for "because the Word of God was given by the Spirit of God it was inconceivable that it should be subject to human fallibility."[180] It is true, as Wood observes, that "Luther pressed the analogy between the incarnation and the nature of Scripture" in such a way that "the human element of Scripture for him was no more liable to error than was the human nature of Christ."[181]

This is a point that much modern theology only grudgingly concedes to be true in Luther, but there is no question that this was Luther's stance vis-à-vis the Scriptures. It is also the ground for Luther's arguing in behalf of Holy Scripture's capacity to take care of itself in defense both of its divine character and also its divine content. In this respect Luther spoke of it as a lion, needing no outside help to fend off any enemy. Also, this accounts for Scripture's capacity to be its own best interpreter, since its "basic perspicuity" must be granted; and Luther cautions that "the man who seeks to impose his own will on Scripture will find it closed and barred to him."[182]

The *sensus literalis, grammaticus, historicus*, states Brian Gerrish, was self-evident in view of the fact that Scripture was queen in every sense of the word for Luther.[183] Careful philology was a *sine qua non* for Luther, but the meaning of any text or passage was itself preeminent, for God wanted it to be understood. Biblical helps, lexicons, and the like were always at Luther's side, but both text and sense were to make common cause; never was it a case of one at the expense of the other.[184] *Sola Scriptura* and *scriptura sui ipsius interpres*, states Gerrish, were inseparable companion principles for Luther, as was their link with the key Reformation doctrine on justification *sola gratia/fide*. "And if mysteries remain—even to reason illuminated by the Spirit—Luther's last retort is that all apparent irrationalities in God's dealings with us will one day become clear," in the glory of heaven, as he wrote to Erasmus.[185] It is significant that Gerrish, a Calvinist, should acknowledge this, since Calvin himself would have argued somewhat differently concerning the capacities of regenerate reason.

According to some students of Luther's works, however, the Reformer's stand upon the Bible was not entirely without ambivalence and ambiguity. On the one hand, he spoke of the Bible as his bride, while, on the other hand, he also often spoke of the distance still remaining between him and the understanding of Scripture, so that he remained as it were "a beginning student" each time he read it.[186] The authors of this judgment, all Roman Catholic, abide by Lortz's verdict that "he [Luther] who proposed to tie himself so thoroughly to the Word of God, never really became its listener in the fullest sense of the word," a stance that they claim "overshadowed Luther's life to the end" and on the basis of which they, like Lortz, conclude that after all Luther "was cut from the roots on out a subjectivist."[187] This severe undercutting of Luther's biblical theology has, however, largely been rejected by scholars steeped in Luther research.

Ernst-Wilhelm Kohls is another scholar who has acknowledged that Luther upheld the Bible's testimony concerning itself, its *Selbsttätigkeit*, and the inherent power it had to "interpret itself and work what God intended."[188] In his second volume under the same title, Kohls notes how Luther inscribed in his personal Bible, in 1542, the words: "Were your word, Lord God, to leave me without comfort, I would succumb. It is this book of the Bible, which teaches God's Word, and in which God himself is speaking with us, that can accomplish this, as a man's best friend."[189]

Wilhelm Pauck recounts that Luther became like a Samson when confronted with the perversion of God's Word, "infuriated" by the assault, capable of "unhinging the gates."[190] "If his opponents abandoned certain parts of Christian doctrine or interpreted them differently, as for example the freedom of the will," states Pauck, "Luther could only conclude that they had never looked down into the ultimate abyss," by which he meant life's *Anfechtungen*, and then also had never plumbed Scripture's depths.[191] Luther was even critical of his own heroic stand at Worms, viewing his performance as a kind of waffling when he should have spoken out even more fiercely, like Elijah against the false prophets.[192] Yet he never tried to take control of the Saxon church in the manner Calvin did at Geneva; and as a result, he goes down in history as a man who had "learned to consider himself nothing before God, but at the same time to exult 'foolishly' in God," a lesson he learned well from the apostle Paul.[193]

It is one of the strange anomalies of Luther study that those who today stand closest to Luther in respect and support of the Bible's unassailable nature as the genuine Word of God should be lightly and patronizingly swept to the side as obscurantists, repristinationists, biblicists, and labels of equally pejorative connotation. The critics, as a matter of fact, think that they have taken care of two fronts with one fell swoop by equating supporters of the conservative viewpoint on Luther's theology of the Word with Lutheran orthodoxy's, which in turn they trace to Melanchthon rather than to Luther.

It is my considered judgment, after dealing firsthand with Luther at length and also with the orthodox theologians like Martin Chemnitz, John Gerhard, John Quenstedt, and the like, that there is remarkable harmony between them. The notion that the so-called orthodox theologians of the seventeenth century added to or developed Luther's theology of the Word in a kind of scholasticism is unfounded. What these orthodox theologians said in a systematic treatment is a fair and honest statement of Luther's position. It is to be feared that modern scholarship has thus simply regurgitated from writer to writer, since the time of Schleiermacher, Ritschl, Harnack, et al., the unfounded notion that orthodoxy has distorted Luther's position on Scripture.

VII. ROMAN CATHOLIC LUTHER STUDIES

The *Lutherjahrbuch 1967* commemorated the 450th anniversary of the Reformation. Included in that special issue was Walther von Loewenich's essay.[194] Loewenich traces Luther studies among Catholic scholars from the beginning of the twentieth century, from the time of Denifle and Grisar onward. He notes how Pope Leo XIII, in an 1897 encyclical, *Militantis ecclesia*, had characterized the Lutheran Reformation as the "Lutheran rebellion" out of which flowed the "ultimate ruin of morals." Loewenich notes the great influence of Otto Scheel and Karl Holl on Luther studies in the early part of the twentieth century, even on Roman Catholic scholars. Among the latter, Joseph Lortz's name stands out as founder of a school of disciples who tended to evaluate Luther with generally kinder and more gentle judgment in view of the circumstances he faced in the sixteenth-century church. But Loewenich also points out that Lortz's judgment of Luther remained firm on this point: however justified he may have been in some of his criticisms of the church, he nonetheless was guilty of "radical subjectivism" and was never in the full meaning of the word a *Vollhörer* ("a full hearer") of Holy Scripture. In the final analysis Loewenich agrees with the judgment against Luther and then cites Adolf Schlatter and Paul Althaus to buttress his case.[195]

Of equal interest is the fact that Ebeling is mentioned by Loewenich as having found the roots of his "new hermeneutic" in Luther's doctrine of the Word.[196] There is no substance to this claim, as we have tried to show. Luther's understanding of the Scripture may indeed have been existential, in the sense that it was the living, efficacious Word of God, but hardly existentialist, in the sense of the individual finding authentic existence within himself through the so-called Word-event. Bultmann's shadow, and to some extent Barth's, show themselves in this sort of thinking, rather than Luther's. Luther always seeks the text's meaning as given by God. What does the text say? Surely not simply what it can possibly say to me, that is, what meaning I can find in it, as though this were a different matter for each individual and the text's meaning were not a stable, consistent content from person to person, from generation to generation, beginning with God's own inspiration through prophet and apostle. Apparently Loewenich agrees also with Lortz in saying that Luther was really the father of modern liberal Protestantism, albeit against his will.[197]

It was in his prestigious *Geschichte der Kirche* that Lortz first performed his major surgery on Luther.[198] The Reformation was the "greatest catastrophe" that had ever befallen the church, "destroying its unity."[199] Never had the church faced such an attack as to its true form and structure as it did with the single person of Martin Luther, a condemned heretic, who inflicted deeper wounds on the church than any other individual in history.[200] Luther was an "introverted, subjectivistic, self-willed, self-centered" foe of the church.[201] How could a faithful Catholic monk become a revolutionary who set himself in the name of God against long-established tradition? Lortz finds the answer in part in the claim that Luther was a very complex, ambivalent person, with many sides to his personality. "There is no such thing as one Luther," states Lortz, as he tries to pin a sort of double-mindedness on the Reformer.[202] Luther's earnest, humble, honorable striving for the truth of man's salvation through the justifying work of Christ, Lortz does not fault, but he claims, on top of it, that Luther's doctrine *sola gratia/fide* was rooted all the time in old Catholic theology.[203] He makes the same claim as regards Luther's fixation on *sola Scriptura*, that Holy Scripture is the authoritative and only norm in the church.[204]

Lortz's indictment of Luther was stated earlier in his *The Reformation in Germany*,[205] which originally appeared in the 1940s. By Luther's "rejection of a living teaching office," Lortz accuses him of opening the floodgates "to lead each man to his own opinion"; and, as a result, "Protestantism became increasingly, alarmingly, unsure of what exactly Christianity is."[206] Luther actually brought aid and comfort to "humanist secularism" that not only "destroyed unity" but led to "the fatal splintering of Protestantism itself."[207] Lortz later wrote a postscript to this volume in which he continued his excoriation of Luther but also took notice of the fact that Vatican II, while not canonizing Luther, did refrain from calling him a heretic, even "allowing many important Reformation doctrines to come into their own."[208] In his estimation the Reformation has thus come to fruition in "none other than the Catholic Church," and "the urge toward unity has now begun to reverse the trend toward schism."[209]

In Lortz's latest assessment of Luther, he does not question the key role that Luther played in the Reformation.[210] In fact, "Luther is the Reformation" and a theologian of first rank.[211] Thereby Lortz reverses what he earlier denied. Yet he still cannot refrain from labeling Luther as "thoroughly ego-oriented" nor from charging that Luther "never viewed Scripture as a unity, nor as containing a single binding meaning."[212] It is an unfounded charge; but one can understand where Lortz is coming from and to what end he is pointing when he concludes: "It was the Church which, in an eternally memorable life-process and without single authoritative direction determined the canon of binding apostolic writings and thus made herself the normative interpreter."[213] Clearly he fails to recognize that it was this usurpation of power to itself that Luther was challenging as having been given by God to any earthly, manmade structure like the church of Rome, for it was a power that he himself retained and located in his inspired Word, Holy Scripture.

Other Catholic scholars with essays in the same volume include Erwin Iserloh, who attempts to show that Luther always remained a mystic,[214] in spite of what Bornkamm and Aland, among others, sought to show, namely, that a "Christ in us" sort of theology was fundamentally contrary to Luther's theology on how sinners are justified *coram Deo*. O. Hermann Pesch virtually claims the same mystical roots for Luther going back to Occamist tradition.[215] More importantly, however, he seeks a reconciling, synthetic bridge between what he calls the "existential theology of Luther" and "the sapiential theology of Aquinas," explaining:

> Luther is in posture of confession, where he addresses God and gives an account of himself before God. Thus he must speak primarily of his own nothingness and sin and seek a word of pardon. In contrast, St. Thomas looks on the world from God's own vantage point. He sees all creation in the divine perspective of its movement out from God and its return to God under his sovereign influence. Charity is the form in which a man makes his return to God.[216]

Those who know Luther's emphasis on what Scripture in fact teaches in answer to the fundamental question, "How do I know that God is gracious to me?" recognize the wide disparity between Luther's teaching on justification and Aquinas's.

The other essays in this volume have less bearing on Luther's doctrine of Scripture.

Hermann Pesch has contributed a valuable essay.[217] He offers some criticism of some of his colleagues in the Roman Catholic camp, including Joseph

Lortz and Hubert Jedin, particularly on the score of Luther not being a "good listener" of the Bible. Pesch shows some sympathy for Leif Grane's vocalized discontent with Lortz's "extremely hard criticism" of Luther, which "went farther than Denifle only in style, and not essentially."[218] Pesch also refers, perhaps somewhat doubtfully, to Hans Küng's attempt, following Hans Urs Von Balthasar, to show that Karl Barth was more in tune with the Reformation of the doctrine of justification than were the Lutherans themselves.[219] Pesch, too, raises literary eyebrows about Ebeling's "use" of Luther to justify his own "word-event" notion on Luther's stance toward and exegesis of the biblical Word.[220]

Gordon Rupp gives telling criticism of Lortz's handling of Luther. On the one hand, he says, Lortz "pays repeated tribute to Luther's creative energy, to the vast, genial flood of his conceptions," and then in the same breath wipes everything off the board with one fell swoop by categorizing his work as "uncoordinated jumbles of paradox and insight, unrestrained and toppling over into the subjectivism and one-sidedness" which constituted Luther's key error, or fault.[221] Moreover, Rupp is on the right track in understanding Luther's struggle with the Roman church when he states that "for Luther the paramount authority was that of Scripture," a stance that "led him to drastic criticism of the tradition in which he had been trained." But ever and always "subject to the over-riding authority of Holy Scripture, he in no wise repudiated either the language or the categories of Christian theology."[222]

Albert von Brandenburg is another contemporary Catholic scholar enjoying considerable reputation in Luther studies. He appeared as a panelist at the Fifth International Luther Congress in Lund, Sweden, in 1977. Brandenburg stated that even when Pope Paul VI placed his blessing upon the assertion that Luther was our common teacher in many respects, he by no means was granting that Luther was "a teacher of the church in the Catholic Church."[223] Nor should it be claimed, states Brandenburg in the same context, that the Gospel Luther "discovered" was something new in the church. Brandenburg closes his essay recommending that Luther's theology be studied afresh without the encumbrance of the Lutheran Confessions, that the close link between Luther and Bultmann be acknowledged, and that Luther's view of the Word be seen more as a "mystery" than as something to be identified with the biblical text.[224]

Some of the same thoughts appear in Brandenburg's book, published in the same year as the Congress.[225] That which separates Luther from the Roman Catholic Church, Brandenburg frankly states, has to do with Luther's contention that "God's Word speaks for itself and interprets itself, while for Romanists, Scripture's meaning comes under the teaching authority of the church. The word that comes forth from the Scripture is time-bound, while the teaching voice of the church continues to move existentially with the times.[226] "An unavoidable question," says Brandenburg, that has to be leveled at Luther is, *who* or *what* guarantees that the word of Gospel will be proclaimed pure and without falsity? If it is not the church (Roman) nor the teaching authority of that church, then ultimately it has to be the "personal 'I' of the person who has had the experience of Christ in his life."[227] Thus Brandenburg closes with the same label of "subjectivist" for Luther, as does Lortz.

In his preface to Harry McSorley's work,[228] Heinrich Fries defines the rudiments of ecumenical theology today, stating among other things that "the Christian concerns and realizations which are alive in the other confessions can also be represented and accepted within the Catholic Church in order that they might *again find their home, in all their integrity*."[229] It is an ecumenical gesture in tune with Vatican II, which likewise called the "separated brethren" home to Rome's bosom. But the fact remains that the "foolish theological rivalry" to which Fries refers can never be resolved as long as Rome, too, views the Bible's content as having merely relative authority, determined in fact by the church (Roman). For his part McSorley's argument does not square with the facts of the Reformation or of contemporary history when he avers that "many of the theological issues which are today regarded as separating factors were not at all the issues that led Martin Luther to precipitate the separation in the sixteenth century," to wit, "the relationship of Scripture and Tradition, the ministry, papal infallibility and the nature of the sacraments."[230] On the contrary, each of these were major concerns for Luther, simply because they were close to the "hinge" doctrine on which everything turned, as he told Erasmus, the issue of the human will versus Scripture's teaching concerning justification *sola gratia/fide*.

There are more dispassionate and accurate Catholic treatments of Luther. Among Catholic scholars, Peter Manns remains one of the foremost leaders in actually listening to what Luther in fact is saying, by firsthand reading of his works, rather than dependence upon secondary sources.[231]

Wolfgang Seibel and O. Hermann Pesch trace the gap between orthodox Lutheran views of Luther's significance in Reformation history and those of his Catholic opponents, from Bellarmine and Cochlaeus down to Denifle, Grisar, and Lortz, especially also the latter's disciples.[232] Pesch, for his part, indicates that the future is open to Luther studies and that there is potential value for all, including the Catholic Church, in such research. Even though it need not lend comfort and aid to a kind of hero cult, Pesch contends that there is much to learn from Luther's fundamental emphasis on what it is that gives freedom to the Christian man or believer. What Luther said and taught in his *Galatians Commentary* (1531–35) is just as pertinent today as it was in the sixteenth century. But it is probably wishful thinking on Pesch's part to think that Vatican II actually furthered this concern of Luther or that Rome today has moved closer to Luther's evangelical center.

VIII. CONCLUSION

The primacy of the Word of God, Holy Scripture, was for Luther axiomatic. Everything he wrote or said theologically took its bearing point from this pole star. The Reformation cannot really be understood apart from this commitment to Scripture's authority. It was the touchstone by which all things purporting to be religious and Christian were to be judged. By it came the rediscovery and the authenticating of the companion truths, that salvation is grounded on the verities of *sola gratia* and *sola fide*, and that all of them stand linked together under the overarching truth of *solus Christus*. The Bible reinforced these teachings for Luther, and, as Heinrich Bornkamm states, Luther "read Holy Writ as though it had been written yesterday" and was addressed by God to him alone.[233]

Luther was convinced that God's holy church, the *una sancta*, had survived in spite of all of the encumbrances of the institutional structure of Rome with its popes and councils. Nothing could finally, once and for all, submerge and drown the evangelical faith. It was like a living stream running down through the centuries, having its source in God's imperishable Word, quite independent of human institutions and things like the touted "apostolic succession." The church, after all, took its beginning and birth from the Word; the Scriptures stood with a unique, divine authority in the church. God's Word was there first, and then the church. Therefore, not the authority of the church, nor the testimony of the church, established the Word's authority but vice versa: the church exists by the agency and power of the Word. This was so already in the Old Testament when God gave His Word directly to the patriarchs, and it continued when by God's own initiative and inspiration the Word was channeled through His chosen spokesmen, the prophets, and then ultimately through the apostles. God thereafter bound His church to the prophetic and apostolic *written* Word.

It is the primacy of this written word of Holy Scripture that has largely been the focal point of attack by modern skepticism. Other forces have sought to sap the church's strength in our day, it is true; but no attack has been more radical and destructive of evangelical Christianity than that which bores away from the inside, the erosion of biblical authority within the church itself.

The Reformation was a call back to a bona fide *sola Scriptura* stance. Luther was intent on not rupturing the church but calling it back from what was seducing it, scholastic philosophizing, uncontrolled and uncontrollable secular humanism of the Renaissance mind, and the incredible proliferation of all manner of pious exercises in the name of God and Christianity that had no grounding in God's Word but were brazenly idolatrous. To achieve that goal it was necessary for the church to anchor itself squarely and solely on the authoritative Word of God, the Scriptures. Luther had no other purpose than that, for he was convinced of the prophet's word, that "the grass withers and the flowers fade, but the Word of our God stands forever" (Isa. 40:8). It is to be regretted, therefore, that a scholar of Heinrich Bornkamm's stature should feel compelled to say that Luther's "faith in God's Word did not need the crutch of the dogma of inspiration."[234] For Luther it was not a crutch but simply an ontological fact. Paul Althaus makes a similar effort at showing that Luther was not to be connected with so-called scholastic orthodoxy on the doctrine of inspiration. But quite ambivalently, and to his credit, Althaus describes Luther's view of Scripture as follows:

> Although Luther criticized the Bible in specific details, he nonetheless followed the tradition of his time and basically accepted it as an essential infallible book, inspired in its entire content by the Holy Spirit. It is therefore "the Word of God," not only when it speaks to us in law and gospel and thereby convicts our heart and conscience but also—and this is a matter of principle—in everything else that it says. Seen as a totality, its historical accounts, its world-view, and all

the miracle stories are "God's word" given by the Holy Spirit; they are therefore all unquestionable truth, to be "believed" precisely because they are contained in the book.[235]

Luther always stood in awe of what God had given him and all men in Holy Scriptures. He recognized no other authority in the church than the God-given, inspired word of Scripture. He literally lived out of the content of this blessed Word, as few men in history have ever done, drawing in its truths as a bee draws nectar from the flower. "The Bible, or the Holy Scriptures," he said, "are like a very large and extensive forest in which there are many and diverse kinds of trees from which one can pluck many kinds of berries and fruits." They are rich in "abundant comfort, doctrine, instruction, exhortation, admonition, promise, and warning," and of them I can honestly say: "In this forest there is not a single tall tree which I have not shaken, and plucked from it a few apples or pears."[236]

Luther was no dilettante who picked here or there, wherever he pleased or where it suited him, but a profoundly dutiful servant of the Lord who like a magnet drew every word God had ever spoken and recorded in Holy Writ to himself in humble trust. Thus, when he came to the last moments of his life, he wrote on a scrap of paper, apparently the final written words from his eloquent and obedient pen:

> Nobody can understand Virgil in his Bucolics, unless he has been a shepherd for five years. Nobody can understand Virgil in his Georgics, unless he has been a plowman for five years. Nobody can understand Cicero in his Epistles unless he has lived for twenty-five years in a large commonwealth. Let no one think he has sufficiently grasped the Holy Scriptures unless he has governed the churches for a hundred years with prophets like Elijah and Elisha, John the Baptist, Christ, and the apostles. Don't venture on this divine Aeneid, but rather bend low in reverence before its footprints! We are beggars! That is true.[237]

If ever a Reformation watchword was needed for our times, by all Christians, it is Luther's humble plea: "Bend low in reverence before its footprints! We are beggars! That is true."

CURRENT STUDIES

CHAPTER SIX

THE RATIONALITY OF BELIEF IN INERRANCY

J. P. Moreland

In recent years, scholars arguing against a conservative understanding of biblical inerrancy have appealed to a wide range of issues. It has been argued, for
example, that belief in inerrancy should be abandoned or redefined because inerrancy is not taught by the Bible and it was not the view of many leaders in the
history of the church. Others argue that the concept of inerrancy is not adequate
to capture the nature of the Bible as revelation.

As important as these and related issues are, one suspects that Donald
Dayton put his finger on the central reason why some scholars feel a need to
abandon or redefine inerrancy: "For many, the old intellectual paradigms [in-
cluding inerrancy] are dead, and the search is on in neglected traditions and
new sources for more adequate models of biblical authority."[1] Simply put,
many no longer think that it is rational to believe that inerrancy is true.

What are we to make of this objection? Is it no longer possible to hold that
belief in the inerrancy of Scripture is a rational position to take? The purpose
of this paper is to argue that belief in inerrancy *is* rational; one is within his or
her epistemic rights in believing that inerrancy is true.[2] In what follows, I will
clarify the objection that belief in inerrancy is not rational. Then, some relevant
features of the theory of rationality will be sketched and applied to the question
of the rationality of inerrancy. For the sake of argument, let us assume that we
possess a clear definition of inerrancy as it is understood by, say, the Evangelical Theological Society. This is not to imply that no more work is needed in
clarifying all the aspects of a definition of inerrancy. But the doctrine of inerrancy, as it is held by the ETS and other conservative evangelicals, is sufficiently clear for our purpose. After all, proponents and opponents of inerrancy
have understood the doctrine well enough to argue about it. The question
before us is whether or not belief in inerrancy, so understood, is rationally
justifiable.

I. INERRANCY IS NOT RATIONALLY JUSTIFIABLE

The view that inerrancy is not rationally justifiable involves at least four
distinct theses.

1. Inerrancy is not rationally justifiable because it is not supportable when a
genuinely inductive method is applied to the phenomena of Scripture (where
"phenomena" refers to all the relevant data inside and outside the Bible, e.g.,
problem passages, archaeological discoveries, scientific facts and theories, etc.).
The "inductive" method here often means what philosophers call enumerative

induction.[3] So understood, "induction" has two important features relevant to our discussion.

First, each particular fact in the phenomena carries equal weight. Second Timothy 3:16 and the problem of harmonizing the genealogies are two equally relevant facts that must be used in forming our doctrine of Scripture. The doctrine of inerrancy resembles a scientific law in that both are codified generalizations of particular facts.[4]

Second, the proper understanding of each particular problem in the phenomena should be reached by considering that particular problem on its own terms. Each particular problem should be evaluated in isolation from other parts of the phenomena. Further, the doctrine of inerrancy should not be used to settle a problem passage when an inductive evaluation of that passage would lead one to see it as an error.

As an example of this last point, consider the following statement by Daniel Fuller. Fuller is criticizing E. J. Young for allowing his doctrine of inerrancy to prevent him from adequately treating the problem of Stephen's chronology in Acts 7:1–4 when it is compared with Genesis 11:26–12:4. Says Fuller:

> Now a historian, unfettered by the necessity to uphold Young's doctrine of inerrancy, would immediately declare it was highly probable that Stephen's peculiar chronology in Acts 7:1–4 stemmed from both his and his hearers having been nurtured in a text that is today extant in the Samaritan Pentateuch. But Edward Young, historical scholar that he was, could not follow this highly probable pathway of historical reasoning. . . . But to be unwilling to let historical data supply a highly probable solution is to reject historical data in the interest of theological dogma.[5]

In other words, proper historical methodology treats Acts 7:1–4 on its own without reference to Genesis 11:26–12:4 or the concept of inerrancy.

2. The doctrine of inerrancy is not rationally justifiable because it places the Christian apologist in an untenable epistemic situation: he cannot be rationally justified in believing inerrancy until he has solved all the problems in the phenomena. On the other hand, a critic of inerrancy *is* rationally justified in denying inerrancy if he can find just one problem that defies "rational" solution. Clark Pinnock puts the point this way:

> For my part, to go beyond the biblical requirements to a strict position of total errorlessness only brings to the forefront the perplexing features of the Bible that no one can completely explain and overshadows those wonderful certainties of salvation in Christ that ought to be front and center. It makes us into sitting ducks for the liberal critics like James Barr and postpones our ability to be certain about the Bible to that remote time when the experts will be able to say, "At last we have proved the Bible in every respect."[6]

3. The doctrine of inerrancy is not rationally justifiable because it fails to take seriously the falsifying problems in the phenomena. Whenever a "crucial experiment" for inerrancy is conducted and the results falsify inerrancy,

proponents of inerrancy engage in a variety of activities that are epistemically suspect. Proponents of inerrancy create *ad hoc* hypotheses, they offer implausible harmonizations, and they engage in special pleading, opting for a suspension of judgment. The following statement by Timothy Phillips is representative of this objection: "The inability of discordant data to conclusively test even the historical knowledge inferred from Scripture is evident from the well-known mental gymnastics in which inerrantists take part, thereby avoiding the conclusion that Scripture errs."[7]

4. The doctrine of inerrancy is not rationally justifiable because its proponents offer no criteria for telling us when they will admit that inerrancy is falsified and must be given up. In the absence of such criteria, the inerrantist's appeal to suspended judgment becomes a deductive dogma, untestable by evidence. Dewey Beegle raised this objection long ago, and it is alluded to frequently.[8]

Underlying this objection seems to be the assumption that in order to know (or have a reasonable belief) that p, I must have criteria for knowing that p or perhaps that ~p [not p]. In this absence of such criteria, one is no longer rational in knowing or believing that p.[9]

Taken together, these four theses constitute a major objection to the rationality of belief that inerrancy is true. Can these objections be answered? I believe they can, and to show this, let us turn to a consideration of some key aspects of a theory of rationality.

II. FEATURES OF A THEORY OF RATIONALITY

In this section, there will be an attempt to reach limited goals. I will not try to give an ontological analysis of acts of rationality,[10] nor will I attempt to resolve the dispute between foundationalist and coherentist theories of epistemic justification. While I hold to a certain form of foundationalism, much of what I say here could be embraced, with adjustments, by a coherentist.[11] My goal is to state certain features of a theory of rationality that are relevant to the objections raised in the previous section.

What is a theory of rationality? At this point it will be helpful to introduce, with some modification, the notation of what Alvin Plantinga calls a noetic structure.[12] A person's noetic structure is the set of propositions he believes, along with certain epistemic relations that hold between him and these propositions and among the propositions themselves. A theory of rationality involves, among other things, an analysis of a person's noetic structure in such a way that light is shed on what it is for some epistemic states to be preferable to others. So conceived, a theory of rationality is a normative endeavor to answer questions like: What is it to be justified in knowing that p? When is a belief that p rational or irrational? How does one justify beliefs? When is it reasonable to give up a belief that p?

With this in mind, I now want to describe five features of a theory of rationality relevant to our discussion of inerrancy.

1. Epistemic concepts of appraisal. Our beliefs evidence different degrees of rationality. Some beliefs, e.g., the belief that I exist, are certain for me. Other beliefs, e.g., that the Kansas City Royals are one of baseball's best teams, are rational to a lesser degree than that of certainty. The following three epistemic

concepts express different degrees of rationality.[13] Let us assume that we are trying to decide whether or not it is rational to believe some belief p. Let us also assume that if we *withhold* our belief that p, we are in a state of suspending judgment regarding p. That is, we neither affirm p, nor do we affirm ~p.

a. Having some presumption in its favor: If p has some presumption in its favor, then it is better to believe p than to believe ~p (although it may be equally good or better to withhold belief that p than to believe p).

b. Acceptability: It is not the case that withholding belief that p is better than believing that p (although it may be equally good to withhold as to believe that p).

c. Being beyond reasonable doubt: Believing that p is more reasonable than withholding belief that p.

Points (a) through (c) are listed in order of increasing rationality. If p has some presumption in its favor, it is less reasonable to believe p than if p were beyond reasonable doubt. If p is "The conservative, classical doctrine of inerrancy is true," which epistemic concept must a defender of the rationality of inerrancy use?

Consider (a). If one holds that p has some presumption in its favor, then it could still be more reasonable to withhold belief that p. This does not seem to be strong enough to match what most defenders of inerrancy want to say about their belief that p. On the other hand, most critics of inerrancy imply that the current state of scholarship makes it better to believe ~p than to believe p. So if the defender of inerrancy could show that p has some presumption in its favor, he could at least argue for a suspension of judgment as opposed to a denial of inerrancy.

What about (c)? If the defender of inerrancy could show that p is beyond reasonable doubt, then of course he would be within his epistemic rights in believing p. This may be a good line of approach, but I do not think that the defender of inerrancy needs to argue for this strong a notion of rationality. In claiming that it is rational to believe in inerrancy, it seems to me one is affirming that belief in inerrancy is acceptable as defined above. The defender of inerrancy is arguing that belief in inerrancy is more rational than the belief that inerrancy is false. He is also arguing that it is at least as rational (perhaps more so) to believe p than to withhold p. Further, if one could show that p has some features in common with Pascal's wager and William James's discussion of live options, namely, that withholding p is not an option, for to withhold p is really to choose against p, then "acceptability" reduces to "having some presumption in its favor." In that case, defending the acceptability of inerrancy would involve showing it had some presumption in its favor.

The upshot of my analysis of rationality is this. In order to argue that belief in inerrancy is rational, one need not show that such a belief is certain, evident, or (perhaps) beyond reasonable doubt. One can be well within one's epistemic rights in believing the truth of inerrancy without adopting such a strong notion of rationality that makes it incumbent on one to answer all problem passages and remove all doubts, puzzles, and objections. One does not need to solve the problem in Acts 7:1–4 *before* one can be rational in affirming inerrancy. If the defender of inerrancy were arguing that belief in inerrancy is absolutely certain or beyond reasonable doubt, his epistemic situation would be different. But I see no reason why the defender of inerrancy needs to adopt such a strong concept of rationality. His task, it seems to me, is less demanding. This will become more evident as we consider further features of a theory of rationality.

2. The proper context of evidence. In most cases a belief is deemed a rational one because it is supported by some appropriate backdrop of evidence.[14] Ontologically, for some belief p, there would exist a set T consisting of all and only the evidence relevant to p. However, one may not know T, and the rationality of believing p depends on the evidential context I select and on whether this is a good evidential context.

Suppose I come home from work and I see toys and doll clothes scattered throughout the living room. Suppose further that I know these items belong to my two little girls. I also know they are in the habit of leaving toys scattered, and I see them in the room playing with the toys and clothes. Given this evidential context, I would be rationally justified in forming the belief p at time t_1 "My girls messed up the living room by scattering their toys and doll clothes." Suppose at some time later, t_2, my wife tells me my daughters had been gone all day and that our neighbor's children had been playing in our house all day with the doll clothes and toys. Furthermore, my wife tells me that my girls had just come home three minutes before I walked in the door. While p was rational for me at t_1, p is no longer rational for me at t_2. What has changed? At t_2 I have a different body of evidence in the relevant evidential context.

Now consider a theist who is trying to defend the rationality of belief that God exists. Suppose an atheist argues that such a belief is not rational given the problem of evil. The theist could agree but go on to argue that this is not the appropriate evidential context. In other words, given that the problem of evil is the only relevant evidence for deciding the rationality of belief that God exists, it could follow that such a belief is not rational. But if the problem of evil is only one piece of relevant evidence in a much broader set of relevant evidence (metaphysical arguments for God, miracles, religious experience, etc.), then the belief that God exists may be rational against *that* backdrop of evidence.

It is very important, then, in deciding whether some belief is a rational one, that I base my answer on the proper set of relevant evidence. We will see shortly that in deciding whether a problem in the phenomena of Scripture is a real or apparent error, the relevant set of evidence includes *other* passages of Scripture *and* the doctrine of inerrancy itself. Only a misunderstanding of induction and its normal role in science and other "inductive" enterprises would cause someone like Fuller to think that Genesis 11:26–12:4 and the doctrine of inerrancy are not members of the proper evidential set for deciding about what to make of Acts 7:1–4.

For now, I want to offer one application for the inerrancy debate, of choosing the appropriate evidential context for justifying a belief. In ranking the plausibility of a variety of hypotheses explaining why an airplane crashed (a Martian did it, the pilot was drunk, the brakes failed, etc.), one implicitly or explicitly appeals to one's background knowledge about the way things normally go in cases like these.[15] These background constraints usually constitute the accumulated tacit and explicit knowledge that resides in an appropriate community of practitioners. One need not accept conceptual relativism nor reduce intellectual history to the sociology of knowledge to appreciate the social component of knowledge and rationality.[16] This is why church history is relevant to the *rationality* of belief in inerrancy and is not merely of historical interest. If one could show that the great majority of theologians and biblical scholars in the history of the church have held to inerrancy, and if this group forms the relevant community of practitioners, then their beliefs provide background constraints for ranking the plausibility of the doctrine of inerrancy vis-à-vis other views of biblical authority.

I am not presenting this as a knockdown argument. Communities can be wrong and background constraints can be mere biases. But the relevant evidential set for deciding the rationality of belief in inerrancy should include the background constraints provided by church history. This would at least make belief in inerrancy *prima facie* justified[17] and contribute to placing the burden of proof on those who deny inerrancy.[18]

3. Depth of ingression. A person's noetic structure contains what Alvin Plantinga has called an index of depth of ingression. Plantinga argues:

> Some of my beliefs are, we might say, on the periphery of my noetic structure. I accept them, and may even accept them firmly, but I could give them up without much change elsewhere in my noetic structure. I believe there are some large boulders on the top of the Grand Teton. If I come to give up this belief (say by climbing it and not finding any), that change need not have extensive reverberations throughout the rest of my noetic structure; it could be accommodated with minimal alteration elsewhere. So its depth of ingression into my noetic is not great.[19]

One can think of a noetic structure as a web of beliefs. The more depth of ingression a belief has in one's noetic structure, the more it exhibits two important features. First, it is more closely and complexly interrelated with other beliefs in my noetic structure. It is less independent than a belief on the periphery. Second, it is an epistemically important belief in my noetic structure. It provides mutual support for other important beliefs deeply ingressed, and it provides epistemic support for a number of beliefs closer to the periphery.

The concept of such depth ingression has important consequences for a theory of rationality. The deeper a belief is ingressed, the greater the evidence required to justify giving up that belief. One *should* not give up a deeply ingressed belief without requiring a greater number and quality of defeaters than one would require of a less ingressed belief. The doctrine of inerrancy is unquestionably a belief that should be deeply ingressed in one's noetic structure. If belief in inerrancy is given up, a number of other beliefs are weakened or need to be given up as well.

I am not here using a domino argument and saying that if the Bible is not true in all points we cannot know that it is true in any point.[20] I am simply making the point that inerrancy is clearly a belief which should be closer to the center of one's noetic structure than to the periphery. This means that one is rationally justified in requiring a good deal of evidence before giving it up.

Critics who argue, under the banner of induction, that particular problems in the phenomena should be treated strictly in their own terms, simply have a naive view of the way rationality fleshes itself out in one's system of beliefs. Similarly, the charge that defenders of inerrancy engage in special pleading, implausible harmonizations, and a suspension of judgment is too simplistic.

It is a simplistic scenario of the epistemic situation merely to look at a set of problem passages and the various explanations of them in determining whether or not those explanations are rational. The role of inerrancy in one's entire set of theological beliefs is also relevant to the rationality of the situation. An interpretation of a problem passage that harmonizes it with another text, and thus preserves inerrancy, may not be as rational as an interpretation that admits an error in the text if one only considers this particular problem in isolation from other epistemically relevant considerations. But if one considers the depth of ingression of inerrancy as well, then the rationality of preserving belief in inerrancy in one's noetic structure (as opposed to denying it and having to readjust a large part of one's structure) can justify suspending judgment or believing a harmonization.

There are many times I have prayed and not received an answer to my prayer. On many of those occasions I thought I had correctly claimed a promise of God. How do I harmonize this lack of an answer with the promises of Scripture? If I take a case on its own terms, I may judge that I was sincere, prayed scripturally, and this falsifies the promises of God to answer according to his word. However, my belief in God's faithfulness is a deeply ingressed one. It is supported by the general evidence I have for Christian theism, past answers to prayers, and so on. If I give up my belief in God's faithfulness, I will have to seriously readjust my noetic structure. But this would be irrational for me, given the role that belief plays in my noetic structure, supporting and being supported by other beliefs.

So I am rationally justified either in harmonizing this unanswered prayer with my doctrine of God's faithfulness or in suspending judgment. The rationality of belief in inerrancy, I suggest, is similarly justified. The defender of inerrancy is not being irrational in calling for suspension of judgment, etc., because of the depth of ingression of belief in inerrancy. At the very least, critics of the rationality of inerrancy should consider this before they criticize as irrational the various attempts to harmonize ages and the like.

4. Insights from the philosophy of science. In our culture, science has been held to be *the* paradigm of knowledge. Whether or not one agrees with this judgment, there can be no doubt that a vast amount of work has been done studying the history, epistemology, and ontology of science. Because science shares various methodological features with historical study, exegesis, and theology (all form and test hypotheses, for example), then insights from philosophy of science can be applied *mutatis mutandis* to these latter fields of study.[21] Since this area of study is so massive, I can only state, without much proof, certain generally agreed-upon principles in the philosophy of science relevant to the inerrancy debate.

First, it is generally agreed that the sort of inductive method Fuller assumes, enumerative induction, is not the major way scientists form and test hypotheses.[22]

Laws are not empirical generalizations formed by taking one fact at a time. Laws and theories are formed in a variety of ways. There is no formalized psychology of discovery. Nevertheless, in forming a hypothesis it is best to start from clear cases or exemplars of the phenomenon to be explained. One does not start with borderline cases.[23] Similarly, scientific hypotheses are tested by a hypothetico-deductive method or abductively. In the former case, implications are deduced from a hypothesis and an attempt is made to falsify or, perhaps, confirm the hypothesis. In the latter case, a hypothesis is seen as a conceptual web or Gestalt that explains facts by fitting them into a coherent picture.

In either case, scientific testing and explanation involves testing particular cases against the backdrop of a hypothesis. Particular experiments are not judged in isolation from this general hypothesis nor in isolation from other experiments involving the same kind of phenomena.

Second, trends in the philosophical studies of language, perception, and science have tended to break down the observation/theory distinction.[24] I do not agree with an absolute denial of the distinction for a variety of reasons that do not concern us here. Nevertheless, it does seem true that the fact/theory distinction is not always easy to make.[25] If this is granted, then the interplay between theory and fact becomes much more complex than Fuller pictures it in his treatment of Acts 7:1–4. The disconfirmation of a theory is generally a very complicated affair. It is *not* a simple matter of a crucial experiment that falsifies the theory. As Larry Laudan points out, the rationality of a theory is multifaceted.[26] It involves much more than the presence or absence of anomalies. The status, nature, weight, and quantity of anomalies defy a simple characterization. Conceptual problems internal to the theory are also relevant. The way the theory fits into rational beliefs (scientific, metaphysical, theological) is also a factor in judging the rationality of a theory. Further, the presence and nature of a rival paradigm is also relevant in judging the rationality of a theory.

In short, studies in the philosophy of science show that it is very difficult to characterize when it is no longer rational to believe a scientific theory in the presence of anomalies. Studies in the history of science confirm this conviction.[27] It is, then, very difficult to give a simple treatment to falsification, *ad hoc* hypotheses, crucial experiment, theoretical simplicity, and the like.[28]

Third, when scientists study some entity—a substance, property, relation, or event—they treat that entity as though it were a universal.[29] When scientists are trying to learn something about dogs by studying Fido, they do not study Fido *qua* particular, but *qua* example of a kind or member of a class. The experimental evidence from studying Fido is *not* evaluated in isolation from knowledge of other examples of that kind. Further, scientists reason from clear exemplars of the class of entity they are studying to problem or borderline cases.

These three features of science are very important clues for understanding the rationality of hypothesis formation, testing, and acceptance. Scientists can be rational in believing a hypothesis in the presence of anomalies by treating them as *alleged* counterinstances rather than real counterinstances. This is true even if some anomaly—considered on its own—would more plausibly be understood as a refuting case of the hypothesis. The scientist is often within his epistemic rights to suspend judgment, use *ad hoc* hypotheses, and refuse to give up the hypothesis in the presence of what appears to be a well-confirmed counterexample.

Consider an example. A standard organic chemistry test by Morrison and Boyd discusses a certain kind of chemical reaction known as halohydrogenation. This kind of reaction was supposed always to happen in a certain way based on scientific theories explaining halohydrogenation. However, a clear, refuting counterexample was found which, if judged simply by the evidence for that case in isolation from the evidence for the hypothesis, provided a refutation of the hypothesis. But scientists suspended judgment on this case and engaged in *ad hoc* harmonization attempts from 1869–1933. At that time they discovered a new, hitherto unknown factor which severed the counterexample from its class.

Why were they rational in doing this? Because the evidence for treating the counterexample as a real refutation had to be sufficiently strong to overturn the combined evidence from a variety of sources that the hypothesis was true. If the counterexample was judged on its own terms, various interpretations that harmonized it with the hypothesis would have been ruled out. But this is not the correct epistemic situation. The counterexample was a member of a class, and the evidence supporting the hypothesis from the rest of the class was relevant to the situation.

The same is true of inerrancy. As Warfield argued,[30] before I am rationally justified in believing that an alleged error is a real one, the evidence for this error must be sufficient to overturn all the evidence I have for the inerrancy of Scripture. Why? Because this problem text should not be rationally appraised *qua* particular but *qua* member of the class "Scripture." This is not theological dogmatism or presuppositional apologetics. This is a proper understanding of "induction" as it is used in any discipline which methodologically resembles science.

For example, in forming or testing the doctrine of the sinlessness of Christ or His deity, one does not rationally evaluate problem passages (cases of Jesus' anger, his lack of knowledge, etc.) in isolation from other considerations. Instead, one starts with clear cases (1 Peter 2:22), formulates a hypothesis, and uses the hypothesis and other cases in a rational appraisal of problem passages. This is a rational procedure, and this is what most defenders of inerrancy do.

It may be instructive at this point to mention the problem of miracles. Theists argue that a particular miracle should be evaluated on its own terms and *not* in light of the general evidence from the majority of natural events in the flow of history. If this procedure is correct—and I think it is—does not this constitute one example of evidence evaluation which is just the opposite of the view I have been presenting?

No, it does not. In fact, the case of miracles further clarifies my argument. The theist does not exactly treat the miracle in its own terms. Rather, he argues that it is an *alleged* example of a new class, "supernatural event," and as such, it should be evaluated apart from the evidential support of an irrelevant class, "natural event." In other words, when the naturalist brings evidence to bear on the miracle from natural events, he is committing a category fallacy. The miracle *claims* to be an example of a *different* class, and thus it should be investigated apart from the class "natural event" to keep from begging the question.

If errantists wish for passages like Acts 7:1–4 to be appraised independently from other texts or the doctrine of inerrancy, this is what they must do. They must sever the problem passage from the class "Scripture." That is, they must find independent reasons (to keep from begging the question) for why the problem passage should not be in the canon. If it can be sustained that this text at least *claims* to be noncanonical, by some criteria other than its status as an alleged error, it becomes severed from the class "Scripture." Then the combined evidence for the truthfulness of Scripture *would* be irrelevant to the problem text.

In sum, insights from the philosophy of science show that one can be rational in affirming inerrancy in the presence of a number of anomalies even if this involves suspending judgment or using *ad hoc* hypotheses. This activity can be rational because (1) hypotheses are not formed or tested by enumerative induction (where cases are evaluated in their own terms) but by hypothetico-deduction or abduction (where the particular cases are judged against the backdrop of the hypothesis); (2) the fact/interpretation distinction, though a genuine one, is not always easy to draw; the rationality of theory change, therefore, is not a simple matter of falsification, but rather a very complex affair that defies simplistic treatment; and (3) problem cases are not treated *qua* particulars but *qua* members of a class, and thus the evidence of this whole class must be overthrown before the case can rationally be judged as a falsifying instance of that class.

5. Criteria of knowledge. It could be objected that nowhere have I stated any criteria for knowing when there would be enough problems with inerrancy to justify giving it up. Thus, I cannot rationally claim to know that inerrancy is true.

I can only offer two brief but important responses. First, as has already been argued, there are no acceptable criteria in the philosophy of science that can be applied in a simple, algorithmic way to all or most cases of theory change in science. The simple fact is that the rationality of theory change is a very multifaceted affair. The same can be said of theological systems. No simple set of criteria can be given for when one theological construct should be given up and another believed. This is not to say that there are no cases where theological or scientific hypotheses should be abandoned. But determining *when* that point is reached and *how* one knows it has been reached is another matter. Theological constructs (first order or second order), inerrancy included, are no different from scientific theories in this regard. So I can offer no adequate criteria for when inerrancy should be abandoned. But this is not surprising, nor is it because I am engaging in a special pleading. This is just the way it often is with hypotheses.

Second, as Roderick Chisholm has pointed out,[31] there are many things one can know without having criteria for knowing them. If this were not the case, I would never know anything, since to know I would have to have criteria for knowledge. But to know my criteria, I would have to have criteria for my criteria. This is a vicious regress.[32] So I can know some things without giving criteria for knowing them or for falsifying them.

As an example, consider a puzzle from the ancient Greeks, known as the sorites problem.[33] Given a small heap of wheat, can I get a large heap by adding one grain? It seems not, for how could one go from a small to a large heap by merely adding one grain? But then it seems that one could add grains of wheat to a small heap and never reach a large heap.

Consider another puzzle. If one gradually changes the shade of a color from red to orange, can one tell when the color changes from red to orange? Probably not. But in the absence of such a criterion, how can I know when I see red or orange?

The problem with both puzzles is this: they assume that in the absence of clear criteria for borderline cases, one cannot have knowledge of clear cases. Without being able to judge when the heap becomes large, I can never know that it is large. Without being able to judge when the color changes to orange, I can never know that it is orange. But the fact is, I can know a large heap or an orange color even if I have no criteria.

I am not dismissing criteria altogether. Indeed, they are important in an overall theory of rationality. But I do not need criteria in all cases to know something.

In the case of inerrancy, the issue is complicated enough that I do not think one needs to give criteria for knowing when to believe errancy or to accept the falsification of inerrancy. It does not follow from this that it would never be rational to give up belief in inerrancy. It may. But giving criteria for this is not easy.

III. SUMMARY

I have tried to analyze the objection that it is no longer rational to believe that inerrancy is true. I have tried to meet this objection by clarifying what the objection is and then by sketching and applying some important features of a theory of rationality. The reader may not agree with the arguments I have used. But I hope enough has been said to show that the rationality of belief in general, and of inerrancy in particular, involves a number of complicated issues. If this is so, then critics of inerrancy should be cautious. A naive appeal to problem passages and "implausible" harmonizations simply does not capture the situation accurately.

CHAPTER SEVEN

THE CULTURAL RELATIVIZING OF REVELATION

Carl F. H. Henry

Charles H. Kraft's controversial *Christianity in Culture*,[1] a study in "dynamic biblical theologizing" in cross-cultural perspective, appeared at a time when the volatile controversy over biblical authority was finding new focus. The issue of the culture-relatedness of the Judeo-Christian revelation has become a matter of high debate. Kraft, the professor of anthropology and African studies at the Fuller School of World Mission, writes in a day when some professedly evangelical spokesmen openly contend that the Koran is for Muslims an acceptable cross-cultural equivalent of the Bible.

Kraft has studied anthropology, has served briefly as a missionary in northern Nigeria, and has engaged in linguistic and ethnological research particularly among the Hausa tribespeople. Some of his Fuller colleagues view Kraft as a sensationalist whose significance should not be overrated. But his book is a well-documented and carefully organized work. It gains power through a rejection of extremist and unbalanced views and from a serious wrestling with many dilemmas that face the missionary task force.

Kraft assures his readers that he is an evangelical Protestant committed to biblical Christianity. He proffers "a culturally informed perspective on Christianity and Christian theology,"[2] one sensitive to the diversity of culture and to the mounting impact of the behavioral sciences. He disavows "absolute cultural relativism" that precludes any and all evaluation of cultural behavior;[3] instead, he promotes "relative cultural relativism."[4] His central concern is the cultural yet transcultural character of revelation and of Scripture, along with the related issues involved in communication and contextualization of the Gospel to, and in, some 6,000 cultures of the modern world.

The Bible is, as we know, itself a multicultural book. But the "cultural distance" between Hebrew culture and European cultures, Kraft holds, makes it "likely that American understandings" of Scripture "will be further from the intent of the original authors than African and Asian understandings."[5] Kraft is disturbed that Western theology has posted a "heresy" sign over other approaches to Christianity than its own. He stresses the crucial importance of divergent "thought patterns" in different cultures, warns against "Greek-type thinking," and sounds a call for conversion to a new perception of the nature of Christ's work. Cultural perspectives differ because of different governing assumptions. But the assumptions of others may be "just as valid" as ours.[6]

No reader will be surprised that the outlook of Africans or Asians often differs sharply from that of Americans or Europeans, who of course also differ sharply from each other about many things. But an anthropological-theological perspective, Kraft tells us, requires taking other views seriously. "What should we do," he asks, if people "show no perceptible guilt over sin from which to be saved?"[7] Many missionaries have given up, he tells us, because they cannot cope with such questions.

Kraft acknowledges that anthropology makes no claim to deal with ultimate truth.[8] The question we soon face is whether *theology* retains any final truths once Kraft integrates it into "a cross-cultural anthropological perspective."[9] Is the truth of special biblical revelation invalidated by the way Kraft relates it to culture? Kraft emphasizes that the anthropological approach is holistic or inclusive of all human experience.[10] He seeks "a cross-culturally valid understanding of Christianity."[11] But this requires "new categories of thought and terrninology" to "broaden and elucidate, rather than to completely displace, traditional evangelical concepts."[12]

Kraft rejects the "staticness that largely characterizes evangelical views of revelation and inspiration."[13] He disavows the "inerrantist model" of Scripture,[14] yet he professes to share most of the major conclusions of inerrantists concerning the "normativeness" of Scripture.[15] Theologians whose views he specially approves include Jack Rogers, David Hubbard, Eugene Nida, Daniel Fuller, Harvey Cox, Bruce Vawter, and later emphases by Bernard Ramm and G. C. Berkouwer. Those he criticizes are B. B. Warfield, Francis Schaeffer, Geerhardus Vos, Carl Henry, J. W. Montgomery, and Harold Lindsell.

Kraft rejects as "either static or applying only to some segment of Euro-American culture" the traditional evangelical methods of theologizing.[16] He prefers, with Richard Quebedeaux, to define evangelical Christianity as "a 'spirit' rather than a well-defined theology" and proposes to incorporate certain liberal characteristics. Kraft depicts what is involved as a shift of method, not of theology. The shift, it develops, involves transmitting not what the Bible means but what it "means *to me* and to people in any culture" and confession of ignorance of "what the Spirit of God wants to teach" others from it.[17]

Kraft writes of legitimate understandings of Scripture by different interpreters in a variety of cultural applications. Along with the anthropologist Monica Wilson, he insists that our ideas must change as societies change[18]—an idea, presumably, that Wilson and Kraft consider impervious to change. Kraft implies that his own principles have the validity of divine absolutes. Kraft proposes, in fact, that we regard his application of anthropological and communicational models to relationships between Christianity and culture as part of the whole truth into which Jesus pledged that the Spirit of truth would lead His disciples (John 16:12–13).

Logical validity, as we know, is universal. But Kraft has a curious and highly ambiguous notion of truth. His notion of "cultural validity"—which anthropologists usually refer to as "cultural relativism"—is confusing. Kraft indicates that no universal criteria are applicable to all cultures and that each culture is valid only for its own participants.[19] None can be regarded as final, and no transcendently absolute criterion is allowed to judge any. Kraft declares this belief in the validity of other cultures to be the equivalent in anthropology of the Golden Rule in theology.[20] Yet cultural validity, Kraft says, does not oblige us to approve of customs like cannibalism, widow-burning, infanticide, polygamy, and premarital sex.[21] On what basis can an emphasis on mere cultural validity identify any practices as universally wicked and sinful? Kraft writes of "the American assumption" that having sexual relations with someone other than one's first wife is adultery.[22] If vices and virtues are conceptually untransferable from one cultural context to another, why should any or all be considered universally normative or abhorrent?

Kraft rightly rejects the Western evolutionary theory that all cultures are slowly evolving toward Euro-American ideals. He urges us not to confuse with "the absolutes of God" for every culture "principles and judgments . . . valid within Western culture."[23] Kraft writes that "no culture, especially not ours, can be regarded as superior in every way to every other culture."[24] One might think that for the sake of balance Kraft would note that American culture at least reflects in some respects more Christian culture than some other cultures do. But in any event he can provide no objective basis for approving monogamy, democracy, capitalism, self-determination, or military preparedness above antithetical views, that is, polygamy, tyranny, communism, enslavement, or military weakness. While he writes of every culture being in some respects "stronger" than others, the term *stronger* cannot reflect objective gradations of truth or morality. Kraft's assumptions provide no basis for regarding any culture as either superior or inferior to any other.

In a grossly ambiguous comment Kraft tells us that cultures are "not only relative to each other but are also relative . . . to the supercultural."[25] In line with other stories that unfold a worldview, Kraft speaks of the Bible as mythology but notes that evangelical Christians insist on historical factuality.[26] Different worldviews involve different assumptions and conclusions[27] and he himself insists on the historicity of biblical events that the writers interpret within their cultural context. The various worldviews serve "an *evaluational*—a judging and validating—function," provide psychological reinforcement for the group,[28] and have an integrating role.[29] Yet the respective worldviews do not "completely determine the perception" of cultural constituencies; the Hebrews, for example, shifted from polytheism to monotheism, and Americans from belief in Yahweh to trust in technology.

God interacts with people in their cultural milieu.[30] Both God's general and His special revelation, we are told, come to us "from cultural and transcultural sources via cultural vehicles."[31] God limits Himself to the capacities of "imperfect and imperfectible, finite, limited" culture, and has done so even in the incarnation of Christ.[32] God uses "human language with all its finiteness, its relativity, and its *assured misperception* of infinity."[33] If Kraft means what he here says, we should distrust his own claims about God and his relations. But Kraft is much more vocal about the infallibility of others than about his own.

Kraft "views God as transcendent and absolute, completely beyond and outside of culture."[34] God is "absolute and infinite."[35] God will not contradict himself.[36] Kraft approves William A. Smalley's emphases that only God is absolute, whereas the revelation of God's will is a "relative absolute"—relative to human finiteness, limitations, personality differences, language, and culture.[37]

Because he denies the existence of any set of "absolute cultural forms,"

Kraft shuns the nouns *superculture* and *supraculture* and concentrates instead on the "supracultural" to designate God's transcendence of all culture.[38] Not even cultural behavior that God prescribes or proscribes for all time is considered supracultural and absolute because all human behavior is cultural behavior. While God is supracultural and His principles are to be constants of the human condition, God's interactions with humans are always cultural.[39]

The question that then arises is whether we encultured humans can know supracultural truth and principles. In view of God's revelation Kraft answers yes, but he insistently declares human understanding to be always fallible. God nonetheless adapts his approach to the cultural, sociological, and psychological limitations of mankind.[40]

It helps Kraft's case little when, in the interest of situation-specific cultural revelation he emphasizes that in Scripture, "The number of highly generalized, cosmic pronouncements (e.g., the Ten Commandments, the Sermon on the Mount) is limited."[41] Not only does he grossly understate the amount of objective doctrinal and ethical teaching that the Bible conveys in specific situations, but the very passages he acknowledges as such contradict the notion that divine truth is to be reformulated in divergent cultural specifications as an internal response.

Let us forget momentarily that Kraft offers his own formulation as the unquestioned epistemic key to the entire revelation-interpretation process, as if like earlier Montanists he was vouchsafed some revelational insight undimmed by the limitations of others. As it stands, his theory holds—contrary to "closed conservatives"—that all human understandings of God's revelation and all behavior-responses are culture-conditioned and none is to be considered universally valid or true.[42]

Kraft's curious insistence that "supracultural truth exists (with God) above and beyond any cultural perception or expressions of it"[43] is noetically justifiable only if Kraft sheds the epistemic skin that he grafts on all other humans and which leads to skepticism unless, in accord with a truly biblical view of God and man, we are able to escape cultural relativity.

God is "above" or outside of culture but chooses to work through and in terms of cultural matrixes. Human perception of supracultural truth, Kraft assures us, is "adequate though never absolute; we are culture-bound in our understandings and interpretations of God's truth."[44]

Kraft, as we have noted, distinguishes "cultural universals" like the Ten Commandments;[45] but he does not inform us how his epistemic theory enables one to insist on such universals and to distinguish them from culturally limited particulars. The fact that known cultures approve or disapprove a given practice does not establish a logical universal. Limited empirical observation of cultural behavior cannot identify universals.

We should not be misled by the fact that, despite these declared culture-limitations, Kraft postulates an absolute God, an absolute revelation, an inspired Bible, and revealed principles. Only a schizophrenic could mentally exempt such postulates from the pervasive culture-limitations on which Kraft insists but which he repeatedly refuses to apply to his own views. It avails little that he appeals to written records of "God's 'bridgings'" of the gap[46] if these records too are fallible and culture-skewed. Kraft makes current prejudices of the behavioral sciences normative for Judeo-Christian revelation instead of challenging those very prejudices either in the name of the culture-relativity they salute or in the name of transcendent biblical revelation.

While Kraft insists on evaluation of cultural behavior, he holds that the "meaning of that behavior is derived *entirely* from within the other's system, never from ours or from some 'cosmic pool' or universal meanings." The fact that God revealed some truths pertaining only to the Hebrews is invoked to justify the notion of the culture-relativity of all revelational information.[48] The implication is that the revelation of God can and must be translated into contrary and perhaps even contradictory "cultural principles" and behavior in divergent societies. Paul's adage "all things to all men" is made to accommodate any and all conflicting beliefs and practices, while the Holy Spirit is held to approve this diversity by "leading 'into all truth'" through divergent culture-bound perceptions.[49]

Astonishingly, Kraft absolutizes the new hermeneutic's devaluation of grammatico-historical exegesis as a welcome development guided by God through the Holy Spirit, even as James Barr (see *Fundamentalism*) similarly sanctifies the whole enterprise of biblical criticism. Like Barr also, Kraft assumes that special divine revelation continues beyond the Bible and that communicators enlightened by behavioral concessions especially enjoy it. Scriptural teachings are devalued as culturally conditioned while modern communication theories are assimilated to the revelation of the Spirit.[50]

Kraft warns us that the New Testament is largely phrased in "*Greek* conceptual categories (rather than in supracultural categories)."[51] If his intention is to suggest that what the writers teach as doctrine is therefore to be stripped of universal truth, then we must warn readers that what Kraft writes is largely phrased in *English* conceptual categories, and he should bear whatever consequences are supposed to follow.

To accommodate culture-relative meaning in the biblical texts Kraft shifts from grammatico-historical interpretation to ethno-linguistic interpretation[52] and then reads into the texts the culture-relativism that humanistic behavioral science requires. Secular humanism banishes the living God in His intelligible revelation and refers statements about God to the not-God. Kraft emphasizes that God is not bound by human culture but rather views culture "primarily as a vehicle to be used by him and his people for Christian purposes, rather than as an enemy to be combatted or shunned."[53]

Kraft rejects the view that God's transcendent relation to culture requires the Christian to prescribe a system of theology valid for all cultures.[54] "Theology (as well as anthropology) is human-made and culture bound."[55] Kraft emphasizes that "the monoculturalness of most Western theology" extremely limits its ability to deal with issues cross-culturally and that Christianity must translate its message into indigenous cultural forms.

Kraft denies that he espouses "an abandonment of theological absolutes (or constants)."[56] But he differentiates these from "the wording of creeds" or from less than "absolute understandings of God's absolute models." For Kraft, the "functions and meanings behind" the doctrinal forms hold priority. He leaves "largely negotiable" in terms of divergent cultural matrixes "the cultural forms in which these constant functions are expressed."[57] "There is, I believe, no absoluteness to the human formulation of . . . doctrine," he says, but "the meaning conveyed by a particular doctrine . . . is of primary concern to God."[58] Here Kraft deflates and relativizes the doctrines of the Bible and the creeds of Christendom. Meanwhile he presumes not only to articulate the supracultural mind of God but also to entrench his own debatable doctrine as the rule to which he accommodates all else. He ranges Jesus against the Pharisees and against evangelical doctrinal orthodoxy and contends that Jesus considered beliefs and practices "simply the cultural vehicles" through which "the eternal message of God" is to be expressed and that must be continually updated to fulfill this function.[59]

To be sure, Kraft holds that "denial of . . . the existence of God, human sinfulness, God's willingness to relate to humans on certain conditions, the necessity of a human faithfulness response to God as preconditional to salvation, and the like would put one outside the biblically allowed range of acceptable variation."[60] Are we to consider the eternal sonship of Christ, his incarnation and bodily resurrection, justification by faith, and other scripturally basic concepts dispensable cultural relativities? Or do they fall under the category of "the like"?

Revelation, Kraft insists, occurs only in personal interaction.[61] Kraft extends revelation, as does Barth, beyond its apostolic inscripturation to the continuing "discovery of revelation" in subjective response, so that not only prophets and apostles but we also, like them, are recipients of revelation. Kraft gains sympathy for his position by unjustifiable exaggerations, as that evangelical orthodoxy implies that God ceased to reveal Himself after the first Christian century.[62] In fact, it is Barthians and not evangelicals who deny the reality of universal general revelation; and Kraft himself compromises its cognitive content. Kraft considers it unreasonable to argue that God now limits His special revelation to the biblical record;[63] but were that the case, postapostolic Christians would still be writing Scripture. The misconception of continuing special revelation may explain why Kraft thinks his interpretative principles have a universal validity he denies to other culture-conditioned understandings. While Kraft urges an unabridged missionary proclamation of the Gospel calling for faith in God, he does not rule out the possibility that God may even now reveal Himself specially and directly to individuals in different cultures, as He did to Abraham and Melchizedek.[64] If revelation continues within a range of variation, why may not Muhammad and Joseph Smith and Charles Kraft then be God's updating prophets?

Kraft denies that we have knowledge of God-in-Himself. The doctrine of an ontological Trinity would require such knowledge. Kraft approves the conception of God "as one in form but three in function or activity," although he disavows any "blanket" endorsement of modalism. Kraft affirms that the notion of one God playing three parts or roles is an interpretation "within the scripturally allowed range."[65] This emphasis has prompted some of Kraft's former students now on mission fields to suggest that Muslim conceptions of Allah are for Arabs a dynamic cultural equivalent of the Christian doctrine of

God. We are told that Christ functions in the Johannine prologue as "a human embodiment of God."[66] Elsewhere Kraft affirms that Christ became "a human being"[67] and that God has witnessed powerfully in and through human beings and supremely in and through *The* Human Being, Jesus Christ.[68]

On the one hand, Kraft insists that "contemporary revelation will never contradict scripturally recorded revelation";[69] on the other hand, he deplores any static view that later revelation cannot update and alter earlier revelation.[70] Indeed, he asserts that the revelation process today must take precedence over static models of revelation that "allow for 'no new truth' to be conveyed."[71]

To test contemporary revelations for legitimacy Kraft proposes their reference to the Bible as a "measure."[72] The companion notion of Scripture as a "tether," as Kraft expounds it, allows him to draw the line wherever he prefers against alternatives both on the right and left, but it imposes on other researchers no objective basis for maintaining the same agenda. The Bible is revelatory, says Kraft—that is, it carries the Word of God to us—only if we use it properly, that is, within the range of variation that God approves.[73] But where will we gain objective information about that range? How can we measure one internal response against another if there is no revelation without inner response and the teaching of the Bible is itself fallible and culture-skewed? Kraft insists that the Bible contains "a range of ideal, sub-ideal but acceptable, and unacceptable behavior and belief" and that its teaching lacks universal truth. What help can it then afford to measure "dynamically equivalent" contemporary revelation if special revelation occurs today and past revelation and present revelation are both culture-skewed? Kraft writes: "God will not (we believe) contradict himself." This emphasis is commendable, but other theologians—including some of Kraft's theological colleagues at Fuller—reject propositional revelation for dynamic revelation and insist that God is no respector of logical consistency. And if God puts a premium on logical consistency, should not professors of missiology? The more one examines Kraft's proposals the more one has the uneasy feeling that he is playing a shell game with us.

Kraft proposes a "conceptual translation" of theological and biblical content so that their communication will "carry the proper meaning and impact."[74] He is critical of "the conservative mentality" that disallows a search for "new meanings."[75] Insofar as theologians or exegetes are prone to dignify their own interpretations as a "theology of glory," this has its point. But if meaning is culture-relative, not even "new meanings" could escape the deficiencies of the old.

Kraft asks for a redefinition of heresy that does not preclude new approaches to truth and is not bound by the orthodoxy of the past.[76] But if truth is fluid and culture-relative, on what basis would such theological innovation be welcomed as "better" or "truer"? Can Kraft's desire to rescue the deity from a perception that God is "behind the times" lead on Kraft's premises to anything other than to a perpetual salvage operation that relativizes the absolute? Objective meaning is not subject to adolescence or to senility, and "growing" meaning should not be dwarfed into Kraft's formulations. Kraft tells us that "perhaps . . . linguistic forms such as words are . . . important only insofar as their function is important." But the structure of his argument presumes that Kraft's own principles hold an abiding cognitive or doctrinal import that is normatively decisive for the character of missiology. If there is no truly objective meaning, Kraft should desist from communication that implies that his own culture-skewed notions miraculously escape the defects he attributes universally to the views of all others.

In the absence of meaning and truth objective to all cultures it is futile for Kraft to write of Christians "maturing . . . into a much more ideal understanding" that "may eventually approach . . . the supracultural ideal that lies outside culture."[77] For, on his approach, our fallible culture-skewed understanding precludes knowing the supraculture and hence knowledge that we are approximating it. The same factors preclude Kraft's judgment that "God has made himself successively better known to his people."[78]

Kraft recognizes that the biblical messages and meanings, like all communication, require an informational context for their intelligibility. In line with champions of the new hermeneutic, he insists that the relation between message and meaning is dynamic rather than static.[79] He rejects the evangelical view that the interpreter is to ferret out a textually given meaning for all readers of the Bible; instead, all that the text teaches is viewed as context. The meaning differs for different cultures.[80] "No cultural symbols have exactly the same meanings in any two cultures."[81] Kraft apparently does not intend to say that his own use of cultural symbols invalidates or precludes an understanding of his meaning; the meanings Kraft forges at Fuller Seminary presumably are reduction-resistant.

Kraft concedes that the meaning of some biblical propositional statements, e.g., "God is love," is culturally transferable "with most (never all) of its meaning intact."[82] But if the original recipient culturally skewed the revelation and the hearer and translator also culturally skewed it, an almost "intact" meaning would be little short of a miracle. Kraft does not exempt prophets and apostles (or Jesus?) when he says that God accepts "understandings of himself and of his truth" that involve divergent meanings. "Even through inspired Scripture, therefore, it is highly unlikely that any . . . people will perceive exactly the same meaning from any given portion."[83] Kraft speaks naively of properly understanding "the meaning of the message . . . for its time or for ours"[84] and postulates "a range of allowable variation as measured by the biblical yardstick—reasonably equivalent to the original intent but not corresponding exactly."[85] But if no universally valid meaning inheres in the biblical text or in our understanding of it, it is futile to speak of normative meaning and of restricted variation, since the text necessarily means different things in different cultures.

In some mediating circles today the empirically formulated claims of secular scholars are elevated to the status of general divine revelation. Kraft is critical of conservative Christian claims that secular anthropologists, sociologists, psychologists, and communications specialists can formulate no valid conclusions on the basis of a naturalistic worldview.[86] "Traditional Christian understandings of the sinfulness of human beings are felt to be incompatible with perspectives that assume that human beings are essentially good,"[87] he notes. Is Kraft telling us that the universal sinfulness of man is noetically irrelevant? Kraft affirms that human beings "are pervasively infected by sin."[88] "As far as anthropology can tell," he remarks, there has never been a human being "not totally immersed in and pervasively affected by some culture."[89] But these several affirmations involve notably different nuances. Evangelical theology holds that even after the Fall man retains noetic competence for revelatory knowledge of the nature and will of the self-revealing God and that man's revolt against objective knowledge of God is basically volitional. Kraft, on the other hand, denies that human beings, even on the basis of creation and even when gifted with special revelation, have such epistemic competence; and he bases this disavowal of objective knowledge of God as He is in Himself on man's supposed universal cultural entrapment. Kraft's treatment even of Jesus Christ in this context is highly ambiguous.

What then is absolute? What is the relation between revelation and the linguistic statements of Scripture? What is the nature of the "revealed truth" that Christianity is to communicate to all mankind? Kraft professes to hold strongly to "biblical authority and inspiration" while attributing valuable insight to those who reject a high view of Scripture. By this he means not that the Bible is revelatory but rather that it is "both inspired by God and an accurate *record of the Spirit-guided perceptions of human beings* who are committed to God."[90] Inspiration therefore does not guarantee the truth of the biblical teaching. Kraft insists that in addition to its historico-cultural specificity, the biblical content "has a cross-cultural relevance that the original cultural forms do not have," but that this must also be expressed "in the linguistic and cultural forms" of the intended receivers.[91]

Kraft proposes to take the Bible "seriously" in a nonstatic, dynamic, and adaptive role. He champions adventuresome experimentation in contrast to evangelical interest in perpetuating orthodox doctrinal formulations and lifestyles.[92] Kraft thinks it a culturally prejudiced Western view when evangelicals regard "the faith once for all delivered" (Jude 3) as a system of doctrine rather than a relationship to God.[93] But a relationship can hardly be delivered once for all; propositional truths can be. The reference that now we see only a "dim image in a poor mirror" (1 Cor. 13:12 TEV) Kraft takes to mean that even biblically informed Christians have no universally valid information about God.

Kraft deplores "the excessive informationalizing of revelation."[94] In expounding the principles of biblical communication he routinely assumes that the intention of the inspired writers was not to convey objectively valid truths.[95] Hence transmission of their content is concerned not with meanings but with messages; meanings are to be supplied by the receptor.[96]

Kraft echoes the neo-orthodox cliche that "truth is not informational but personal" and clothes this dogma with the authority of Jesus.[97] That biblical truth is to be "done" and has as its ultimate goal the salvation of sinners, is made a basis for minimizing the fact that revelation has for its proximate end the divine communication of universally sharable truths. Consequently Kraft deplores "static" revelation and promotes dynamic revelation and dynamic concepts. He contends that "eternal truths" (presumably, even Christ's death for sinners—a proposition revealed in time yet eternally true) are inappropriate until we personally appropriate them.[98] Divine revelation, he tells us, "is more properly defined as . . . *stimulus to action*, than as the mere transmission of information."[99] Kraft not infrequently blurs the qualifier *mere;* even where he retains it, he devalues the cognitive importance of divine disclosure.

Kraft asserts that "the totality of the Bible (forms as well as meanings) is inspired," but while it is not full of errors no track of its content is wholly free from error.[100] Kraft joins nonevangelical critics in the canard that inerrancy would require dictation. He approvingly quotes the Roman Catholic scholar Bruce Vawter in an attack on the fixity and finality of biblical truth[101] and insists on a nonevangelical distinction between the words and the Word of God. Scripture is "the product of the Spirit-led recordings and canonization of divine-human interactions."[102] God inspired many humans in the same way, leading some to record these divine-human interactions. The Spirit continues such interaction with readers and hearers of their writings.[103]

Kraft veers toward a "functional understanding of the nature of Scripture."[104] He rejects any "objective" inscripturation of past revelation.[105] He calls the Bible "revelation" only in a "potential sense"[106] and prefers actually not to call it revelation without personal response.[107] He ascribes the obtuseness of the Pharisees to their view that the Old Testament was revelation rather than to their rejection of its revelation (cf. Jesus' warning, "If they hear not Moses and the prophets . . .").

Kraft has no tolerance for "closed evangelicals and fundamentalists" who insist on a particular theory of inspiration or atonement, quibble over biblical criticism, or insist on a specific metaphysical philosophy.[108] He pleads (as we have noted) the cause of theological experimentation against closed conservatism. But he too is closed to certain traditional evangelical options. He assures readers of the orthodoxy of his views and asks them to overlook whatever they consider heretical. Kraft thus rejects traditional evangelical theology as ethnocentric, eviscerates evangelical theism of some of its historical commitments, and commends his reductionistic view as if it were exempt from such limitations.

Kraft's major aim is to facilitate the use of "dynamic" or "functional" equivalence in Bible translation.[109] Kraft rightly argues that formal-correspondence translation may obscure the sense and that the Bible is to be translated into the idiom of the people. He questions whether most if not all earlier translations adequately convey God's message.[110] He criticizes the RSV, ASV, KJV, NASV, and largely NIV also for too limited a break with formal correspondency translation[111] and promotes dynamic equivalence transculturation into the receptor's cultural setting.[112] Transculturation aims "to represent the meanings" or past events as if they were clothed in contemporary events.[113] But if the meaning of the original is culture-imbedded, can we speak of conveying an objective or normative meaning? Would not one culture-imbedded meaning be as valid or relative as another, since none is objectively normative?

As Kraft sees it, theology is an attempt to understand God based on these culture-imbedded meanings.[114] Kraft implies that different languages reflect and require different worldviews,[115] whereas the same language can obviously be used to present divergent worldviews. Theology is not for Kraft ideally a systematizing of scripturally revealed truths but a human effort not to be confused with "the changeless, absolute truth that remains in the mind of God" and is "beyond our reach."[116] Kraft insists that most "heresies" are really cultural adaptations that we ought not to fear[117] and that theological truth must be perpetually "recreated like a dynamic-equivalence translation of transculturation."[118] If culture and subculture pervasively affect the inspired prophets' and apostles' understanding of God, and additionally affect the theologians' communication of that message, and the receptors' perception of that communication also,[119] one would think that theology would be automatically recreated without need of creative effort. But, says Kraft, theology written in one culture must be aggressively transculturated into the concepts and language framework of another if it is to be of value and must be deprovincialized also into the concepts and language of different academic disciplines in the same culture.[120]

Now the relevant comment here is not that Augustine, Calvin, or any other theologian has bequeathed to us the unadulterated truth of God. But Judeo-Christian theology historically has claimed for the inspired biblical prophets and apostles, and especially for Jesus Christ, a role in the conveyance of objective divine truths that Kraft obscures. And if cultural differences require the radical treatment that Kraft demands for their proper intelligibility in paradisciplinary and paracultural circles, it is amazing that we find so readily understandable what Kraft writes as an anthropologist, communicator, or missionary who professes to have jumped outside a Western mold. Our problem is usually not with the meaning of what Kraft says but with his departures from the truth of historic evangelical theology in respect to the doctrines of revelation, inspiration, the Trinity, and the evidently marginal role he gives to the deity and the bodily resurrection of Jesus Christ in communicating the Christian message.

The core of concern over Kraft's notion of "dynamic equivalence" translation is the matter of "paradigm shifting" through which Kraft proposes to defend the validity of divergent interpretations in different cultural contexts; and this in view of behavioral science perspectives: "*Valid* theologizing may be done on the basis of a variety of cultural, subcultural and disciplinary models."[121] The questions that here arise are to what extent, if any, we may consider divergent representations to be true and on what basis any of them is in certain identifiable respects to be considered normatively true for all cultures and disciplines. Or is the discussion of universally valid meaning and shared truths wholly extraneous to authentic theologizing? And if so, why is Kraft then wasting his time by telling us all how the game must everywhere be played?

Kraft proposes to treat the biblical revelation as a conceptual model or theory or worldview to account for the data of life and experience, and in this connection he notes the role of explanatory models in science. By their perpetual revision of inferences based on limited data empirical scientists have been forced to declare that their theoretical statements are not literally true statements about the real world. But is this a conclusive reason to compress into this same scientific pattern of postulation and tentativeness claims about

God grounded in divine self-revelation? Anyone who thinks that the biblical writers offer only a paradigmatic worldview or model of reality projected as by natural or behavioral scientists on the basis of human perception has yet to learn the most elemental distinction between divine revelation and human reasoning. Kraft's emphatic insistence that "we see reality *not as it is but always from inside our heads*"[122] implies that we would have to be headless or mindless to know reality as it truly is. If, as Kraft insists, human description of "the ordered reality (out there)" involves not only an internal psychological ordering based on assumptions, as indeed it does, but also and always involves individual distortion of perceived reality—even by divinely inspired writers—then the outcome can only be skepticism and with it the loss of a universal missionary imperative to communicate the teaching of Jesus and other biblical truths. Kraft emerges in this context, moreover, either as a transcendent divine voice that escapes these human limitations and that informs us what is objectively and everywhere the case, or he is naively self-deceived. If Kraft can tell us what is objectively the case, and in 404 small-type pages at that, surely the inspired prophets and apostles can, and not least of all the self-revealing God.

We have yet to find evidence that Kraft's synthesis achieves his goal of more effectively "communicating the Christian message in a multi-cultural world."[123] Instead of providing a cure-all for the problems of Christian proclamation, the universal culture-skewing of divine revelation asserted by behavioral scientists ventures to resolve the besetting problems of missions by liquidating the distinctive claims of Judeo-Christian religion.

What Kraft's exposition blurs is the singular uniqueness of God's self-revelation to Israel, the universal significance of the law in the Old and New Testaments, the irreducible and incomparable incarnation of God in Jesus Christ, and other Judeo-Christian distinctives as well—distinctives that the search for conceptual cultural equivalents can only obscure. The normativity of biblical theology cannot survive alongside the normativity of humanistic anthropology. To exaggerate the role of the behavioral sciences, as Kraft does, constitutes a disservice to both biblical theology and anthropology. For it clouds not only the nature of biblical revelation but also the very proper service that anthropological science can render the Christian missionary community.

ENDNOTES

Chapter 1

1. These scholars include Timothy Smith (John Wesley), Donald Dayton (Bengel and the Pietists), Mark Noll and George Marsden (nineteenth century Presbyterians), Robert Webber (church fathers). Mark Noll and Nathan Hatch are interested in how people have treated the Bible, not solely with what they said they believed about it. This functional approach is very important for any study of the role of biblical authority in a church or culture. An individual or group may profess a high view of biblical authority without living under the dictates of Holy Writ. They may take their ethics and political theory from sources other than Holy Writ while describing themselves as "Bible believers." However, the conceptual problems involved in the functional approach are complex. At what point do the actions of an individual or group either disprove or prove the sincerity of formal belief statements? Is it not possible that an individual or group may hold a certain belief without maintaining it consistently in practice? The vast literature on "secularization" should be considered when a historian uses a functional approach to these questions (see the works of Michel Vovelle, David Martin, and others).

2. Protestant apologists frequently argued that they were reestablishing orthodoxy because Roman Catholics had innovated in doctrine and practice, particularly from the eighth and ninth centuries on. The Reformers did not see themselves as genuine innovators but as the restorers of biblical Christianity.

3. How to establish the criteria by which these kinds of judgments could be made became a focal point of controversy between Roman Catholics and Protestants in the sixteenth and seventeenth centuries. Roman Catholics claimed that they followed church tradition as amplified by the Vincentian canon (A.D. 434): "Now in the Catholic Church itself we take the greatest care to hold that which has been believed everywhere, always and by all." Protestants stressed their use of the analogy of faith and their reliance upon the Holy Spirit, regenerated reason, and the witness of the church.

4. See, for example, the debate between the Reformed pastors of France and Roman Catholic apologists concerning the Eucharist (Remi Snoeks, *L'argument de tradition dans la controverse eucharistique entre catholiques et réformés français au XVIII siècle* [Louvain: Editions J. Duculot, 1951]; Georges Tavard, *La tradition au XVIIIë siècle en France et en Angleterre* [Paris: Cerf, 1969]).

5. Consult Wayne Grudem's essay on the Bible's claims about its own authority in *Scripture and Truth* (ed. D. A. Carson and John D. Woodbridge; Grand Rapids: Zondervan, 1981). See also Paul Feinberg, "The Meaning of Inerrancy," in *Inerrancy* (ed. Norman Geisler; Grand Rapids: Zondervan, 1979), 267–304.

6. The authors write: "We will be grateful for every contribution to our understanding of this extensive and essential topic" (xii).

7. Jacques Le Brun, "Das Entstehen der historischen Kritik im Bereich der

178

religiösen Wissenschaften im 17. Jahrhundert," *Trierer theologische Zeitschrift* 89 (1980): 100–17. Professor Le Brun and the present author have edited a lost manuscript of the biblical critic, Richard Simon (1638–1712): *Additions aux "Recherches curieuses sur la diversité des Langues et Religions" d'Edward Brerewood* (Amsterdam: Quadratures, 1981).

8. For example, the French researcher, François La Planche, is writing a *doctorat d'état* on the attitudes of French Reformed theologians toward Scripture during the first half of the seventeenth century.

9. Scholars have on occasion taken pivotal passages out of their contexts. These statements lose their integrity when disassociated from the cultural givens of a day and the intellectual mindset of their authors. Some writers have made too facile comparisons in attempting to demonstrate the similarities or dissimilarities of belief between individuals from different centuries and cultures.

10. H. D. McDonald's *Ideas of Revelation: An Historical Study A.D. 1700 to A.D. 1860* (London: Macmillan, 1959) represents a competent analysis by an evangelical scholar.

11. Rogers and McKim's discussion of this point throws them into an epistemological quandary. If the Hebrew writers of the O.T. did not function with the laws of logic in some sense, then it is highly doubtful that St. Augustine, the Reformers, or contemporary Christians could have understood their writings with any accuracy. For helpful comments about the common attitudes toward "truth" shared by the Hebrews and the Greeks, see Anthony C. Thiselton, *The Two Horizons: New Testament Horizons and Philosophical Descriptions* (Grand Rapids: Eerdmans, 1980), 411–15. See also Roger Nicole's essay, "The Truth of Scripture," in *Scripture and Truth*.

12. Introduction, xvii–xxiii.

13. Since the pioneering studies of Arnold van Gennep, Gabriel Le Bras, and others, historians of religion have tended to speak of orthodoxies rather than orthodoxy. They want to describe accurately a faith's history and beliefs rather than argue about the ontological truthfulness of the belief system itself. Because Rogers and McKim wish to defend a theological stance through historical argumentation, their volume finds its place in the centuries-old heritage of historical apologetics.

14. To describe a history of a doctrine is a legitimate enterprise. How to do so in a methodologically responsible fashion remains a difficult problem for church historians. The present writer has also written in a way which some might deem apologetic in intent: John Woodbridge, Mark Noll, Nathan Hatch, *The Gospel in America* (Grand Rapids: Zondervan, 1979), 99–134.

15. Why does one thinker represent the "church's position" whereas another does not? The criteria by which a historian designates his representatives for any doctrinal development should be carefully explicated. Rogers and McKim fail to establish carefully these criteria and thereby leave themselves open to the charge of selecting arbitrarily their representatives and data. Even when the authors treat Reformed "traditions," they are quite arbitrary in their selection procedure. For example, Dutch and French Reformed Christians receive relatively little notice compared to the lavish commentary upon the English Puritans, the American Princetonians, and the later Berkouwer.

16. Paul Dibon, *La philosophie néerlandaise au siècle d'or* (Paris: Elsevier, 1954), 1:258.

17. Professor Armstrong writes: ". . . like Puritanism, Protestant scholasticism is more a spirit, an attitude of life, than a list of beliefs. For this reason it practically defies precise definition" (*Calvinism and The Amyraut Heresy: Protestant*

Scholasticism and Humanism [Madison: The University of Wisconsin Press, 1969], 32). Armstrong does present an important set of characteristics by which he defines scholasticism (32).

18. See Dominique Bourel's entertaining though acerbic essay on this form of deficient historical writing: "Orthodoxie, piétisme, Aufklärung," *Dix-huitième siècle* 10 (1978): 27–32. Or consult the entire 1978 edition of the *Dix-huitième siècle* dedicated to the question, "Qu'est-ce que les lumières" where the problem of defining the "Enlightenment" is evoked. The historiography concerning the definition of the Renaissance is equally abundant and complex.

19. For example, if a thinker says that the Bible is not a scientific textbook, Rogers and McKim assume that he or she does not believe that the Scriptures' incidental teaching about the external world is inerrant. In point of fact many Christians ranging from St. Augustine to Charles Hodge denied that the Bible was a scientific textbook but nonetheless affirmed the complete infallibility of Holy Writ.

20. Some individuals, however, may advocate views which are logically incompatible with each other. Human beings do not always sort out their own thought with care.

21. J. W. Montgomery rightfully labels this the "Platonic fallacy": "In the Western tradition, the metaphysical insistence that man must err always and everywhere has its source in Platonic idealism: the realm of forms or ideas or ideals is transcendent and can be represented only inadequately and fallibly on earth. . . . The center and theme of Christian revelation is that the perfect does come to earth: perfect God becomes perfect Man, with no loss of Godhead. But the pagan Platonist—and the naive Christian who has absorbed Platonic categories without realizing it—will not permit unqualified perfection to come to earth even when God himself is responsible for it, as He is in the production of inerrant Scripture" (J. W. Montgomery, ed., *God's Inerrant Word: An International Symposium on the Trustworthiness of Scripture* [Minneapolis: Bethany Fellowship, 1974], 34). See also John Frame, "God and Biblical Language: Transcendence and Immanence," *God's Inerrant Word*, 159–77.

22. For a good illustration of what the social history of ideas might represent, see Robert Darnton, "Reading, Writing, and Publishing in Eighteenth-Century France: A Case Study in the Sociology of Literature," *Historical Studies Today* (ed. Felix Gilbert and Stephen Graubard; New York: W. W. Norton Company, 1972), 238–80. The *Annales School* literature does not figure in their bibliography. Consult Jacques Le Goff and Pierre Nora, *Faire de l'histoire: Nouvelles approaches* (Paris: Gallimard, 1974).

23. See the classic work by Emmanuel Le Roy Ladurie, *Montaillou: The Promised Land of Error* (New York: George Braziller, 1978). Consult also Timothy Tackett, *Priest & Parish in Eighteenth Century France* (Princeton: Princeton University Press, 1977); John Woodbridge, "L'influence des philosophes français sur les pasteurs réformés du Languedoc pendant la deuxième moitiè du dix-huitième siècle" (Doctorat de Troisième Cycle; University of Toulouse, 1969); Jean Delumeau, *Le catholicisme entre Luther et Voltaire* (Paris: Presses Universitaires de France, 1971), 9–30 (a bibliography). For the United States, see, for example: Jackson Carroll, Douglas Johnson, Martin Marty, *Religion in America 1950 to the Present* (New York: Harper and Row, 1979); Donald Matthews, *Religion in the Old South* (Chicago: The University of Chicago Press, 1977).

24. Consult Robert Mandrou, *De la culture populaire aux 17ë et 18ë siècle: La Bibliothèque bleue de Troyes* (Paris: Stock, 1975); Geneviève Bollème, *Les*

Almanachs populaires aux XVIIë et XVIIIë siècles: Essai d'histoire sociale (Paris: Mouton, 1969); Michel Vovelle, *Piété baroque et déchristianisation en Provence au XVIIIë siècle* (Paris: Plon, 1973); Natalie Davis, *Society and Culture in Early Modern France* (Stanford: Stanford University Press, 1975).

25. See: Robert Darnton, *The Business of Enlightenment: A Publishing History of the Encyclopedie* (Cambridge, Mass.: Harvard University Press, 1979); Henri-Jean Martin, *Livre pouvoirs et société à Paris au XVIIë siècle* (1598–1701) (2 vols.; Geneve: Droz, 1969); Raymond Birn, "Livre et société after ten years; formation of a discipline," *Studies in Voltaire and the Eighteenth Century* CLI–CLV (1976), 287–312; F. Furet, ed., *Livre et société dans la France du XVIIIë siècle* (2 vols.; Paris: Mouton, 1970); Paul Korshin, ed., *The Widening Circle* . . . (Philadelphia: University of Pennsylvania Press, 1976); J. Woodbridge, "Censure royale et censure épiscopale: Le conflit de 1702," *Dix-huitième siècle* 8 (1976): 335–55; idem, "The Parisian Book Trade in the Early Enlightenment: An Update on the Prosper Marchand Project," *Studies in Voltaire and the Eighteenth Century* (a forthcoming article); Horst Meyer and Werner Arnold, ed., "Bibliographie," *Wolfenbütteler Notizen zur Buchgeschichte* 5 (1980): 162–92; Daniel Roche, *Le siècle des lumières en province Académies et académiciens provinciaux, 1680–1789* (2 vols.; Paris: Mouton, 1978); Elizabeth Eisenstein, *The Printing Press as an Agent of Change* (New York: Cambridge University Press, 1980).

26. A summary book concerning methodological pitfalls in doing good history is David Fischer's *Historians' Fallacies: Toward a Logic of Historical Thought* (New York: Harper and Row, 1970).

27. Stephen Neill writes: "Nothing is more notable than the anonymity of the early missionaries . . ." (*Christian Missions* [Grand Rapids: Eerdmans, 1965], 24).

28. A reading of J. N. D. Kelly's *Early Christian Doctrines* (New York: Harper and Row, 1960) takes one into the raging swirl of these disputes. See also the standard studies by Bertold Altaner, Johanes Quasten, Jean Danielou, and others.

29. On the church fathers' attitudes toward Scripture, see Geoffrey Bromiley's essay on the subject in *Scripture and Truth*. Bromiley writes: "If the Fathers did not give any particular emphasis to the term 'inerrancy,' they undoubtedly expressed the content denoted by the word." See also Edwin Yamauchi, "Inerrancy and the Ante-Nicene Fathers" in a publication of the International Council on Biblical Inerrancy.

30. Bruce Vawter, *Biblical Inspiration* (Philadelphia: Westminster, 1972), 132–33. Vawter himself is not a proponent of biblical inerrancy.

31. Cited in Cyril Richardson, ed., *Early Christian Fathers* (New York: Macmillan, 1970), 64.

32. Cited in Alexander Roberts, ed., *The Ante-Nicene Fathers . . . : The Apostolic Fathers-Justin Martyr-Irenaeus* (Grand Rapids: Eerdmans, 1973), 1:230.

33. Cited in John Walvoord, ed., *Inspiration and Interpretation* (Grand Rapids: Eerdmans, 1957), 20.

34. See, for example, Cardinal Augustinus Bea, *De Inspiratione et Inerrantia Sacrae Scripturae* (Rome: Pontificum Institutum Biblicum, 1954); Sebastianus Tromp, *De Sacrae Scripturae Inspiratione* (Rome: Apud Aedes Universitatis Gregorianae, 1953).

35. The comments of Professor Wells are found in a review of Rogers and McKim's book in *The Westminster Theological Journal* 43 (fall 1980): 152–55.

36. Rogers and McKim refer to Vawter's study on 51, n. 31. They also mention in passing works by Tholuck and Gogler.

37. See this review, n. 21. Consult also J. I. Packer, "The Adequacy of Human Language," *Inerrancy*, 197–226.
38. Origen, "Origen Against Celsus," *The Ante-Nicene Fathers* 4:395–669.
39. Augustine, *Letters* 28.3.
40. Ibid. 28.5. Augustine adds to this statement: "from considerations of duty; unless, perchance, you purpose to furnish us with certain rules by which we may know when a falsehood might or might not become a duty."
41. *Letters* 82.3. Augustine continues: "And if in these writings I am perplexed by *anything* [italics mine] which appears to me opposed to truth, I do not hesitate to suppose that either the MS is faulty, or the translator has not caught the meaning of what was said, or I myself have failed to understand it. . . . I do not need to say that I do not suppose you [Jerome] to wish your books to be read like those of prophets or of apostles, concerning which it would be wrong to doubt that they are free from error."
42. *De civitate Dei* 21.6.1. See also this chapter, n. 260.
43. A. D. R. Polman, *Word of God According to St. Augustine* (Grand Rapids: Eerdmans, 1961), 66. See also Charles J. Costello, *St. Augustine's Doctrine on the Inspiration and Canonicity of Scripture* (Washington: Catholic University of America, 1930).
44. Ibid., 56.
45. St. Augustine, in fact, did not allow for such inadvertent "errors" as Bruce Vawter (*Biblical Inspiration,* 133) points out: "Even his *Gen. ad. litt.*, which is often, and rightly, held up as a patristic example of a felt need to adjust scriptural interpretation to some of the facts of human experience, is for the most part an exercise in concordism, premised on the assumption of a sacred text that must have been infallible in every respect. 'The evangelists could be guilty of no kind of falsehood, whether it was of the type designed intentionally to deceive or was simply the result of forgetfulness' (*Cons. evang.* 2.12.29, PL 34:1091)." Or Augustine declares: "At the same time, as I have said already, it is to the canonical Scriptures alone that I am bound to yield such implicit subjection as to follow their teaching without admitting the slightest suspicion that in them any mistake or any statement intended to mislead would find a place" (*Letters* 22).
46. Cited in Polman, *Word of God*, 59–60.
47. See Rogers and McKim's references to Polman, 64, n. 121. For Polman's introductory commentary, see *The Word of God,* 61.
48. Writes Polman on the science matter: "True, the Bible does not describe the Creation in detail, but merely tells us what the Holy Ghost in the Biblical author saw needful to report [*De Genesi ad litteram* 5.23]. What the Scriptures say on this subject is completely reliable, and even when they tell us that a single source watered the whole earth we have no reason for disbelief. . . . When the Bible tells us that there were waters above the firmament, waters there must have been. In any case, the authority of the Scriptures surpasses the capacity of all our reason [*De Genesi ad litteram*, 2.9]. This is equally true of the purely historical accounts" (*The Word of God*, 52).
49. Ibid., 60.
50. Rogers and McKim, *Authority and Interpretation*, 65 n. 136.
51. Vawter, *Biblical Inspiration,* 38–39.
52. Hans Küng, *Infallible? An Enquiry* (London: Collins, 1972), 173–74; see Robert Preus's discussion of the oracle theme on Augustine in *Inerrancy*, 478 n. 17.
53. H. Sasse, "Sacra Scriptura—Bemerkungen zur Inspirationslehre Augustins,"

Festschrift Franz Dornsieff (Leipzig: VEB Bibliographisches Institut, 1953), 262–73.

54. Wrote Wycliffe: "whanne Christ seip in pe Gospel pat bope hevene and erpe shulen passe, but His wordis shulen not passe, He undirstandip bi His woordis His wit. And pus Goddis wit is Hooly Writ, pat my on no maner be fals." (Hebert Wirin, ed., *Wyclif—Select English Sermons* [London: Oxford University Press, 1929], 19). In this statement p=th. James O'Connor alerted the author to the use made by Rogers and McKim of the Mallard article.

55. Kenneth Davis, a leading Anabaptist scholar and the author of *Anabaptism and Asceticism: A Study of Intellectual Origins* (Scottdale, Penn.: Herald Press, 1974) has indicated that many of the early Anabaptists believed in complete biblical infallibility (communications with J. Woodbridge, spring 1980).

56. On this issue, consult Rupert E. Davies, *The Problem of Authority in the Continental Reformers* (Westport, Conn.: Hyperion Press, 1976 [reprint of 1946 edition]).

57. Roman Catholics claimed that representatives of the church had the sole right to interpret Scripture. Luther reacted strongly against this notion.

58. Cited in Ernst F. Winter, ed., *Erasmus—Luther Discourse on Free Will* (New York: Frederick Ungar Publishing Co., 1966), 59.

59. Ibid., 59–60. Earlier Erasmus declared: "I know, when investigating truth, there is no harm in adding to the diligence of one's predecessors. I admit that it is right that the sole authority of Holy Scriptures surpasses the voices of all mortals. But we are not involved in a controversy regarding Scripture. The same Scripture is being loved and revered by both parties. Our battle concerns the sense of Scripture" (ibid., 15).

60. Jacques Chomaret, "Les *Annotations* de Valla, celles d'Erasme et la grammaire," *Histoire de l'exégèse au XVIë siècle* (ed. Olivier Fatio and Pierre Fraenkel; Genève: Droz, 1978), 209–10. In a conflict with Spanish monks Erasmus claimed that he had proposed the limited biblical infallibility viewpoint "per fictionem." He claimed complete infallibility "in truth."

61. Cited in Robert Preus, "The View of the Bible Held by the Church: The Early Church Through Luther," *Inerrancy* 380 (W^2 9.356). Preus relies heavily upon Reu and Walther in his discussion of Luther. His excellent article should be studied with care.

62. Cited in Paul Althaus, *The Theology of Martin Luther* (Philadelphia: Fortress Press, 1966), 6 n. 12 (*Weimar Ausgabe* [hereafter WA] 7:315).

63. Cited in Preus, "The View of the Bible. . . ," 380 (WA 54:158).

64. Ibid. (W^2 20.798).

65. Althaus, *The Theology of Martin Luther*, 6.

66. WA 40:2.52. Luther also wrote: "For if they believed they were God's words they would not call them poor, miserable words but would regard such words and tittles as greater than the whole world and would fear and tremble before them as before God Himself. For whoever despises a single word of God does not regard any as important" (from Luther's *Vom Abendmahl Christi*, cited in M. Reu, "Luther and the Scriptures," *The Springfielder* [1960], 32). Or he declared: "Not only the words but also the expressions used by the Holy Spirit and Scripture are divine" (WA 40:3.254).

67. *Luther's Works* 47:308.

68. Rogers and McKim, *The Authority and Interpretation of the Bible,* 77–79.

69. Ibid., 133 n. 112. Reinhold Seeberg, *The History of Doctrines* (Grand Rapids: Baker, 1978 [reprint]), 2:300.

70. M. Reu, *Luther and the Scriptures* (Columbus: Wartburg, 1944). This chapter

has been reprinted in *The Springfielder* (1960). Consult also Wilhelm Walther, *Das Erbe der Reformation* (Leipzig: Duchert, 1918).

71. Reu, *Luther and the Scriptures,* 41.

72. Writes Reu: "If Luther, indeed, has never directly admitted that an actual mistake is to be found in a Scripture passage, and if instead, when an incorrect historical allusion or a contradiction of another Scripture passage seems to be evident, he sought some expedient that might remove the difficulty and frequently in doing so ventured to propose dating hypotheses, he did not mean by his expressions, 'that is a matter of no importance,' or 'that does not affect the matter,' that it was a matter of indifference to him as to whether an actual error occurred or not. . . . In these statements Luther does not say that it is a matter of indifference to him whether they contain errors or not but only that his faith would not be endangered, if, in spite of his best effort, he would be unable to solve the apparent contradictions or *to prove the inconsequence of all skeptical questions.* He dismisses the matter if he cannot prove it conclusively, but his inability to do so neither commits him to the opinion that these passages really contain error, nor is his faith in salvation thereby imperiled" (ibid., 49–50).

73. Ibid., 58.

74. Brian Gerrish, whose authority Rogers and McKim also invoke, takes a different stance than Heick. He argues that Reu generally understood correctly Luther on infallibility. Gerrish does not believe that Seeberg's list of "critical opinions" demonstrates that Luther admitted the reality of "errors" in the original autographs: "Of the examples given by Seeberg one (the first) relates to textual or 'lower' criticism; three (nos. 4, 6, 8) relate to authorship; and four (nos. 5, 9, 10–11) to canonicity. Only three (nos. 2–3, 7) appear to relate to errors in the original text of the canonical writings, and there are some Luther-scholars (M. Reu, for example) who find it possible to maintain that even these three are inconclusive. . . . Certainly, Luther is extremely reluctant to admit error in Scripture, and on the whole I think that Reu has understood him correctly. It seems, in fact, that Luther never really questioned the medieval theory of inspiration, although he did provide a way of escape from it ("Biblical Authority and the Continental Reformation," *SJT* 10 [1957]: 345–46).

75. J. Theodore Mueller, "Luther and the Bible," *Inspiration & Interpretation,* ed. John Walvoord (Grand Rapids: Eerdmans, 1957), 87–114.

76. One can find a convenient listing of scholars who affirm that Calvin believed in either complete or limited biblical infallibility in J. S. K. Reid, *The Authority of Scripture: A Study of the Reformation and Post Reformation Understanding of the Bible* (New York: Harper & Brothers, n.d.), 55; see also H. Jackson Forstman, *Word and Spirit: Calvin's Doctrine of Biblical Authority* (Stanford: Stanford University Press, 1962), 1–6.

77. Ford Lewis Battles wrote the Foreword for Rogers and McKim's study. He translated Calvin's *Institutes* (McNeill edition) and wrote an important article on the concept of accommodation in Calvin: "God was Accommodating Himself to Human Capacity," *Int* 31 (1977): 19–38. John McNeill authored, among other essays, *The History and Character of Calvinism* (New York: Oxford University Press, 1967) and "The Significance of the Word of God for Calvin," *CH* 28 (1959): 131–46. T. H. L. Parker's *John Calvin* (Philadelphia: Westminster, 1977) is important for its dating of events in Calvin's life (New York: Harper and Row, 1963) and is one of the finest analyses of Calvin's thought save for the author's discussion of Calvin and biblical authority.

78. Scholars have argued strenuously about Calvin's view of the Holy Spirit's

interaction with external biblical evidences in confirming biblical authority. For a good discussion of this question, see Kenneth Kantzer, "John Calvin's Theory of the Knowledge of God and the Word of God" (Ph.D. dissertation, Harvard University, 1950), 427–62.

79. Gerrish, "Biblical Authority and the Continental Reformation," 354–55. Gerrish cites Warfield concerning the "original document" hypothesis.
80. Forstman, *Word and Spirit*, 65.
81. McNeill, "The Significance of the Word of God," 131–46.
82. Ibid., 140.
83. Kenneth Kantzer, "Calvin and the Holy Scriptures," *Inspiration and Interpretation*, 137–42.
84. Calvin, *Commentaries on the Epistle of Paul the Apostle to the Romans*, ed. John Owen (Edinburgh: Calvin Translation Society, 1849), 117.
85. Calvin, *Calvin's Commentaries: The Epistle of Paul the Apostle to the Hebrews*, ed. David Torrance (Grand Rapids: Eerdmans, 1963), 136. The John Owen translation of this passage limits the specific context for Calvin's remark: "But the Apostle followed the Greek translators when he said, 'A body hast thou prepared'; for in quoting these words the Apostles were not scrupulous . . . ," 227).
86. Calvin, *Commentary upon the Acts of the Apostles*, ed. Henry Beveridge (Edinburgh: Calvin Translation Society, 1844), 265. See also page 182 of the Torrance edition. As Robert Godfrey points out, the Latin edition does not indicate that the error should be attributed to Luke. Elsewhere Rogers and McKim declare: "In his commentary on Hebrews 2:7 Calvin acknowledged that some felt that the phrase, 'a little lower than the angels' was not used by the author of Hebrews in the same sense as David had meant it in Psalm 8" (109–10). The authors do not note Calvin's continuing comment on this passage: "David's meaning is this: . . . The apostle has no intention of overthrowing this meaning or of giving it a different turn; . . ." (Calvin, *Commentary on Hebrews* [Torrance edition], 23).
87. This discussion concerns Calvin's commentary upon Genesis 1:16.
88. Calvin, *Commentaries on the First Book of Moses Called Genesis*, ed. John King (Edinburgh: Calvin Translation Society, 1847), 1:87.
89. St. Augustine had taken the same stance earlier concerning the two great lights question (Gen. 1:16): "Similarly with the great lights mentioned in Genesis 1:16. We must certainly agree that, to our eyes, these two lights shine more brightly on the earth than all the others" (*De Genesi ad litteram* 2.34, as cited in Polman, *The Word of God*, 60).
90. Calvin commented upon Psalm 93:1 using what Edward Rosen called "pre-Copernican" categories (E. Rosen, "Calvin's Attitude Toward Copernicus," *Journal of the History of Ideas* 21 [1960]: 438–39).
91. Dowey, *The Knowledge of God in Calvin's Theology*, 91.
92. Davies, *The Problem of Authority in the Continental Reformers*, 16. Emile Doumergue's list of "errors" which Calvin allegedly admitted has played a similar role as Seeberg's list of "errors" which Luther allegedly admitted.
93. Martin Luther, *Luther's Works Table Talk*, ed. Theodore Tappert (Philadelphia: Fortress, 1967), 54.358–59.
94. Rogers and McKim, *The Authority and Interpretation of the Bible*, 166.
95. Nonetheless Luther scholars have consistently relied upon the collection of sayings by the Reformer.
96. Edward Rosen, "Calvin's Attitude toward Copernicus," *Journal of the History of Ideas* 21 (1960): 431–41; Rosen, "A Reply to Dr. Ratner: Calvin's Attitude

toward Copernicus," *Journal of the History of Ideas* 22 (1961): 386–88. Rosen argues that Calvin was a pre-Copernican but not an anti-Copernican. Ratner suggests that Calvin was an anti-Copernican. In the discussion of the relationship between the Bible and "science," Rogers and McKim do not carefully define what science means in a sixteenth-century context.

97. Stauffer has emerged as one of the leading Calvin scholars in the world due to his systematic study of Calvin's published and unpublished sermons.

98. Rosen seeks to sort out the origins of this comment in his "Calvin's Attitude Toward Copernicus," 433–38.

99. In his *Religion and the Rise of Modern Science* (Grand Rapids: Eerdmans, 1972), R. Hooykaas also argues that Calvin never referred to Copernicus (121). Hooykaas, a fine scholar, has surprisingly misunderstood Calvin's concept of accommodation and biblical infallibility. He assumes that Calvin may have admitted the possibility of a factual error in the original text (Acts 7:16) (120). This is a tenuous piece of evidence upon which to base an interpretation. We discussed Calvin's treatment of that passage earlier in this chapter (n. 86).

100. According to Rosen, Professor Ratner found it "incredible that Calvin 'never heard' of Copernicus . . ." (Rosen, "A Reply to Dr. Ratner . . . ," 386). We too find that idea a difficult supposition, even though Rosen defends it.

101. Cited in Dowey, *The Knowledge of God in Calvin's Theology*, 140, n. 443. See Calvin, *Commentaries on the First Book of Moses Called Genesis*, 1:61, where the Reformer takes note of Saint Augustine's warning to Christians not to "push their inquiries respecting duration, any more than respecting the infinity of space."

102. Cited in Hugh Kearney, *Science and Change 1500–1700* (New York: McGraw Hill, 1974), 104. On Brahe (1546–1601), see Kearney, 130–32.

103. Ibid., 104.

104. Cited in Edward Rosen, "Copernicus and Renaissance Astronomy," *Renaissance Men and Ideas*, ed. Robert Schwoebel (New York: St. Martin's Press, 1971), 100. In the introduction to his famous *New Astronomy,* Johannes Kepler (1571–1630) argued that Copernicus's views were compatible with scriptural teachings (ibid., 99–101).

105. See the Council of Trent, Decree concerning the Canonical Scriptures, April 8, 1544 (*The Creeds of Christendom*, ed. Philip Schaff [Grand Rapids: Baker, n.d. (reprint)], 2:79–83).

106. Vawter, *Biblical Inspirations*, 63–68.

107. Other matters such as Lessius's attitude toward the inspiration of canonical Scriptures were also hotly contested (ibid.).

108. Cited in Richard Popkin, *The History of Scepticism: From Erasmus to Descartes* (New York: Harper and Row, 1968), 69.

109. This is not to deny the impact of Aristotelianism upon the thought patterns of some Roman Catholic apologists. Consult Robert Richgels, "Scholasticism Meets Humanism in the Counter-Reformation: The Clash of Cultures in Robert Bellarmine's Use of Calvin in the Controversies," *Sixteenth Century Journal* 6 (1975): 53–66. In fact some of the Aristotelian apologists resorted to the pyrrhonical apologetic as well.

110. Popkin, *The History of Scepticism*, 69.

111. The Jesuit François Veron (1575–1625) borrowed this tactic from another Jesuit, Jean Gontery (1562–1616). Louis Bredvold notes that Veron's *machine de guerre de nouvelle invention* "had its effect upon thousands and caused his name to be remembered, with both reverence and execration, for a century"

(*The Intellectual Milieu of John Dryden* [Ann Arbor: The University of Michigan Press, 1966 (reprint of 1934 edition), 80]). See Bibliothèque nationale D 54285: François Veron, *Briefve mèthode pour reduire les devoyez et convaincre les ministres de la parole de Dieu réformée* (Lyon: Jean Lautret, 1618); B.N. 54291: Veron, *Combat contre tous les Ministres de France, Specialement contre le Sieur du Moulin, et ses colleagues de Charenton* (Paris: Cotteria, 1620).

112. Cited in Popkin, *The History of Scepticism*, 71.

113. B.N. D²6979: Jean Daillé, *La Foy fondée sur les saintes Escritures contre les nouveaux Methodistes* (Charenton: Samuel Perier, 1656 [2d ed.]), 2.

114. Even Amyraut stressed reason's rights in the context of debate with Roman Catholic fideists. Notes Armstrong: "Rex [Walter] and Sabean [David] have shown that *De l'élévation de la foy et l'abaissement de la raison en la créance des mystères de la religion* of 1640 is an attack on the fideism of the Roman Catholic theologians by means of an assertion of the reliability of reason" (Armstrong, *Calvinism and the Amyraut Heresy*, 273).

115. B.N. D 2204: Balle, *Catechisme et abbrege des controverses de nostre temps* (Paris: Pierre Chevalier, 1607), 19–20.

116. Rogers and McKim, *The Authority and Interpretation*, 464–65.

117. Ibid., 122.

118. Ibid., 465–66.

119. Ibid., 120–21. The authors do not cite chapter 20 in their presentation of the Scots Confession, 1560 (465). This chapter can be found in Schaff, ed., *The Creeds of Christendom*, 3:465–66.

120. Protestant writers of the sixteenth and seventeenth centuries identified "men" as those who could "err" (e.g., not tell the truth on all occasions), whereas they thought the writers of Scripture under the inspiration of the Holy Spirit were men who did not err.

121. B.N. D² 3400²: Pierre Viret, *Sur les conciles et les commandements* (Genève: n.d.), 19v.

122. Ibid., 21v.

123. B.N. D² 4274: Pierre du Moulin, *Du juge des controverses* (Sedan: Jean Iannon, 1630). On Du Moulin, see Lucien Rimbault, *Pierre du Moulin 1568–1658: Un Pasteur classique à l'âge classique* (Paris: Vrin, 1966). On Reformed apologetics in the seventeenth century, see Walter Rex, *Essays on Pierre Bayle and Relious Controversy* (The Hague: Martinus Nijhoff, 1965).

124. Wrote Du Moulin: "Our adversaries especially want to attack the original Hebrew and Greek texts which they have denigrated and have attempted to render suspect, as being corrupted. They have ordered that the Latin vulgar version, received in the Roman Church, be the only one held as authentic (*Du juge des controverses . . .*, 19)."

125. For Rogers and McKim's treatment of Pierre du Moulin, see pp. 163–64.

126. Philip Hughes, *The Theology of the English Reformers* (Grand Rapids: Eerdmans, 1966), 16.

127. Bellarmine reportedly kept a portrait of Whitaker, so much did he admire the man's learning and ingenuity (William Whitaker, *A Disputation on Holy Scripture . . . ,* ed. William Fitzgerald [Cambridge: Cambridge University Press, 1849], x). The Roman Catholic Richard Simon also thought Whitaker was one of the most influential Protestant disputants of the sixteenth century. Wrote Simon: "In addition, I have gone into more detail about the sentiments which Whitaker had of Bellarmine and other Jesuits, because that ought to serve as a key for understanding countless books which have been written thereafter by

188 / Biblical Authority and Conservative Perspectives

Protestants of France, England, and Germany against the books of Bellarmine"
(*Histoire critique du Vieux Testament* [Rotterdam: Renier Leers, 1685], 472).

128. Hughes, *The Theology of the English Reformers*, 16.
129. Whitaker, *A Disputation on Holy Scripture*, 660–61. Bishop John Jewel is just
as explicit in his *A Treatise of the Holy Scriptures* prepared eighteen years
earlier (1570): "Many think the apostle's speech is hardly true of the whole
scripture, that all and every part of the scripture is profitable. Much is spoken
of genealogies and pedigrees, of lepers, of sacrificing goats and oxen, etc.:
these seem to have little profit in them, but to be vain and idle. If they shew
vain in thine eyes, yet hath not the Lord set them down in vain. 'The words of
the Lord are pure words, as the silver tried in a furnace of earth fired seven
times.' There is no sentence, no clause, no word, no syllable, no letter, but it is
written for thy instruction: there is not one jot but it is sealed and signed with
the blood of the Lamb. Our imaginations are idle, our thoughts are vain: there
is no idleness, no vanity in the word of God. Those oxen and goats which were
sacrificed teach thee to kill and sacrifice the uncleanness and filthiness of thy
heart: . . . That leprosy teacheth thee to know the uncleanness and leprosy of
thy soul. Those genealogies and pedigrees lead us to the birth of our Saviour
Christ. So that the whole word of God is pure and holy; no word, no letter, no
syllable, no point or prick thereof, but is written and preserved for thy sake"
("A Treatise of the Holy Scriptures," in *The Works of John Jewel Bishop of
Salisbury* [Cambridge: The University Press, 1850], 4:1175). For a discussion
of Jewel, see W. M. Southgate, *John Jewel and the Problem of Doctrinal Authority* (Cambridge, Mass.: Harvard University Press, 1962). Jewel had a great
appreciation for the patristic writers' understanding of Scripture.
130. Whitaker, *A Disputation on Holy Scripture,* 294–95.
131. Ibid., 295. Whitaker saw himself as a follower of St. Augustine in his commitment to complete biblical infallibility (ibid., 36–37): "we cannot but wholly
disapprove the opinion of those who think that the sacred writers have, in some
places, fallen into mistakes. That some of the ancients were of this opinion appears from the testimony of Augustine, who maintains, in opposition to them,
'that the evangelists are free from all falsehood, both from that which proceeds
from deliberate deceit, and that which is the result of forgetfulness (*De Cons.
Ev. Lib.* II. c. 12.).'" Whitaker also denied that Stephen had erred in Acts 7:16.
The contention made by Rogers and McKim that Augustine believed in limited
biblical authority does not accord with Whitaker's analysis of that church father.
Moreover, Whitaker's commitment to complete biblical infallibility does not
accord with our authors' interpretation that the English Puritans held to limited
biblical infallibility. Although an Anglican, Whitaker was known for his Puritan
sympathies. And once again, his book on the Holy Scriptures was the classic
study by an Englishman in the last half of the sixteenth century.
132. See Jill Raitt, *The Eucharistic Theology of Theodore Beza* (Chambersburg,
Penn.: American Academy of Religion, 1972); Brian Armstrong, *Calvinism
and the Amyraut Heresy;* John Patrick Donnelly, "Italian Influences on the
Development of Calvinist Scholasticism," *Sixteenth Century Journal* 7 (1976):
81–101; idem, *Calvinism and Scholasticism in Vermigli's Doctrine of Man
and Grace* (Leiden: E. J. Brill, 1976).
133. For example, Roger Nicole's perspectives concerning Amyraut's thought are
quite different from those of Brian Armstrong. Consult Nicole, "Moyse
Amyraut (1596–1664) and the Controversy on Universal Grace" (Ph.D. dissertation, Harvard University, 1966). Armstrong attempts to fend off Nicole's
interpretation in *Calvinism and the Amyraut Heresy*, 286–87.

134. See Robert Godfrey's study of this question in *Scripture and Truth*. Professor Godfrey points out that Rogers and McKim misinterpret significantly the Synod of Dort, Francis Turretin, as well as Calvin and Luther.
135. Rogers and McKim, *The Authority and Interpretation of the Bible*, 147–65.
136. Ibid., 202–3.
137. Ibid., 218–23.
138. The authors attempt on several occasions to make what amounts to a monocausational nexus but never do so in a compelling way. See, for example, their discussion of John Owen, 222.
139. The authors are less than fair in their treatment of Theodore Beza: "Beza was a major influence at the Synod of La Rochelle in 1571. The Synod produced a new confession of faith that contained scholastic terminology appearing to contradict the Second Helvetic Confession on the subject of communion. Ramus was infuriated by the confession and wrote to Bullinger denouncing its innovations. The debate over these matters was suddenly cut short by the Massacre of St. Bartholomew's Day on August 24, 1572, in which Ramus and many other French Protestant leaders were killed. The opposition to Beza's scholasticizing was decimated . . ." (164). The authors do not tell us that in his own correspondence with Bullinger, Beza indicated that he was quite willing to give up the controverted word *substance*. Writes Robert Kingdon: "He [Beza] insists that its use was required only to undercut the wild doctrines of a group of Italian troublemakers in Lyon. He declares himself personally willing to forego use of the word, if the description of what takes place in the sacrament is expressed with the care which the Zurichers normally use" (Robert Kingdon, *Geneva and the Consolidation of the French Protestant Movement 1564–1572* [Madison: The University of Wisconsin Press, 1967], 104). Rogers and McKim's portrayal of the relationship between Ramus and Beza is misleading. Kingdon's book gives a competent analysis of the multiple issues which troubled that relationship.
140. Robert Preus, *The Theology of Post-Reformation Lutheranism: A Study of Theological Prolegomena* (St. Louis: Concordia Publishing House, 1970); idem, *The inspiration of Scripture: A Study of the Seventeenth-Century Lutheran Dogmaticians* (Edinburgh: Oliver & Boyd, 1957).
141. Writes Preus: "There is nothing new about the doctrine of the truthfulness of Scripture as taught by the Lutherans during the late period of orthodoxy. The same position was shared by Gerhard, Flacius, Luther, the Scholastics, and the early church fathers. What is new is a rather marked preoccupation with the doctrine and a greater emphasis on it by Calov, Scherzer, Dannhauer, Quenstedt, and others at about the middle of the 17th century" (ibid., 347; see n. 259, p. 397 for documentation concerning this contention).
142. This is a Thèse de Doctorates Sciences Religieuses. The thesis deserves publication. Robinson writes judiciously and with a mastery of his subject matter.
143. Rogers and McKim tend to emphasize John Owen's and Francis Turretin's commitment to biblical infallibility as if the two men espoused a new doctrine. Robinson's thesis reveals clearly that a belief in complete biblical infallibility was commonplace among even the first theologians he studies.
144. For example, as Sarah Hutton has pointed out, Platonism was compatible with the thought of the Dutch Arminians known for their rationalistic tendencies: "Its Dutch aspect suggests a connection between Arminianism and Platonism which fits well with Rosalie Colie's observations of the strong links between the Cambridge Platonists and the Dutch Remonstrants" ("Thomas Jackson, Oxford Platonist, and William Twisse, Aristotelian," *Journal of the History of*

Ideas 39 [1978]: 652). Consult Rosalie Colie, *Light and Enlightenment: A Study of the Cambridge Platonists and the Dutch Arminians* (Cambridge: Cambridge University Press, 1957).

145. Dibon notes that in the universities of the United Provinces toward 1620 there was "a strong tendency to the 'aristolelico-ramiste' conciliation" in logic (*La philosophie néerlandaise au siècle d'or...*, 1:258). On Ramism, see Walter Ong, *Ramus: Method, and the Decay of Dialogue; from the Art of Discourse to the Art of Reason* (Cambridge, Mass.: Harvard University Press, 1958).

146. Rogers, *Scripture in the Westminster Confession* (Grand Rapids: Eerdmans, 1967), 224.

147. Dibon writes concerning the Dutch theologians: "The historical Aristotle, to whom our professors maintain their fidelity and whom they do not fail to oppose to the fictional Aristotle of the scholastic tradition, remains, concerning the issue of 'lumiere naturelle,' the master thinker, but not an infallible master" (*La philosophie néerlandaise au siècle d'or*, 258).

148. Ibid., 259. Observes Dibon: "It is striking to see with what frequency there appears in the writings of philosophers as well as theologians friend Plato, friend Aristotle, but greater friend, truth."

149. Ibid., 248.

150. In his *Pia desideria* (1675) Jacob Spener criticizes sharply those German Lutheran theologians of his day who had become caught up in writing showy metaphysical tractates. Other theologians were more obviously concerned about the health of the Lutheran churches when they wrote.

151. Geoffrey Bromiley, *Historical Theology: An Introduction* (Grand Rapids: Eerdmans, 1978), 328. Bromiley specifically challenges (327–28) the kinds of criticism Rogers and McKim make concerning Lutheran and Reformed theologians.

152. Rogers and McKim, *The Authority and Interpretation of the Bible*, 198 n. 251. Cf. Geoffrey Bromiley, "The Church Doctrine of Inspiration," *Revelation and the Bible: Contemporary Evangelical Thought*, ed. Carl F. H. Henry (Grand Rapids: Baker, 1958), 213–14.

153. Grand Rapids: Eerdmans, 1967.

154. John Gerstner, "The Church's Doctrine of Biblical Inspiration," *The Foundation of Biblical Authority*, ed. James M. Boice (Grand Rapids: Zondervan, 1978), 42–45. Rogers and McKim, *The Authority and Interpretation of the Bible*, xxiv n. 11; 250 n. 32; 373 n. 95.

155. Consult B. B. Warfield, *The Westminster Assembly and Its Work* (New York: Oxford University Press, 1931). See also Charles Briggs, *Whither? A Theological Question for the Times* (New York: Charles Scribner's Sons, 1889); idem, *General Introduction to the Study of Holy Scripture* (Edinburgh: T & T Clark, 1899).

156. Rogers and McKim, *The Authority and Interpretation of the Bible*, 206–8. Rogers and McKim also rest their case upon the disjunction that because the Westminster divines (e.g., Rutherford) did not see the Scriptures as a rule in astronomy, they did not view the Scriptures as completely infallible. This does not follow, however. See n. 162, *infra*, where they acknowledge that Rutherford on occasion spoke the language of a dictation theory of inspiration.

157. Rogers, *Scripture in the Westminster Confession*, 90–95.

158. On the career of William Ames, see Keith Sprunger, *The Learned Doctor William Ames: Dutch Backgrounds of English and American Puritanism* (Urbana: University of Illinois Press, 1972) and the many books of Perry Miller.

159. William Ames, *The Marrow of Sacred Divinity*, ed. John Eusden (Boston: Pilgrim Press, 1968 [reprint]), 185–86.
160. Bromiley, *Historical Theology*, 327.
161. Ames, *The Marrow of Sacred Divinity,* 188–89. In paragraph 27, Ames distinguishes between interpreters and prophets. For him interpreters were translators/copyists who could err. Prophets were the biblical authors who did not err. Ames' distinction is found in earlier English writers of the sixteenth century.
162. In this light Rogers and McKim's attempts to evade some of the Westminster Divines' statements lose much of their force. Concerning Samuel Rutherford, they note: "Rutherford was, on occasion, driven to a theory of dictation. He contended, in controversy, that the biblical writers, 'in writing every jot, tittle or word of Scripture, they were immediately inspired as touching the matter, words, phrases, expression, order, method, majesty, stile and all: so I think they were but Organs, the mouth, pen and Amanuenses; God as it were immediately dying, and leading their hand at the pen'" (250 n. 23). Rutherford's language resembles very closely that of Bishop John Jewel who wrote decades before him.
163. The stance of Ames concurs with the position of other English divines of the sixteenth century.
164. Consult Rogers's sources on Ames: *Scripture in the Westminster Confession*, 92–95. McKim has evidently studied Ames's writings in greater detail.
165. Warfield, *The Westminster Assembly,* 264–73
166. Philip Schaff, ed., *The Creeds of Christendom: The Greek and Latin Creeds* (Grand Rapids: Baker, n.d. [reprint]), 80–82.
167. Whitaker, *A Disputation on Holy Scripture*, 135. John Jewel argued that God's word had been preserved so well that "it yet continueth still without adding or altering of any one sentence, or word or letter" ("A Treatise of the Holy Scripture . . . ," *The Works of John Jewel,* 4:1165). Some Englishmen did think their Bibles perfectly reflected the originals.
168. Wrote Whitaker: "We must hold, therefore, that we have now those very ancient Scriptures which Moses and the other prophets published, although we have not, perhaps, precisely the same forms and shapes of the letters" (*A Disputation on Holy Scripture*, 117).
169. Elsewhere Whitaker declared: "Now then, if the originals of sacred Scripture have not been so disgracefully corrupted by any malice of Jews or adversaries, as some people have ignorantly suspected; and if no mistakes have crept into the originals, but such as may casually be introduced into any book (which our opponents expressly allow) . . ." (Ibid., 161). Whitaker used the verb *creep* concerning problems of textual transmission.
170. Some Roman Catholic apologists argued that because the "originals" had been lost, Protestants could never recreate a completely infallible text. Concerning St. Augustine's stance, see *Letter 82* and *Doct. Christ.*, lib. 2. Augustine was prepared to correct the Latin text with the Septuagint, so taken was he by its supposed divine inspiration. Later he moderated his commitment to the Septuagint's inspiration. Bruce Metzger argues that the quest to establish "the original text of the New Testament" began in the late second century (*The Text of the New Testament: Its Transmission, Corruption and Restoration* [New York: Oxford University Press, 1968], 150).
171. For a bibliography on Grotius, see: Jules Basdevant, ed., *La vie et l'oeuvre de Grotius (1583–1645)* (Paris: Institut Néerlandais, 1965); Hugo Grotius, *The Truth of the Christian Religion in Six Books by Hugo Grotius Corrected and*

Illustrated with Notes by Mr. Le Clerc, ed. John Clarke (Cambridge: J. Hall, 1840).

172. Richard Popkin, "Scepticism, Theology and the Scientific Revolution in the Seventeenth Century," *Problems in the Philosophy of Science*, ed. L. Lakatos and Alan Musgrave (Amsterdam: North Holland Publishing Company, 1968), 3.21–25.

173. In his *Divinai fidei analysis* (1652) Holden restricted "not only inerrancy but inspiration itself to the doctrinal matters of Scripture . . ." (Vawter, *Biblical Inspiration*, 134). Professor Jacques Le Brun (Hautes Etudes, Paris) has studied the impact of Holden's writings upon Richard Simon. See the controverted passages of Holden's *Divinae fidei analysis* 1.5 and 2.3. Holden was one of the first to limit infallibility to matters of doctrine.

174. On Spinoza's perspectives concerning biblical criticism, consult Sylvain Zac, *Signification et valeur de l'interprétation de l'écriture chez Spinoza* (Paris: P. U. F., 1965); Leo Strauss, *Spinoza's Critique of Religion* (New York: Schocken, 1965); A. Malet, *Le Traité Theologico-Politique de Spinoza et la pensée biblique* (Paris: Belles Lettres, 1966).

175. Socinus wrote: "Christ and the apostles were influenced by the opinions of men, and in certain matters they are able to adapt and accommodate themselves to those opinions that flourished at that time. As a result, some of the divine writers upheld the truth better than others do, and sometimes in a minor way a writer had been mistaken about those things that only slightly deal with what we are to believe or do" (Cited in quotation of Calovius in Robert Preus, *The Theology of Post-Reformation Lutheranism: A Study of Theological Prolegomena* [St. Louis: Concordia, 1970], 190). This statement of Socinus is found in *De Auctoritate S. Scripturae*, Cap. I. Seventeenth-century Lutherans struggled with "Socinians" as well. Moreover, the expression *Socinian* became a theological swear word with which apologists cursed anyone to their theological left. Cf. R. Florida, *Voltaire and the Socinians* (Oxfordshire: Voltatre Foundation, 1974); George H. Williams, ed., *The Polish Brethren* (2 vols.; Missoula, Mont.: Scholars Press, 1980).

176. Contemporaries made this distinction. Sometimes intellectual libertines were falsely accused of moral improprieties. See the entire issue of the *XVIIë siècle* 32 (1980) devoted to an important discussion of *libertinage* by René Pintard, Roger Zuber, Georges Couton, Pierre Rétat, Bernard Toranne, and others. See also Lucien Febvre, *Le problème de l'incroyance au 16ë siècle: La religion de Rabelais* (Paris: Albin Michel, 1968).

177. On Mersenne, see Robert Le Noble, *Mersenne ou la naissance du mécenisme* (Paris: Vrin, 1943); idem, *Esquisse d'une histoire de l'idée de nature* (Paris: Albin Michel, 1969).

178. Popkin, *The History of Scepticism*, 197–217.

179. Notes Simon: "He [Morin] declared at the beginning [of his *Exercitations*], that his purpose is to combat Protestants, who boast that they have no other rule in their Religion than the originals (*originaux*) of the Bible; as if it is not evident that the first originals have been lost. . . . This is why the opinion of P. Morin must be modified, who under the pretext of defending the authority of ancient translations received by a long usage in the Church, tried to destroy the authority of the Hebrew text, as it was given to us by the Jews" (*Histoire critique du Vieux Testament*, 465).

180. Robinson, "The Doctrine of Holy Scripture in Seventeenth-Century Reformed Theology," 106. (This is Polanus's perception of Levita's position.)

181. Ibid., 108.

182. On Aben Ezra, see article "Ibn Ezra, Abraham," *Encyclopaedia Judaica* (New York: Encyclopaedia Judaica Company, 1971), 8:1163–70.

183. Some doubt remains about Aben Ezra's intentions in raising questions about the Mosaic authorship of the Pentateuch. Did he do so to provoke research or to undermine biblical authority? Richard Simon believed that Aben Ezra merely "wondered" about the objections he proposed against a full Mosaic authorship of the Pentateuch.

184. Baruch Spinoza, *The Chief Works of Benedict de Spinoza*, ed. R. H. M. Elwes (London: George Bell and Sons, 1883), 1:7–8. On the spread of Spinoza's thought, see Jean Orcibal, "Les Jansenists face à Spinoza," *Revue de littérature comparée* 23 (1949): 441–68; Paul Vernière, *Spinoza et la pensée francaise avant la Révolution* (2 vols.; Paris: P. U. F., 1954).

185. John Woodbridge, "The Reception of Spinoza's *Tractatus-Theologico Politicus* by Richard Simon (1638–1712)," paper delivered in May 1980 at the Lessing Akademie, Wolfenbüttel, West Germany. See Simon, *Histoire Critique du Vieux Textament*, 1:7, and his *De l'inspiration des livres sacrez* (Rotterdam: Renier Leers, 1687), 43–49.

186. In the sixteenth century the exegetical studies of several rabbis obliged some Christian theologians to reconsider their own approaches to Scripture. Then again, the influence of Rabbi David Kimchi's works is evident in the writings of Michel Servetus. Consult Jerome Friedman, "Servetus and the Psalms: The Exegesis of Heresy," *Histoire de l'exégèse au XVIë siècle,* 173. For a more positive contribution of Jewish exegetical studies to Christians' research see A. F. Von Gunten, "La contribution des 'Hébreux' à l'oeuvre exégétique de Cajétan," *Histoire de l'exégèse au XVIë siècle*, 46–83.

187. This is clear from the records of the Company of Pastors, State Archives, Geneva. The present author has studied the originals of the proceedings of the Company of Pastors for the decade 1670–1679.

188. Richard Simon describes the flap which occurred because Morin helped in the publication of the *Critica sacra*. Protestant apologists such as Bootius accused Cappel of having consorted "avec le P. Morin pour detruire les Originaux de la Bible . . ." (*Histoire critique du Vieux Testament*, 477).

189. Popkin, "Scepticism, Theology, and the Scientific Revolution," 17. Bishop Ussher's attempt to establish a precise date for creation indicates his confidence that the words of Scripture are historically reliable. Galileo was able to write rather freely after Cardinal Maffeo became pope in 1623, taking the name of Urban VIII. On the role of printing in the birth of "modern science," see Eisenstein, *The Printing Press as an Agent of Change . . .*, 685–708 (note also her excellent bibliography).

190. Ibid. 18. Concerning La Peyrère, see David R. McKee, "Isaac de La Peyrère, a Precursor of Eighteen Century Deists," *PMLA* 59 (1944): 456–85.

191. Consult the Latin edition: *Prae-adamite* (1655; Bibliothèque nationale A 10951).

192. B. N. M. 18646: I. de la Peyrère, *Relation de l'Islande* (Paris: L. Billaine, 1663); B. N. 18667: La Peyrère, *Relation de Groenland* (Paris: Augustin Courbé, 1647).

193. Popkin, "Scepticism, Theology, and the Scientific Revolution," 19.

194. B. N. D. 40449: La Peyrère, *Lettre de la Peyrère, à Philotime* (Paris: Augustin Courbé,1657).

195. Simon wrote at least seven letters to La Peyrère in the years 1670–1671 (*Lettres choisies*, 1730 ed.). Simon tried to deny any dependence upon La Peyrère.

196. For a sensitive history of the early modern "scientists," see Robert Mandrou, *Des humanistes aux hommes de science XVI et XVII siècles* (Paris: Seuil, 1973).

197. The first edition of this book was published by John Bill. See the edition (1981) of Richard Simon's commentary upon it (ed. Jacques Le Brun and J. Woodbridge). On travel literature, see, among others, G. Atkinson, *The Extraordinary Voyage in French Literature before 1700* (New York: Columbia University, 1920); Pierre Martino, *L'Orient dans la littérature française au XVIIë et au XVIIIë siècle* (Paris: Hachette, 1906); plus the hundreds of travel reports from the sixteenth and seventeenth centuries. Concerning new perspectives on knowledge, see George Sarton, *The Appreciation of Ancient and Medieval Science During the Renaissance* (Philadelphia: University of Pennsylvania Press, 1955); H. T. Pledge, *Science Since 1500* (London: Her Majesty's Stationary Office, 1966); D. W. Waters, *The Art of Navigation in England in Elizabethan and Early Stuart Times* (New Haven: Yale University Press, 1958); Marie Boas, *The Scientific Renaissance 1450–1630* (London: Collins, 1962); Mark H. Curtis, *Oxford and Cambridge in Transition (1558–1642)* (Oxford: Clarendon Press, 1959); the multiple works of Margaret Jacob, Christopher Hill, John Redwood, Herbert Butterfield, Roger Hahn, William Shea, and others. Consult especially Richard S. Brooks, *The Interplay Between Science and Religion in England 1640–1720: A Bibliographical and Historiographical Guide* (Evanston: Garrett-Evangelical Theological Seminary, 1975) which updates considerably the bibliography out of which Rogers and McKim work. The study of the history of "science" has become a genuine industry. Rogers and McKim do not give much indication of keeping abreast with its surging advances.

198. Jean Le Clerc critiques Simon's *Histoire critique du Vieux Testament* in an important volume, *Sentimens de queleques théologiens de Hollande* (1686). A flurry of volumes by the two disputants followed. On this debate, see the M.A. thesis in church history by Martin Klauber (Trinity Evangelical Divinity School). Concerning Le Clerc, consult Annie Barnes, *Jean Le Clerc (1657–1736) et la République des Lettres* (Paris: Droz, 1938); idem, *Lettres inédites de Le Clerc à Locke* (ed. Gabriel Bonno; Berkeley: University of California Press, 1959). On the career of Richard Simon, see Paul Auvray, *Richard Simon 1638–1712* (Paris: P. U. F., 1974); Jean Steinmann, *Richard Simon et les origines de l'exégèse biblique* (Paris: Desclée de Brouwer, 1960); Henri Margival, *Essai sur Richard Simon et la critique biblique au XVIIë siècle* (Genève: Slatkine, 1970 [reprint]); Auguste Bernus, *Richard Simon et son histoire critique du Vieux Testament* (Genève: Slatkine, 1969 [reprint]); R. Saverio Mirri, *Richard Simon e il metodo storico-critico de B. Spinoza* (Firenze: Felice Le Monnier, 1972). Concerning Locke and religion, see the studies of John Yolton.

199. On Bayle, see Paul Dibon, ed., *Pierre Bayle, le philosophe de Rotterdam* (Amsterdam: Elsevier, 1959); Elisabeth Labrousse, *Pierre Bayle* (2 vols.; La Haye: Nijhoff, 1963–1965) and the studies of Pierre Rétat, Jacques Solé and others. Consult also the works on other early modern students of the Bible: Alphonse Dupront, *Pierre Daniel Heut et l'exégèse comparatiste au XVIIë siècle* (Paris: Leroux, 1930); Leonard E. Doucette, *Emery Bigot: Seventeenth-Century French Humanist* (Toronto: University of Toronto, 1970); see also books and articles on Henri Justel, E. Du Pin, Scaliger, Menage, Hobbes, Limborch, Bekker, Arnauld, Pierre Nicole, John Dryden, Dom Calmet, and other members of the Republic of Letters.

200. Norman Geisler associates the emergence of attacks on inerrancy with the influence of inductive methodology in biblical studies (Geisler, "The Philosophical Presuppositions of Biblical Inerrancy," *Inerrancy*, 307–34). The "Battle

between the Ancients and the Moderns" should be considered in any discussion of these matters. The impact of radical German Pietism upon developments in biblical criticism is also significant.

201. For a review of the state of biblical criticism in France for the year 1778, consult Marie-Hélène Contoni, "La critique biblique en 1778," *Dix huitième siècle* 11 (1979): 213–33; Bertram Schwarzbach, *Voltaire's Old Testament Criticism* (Geneve: Droz, 1971); René Pomeau, *La religion de Voltaire* (Paris: Nizet, 1969 [re-edition]); on Germany, see in particular Walter Grossmann, *Johann Christian Edelmann: From Orthodoxy to Enlightenment* (The Hague: Mouton, 1976), which studies Edelmann's relationship to Lessing and Reimarus. See Lessing's attack on biblical inerrancy in Gotthold Lessing, "On the Proof of the Spirit and of Power," *Lessing's Theological Writings*, ed. Henry Chadwick (Stanford: Stanford University Press, 1967), 55. In the Anglo-Saxon world there is an unfortunate tendency to locate the origins of biblical criticism in the eighteenth century rather than in earlier centuries.

202. One of the professors at the French Seminary at Lausanne (where future pastors of the Church of the Desert trained) noted fourteen reasons why the Bible contains no error (University of Geneva Archives: Collection Court No. 23, folios 18–23). On the French Reformed pastors of the Church of the Desert, see Woodbridge, "L'influence des philosophes français." On the "Pietists," see the works of Ernest Stoeffler, James Tanis, Richard Lovelace, August Langen, Heinrich Bornkamm.

203. A competent study on Francis Turretin remains to be written. The Turretin family archives were used only selectively in the older biographies. Unfortunately, these archives are located in a small Swiss town and cannot be easily consulted. American scholars have been prone to write much about Francis Turretin without having studied his papers.

204. See Sydney Ahlstrom, "The Scottish Philosophy and American Theology," *Church History* 24 (1955): 257–72; Theodore Bozeman, *Protestants in an Age of Science* (Chapel Hill: University of North Carolina Press, 1977); John C. Vander Stelt, *Philosophy and Scripture: A Study in Old Princeton and Westminster Theology* (Marlton, N.J.: Mack Publishing Company, 1978).

205. John Gerstner, "The View of the Bible Held by the Church: Calvin and the Westminster Divines," *Inerrancy*, 400–408.

206. In his diary (May 2, 1709), William Byrd of Westover noted: "In the evening we talked about religion and my wife and her sister had a fierce dispute about the infallibility of the Bible" (cited in Carl Bode, ed., *American Literature: The 17th and 18th Centuries* [New York: Washington Square Press, 1973], 230). Or the American Puritan divine, Samuel Willard, declared: "Truth is self-consenting, but error is self-contradictory. There is a sweet harmony in the whole Word of God. There are no contradictions to be found there. If any shall judge that there are such, the mistake is not in the Scriptures, but in their deceived understandings" (cited in Ernest B. Lowrie, *The Shape of the Puritan Mind: The Thought of Samuel Willard* [New Haven: Yale University Press, 1974], 35–36). On the founding of Princeton Seminary in 1812, see Mark Noll, "The Founding of Princeton Seminary," *The Westminster Theological Journal* 42 (1979): 72–110.

207. Samuel Taylor Coleridge, *Confessions of an Inquiring Spirit* (Boston: James Monroe and Company, 1841). On Coleridge, see among other studies, Basil Willey, *Nineteenth Century Studies Coleridge to Matthew Arnold* (New York: Harper and Row, 1966), 1–50.

208. Coleridge, *Confessions of an Inquiring Spirit*, 79–80.

209. Ibid., 81.
210. Charles Hodge, *Systematic Theology* (New York: Charles Scribner's Sons, 1871), 1:180. Historians have tended to overlook the controversy that ensued among American theologians concerning Coleridge's posthumous *Confessions of an Inquiring Spirit*. Evangelicals wrestled with Coleridge decades before they encountered Darwin. Evangelicals sometimes debated the mode of inspiration, but not one of its results, complete biblical infallibility.
211. This particular edition was published by William Collins of Glasgow. Writes Andrew King: ". . . but in reference to these alleged contradictions it may be observed, that some of them are to be found only in our translation—they do not attach to the Scriptures in their original languages. You are fully aware, we trust, that we are far from maintaining that the translations of them have been made by inspiration . . ." (ibid., 125).
212. Beck, "Monogramata Hermeneutics N. T.," *Biblical Repertory* 1 (1825): 27. The fact that Charles Hodge wanted to publish Beck's article (1–122) with its review of the history of biblical interpretation indicates the breadth of the Princetonian's own interests in the field. Beck makes but few allusions to Francis Turretin in his survey. In Scotland, Reverend John Dick wrote about the lost "original documents" in his *Lectures on Theology* (Oxford: David Christy, 1838), 635. Dick's Theology was also published in America.
213. L. Gaussen, *Theopneustia The Bible: Its Divine Origin and Inspiration* (Cincinnati: George Blanchard, 1859), 195–96, 207. This volume, originally published in French, was cited in the United States by the 1840s.
214. John Henry Newman, *The Theological Papers of John Henry Newman on Biblical Inspiration and Infallibility*, ed. J. Derek Holmes (Oxford: Clarendon Press, 1979), 10.
215. In 1893, Thomas Huxley commented about the long-standing commitment of some of his fellow citizens to complete biblical infallibility: "The doctrine of biblical infallibility . . . was widely held by my countrymen within my recollection: I have reason to think that many persons of unimpeachable piety, a few of learning, and even some of intelligence, yet uphold it. But I venture to entertain a doubt whether it can produce any champion whose competency and authority would be recognized beyond the limits of the sect, or theological coterie, to which he belongs. On the contrary, apologetic effort, at present, appears to devote itself to the end of keeping the name of 'Inspiration' to suggest the divine source, and consequently infallibility, of more or less of the biblical literature, while carefully emptying the term of any definite sense. For 'plenary inspiration' we are asked to substitute a sort of 'inspiration with limited liability,' the limit being susceptible of indefinite fluctuation in correspondence with the demands of scientific criticism" (cited in John C. Greene, "Darwin and Religion," *European Intellectual History since Darwin and Marx*, ed. W. Warren Wagar [New York: Harper and Row, 1966], 15–16). To our mind George Marsden, a fane historian, has perhaps exaggerated some of the conceptual differences which existed between English and American evangelicals toward biblical authority (Marsden, "Fundamentalism as an American Phenomenon: A Comparison with English Evangelicalism," *Church History* 46 [1977]: 215–32). See James Moore, *The Post-Darwinism Controversies* . . . (London: Cambridge University Press, 1979). Moore proposes the paradoxical thesis that the "orthodox" were better prepared to accept Darwin's thought than Protestant "liberals." Moore's bibliography on this topic is superb.
216. See Woodbridge, Noll, Hatch, *The Gospel in America*, 99–134. Washington Gladden, no friend to biblical inerrancy, noted in the 1890s that most Ameri-

can Protestants believed that the Bible was "free from all error, whether of doctrine, of fact, or of precept" (Charles Hodge's expression). He wrote: "Such is the doctrine now held by the great majority of Christians. Intelligent pastors do not hold it, but the body of the laity have no other conception" (*Who Wrote the Bible? A Book for the People* [Boston & New York: Houghton, Mifflin, 1891], 357). In a blurb for William Newton Clarke's *Sixty Years with the Bible: A Record of Experience* (New York: Charles Scribner's Sons, 1910), a reviewer noted that Clarke had given up "the common view [complete biblical infallibility] which all evangelicals held a half century ago . . ." Clarke himself wrote: "I have dated this conviction against the inerrancy of the Bible here in the Seventies, and here it belongs . . ." (ibid., 108.) See also: T. F. Curtis, *The Human Element in the Inspiration of the Sacred Scriptures* (New York: D. Appleton & Company, 1867), 36–38. Curtis called for a new "Reformation" in which Protestants would give up their commitment to complete biblical infallibility. Curtis acknowledged that the latter belief dominated Protestantism in his day.

217. Cited in John H. Leith, ed., *Creeds of the Churches* (New York: Anchor Books, 1963), 334–35.

218. Norman Maring, "Baptists and Changing Views of the Bible, 1865–1918," *Foundations* 1 (1958): 52. Less creedally oriented churches refrained from establishing statements where biblical authority was delimited with precision. Their members usually read the Scriptures as if they were infallible, however.

219. Cited in G. F. Wright, *Charles Grandison Finney* (Boston: Houghton, Mifflin, 1891),182–83.

220. Charles Finney, *Skeleton Lectures* (1840; published 1841), 52. See the M.A. thesis in church history by David Callen (Trinity Evangelical Divinity School), which is devoted to Finney's view of Scripture. The author is indebted to Mr. Callen for the Finney data. Finney shared with the Princetonians and others a commitment to Common Sense Realism.

221. On Wesley's view of biblical authority, see the M.A. thesis in church history by Timothy Wadkins (Trinity Evangelical Divinity School) which is devoted to this subject. Professors Donald Dayton and Timothy Smith do not agree with our assessment. Wesley made statements like these which Wadkins is attempting to study in their contexts: "Nay, will not the allowing there is any error in scripture, shake the authority of the whole way;" "Nay, if there be any mistakes in the Bible, there may as well be a thousand." Concerning Wakefield, see his *Complete System of Christian Theology* (Cincinnati: Cranston and Stowe, 1869), 77–78.

222. Cited in Kurt Marquart, *Anatomy of an Explosion: A Theological Analysis of the Missouri Synod Controversy* (Grand Rapids: Baker, 1978), 45.

223. Randall Balmer has surveyed the books on biblical inspiration published in America (1800–1880). He documents this contention in his M.A. thesis in church history devoted to Ernest Sandeen's interpretation.

224. Ernest Sandeen, *The Roots of Fundamentalism British and American Millenarianism, 1800–1930* (Grand Rapids: Baker, 1978 [reprint 1970]), 103–31.

225. See Randall Balmer and John Woodbridge in *Scripture and Truth*. For other criticisms of Ernest Sandeen's proposal, see George Marsden, "Defining Fundamentalism," *Christian Scholar's Review* 1 (1971): 141–51; Ernest Sandeen, "Defining Fundamentalism: A Reply to Professor Marsden," *Christian Scholar's Review* 1 (1971): 227–33.

226. This quotation is found in Ernest Sandeen, *The Origins of Fundamentalism: Toward a Historical Interpretation* (Philadelphia: Fortress Press, 1968), 14.

198 / Biblical Authority and Conservative Perspectives

227. Sandeen, "The Princeton Theology: One Source of Biblical Literalism in American Protestantism," *Church History* 31 (1962): 314; also cited in Sandeen, *The Roots of Fundamentalism*, 127.
228. Archibald Alexaner, *Evidences of the Authenticity, Inspiration and Canonical Authority of the Holy Scriptures* (Philadelphia: Presbyterian Board of Publications, 1836), 230.
229. Sandeen, *The Roots of Fundamentalism*, 126–28.
230. This chapter has been reprinted in book form: A. A. Hodge and B. B. Warfield, *Inspiration* (Introduction by Roger Nicole; Grand Rapids: Baker, 1979).
231. Sandeen, *The Roots of Fundamentalism*, 28.
232. Roger Nicole aptly summarizes Charles Hodge's use of the Parthenon illustration: "Its meaning in keeping with the context must be simply that he [Hodge] was not deterred from confessing the infallibility of the Bible by his inability to provide a fully satisfactory explanation in every one of the cases where a discrepancy is alleged" (A. A. Hodge and B. B. Warfield, *Inspiration*, Appendix 5, 95).
233. B. B. Warfield, *The Inspiration and Authority of the Bible*, ed. Samuel Craig (Philadelphia: Presbyterian and Reformed, 1964), 220–21.
234. Rogers and McKim's commentary misses the point of Hodge's argument. Hodge did not "admit" that the problem concerned his own theory of biblical inspiration because he believed that he understood that doctrine correctly.
235. Archibald A. Hodge, *A Commentary on the Confession of Faith* (Philadelphia: Presbyterian Board of Publication, 1885 [reprint 1869]), 58–59.
236. Rogers and McKim, *The Authority and Interpretation*, 302.
237. Ibid., 303–5.
238. Hovey, *Manual of Systematic Theology and Christian Ethics* (Philadelphia: American Baptist Publication Society, 1877), 77–84.
239. A. A. Hodge, *A Commentary on the Confession of Faith*, 65. Hodge continues: "That the original sacred text has come down to us in a state of essential purity" (ibid.).
240. See this chapter, n. 212.
241. Cited in Dennis Okholm, "Biblical Inspiration and Infallibility in the Writings of Archibald Alexander," *TrinJ* 5 (1976): 84. See also Archibald Alexander, "Review of Woods on Inspiration," *Biblical Repertory and Theological Review* 3 (January 1831):10.
242. Cf. Sandeen, *The Roots of Fundamentalism*, 127–30.
243. Randall Balmer has studied the circumstances surrounding the creation of the 1881 "Inspiration" article by A. A. Hodge and B. B. Warfield. He has found no indications of "conspiratorial thinking" in their correspondence or other writings.
244. Sandeen, *The Roots of Fundamentalism*, 289
245. Charles Hodge, for one, had a broad culture. Rogers and McKim note some aspects of his reading fare.
246. Mark Noll and George Marsden have done research on this complex question. See also Herbert Hovenkamp, *Science and Religion in America 1800–1860* (Philadelphia: University of Pennsylvania, 1978). Mark Noll writes aptly about some of the problems Common Sense Reason engendered for evangelical Protestants of the nineteenth century. The Common Sense Realist ". . . was unwilling to rest with traditional tensions in Christian thought; for example, how divine sovereignty and human responsibility could exist together, or how the sacraments could be valuable for salvation without denying justification by faith. Most theologians in the nineteenth century were not content until they had 'settled' these difficulties" (*The Gospel in America*, 40).

247. Like Calvin, the Princetonians relied upon the Holy Spirit's witness to the "truth" of Scripture and also used the law of noncontradiction.
248. Charles Hodge recognized the decisive role of the Holy Spirit in doing theology: "The distinguishing feature of Augustinianism as taught by St. Augustine himself, and by the purer theologians of the Latin Church throughout the Middle Ages, which was set forth by the Reformers, and especially by Calvin and the Geneva divines, is that the inward teaching of the spirit is allowed its proper place in determining our theology. . . . The effort is not to make the assertions of the Bible harmonize with speculative reason, but to subject our feeble reason to the mind of God as revealed in his Word, and by his Spirit in our life" (*Systematic Theology,* 1:16).
249. Theodore Bozeman, *Protestants in an Age of Science: The Baconian Ideal and Ante-bellum American Religious Thought* (Chapel Hill: The University of North Carolina Press, 1977), 209 n. 12.
250. Charles Hodge wrote concerning the biblical writers and their knowledge: "As to all matters of science, philosophy, and history, they stood on the same level with their contemporaries. They were infallible only as teachers, and when acting as the spokesmen of God. Their inspiration no more made them astronomers than it made them agriculturists" (*Systematic Theology,* 1:165). Hodge identified an erroneous doctrine of accommodation with the thought of the German critics Semler and Van Hemert. He cites Van Hemert's remark: "If anything be taught which is contrary to reason, it is an accommodation . . ." (*Biblical Repertory,* 1:126). He also proposed what he thought was a proper definition of accommodation: "The sacred writers were not machines. Their self-consciousness was not suspended, nor were their intellectual powers superseded. . . . It was men, not machines; not unconscious instruments, but living, thinking, willing minds, whom the Spirit used as his organs. Moreover, as inspiration did not involve the suspension or suppression of the human faculties, so neither did it interfere with the free exercise of the distinctive mental characteristics of the individual. . . . It lies in the very nature of inspiration that God spake in the language of men; . . ." (*Systematic Theology,* 1:157). On the devotional life of the Princetonians, see the important article by W. Andrew Hoffecker, "The Devotional Life of Archibald Alexander, Charles Hodge, and Benjamin B. Warfield," *WJS* 42 (1979): 111–29.
251. Rogers and McKim lapse into this rare polemical expression (459).
252. Rogers also studied with Professor Berkouwer.
253. Rogers and McKim's debt to Barth is a complex one. Barth did not want to sort out an infallible canon within Scripture. The authors attempt to identify such a canon by limiting it to "matters of faith and practice." On the other hand, Rogers and McKim seem to share with Barth a position which C. F. H. Henry identifies as neo-Protestant: "The recent neo-Protestant attempt, as by Barth, to dispense with inerrant autographs by assigning a larger role to the Holy Spirit, has exchanged the objective validity of the text for a subjective paradoxic Word" (*God, Revelation, and Authority God Who Speaks and Shows* [Waco, Tex.: Word, 1979], 4:250). Moreover, Rogers and McKim point out (420) that Barth acknowledged a tendency within the early church "to insist that the operation of the Holy Spirit in the inspiration of the biblical writers extended to the individual phraseology used by them in the grammatical sense of the concept." Barth did not like this tendency, but he at least recognized his own departure from it. Neither Barth nor Rogers and McKim have much claim on the patristic writers as precursors.
254. Must reading for those who would understand the later thought of Berkouwer

(and therefore the thinking of Rogers and McKim) includes, among others, Geoffrey Bromiley, "Biblical Authority," *Christianity Today* 20/4 (November 21, 1975): 42–45; Henry Krabbendam, "B. B. Warfield vs. G. C. K. Berkouwer," *Inerrancy*, 413–46. Krabbendam makes particularly blunt statements: "Berkouwer and his followers are in the grip of a dialectic that arises from apostasy and can arise only from apostasy" (ibid., 446). Charles Briggs's interpretation of the Westminster Divines apparently influenced Rogers and McKim as well, even though Briggs either misquoted or misinterpreted his sources on more than a few occasions.

255. We would recommend that each page of the authors' study should be evaluated by referring to the sources they used as well as to other competent analyses on the subject matter under consideration.

256. It is possible that some of the issues motivating the authors' efforts was their genuine desire to uphold some form of biblical authority while letting diverse forms of biblical criticism take them where they would.

257. If we had attempted to write a book with the title the authors give to their own volume, we would have followed a more carefully defined route, taking into consideration the methodological problems which can wreck such a bold enterprise. Moreover, we would have attempted to move beyond our own areas of specialization in order to provide a more comprehensive bibliographical backdrop to the undertaking.

258. We have relied essentially on the authors' own sources so that they cannot claim that our review is based on a historiographical tradition of "Warfieldian writers." The authors dismissed out of hand the works of some fine scholars apparently on the basis that they personally held to Warfield's position on Scripture. See, for example, their comments on Ronald Nash's *The Light of the Mind: St. Augustine's Theory of Knowledge* (Lexington: University Press of Kentucky, 1969), 61 n. 93.

259. The Continental Reformers stressed finding Christ in the Scriptures. But they also maintained that all the Bible was a rule of faith. As we saw, the English Reformers thought in the same terms.

260. Cited in Newman, T*he Theological Papers of John Henry Newman*, 7–8. This kind of argument was proposed by Augustine in writing to Jerome (Letter 40): "In your exposition of the Epistle of Paul to the Galatians I have found one thing which causes me much concern. For if it be the case that statements untrue in themselves, but made, as it were, out of a sense of duty in the interest of religion, have been admitted into the Holy Scriptures, what authority will be left to them? If this be conceded, what sentence can be produced from these Scriptures, by the weight of which the wicked obstinacy of error can be broken down? For as soon as you have produced it, if it be disliked by him who contends with you, he will reply that, in the passage alleged, the writer was uttering a falsehood under the pressure of some honorable sense of duty and where will anyone find this way of escape impossible, if it be possible for men to say and believe that, after introducing his narrative with these words, 'The things which I write unto you, behold, before God, I lie not,' the apostle lied when he said of Peter and Barnabas, 'I saw that they walked not uprightly, according to the truth of the gospel'? For if they did walk uprightly, Paul wrote what was false; and if he wrote what was false *here*, when did he say what was true? Shall he be supposed to say what is true when his teaching corresponds with the predilection of his reader, and shall everything which runs counter to the impressions of the reader be reckoned a falsehood uttered by him under a sense of duty? It will be impossible to prevent men from finding

reasons for thinking that he not only might have uttered a falsehood, but was bound to do so, if we admit this canon of interpretation."

261. The authors attempt to skirt this problem in a brief note (xxiv n. 12): "The use of 'salvation' to designate the primary purpose of Scripture should not be taken to exclude, for example, social and ethical concerns. It is not meant to make the Bible only a book of personal piety. Scripture certainly deals with the relationships of persons to God, to themselves, and to their neighbors. What 'salvation' is meant to exclude is the post Reformation scholastic notion that the Bible is a competing and superior source of technical information in the various sciences." Given this perspective, the Bible student is obliged to use his or her understanding of "science" and other disciplines to sort out infallible "salvation truths" from fallible materials. This operation necessitates that one's reason and culture judge revelation in a most unfortunate way. Many Christians believe that the Bible is completely infallible but that it is not a "scientific textbook" *per se.*

262. The alert reader needs to recall that some of the later claims of this volume are based upon misconstrued arguments found earlier in the text. He or she should also recognize the "drumbeat form" of argumentation in the volume. Themes are repeated frequently as if their constant repetition will somehow finally make them true.

263. Kenneth Kantzer's observation about the views of St. Augustine, Calvin, and Luther are appropriate in this regard. These churchmen believed in biblical inerrancy if inerrancy means that the Bible does not wander from the truth in anything it affirms or says when properly interpreted.

Chapter 2

1. The phrase is Augustine's: ". . . Thy books . . . the way which leadeth not only to behold but to inhabit the blessed country" (*Confessiones* 7.20).

2. For example, Etienne Gilson argues that there are no fundamental changes in Augustine's major doctrinal positions: see his *Introduction a l'étude de saint Augustin.* ET *The Christian Philosophy of Saint Augustine* (tr. L. E. M. Lynch: New York: Random House, 1960). Eugene TeSelle (*Augustine the Theologian* [New York: Herder & Herder, 1970], 20) stresses the "continuity" of "becoming" in Augustine. To deal fully with the question of continuity or change in Augustine's basic theological convictions requires a recognition of his historical context, a decision with respect to the systematic nature of several of his more prominent works and, finally, the use of his own *Retractions*, written to correct his early works at various points.

3. Unless otherwise indicated all citations will be taken from the English translation of Augustine's works in the series edited by P. Schaff, *A Select Library of the Nicene and Post-Nicene Fathers of the Christian Church,* first series (8 vols., 1887–92), reprinted by Eerdmans. A guide to the critical and further editions of Augustine's works may be found in Robert Meagher, *Augustine: An Introduction* (New York: Harper and Row, 1979: 1st pub., 1968), 294–301. Note should be made of the fresh English translation of Augustine's work in the series, "The Fathers of the Church," currently in various stages of completion by the Catholic University of America Press.

In any initial study of Augustine's work Meagher writes that one must consider *The Confessions, The City of God,* and *The Trinity* (294). Vernon J. Bourke writes that the major treatises of the mature Augustine are *The Literal Meaning of Genesis,* with respect to God and the created world; *The Trinity,* with respect to God and the human soul; and *The City of God,* with respect to God and society: see V. J. Bourke, *Augustine's Quest of Wisdom: Life and Philosophy of the Bishop of Hippo* (Milwaukee: Bruce Publishing Co., 1945), 202–3. With respect to biblical interpretation itself, Augustine's treatises *On Christian Doctrine* and *On the Harmony of the Evangelists* are also crucial in addition to his correspondence with Jerome as it pertains to these matters.

4. On revelation, particularly as it pertains to Augustine, see A. C. de Veer, "'Revelare,' 'Revelatio' Élements d'une étude sur l'emploi du mot et sur sa signification chez s. Augustin," *Recherches augustiniennes* 2 (1962): 331–57.

5. On various dimensions of the problem of inspiration, see G. Lanczkowski. "Inspiration, Religionsgeschichtlich," *RGG*, 3rd ed. (1959), 3:733–75; O. Weber, "Inspiration, Dogmengeschichtlich," ibid., 775–9; and J. T. Forestell, "Bible, II (Inspiration)," in *The New Catholic Encyclopedia* (1967), 2:381–6.

6. On Scripture, see G. Gloege, "Schriftprinzip," *RGG*, 3rd ed. (1959), 3:1539–43.

7. On Infallibility, see G. Courtade, Inspiration et Inerrance," *Dictionnaire de la Bible*, suppl. 4 (Paris, 1949), cols. 526ff.; and R. F. Smith, "Inspiration and Inerrancy," in *The Jerome Biblical Commentary*, ed. by R. E. Brown et. al (Englewood Cliffs, N.J.: Prentice-Hall, 1968), 2:499–514.

8. E.g., *Confessiones*, 1.1.1; 6.1.1. For a useful contemporary framework in which to view Augustine's understanding of revelation and the associated question of inspiration, see H. D. McDonald, *Theories of Revelation, An Historical Study 1860–1960* (London: George Allen and Unwin, 1963); and J. T. Burtchaell, *Catholic Theories of Biblical Inspiration since 1810: A Review and Critique* (Cambridge: Cambridge University Press, 1969).

9. Aimé Solignac, "L 'Existentialisme de Saint Augustine," *NRT* 70 (1948): 3–17.

10. On the intellectual journey this involved (following *Conf.* V, iii, 3), idem, "Doxographics et manuels dans la formation philosophiques de saint Augustin," *Recherches augustiniennes* 1 (1958): 113–48.

11. Franz Körner, *Dat Sein und der Mensch: Die Existenzelle Seinsentdeckung des Jungen Augustin* (Frieburg: Alber, 1959), 27–40. Cf. "Die Entwicklung Augustins von der Anamnesiszur Illuminationslehre im Lichte seines Innerlichkeitsprinzips," *Theologische Quartalschrift* 134 (1954): 397–447.

12. Caroline E. Schuetzinger ("Franz Körner's Existential Interpretation of the Young Augustine," *Augustinian Studies* 1 [1970]: 19–29) writes: "Again, why did Augustine after his Milanese experience express his ideas in a Neoplatonic way, whereas later, at the apex of his literary productivity, he uses the language of the Bible?"

13. Gerard Verbeke, "Connaissance de soi et connaissance de Dieu chez saint Augustin," *Augustiniana* 4 (1954): 495–515. The fruitfulness of this existential approach receives different nuances in R. Berlinger, *Augustins dialogische Metaphysik* (Frankfurt: M: Klostermann, 1962); J. Mader, *Die logische Struktur des personalen Denkens: Aus der Methode der Gotteserkenntnis bei Aurelius Augustinus* (Vienna: Herder, 1965); and James W. Woelfel, *Augustinian Humanism: Studies in Human Bondage and Earthly Grace* (Lawrence, Kans.: University of Kansas, 1979).

14. See in John Baillie, *The Idea of Revelation in Recent Thought* (New York: Columbia University Press, 1956), 4–5. See Baillie's references to Thomas Aquinas, *Summa Contra Gentiles*, 4.1; and A. A. Hodge, *Outlines of Theology* (London: T. Nelson. 1863), 49–50.

15. *Confessiones*, 6.5.7–8.

16. Jean-Louis Maier, *Les missions divines selon Augustin* (Fribourg en Swisse: Editions Universitaires, 1960), esp. 218.

17. *Epistula* 147; cf. *De civitate dei*, 22.29.

18. Ibid., 52.
19. *Epistula* 148.4.13.
20. Ibid., 1.1.
21. Ibid., 5.18. The development of the internal understanding of divine manifestation best illustrates Augustine's theological genius according to Maier, *Missions divines*, 218.
22. *Epistula* 148.2.10.
23. Basil Studer, *Zur Theophanie-Exegese Augustins: Untersuchungen zu einem Ambrosius-Zitat in der Schrift De videndo Deo (ep. 147)* (Rome: Herder, 1971). See also L. J. Van der Lof, "L'exégèse exacte et objective des théophanies de l'Ancien Testament dans le 'De Trinitate," *Augustiniana* 14 (1964): 485–99.
24. C. Kannengiesser, "Enarratio in psalmum CXVIII: Science de la révélation et progres spirituel," *Recherches augustiniennes* 2 (1962): 359–81; note the context, 359–64.
25. *Enarratio in psalmum CXVIII* (CXIX), 6: ". . . he desireth that his ways may be made direct to keep the statutes of God. How to be made direct, save by the grace of God? Otherwise he will find in the law of God not a source of rejoicing, but of confusion, if he hath chosen to look into commandments, which he doth not." Kannengiesser ("Enarratio," 372) stresses the practical value of revelation in Augustine's thinking.
26. Maier, *Missions divine,* 103–7.
27. TeSelle, *Augustine the Theologian,* 129. The value of this history is not in itself but in the revelation of God's purposes (*De civitate dei,* 11–18). See Christopher Dawson, "The Christian View of History," *Blackfriars* 22 (1951): 312–27.
28. Ibid., 125. TeSelle cites *De vera religione* 7.13: "The chief argument for following this religion is history."
29. *Epistula* 6.2.
30. *Epistula* 7.1.1.
31. *Epistula* 8.
32. *Epistula* 9.
33. *Epistula* 7.4. These will be further considered in II.
34. Goulvan Madec, "Conaissance de Dieu et action de graces. Essai sur les citations de l'Ép aux Romains 1, 18–25 dans l'oeuvre de s. Augustin," *Recherches augustiniennes* 2 (1962): 273–309; esp. 293–98, 308–9. Madec notes the context of Augustine's argument as he deals with the benefits and deficiencies of Platonism (276–84).
35. P. Lope Cilleruelo, "La memoria dei segun S. Augustin," *Augustinus Magister* 1 (Paris: Études Augustiniennes, 1954): 499–502; "Por qué 'memoria Dei'?" *Revue des études augustiniennes* 10 (1964): 291. I am dependent upon Lorenz, "Zwölf Jahre" 39 (1975), 345; and Madec, "Pour et contra la 'memoria Dei'," *Revue des études augustiniennes* 2 (1965): 89–92.
36. Ragnar Holte, *Béatitude et Sagesse: Saint Augustin et le probleme de la fin de l'homme dans la philosophie ancienne* (Paris: Études Augustiniennes, 1962), 141.
37. *Epistula,* 148.3.12; cf. *Confessiones,* 10.42.67.
38. A. C. de Veer, "'Revelare,' 'Revelatio.' Élements d'une étude sur l'emploi du mot et sur sa signification chez s. Augustin," *Recherches augustiniennes* 2 (1962): 331–57.
39. Rene Latourelle, "L'idée de révélation chez les Pères de l'Église," *Sciences Ecclésastiques* (1959): 297–344.
40. Ibid., 335–40.

41. M. Dulaey, *Le reve dans la vie et la pensee de s. Augustin* (Paris: Études Augustiniennes, 1973).

42. *Epistula* 6 (A.D. 389).

43. Adolf Harnack, "Die Höhepunkte in Augustins Koffessionen," repr. in *Reden und Aufsätze* 1 (Giessen: Ricker, 1904) 51–79; see also his *Lehrbuch der Dogmengeschichte* (3 vols., 1886–89); ET as *History of Dogma* (7 vols., 1884–89). Whereas he argued for the influence of Plato, later scholarship has pointed to the influence of Plotinus or Porphyry or both.

44. Prosper Alfaric, *L'évolution intellectuelle de saint Augustin* (Paris: E. Nourry, 1918).

45. Charles Boyer, *Christianisme et Néo-Platonisme dans la formation de saint Augustin* (Paris: Beauchesne, 1920). See also his *Essais sur la doctrine de saint Augustin* (Paris: Beauchesne, 1932).

46. Pierre Courcelle, *Recherches sur les Confessions de saint Augustin* (Paris: E. DeBoccard, 2d ed., 1968; 1st ed., 1950).

47. Ibid., 138, 159, 168–74 et passim. See further Courcelle's work, "Nouveaux aspects du platonisme chez saint Ambroise," *Revue des études latines* 34 (1956): 220–39.

48. John Burnaby even contends that Augustine was the greatest disciple and profoundest critic of Plotinus. See the preface to his study, *Amor Dei: A Study of the Religion of St. Augustine* (London: Hodder and Stoughton, 1938).

49. Frederick E. Van Fleteren, "Augustine's Ascent of the Soul in Book VII of the Confessions: A Reconsideration," *Augustinian Studies* 5 (1974): 29–72.

50. Ibid., 71. "This is not to throw the question of Augustine's sincere conversion to Christianity in doubt, as others have done. Rather Augustine seems to interpret the Christian path to salvation in terms of ascent or return motif garnered from the Platonists." Van Fleteren holds that "remnants of this anagogic movement" remain in Augustine's later works (72).

51. E.g., F. Joachim von Rintelen, "Augustine: The Ascent in Value towards God," *Augustinian Studies* 2 (1972): 155–78.

52. Robert O'Connell (*St. Augustine's Early Theory of Man, A.D. 386–391* [Cambridge, Mass.: Harvard University Press, 1968], 27) argues that Augustine adopted Neoplatonism in part to throw off the influence of Manichaeism. In doing so Augustine attempted to develop an "intellectus fidei" which did justice to both terms.

53. A. H. Armstrong, "St. Augustine and Christian Platonism," in *Augustine, A Collection of Critical Essays*, ed. R. A. Markus (Garden City, N.Y.: Doubleday 1972), 3–27. Cf. idem, "Spiritual or Intelligible Matter in Plotinus and St. Augustine," *Augustinus Magister* (Paris: Etudes Augustiniennes, 1954).

54. John J. O'Meara, "The Neoplatonism of Saint Augustine," in *Neo-platonism and Christian Thought*, ed. D. J. O'Meara (Albany, N.Y.: State University Press, 1982), 34–41.

55. Ibid., 37.

56. Robert J. O'Connell, *St. Augustine's Confessions: The Odyssey of the Lord* (Cambridge, Mass.: Belknap, 1969).

57. O'Connell, *Early Theory*, iii.

58. Ibid., 27. O'Connell offers more ways in which Augustine altered the Plotinian matrix in "Action and Contemplation," in *Augustine* (ed. R. A. Markus), 38–58.

59. On the continuing importance of Courcelle's work, see the thesis of Eckard König, *Augustinus Philosophus: Christlicher Glaube und philosophisches Denken in den Frühschriften Augustinus* (München: Wilhelm Fink Verlag, 1970).

60. Brown, *Augustine of Hippo*, 79 n. 1.
61. *Confessiones*, 6.9; 20–21; *De vera religione* 3.3; *De Genesi ad litteram* I, 21, 41. A general index of how Augustine used Scripture is important in this regard. See further in III, infra.
62. R. A. Markus, "Introduction," in *Augustine* (ed. R. A. Markus), vii–xv.
63. Markus cites *De Trinitate*, 4.16, 21.
64. *Contra Iuliacum*, 4.14, 72; as cited by Markus, ibid., 9. See also Augustine, *De vera religione*, 5, 8.
65. Ibid., x.
66. Mary Patricia Garvey, *St. Augustine: Christian or Neoplatonist?* (Milwaukee: Marquette University Press, 1939). See her excellent review of some of the earlier literature on this controversy (1–38).
67. John A. Mourant, "The Emergence of a Christian Philosophy in the Dialogues of Augustine," *Augustinian Studies* 1 (1970): 69–88.
68. Ibid., 72. Mourant writes: "The attack of Augustine upon the Academics reflects not merely his own moral certitude that there are eternal and immutable truths, but also his own commitment to truths that are based upon the authority of faith. Out of this discussion emerges the true function of Neoplatonism—the explication of the truths of faith. . . . [It] is Christianity which succeeds in restoring and making possible the adherence to the eternal truths taught by Neoplatonism. The true function of Neoplatonism is explication rather than certification."
69. William A. Christian, "The Creation of the World," in *A Companion to the Study of St. Augustine*, ed. Roy W. Battenhouse (New York: Oxford University Press, 1955); first published in *HTR* 46 (1953): 1–25.
70. Robert Russell, "The Role of Neoplatonism in St. Augustine's De Civitate Dei," in *Neoplatonism and Early Christian Thought*, ed. H. J. Blumenthal and R. A. Markus (London: Variorum Publications, 1981), 161ff.
71. *De civitate dei*, 10.2; as cited by Russell, ibid., 162. In a more negative vein, Russell goes on to write that Augustine's teaching is not identical with that of Plotinus: "For Augustine the source of the soul's illumination is the Supreme Being whereas, for Plotinus, it is not the Plotinian First Principle, the One, but the derived and subordinated Hypostasis called the Divine Intellect (nous)" (162).
72. Ibid., 167.
73. Alfred Warren Matthews, *The Development of St. Augustine from Neoplatonism to Christianity, 386–391* A.D. (Washington, D.C.: University Press of America, 1980), 30–31, 37; and see also Jean-Marie LeBlond, *Les conversions de saint Augustin* (Theologie 17; Paris: Aubrier, 1950).
74. Ibid., 29–30.
75. Ibid., 24–26. Matthews writes: "Only slowly did he begin to understand the significance of his decision in terms of his appreciation for classical Latin authors, ancient Greek philosophies, Manichaeism, Neoplatonism, and the various interpretations of Christian doctrine. His commitment to the authority of Christ was definite. But he did not have a clear idea of the Christ to whom he was devoted nor the means by which His authority was made known to believers. He did not think of his new commitment as excluding his former intellectual endeavors or his new found Platonism" (70). Such a conclusion, Matthews adds, agrees with the assessment of this period in Augustine's life made earlier by B. B. Warfield, *Encyclopedia of Religion and Ethics*, 2:219.
76. Donald Bates, "Sacred Scripture: The Recourse of St. Augustine," *The Tagastan* (Publication of the students of Augustinian College, Washington, D.C.) 20 (1958): 24–42.

77. *De Trinitate,* 13.19: "And those distinguished philosophers of the heathen who have been able to understand and discern the invisible things of God by those things which are made, have yet, as is said of them, 'held down the truth in iniquity' [Rom. 1:23]; because they philosophized without a Mediator, that is, without the man Christ, whom they neither believed to be about to come at the word of the prophets, nor to have come at that of the apostles."
78. *De Genesi contra Manichaeos,* 2.4; cf. *De moribus ecclesiae catholicae,* 1.2.
79. Ibid., 12.15.
80. Ibid., 4.17.
81. Ibid., 4.18.
82. This conclusion is articulated by O'Meara, "The Neoplatonism of St. Augustine," 41.
83. This is made somewhat difficult because the Greek term for "inspire" (θεόπνευτός = "God-breathed") occurs only once in the Bible, 2 Tim. 3:16.
84. Portalié, *A Guide to the Thought of St. Augustine,* 122.
85. R. A. Markus, *Saeculum: History and Society in the Theology of St. Augustine* (Cambridge: Cambridge University Press, 1970), 12.
86. J. N. D. Kelly, *Early Christian Doctrines* (revised ed., New York: Harper and Row, 1978), 63–64.
87. *De Genesi ad litteram,* 12.11.22. Edition used: *St. Augustine: The Literal Meaning of Genesis* (tr. and annotated by John Hammond Taylor; 2 vols.; New York: Newman/Paulist Press, 1982). Book 12 is in 2:178–231.
88. Ibid., 12.7.16–17.
89. Ibid., 12.7.16, 18.
90. Ibid., 12.14.29–30.
91. Ibid., 12.24.50–51.
92. Ibid., 12.25.52.
93. Ibid., 12.26.53.
94. Ibid., 12.26.54. Augustine adds: "And here we are speaking not of the face of the body but of that of the mind." See above, Section I. Augustine makes a similar distinction in *de civitate dei,* 16.6, a passage cited by Karl Barth, *Church Dogmatics* 1/1, 114.
95. *Confessiones,* 6.1.1. Book VI appears to be an account, as later related, of Augustine's despair of finding meaning. Cf. *De utilitate credendi,* 8, 20.
96. Testard, *Saint Augustin et Ciceron,* 1:83.
97. E.g., D. E. Roberts, "The Earliest Writings," in R. W. Battenhouse, ed., *A Companion to the Study of St. Augustine* (New York: Oxford University Press, 1955); John A. Mourant, "Augustine and the Academics," *Recherches augustiniennes* 4 (1966): 67–96; and John Heil, "Augustine's Attack on Skepticism: *The Contra Academicos,*" *HTR* 65 (1972): 99–116.
98. Heil, "Augustine's Attack," 103.
99. "The Earliest Writings," 95–100.
100. TeSelle, *Augustine the Theologian,* 43–55.
101. Charles Cochrane, *Christianity and Classical Culture: A Study of Thought and Action from Augustus to Augustine* (New York: Oxford University Press, 1963) 432–46.
102. Ibid., 435.
103. Frederick Copleston, *A History of Philosophy* (Garden City, N.Y.: Doubleday, 1962), 2/1.67.
104. *De beata vita*; cf. B. Montagues, "Les deux fonctions de la sagesse; ordonner et juger," *Revue des Sciences Philosophiques et Theologigues* 53 (1969): 675–86; and Wolfgang Stein, *Sapientia bei Augustinus* (Köln: Universitats Vierlag, 1973).

105. *De Trinitate*, 15.12.21: cf. Ronald Nash, *The Light of the Mind: St. Augustine's Theory of Knowledge* (Lexington, Ky.: University of Kentucky Press, 1969), 17.
106. *Contra Academicos*, 3.1.1; cf. *Retractiones* 1.1.1.
107. In addition to the cited portions of *De Trinitate*, see, for example, *De Quantitate animaeo*, 33, 70–76. Attempts to outline this working theory and knowledge may be found in most studies of Augustine's thought. See Nash, *Light of the Mind*, 9–10.
108. Frederick E. Van Fleteren acknowledges the controversy that surrounds Augustine's understanding of authority and reason. Following Olivier du Roy, Van Fleteren traces Augustine's ideas here in light of his life experiences. "Authority and Reason, Faith and Understanding in the Thought of St. Augustine," *Augustinian Studies* 4 (1973): 33–71.
109. *Contra Academicos*, 3.1.1; *De libero arbitrio*, 2–3, 7.
110. Gilson, *The Christian Philosophy of St. Augustine*, 27–69; Portalié, *A Guide to the Thought of St. Augustine*, 105–25.
111. *De Trinitate*, 11.9.16.
112. Gilson, *The Christian Philosophy of St. Augustine*, 42.
113. Gerard Verbeke, "Pensée et discernment chez S. Augustin," *Recherches augustiniennes* 2 (1962): 59–80. For a further treatment of this "Cartesian" dimension of Augustine's epistemology, see John A. Mourant, "The Cogitos: Augustinian and Cartesian," *Augustinian Studies* 10 (1979): 27–42.
114. Copleston, *A History of Philosophy*, 2/1.71.
115. Nash as well as others; e.g., Etienne Gilson. Whitney J. Oates argues this. Cf. Nash, *Light of the Mind*, 1–3.
116. *De Libero arbitrio*, 12, 34.
117. *De Genesi ad litteram*, 12.11.22–23; presented more fully in *De quantitate animae* 23.41–43, 69.
118. Ibid., 12.25.52.
119. See the study of Rudolf Lorenz, "Die Wissenschaftslehre Augustins," *Zeitschrift für Kirchengeschichte* 67 (1955–56): 29–60, 213–51. Note his discussion of the different ways of knowing the truth at the level of *scientia*: evidence, authority, and signs. These will be important in Augustine's understanding of Christianity.
120. Nash, *Light of the Mind*, 16. Nash cites *De civitate dei*, 19.18.
121. Gilson, *The Christian Philosophy of St. Augustine*, 29.
122. *De praedestinatione sanctorum* [2], 5.
123. *De utilitate credendi*, compare 26 and 29. Significantly, Augustine tells us that this was the first book he wrote after he had become a priest or presbyter in 391.
124. Ibid., 28. This is particularly true in matters of religion. Note Augustine's argument and his appeal to the wise, those who truly possess God. Cf. Gilson, *The Christian Philosophy of Saint Augustine*, 6.
125. *Confessiones*, 11.14.17; 28.38. We cannot pause to deal with this here but should note that speculation on Augustine's understanding of the nature of time has received lively attention during the ten year period, 1970–1980. See Terry Miethe, *Augustinian Bibliography, 1970–1980*, 74–76.
126. Harry A. Wolfson, *The Philosophy of the Church Fathers*, vol. 1: *Faith, Trinity, Incarnation* (Cambridge, Mass.: Harvard University Press, 1964), 127–40.
127. *De praedestinatione sanctorum* [2].5. Here Augustine writes that thinking is prior to believing. Belief is to think with assent. As we cannot think without God, so we cannot believe without Him.

128. Cf. Robert E. Cushman, "Faith and Reason," *A Comparison to the Study of St. Augustine* (New York: Oxford University Press, 1955), 310.
129. Gordon Lewis, "Faith and Reason in the Thought of St. Augustine" (Ph.D. diss., Syracuse University, 1959).
130. *De moribus ecclesiae catholicae*, 17.31.
131. *De libera arbitrio*, 1.2.4.
132. *Contra Faustum Manichaeum*, 52.19.
133. P. Magnus Löhrer, *Der Glaubensbegriff des Hl. Augustinus in Seinen ersten Schriften bis zu den Confessiones* (Zurich: Benziger Verlag, 1955), 90.
134. *Contra Academicos*, 3.19.42 (edition used: trans. and ed. Mary Patricia Garvey [Milwaukee: Marquette University Press, 1957]). Cf. *Epistula*, 11.4.
135. Markus, *Saeculum*, 187. Markus is citing *De Trinitate*, 3.2.22.
136. Ibid., 187.
137. Löhrer, *Glaubensbegriff des Hl. Augustinus*, 96; cf. Ernst Benz, *Augustinus Lehre von der Kirche* (Wiesbaden: Franz Steiner Verlag, 1954). See Bonner, *St. Augustine of Hippo*, 224–36.
138. R. Heinz, "Auctoritas," in *Vom Geist des Romertums. Auzgewahlte Aufsätze* (3d ed., 1960), 43–58; and K. H. Lütcke, *Auctoritas bei Augustin. Mit einer Einleitung zur römischen Vorgeschichte des Bergriffs* (Stuttgart: Kohlhammer, 1968).
139. Cf. Bonner, *St. Augustine of Hippo*, 231. Note the work of F. Dvornik, "Pope Gelarius and Emperor Anastasius I," *Byzantine Zeitschrift* 44 (1951): 111–16.
140. TeSelle, *Augustine the Theologian*, 32. Lorenz argues ("Wissenschaftslehre," 216–17) for the identity of legitimate authority and truth.
141. Summarized in *De magistro*, 7.19–20.
142. Ibid., 12. 40.
143. Ibid., 14.46.
144. Ann Clark, "Unity and Method in Augustine's 'De Magistro'," *Augustinian Studies* 8 (1977): 1–10.
145. Alan Richardson, *Christian Apologetics* (New York: Harper, 1947), 238.
146. Nash, *Light of the Mind*, 32. Nash cites *De libero arbitrio*, 1.2.4: one should "believe that God exists because that is taught in the books of great men who have left their testimony in writing that they lived with the Son of God, and because they have written that they saw things which could not have happened if there were no God."
147. See Augustine's argument in *De Trinitate*, 4.18 where he argues for the need for temporal things to carry us to eternal things; cf. *De Trinitate*, 12.19.
148. *De beata vita* 1; *Retractiones* 1.1.1 (PL 32, c. 583ff.); cf. B. Montagnes, "Les deuz fonctions de la sagesse: ordonner et juger," *RSPT* 53 (1969): 675–86; and Stein, *Sapientia*.
149. Cochrane, *Christianity and Classical Culture*, 432–46.
150. See Augustine's discussion of Plotinian illumination in *De civitate dei*, 10.2. Andrew Louth presents some differences between Augustinian and Plotinian mysticism in *The Origins of the Christian Mystical Tradition: From Plato to Denys* (Oxford: Clarendon, 1981/3), 134–57.
151. *Confessiones*, 11.4–5; Frederick Copleston, *History of Philosophy*, 2/1 67, 83–88.
152. Vernon J. Bourke (*Augustine's Quest*) writes that a spiritual creature is in an unformed state until it turns toward its Creator: in turning it is illumined. Such illumination makes possible the knowledge of eternal truth. Bourke cites *De Genesi ad litteram*, 1.3.7–1.4.9. As Augustine delineates in *De Trinitate* 12. 15, this is not Platonic reminiscence.

153. Aimé Solignac, "Analyse et sources de la Question De Ideis," *Augustinus Magister* 1 (1954): 307–15.
154. Theodore Kondoleon, "Divine Exemplarism in Augustine," *Augustinian Studies* 1 (1970): 181–95.
155. Viktor Warnach, "Erleuchtung und Einsprechung bei Augustinus," *Augustinus Magister* 1 (Paris: Études Augustiniennes, 1954): 429–50.
156. The following list is based on the summary of different perspectives on illumination found in Portalié, *A Guide to the Thought of St. Augustine*, 24–30, 109–14; cf. Bruce S. Bubacq, "Augustine's Illumination Theory and Epistemic Structuring," *Augustinian Studies* 11 (1980): 35–48.
157. Johannes Hessen, *Die unmittelbare Erkenntnis nach dem A. Augustinus* (Paderborn: Schöningh, 1919). A survey of recent German debate over the question of Augustine's theory of illumination is found in the study by Caroline E. Schuetzinger, *The German Controversy on St. Augustine's Illumination Theory* (New York: Pageant Press, 1960).
158. Ronald H. Nash, "Some Philosophic Sources for Augustine's Illumination Theory," *Augustinian Studies* 2 (1971): 49. These ideas are outlined at length in Nash's study, *The Light of the Mind*.
159. See Charles Boyer, *L'idée de vérité dans la philosophie de s. Augustin*, 2d ed. (Paris: Beauchesne, 1940), in the period prior to the focus of our study.
160. This position is held by Etienne Gilson, *Introduction a l'étude de Saint Augustin* (Paris: Librarie Philosophique J. Urin, 1943), 88–170.
161. See Augustine's discussion of "natural" phenomenon and "miracle" in *De Trinitate* 3.5.
162. *Confessiones* 10.
163. *De moribus manichaeorum* 8.11.
164. Cochrane, *Christianity and Classical Culture*, 437.
165. *De civitate dei*, 18.41. Augustine writes of the concord of the Scriptures in distinction from the discord of the philosophers, that the oracles of God were entrusted to Israel. Cf. *De utilitate credendi*, 13: "Believe me, whatever there is in these Scriptures, it is lofty and divine: there is in them altogether truth, and a system of teaching most suited to refresh and renew minds: and clearly as ordered in measure, as that there is no one but may draw thence, what is enough for himself, if only he approach to draw with devotion and piety, as true religion demands." Cf. *Ennarationes in Psalmos*, 8.7.
166. *De Trinitate* III, ii, 23–24: ". . . when the holy prophet speaks, although we say, The prophet said, we mean nothing else to be understood than that the Lord said; and if we were to say, The Lord said, we should not put the prophet aside, but only intimate who spoke by him." On the agreement of the testaments, see *Contra Adimantum Manichaei disipulam*, 3.3 (*PL* 42, 134).
167. Charles J. Costello, *St. Augustine's Doctrine of the Inspiration and Canonicity of Scripture* (Washington, D.C.: The Catholic University of America, 1930), 3.
168. I am guided here by the work of A. D. R. Polman, *Word of God*, 39–53.
169. *De consensu evangelistarum*, 1.2.3–7. Augustine notes: "But the fact is, that just as they received each of them the gift of inspiration, they abstained from adding to their several labours any superfluous conjoint composition" (I, ii, 4).
170. Ibid., 1.16.24.
171. Ibid., 1.25.54. Note the purpose of the analogy following the cited portion: to promote "unity and . . . concordant service. . . ."
172. Ibid., 2, prologue and compare 2.5.16.
173. Ibid., 2.11.28: cf. 2.37.67; 46.97. These texts are important for the consideration of the question of inerrancy in Augustine and will be taken up in section 4.

174. Further examples may be found in Costello, *St. Augustine's Doctrine*, 6–28.
175. I am dependent on the work of Polman, *Word of God*, 43–46; and Costello, *St. Augustine's Doctrine*, 4–5.
176. Polman (*Word of God*, 44) writes: "Augustin must have taken it [*inspirare*] from 2 Timothy 3:16, where this verb appears in the Latin translation of the New Testament which he was using." Cf. *Collatio cum maximino Arianorum episcopo*, 30.
177. *De gratia Christi et de peccato originali*, 43; *De gratia et libero arbitio*, 3: as cited in Polman, ibid., 45.
178. *De consensu evangelistarum* I, 10, as cited in Polman, ibid.
179. *De Trinitate*, 3, pref., 2.
180. Polman, ibid., 45.
181. Ibid. As in *De consensu evangelistarum*, 1.54 and *Epistula* 82.3; cf. Costello, *St. Augustine's Doctrine*, 16.
182. Costello, *St. Augustine's Doctrine*, 13.
183. Polman, *Word of God*, 51.
184. Warnach, "Erleuchtung und Einsprechung bei Augustinus," 429–50.
185. *Epistula* 150.2.
186. *De Genesi ad litteram*, 12.
187. Rudolf Allers ("Illumination et vérités éternelles. Une étude sur l'a priori augustinien," *Augustinus Magister* 1 [1954]: 477–90) argues that one simply cannot work out an intelligible theory from Augustine's work.
188. Portalié, *A Guide to the Thought of St. Augustine*, 109. Portalié cites *De Trinitate*, 14.12.15.
189. Hermann Sasse, "Sacra Scriptura: Observations on Augustine's Doctrine of Inspiration," *The Reformed Theological Review* 14 (1955): 65–80; esp. 67.
190. Ibid., 71. Sasse cites *De consensu evangelistarum*, 1.20.28.
191. Sasse (ibid., 72) cites Augustine, *De consensu evangelistarum*, 1.35.54.
192. Ibid., 72–73: "However, this personal contribution does not seem fully to have been effaced where the activity of the divine Spirit is understood not as *dictare* but as *suggerere*. In this way Augustine explains the differences in the gospel accounts with regard to the sequence of events, that each of the Evangelists believed it to have been his duty to relate what he had to relate in that order in which it had pleased God to *suggest to his recollection* the matters in which he was engaged in recording."
193. Ibid., 73. Sasse (73–74) adds: "It is one of the greatest tragedies of church history, that Christianity, through the authority of the Fathers of the Church, had to drag along through the centuries a theory which is simply the painfully Christianized form of a pagan doctrine of inspired writings."
194. Bruce Vawter, *Biblical Inspiration* (Philadelphia: Westminster, 1972), 34.
195. Ibid., 21–22.
196. As cited by Vawter, ibid., 22: A. Bea, "Deus auctor Sacrae Scriptunae: Herkunft und Bedeutung der Formel," *Angelicum* 20 (1943): 16–31.
197. Polman, *Word of God*, 51.
198. Ibid., 54–62. For example: (1) Scripture gives a reliable but not complete view of God. (2) Scripture is not a scientific textbook; its aim is moral and soteriological. (3) The historical description in Scripture concerns primarily Christ and His church (the City of God and its Head). (4) There is a need to read the biblical data carefully and correctly.
199. Geoffrey Bromiley, "The Church Fathers and Holy Scripture," in *Scripture and Truth*, ed. D. A. Carson and John D. Woodbridge (Grand Rapids: Zondervan, 1983). The article is similar to his earlier effort, "The Church

Doctrine of Inspiration," in *Revelation and the Bible*, ed. Carl F. H. Henry (Grand Rapids: Baker, 1958), 205–17; esp. 208.

200. Ibid., 208: "We must not exaggerate these weaknesses in relation to the real strength of patristic doctrine and in avoidance of cruder errors especially in relation to pagan ecstaticism. Indeed, even the human element is not altogether lost in the divine, for Augustine can find a place for this side by side with his doctrine of dictation (*De consensu evangelistarum,* 2.12), and it was realized that the unpolished style of some of the authors could not be attributed to the Spirit except by way of condescension."

201. Heinrich H. Vogels, "St. Augustins Schrift De Consensu Evangelistarum," *Bibl. Studien* (Frieburg im Breisgares, 1908), 13:67–68.

202. Markus (*Saeculum,* 187–88) follows and agrees with Vogels. Moreover, he adds a further dimension to his remarks by noting that this example shows the "ecclesial" nature of inspiration, "an emphasis almost forgotten since Augustine until its revival in our own days by Karl Rahner—and tells nothing about what is special about inspiration as distinct from any other action of the Head in his members" (188).

203. J. N. D. Kelly, *Early Christian Doctrines* (rev. ed., New York: Harper and Row, 1978), 60–63.

204. Ibid., 63.

205. Cochrane, *Christianity and Classical Culture,* 476–77. Cochrane writes: "At this point, however, an emphatic warning becomes necessary. By the light of the Spirit Augustine does not mean the ecstatic illumination professed by Tertullian on the basis of the Montainst notions regarding the *Paraclete*" (476).

206. Kelly, *Early Christian Doctrines,* 63.

207. TeSelle, *Augustine the Theologian,* 199. TeSelle does add that later, in *De civitate dei,* "The divine omnipotence and the authority of Scripture" is appealed to more readily.

208. Markus, *Saeculum,* 13. Markus adds: "The form and content of his narrative may be historical; it is his judgment, his interpretation of them in terms of the pattern of the redemptive history into which divine inspiration vouchsafes him insight, that differentiate his history from history as it might be written by a noninspired writer. Inspiration, the gift of prophecy (in this wide sense) is the constitutive difference between 'sacred' and 'secular' history" (14). Markus continues by noting the effect of the transference of the idea of inspiration from the prophet to the prophetic text in Augustine's later thinking.

209. *De Trinitate,* 12.15.24.

210. *De Trinitate,* 1.1–2.

211. *Ennarationes in Psalmos,* 119.105.

212. Ibid. Augustine writes: "Is it He who was in the beginning God with God, that is, the Word by whom all things were made? It is not thus. For that Word is a light, but is not a lantern. For a lantern is a creature, not a creator; and it is lighted by participation of an unchangeable. . . . For no creature, however, rational and intellectual, is lighted by itself, but is lighted by participation of eternal Truth. . . . Since therefore the only-begotten Word, coequal with the Father, is styled a light; and man when enlightened by the Word is also called a light . . . and since no man of these is the Word, and that Word by whom they were enlightened is not a lantern; what is this word, which is thus called a light and a lantern at the same time, save we understand the word which was sent unto the Prophets, or which was preached through the Apostles; not Christ the word, but the word of Christ, of which it is written, 'Faith cometh by

hearing and hearing by the word of God?' . . . What therefore he saith, 'Thy word' is the word which is contained in all the holy Scriptures."

213. *Epistula,* 135.5.18. Augustine writes: ". . . by the condescension of its style, it invites all not only to be fed with the truth which is plain, but also to be exercised with the truth which is concealed, having both in its simple and obscure portions the same truth. . . . By these means wayward minds are corrected, weak minds are nourished, and strong minds are filled with pleasure, in such a way as is profitable to all. This doctrine has no enemy but the man who, being in error, is ignorant of its incomparable usefulness, or, being spiritually diseased, is averse to its healing power."

214. In addition to what was cited there, see Jean Bosc for the place of Scripture in Augustine's growing doctrinal understanding, "Saint Augustin, docteur évangelique," *Foi et Vie* 53 (1955): 201–15; and with respect to his spiritual life, Paul Agaësse, "Écriture Sainte et vie spirituelle Saint Augustin," *Dictiannaire de Spiritualité* 4, fasc. 25 (Paris: Beauchesne, 1958), c. 155–58.

215. TeSelle, *Augustine the Theologian,* 21–22.

216. Oswald Loretz, *The Truth of the Bible* (New York: Herder & Herder, 1968), 72.

217. Van der Meer, *Augustine the Bishop,* 440–50. Van der Meer writes: "The whole work of Augustine owes its very flesh, its very bones and marrow, to the word of God. His whole vocabulary is permeated by the rich and somewhat crude speech of the old translations of the Bible; . . . it would be difficult to point to a man who was more completely filled by the Holy Scriptures than was Augustine. Origen is the learned visionary, Jerome the 'three tongued' scholar, but Augustine is, above all, the believing Bible student" (343).

218. These categories are raised up by Matthews, *The Development of St. Augustine,* 24–25.

219. Polman, *The Word of God,* 74.

220. Ibid., 13.

221. Ibid., 32–33. Matthews (*The Development of St. Augustine,* 3–4) places the major shift a little earlier (with respect to Scripture, cf. 122–23).

222. Ibid., 13.

223. *Confessiones* 6.4.6.

224. I am following the helpful bibliographic work of Julien Ries, "La Bible chez saint Augustin et chez les manichéens," *Revue des études augustiniennes* 7 (1961): 231–43; 9 (1963): 201–15; 10 (1964): 309–29.

225. See Eulogio Nebreda, *Bibliographia Augustiniana* (Rome: Typ Pol. "Curore di Maria," 1928); also the work of Jean Pépin (1954) and particularly H. von Compenhausen, "Neuere Augustin-Literatur," *ThR* (1948): 51–72.

226. Bonner, *St. Augustine Hippo. Life and Controversies,* 193–223.

227. Specifically, note Augustine's work, *Contra Faustum Manichaeum,* written circa A.D. 400. The forms of Faustus's attack upon Christianity came in three areas: (1) the geneological records leading to Christ's birth were divergent, therefore spurious; (2) the present form of the Gospels was the result of Judaizing influences; (3) the immorality of the patriarchs of the Old Testament cast their teachings in doubt. Cf. Bonner, *St. Augustine of Hippo,* 216–23; Ries, "La Bible chez s. Augustin," 9 (1963): 210. Ries writes: "Soucieux de prouver la véracité de la Bible, Augustine trace la frontière entre les livres apocryphes et les livres canoniques, ces derniers marques du sceau de la tradition apostolique" (210).

228. Heinrich J. Vogels, "Die Heilige Schrift bei Augustinus," in *Aurelius Augustinus,* 411–21.

229. P. Lagrange, "Les rétractations exégétiques de saint Augustin," in *Miscellanea Augustiniana* (Rome, 1931), 373–95, cf. Fritz Hofmann, *Der Kirchenbegriff des Hl. Augustinus* (Munich, 1933).

230. Katharina Staritz, *Augustinus Schöpfungsglaube dargestellt nach seinen Genesisauslegung* (Marbourg-Breslau: Inaug. Diss., 1931).

231. Paul Monceaux, "Le manichéen Fauste de Milev: Restitution des ses 'capitual'," *Mémories de l'Académie des Inscriptions et Belles Lettres* (1924); and "S. Augustin et S. Antoine," *Miscellanea Augustiniana* 2 (1932), 61–89. See his older study, *Histoire littéraire de l'Afrique chrétienne*, 7 vols. (Paris: E. Leroux, 1901–1923).

232. Alberto Pincherle, *La formazione teoloica di san Agostino* (Rome: Edizioni italiane, 1947). I am dependent upon Ries, "La Bible chez s. Augustin," 10 (1964): 309.

233. Ibid., 10.

234. *De doctrina christiana,* 3.30.42–37.55.

235. *De civitate dei,* 18.38.

236. Ibid., 11.1–3; 17.1.

237. *De doctrina christiana,* 3.44. This is not said to exclude the influence of the weight of catholic tradition upon Augustine.

238. Markus, *Saeculum,* 188–96.

239. *De vera religione,* 25.46 (*PL* 34); as cited by Markus, ibid.

240. This idea of development in Augustine's concept of the canon needs to be considered very carefully in light of Matthew's discussion (*The Development of St. Augustine,* 122–24) and citations of Scripture in the early Augustine. Here there appears to be a quite authoritative, operative canon. Again we see the need for a compendium of Scripture references in Augustine.

241. Markus, ibid., 188–91; note Augustine's argument in *De civitate dei,* 18.38.

242. Brown, *Augustine of Hippo,* 252.

243. Ulrych Duchrow, *Sprachverständnis und bibisches Hören bei Augustin* (Tübigen: J. C. B. Mohr and Paul Siebeck, 1965), 1–2.

244. See Duchrow's study on the utility of such signs since the Fall and in light of our own: "Signum und Superbia beim jungen Augustin (386–90)," *Revue des études augustiniennes* 7 (1966): 369–72.

245. *De catechizandis rudibus,* 14.8; cf. *De civitate dei,* 11.3.

246. Duchrow, *Sprachverständnis,* 151. Duchrow writes: "Die Heilige Schrift wird auf diese Weise zu einem der Schöpfung parallelen geschichtlichen Hinweissystem auf die geistige Wirklichkeit."

247. I am following R. A. Markus, "St. Augustine on Signs," in *Augustine, A Collection of Critical Essays,* ed. R. A. Markus (Garden City, N.Y.: Doubleday, 1972), 61–85; repr. from *Phronesis* 2 (1957): 60–83.

248. *De magistro,* 11.38 as cited by Markus, ibid., 71.

249. *De doctrina christiana,* 2.1.1.

250. Ibid., 1.2.2.

251. Markus, "St. Augustine on Signs," 73–75.

252. *De doctrina christiana,* 2.1.1.

253. Ibid., 2.3.4.

254. Ibid., 2.5.6.

255. Ibid., preface.

256. Donald E. Daniels, "The Argument of the *De Trinitate* and Augustine's Theory of Signs," *Augustinian Studies* 8 (1977): 33–54.

257. Markus, "St. Augustine on Signs," 80. Markus cites *De Trinitate,* 15.11.20. Markus writes that Augustine has, then, two theories of language, one

approaching the question from the hearer's side and the other from the speaker's or thinker's side (82).

258. *De Trinitate*, 1.1. See also the work of Alfred Schindler, *Wort und Analogie in Augustinus Trinitätslehre* (Tübingen: J. C. B. Mohr, 1965). Schindler takes a different tack from Markus and argues that the concept of the inner word is not important as such to Augustine. It is discussed only because necessitated by the nature of the Trinitarian speculation at hand. He bases his conclusions upon his study of stoic terminology.

259. *De Trinitate*, 12.15.24–25.

260. *De Trinitate*, 1.2. Referring to the different ways of framing one's knowledge of God as cited earlier (1.1), Augustine writes that Scripture uses words from corporeal and spiritual perception so that even the weak may be moved to seek those things that are above . . . (1.1.2). Those who attempt to know God through some form of mystical ascent, apart from the aid He gives "are more mischievously and emptily vain than their fellows . . ." (1.1.2); cf. 4.18 and 12.19.

261. Here we may pose van der Meer's (*Augustine the Bishop*, 438) question: "Does the truth of this particular world consist in the concepts or in the biblical facts that are always transforming themselves into symbols?" His answer: in a sense both.

262. For a helpful description of the current scene in religious language against which one may want to understand Augustine, see Avery Dulles, *Revelation and the Quest for Unity* (Washington & Cleveland: Corpus Books, 1968), 243; see Robert H. Ayers, "Language Theory and Analysis in Augustine," *SJT* 29 (1981): 1–12.

263. Ludwig Wittgenstein, *Philosophische Untersuchungen* (Oxford: Clarendon, 1953), 2. Wittgenstein is critical of Augustine's thought as expressed in *Confessiones* 1.8 for apparently delineating too narrow a referential view of language.

264. Jackson, "The Theory of Signs," in *De Doctrina Christiana*, 92–147.

265. Rudolf Lorenz, "Die Wissenschaftslehre Augustins," *Zeitschrift für Kirchengeschichte* 67 (1955–56): 46–49, but note the argument of the whole, esp. 57–60.

266. Gerhard Strauss, *Schriftgebrauch, Schriftauslegung und Schriftbeweis bei Augustin* (Tübingen: J. C. B. Mohr/Paul Siebeck, 1959).

267. Strauss, ibid., 74–80; cf. Lorenz, "Wissenschaftslehre," 216–28, esp. 218.

268. Duchrow, *Sprachverständnis*, 206ff. For Lorenz's comment, see "Zwölf Jahre" 39 (1975): 274. I am following him here.

269. *De Trinitate*, 9.7.12; 15.11.20. Duchrow (*Sprachverständnis*, 187ff.) remains critical of Warnach ("Erleuchtung und Einsprechung") who argued that illumination comes through language and may be conceived of as judgment.

270. Duchrow (*Sprachverständnis*, 153) notes: "Der Geganstand der Predigt, die Heilige Schrift als Einheit von res und signa, wird nun allerdings von Augustin nicht einfach summarisch dargestellt, sondern tief metaphytisch verankert."

271. As implied Hans-Georg Gadamer, *Truth and Method* (New York: Seabury, 1975), 378–81.

272. Cochrane, *Christianity and Classical Culture*, 75–81, 157–62, 336–37.

273. Douglas W. Johnson, "Verbum in the Early Augustine (386–87)," *Recherches augustiniennes* 8 (1972): 25–53.

274. Ibid., 29. Johnson acknowledges that his conclusions differ somewhat from those of Duchrow and Schindler. The former argues that Augustine's *Verbum* should be associated with illuminism, the latter with logos speculation.

275. Strauss, *Schriftgebrauch*, 129; Duchrow, *Sprachverständnis*, 156.

276. *De doctrina christiana* 2.16.23–26.
277. Peter Stunner, "Charismatische und methodische Schriftauslegung nach Augustins Prolog zu 'Du doctrina christiana,'" *KD* 1 (1955): 59–69, 85–103.
278. Eugene Kevane, "Paideia and Anti-Paideia: The Prooemium of St. Augustine's *De Doctrina Christiana*," *Augustinian Studies* 1 (1970): 153–80.
279. Ibid., 161–62.
280. *Confessiones*, 7.20.
281. Hill, "Augustine as Preacher," 463–71. For a larger view of this work, cf. Henri-Irénée Marrou, *Historie de l'éducation dans l'Antiquité*, 5th ed (Paris: du Seuil, 1960). On Augustine's use of the classics, see Harold Hagendahl, *Augustine and the Latin Classics* (Stockholm: Almquist & Wiksell, 1967).
282. Cochrane, *Christianity and Classical Culture*, 474–77. Cf. *De doctrina christiana* 2.11.16–2.31.48.
283. Ibid., 475.
284. Robert M. Grant (*A Short History of the Interpretation of the Bible*, revised ed. [New York: Macmillan, 1972], 109–11) points to the importance of this word in the development of Augustine's theology.
285. Harry Austryn Wolfson, *The Philosophy of the Church Fathers*, 3d rev. ed. (Cambridge, Mass.: Harvard University, 1976), 68. Cf. *De utilitate credendi* for an early view of Augustine's fourfold exegesis of Scripture. Augustine writes: "All the Scripture therefore, which is called the Old Testament, is handed down four-fold to them who desire to know it, according to history, according to aetiology, according to analogy, according to allegory" (chap. 5). Cf. *De vera religione*, 50.99.
286. For examples of those who defend the literal sense in Augustine, see Costello, *St. Augustine's Doctrine*, 49–52; Wolfson, ibid., 68; Heiko Obermann, *Forerunners*, 283. Note Augustine's own remarks in *De doctrina christiana*, 2.10. Still, what the literal sense meant to Augustine is not always completely clear, as is pointed out in Pontet's comment (*L'Exégése de St. Augustin prédicateur*, 144) that when Augustine set out to expound a text he did not first ask what the historical author had intended, rather what God had intended through the literal and other "senses" of Scripture.
287. Wolfson, *Philosophy of the Church Fathers*, 73–78.
288. Jean Pépin, "Saint Augustin et la function protreptique de l'allégorie," *Recherches augustiniennes* 1 (1958): 245–86. Augustine's knowledge of Philo of Alexandria, so influential upon Origen and the entire tradition of the church in the East, has been demonstrated by Berthold Altaner, "Augustinus und Philo von Alexandrien," in *Zeitschrift für katholische Theologie* 63 (1941): 81–90.
289. James Preus, *From Shadow to Promise: Old Testament Interpretation from Augustine to the Young Luther* (Cambridge, Mass.: The Belknap Press, 1969), 12. Preus cites *De doctrina christiana* 3.37.56 and the work of Gerhard Ebeling for this distinction.
290. J. Barton Payne, "Biblical Problems and Augustine's Allegorizing," *WTJ* 14 (1951–52): 46–53.
291. *Confessiones*, 12.31.42; *De doctrina christiana*, 3.27.38; and *De Genesi ad litteram*, 11.1.2. Cf. Costello, *St. Augustine's Doctrine*, 23–28; and cf. *De doctrina christina* 4.27.38.
292. Portalié, *A Guide to the Thought of St. Augustine*, 23. Cf. TeSelle, *Augustine the Theologian*, 204.
293. See, for example, Berthold Altaner, "Die Benützung von original greichischen Vätertexten durch Augustinus," *ZRGG* 1 (1948): 71–79; "Augustinus und die

neutestamentliche Apokryphen, Sibyllinen und Sextussprüche. Eine Quellenkritische Untersuchung," in *Analecta Bollandiana*, Vol. 67 (Mélanges Paul Peeters; Bruxelles: Société des bollandistes, 1949), 1:236–48.

294. Cornelius Petrus Mayer, *Die Zeichen in der geistigen Entwicklung und in der Tieologie* 2: *Die antimanichäische Epoche* (Würzburg: Augustinus Verlag, 1974).

295. Edwin Leroy Fromm, *The Prophetic Faith of Our Fathers: The Historical Development of Prophetic Interpretation* 1: *The Early Church* (Washington: Review and Herald, 1950).

296. Paula Fredriksen Landes, "Tyconius and the End of the World," *Revue des études Augustiniennes* 28 (1982): 59–75.

297. Preus, *From Shadow to Promise*, 1–12.

298. *De spiritu et littera* as cited by Preus, ibid.

299. Preus, ibid., 16.

300. Indeed, it is central to his Psalms commentary, *Enarrationes in Psalmos*, finished in A.D. 416.

301. John Hammond Taylor, trans. and ed., *St. Augustin: The Literal Meaning of Genesis*, 2 vols. (New York: Newman Press, 1982), 5, 9–12. Cf. Gilles Pelland, *Cinq études d'Augustin sur le début de la Genèse* (Tournai & Montreal: Descleé 1972). Cf. Augustine's introduction to *De Genesi ad litteram* 1.1.1.

302. *Genesi ad litteram* I, xx, 40. See Pontet, *L'Exégése de St. Augustin*, 133.

303. *De doctrina christiana* 2.6.8; 2.9.14 as cited in Preus, *Shadow to Promise*, 12.

304. Portalié, *A Guide to the Thought of St. Augustine*, 122–23.

305. *De Genesi ad litteram* 1.19.39; cf. 1.21.41 and 2.9.20.

306. See his criticism of the Manichaean "tricks for the unwary" in *De moribus ecclesiae catholicae*, 1, 2; cf. 29, 59–61.

307. In both Testaments recourse to authority and the temporal and corporal images found there are designed to carry us to eternal things: cf. *De moribus ecclesiae catholicae* 1.7; *De Trinitate*, 4.18; 12.19.

308. *De doctrina christiana*, 10.1.2; Costello (*St. Augustine's Doctrine*, 3) cites *Contra Adimentum*, 3.3 and 7.5.

309. *De Trinitate*, pref., 1.

310. *De doctrina christiana*, 3.10; 1.34, 40.

311. Ibid., 1.39.43; cf. *De moribus ecclesiae catholicae*, 30.

312. Hermann-Josef Sieben, "Die 'res' der Bibel. Eine Analyse von Augustinus, De doctr. Christ. I–III," *Revue des études augustiniennes* 21 (1975): 72–90. See his conclusions on 80, 85, 90.

313. Dany Dideberg, *Saint Augustin et la première épitre de saint Jean. Une théologie de l'agapè* (Paris: Beauchesne, 1975). Dideberg rejects Nygren's thesis that the *caritas* of Augustine is other than the *agape* of the New Testament. This was first challenged as long ago as 1938 by John Burnaby, *Amor Dei: A Study of the Religion of St. Augustine* (London: Hodder and Stoughton, 1938).

314. Eugene TeSelle, "Some Reflections on Augustine's Use of Scripture," *Augustinian Studies* 7 (1976): 165–78. TeSelle cites Dideberg, ibid., 158–70.

315. *De doctrina christiana* 2.15.22. See Portalié, *A Guide to the Thought of St. Augustine*, 122–23.

316. *De doctrina christiana*, 2.15.22: see J. Jellicoe, *The Septuagint and Modern Study* (Oxford: Clarendon, 1968), 29–58.

317. Heinrich Karpp, "'Prophet' oder 'Dolmetscher'? Die Galtung der Septuaginta in der alten Kirche," *Festschrift für Günther Dehn*, ed. Wilhelm Schneemelcher (Neukirchen Kreis Moers: Buchhandlung des Erziehungsvereins, 1957), 103–17.

318. *Epistula* 28.2.
319. *Epistula* 71.3.5.
320. Ibid. The text goes on to say that for fear he might lose his congregation the poor bishop at Oea reverted to the older translations.
321. *Epistula,* 75.6.20.
322. *Epistula,* 83.5.34–35.
323. *De civitate dei,* 15.13. XVIII, 42–44.
324. Note the strong ecclesial dimension of authority in XVIII, 43.
324. *De Trinitate,* 4.17.
325. Ibid.
326. Ibid., 15.13.
327. Ibid., 18.44.
328. Ibid.
329. The canonical books are listed by Augustine in *De doctrina christiana,* 2.8–9.
330. *De civitate dei,* 18.38.
331. Ibid., 11.1; 18.38.
332. Ibid., 18.381.
333. Ibid., 18.41.
335. *De civitate dei,* 18.41.
336. TeSelle, "Some Reflections on Augustine's Use of Scripture," 174.
337. Bonner, *St. Augustine of Hippo,* 230. Bonner cites Pontet, *L'exégése de S. Augustin prédicateur,* 111–48; and *Conf.,* 8.15.16; *Contr. Faust.* 11.5: *Enarr. in Ps.* 103.1.8; 90.20.1.
338. Ibid. Bonner cites *De doctrina christiana* 3.2.2; *De fide et symbolo,* 1; De 7. 12.
339. Anne-Marie La Bonnardière, *Biblia,* various volumes (Paris: Études Augustiennes, 1955); cf. Francois Chatillon, "Orchestration scripturaire," *Revue du Moyen Age Latin* 10 (1954): 210–18.
340. I am following TeSelle, "Some Reflections on Augustine's Use of Scripture," 175. Howard J. Loewen draws this theology out by arguing that the authority of Scripture is "fused" in Augustine's thinking with a "churchly context," its "signifying function," and "the interiority of the knowledge of faith" ("The Use of Scripture in Augustine's Theology," *SJT* 34 [1981]: 201–24).
341. *De doctrina christiana* 1.39.43–40.44. This in light of *De Trinitate* 1.1.2.
342. Alan Richardson, art. "Scripture, Authority of," *IDB* 4.248.
343. Kelly (*Early Christian Doctrines,* 52–79) is particularly helpful.
344. B. B. Warfield, "Augustine's Doctrine of Knowledge and Authority," in *Calvin and Augustine,* ed. by S. G. Craig (Philadelphia: Presbyterian and Reformed, repr. 1956) 387–477, esp. 432 (orig. *PTR,* 1907).
345. Johannes Schildenberger, "Gegenwartsbedeutung exegetischer Grundsätzes hl. Augustinus," *Augustinus Magister* 2 (Paris: Études Augustiniennes, 1954), 677–90.
346. *De doctrina christiana* preface,
347. *De doctrina christiana,* 1.39.43–46, 44; cf. Pontet, *L'Exégése,* 35–110, 447–514, 578–79.
348. Debate over the interpretation of Galatians 2, reopened in the nineteenth century in the work of F. C. Baur (d. 1860) and in several important monographs in this century, forms a rich and controversial chapter in the early history of the church. Not only are doctrinal and theological or exegetical concerns central to the interpretation, but psychological and historical issues are drawn in as well. Then too is the problem of whether the passage should be read literally or tropologically.
349. Not simply a conflict over practice, Galatians 2:15ff. reveals an underlying

theological problem based upon Paul's concept of the interplay of law and grace: life in the new age is a movement from law-observance to freedom "in Christ." For Paul, Jesus' death on the cross marked the end of the time of law (Gal. 3). A return to the obedience of the law reverses the flow of God's salvific activity and invalidates its corollary, justification. As such the incident presents in brief many of the questions raised of Scripture by the Manichaeans and by Porphyry in an effort to discredit Christianity. According to J. Schmid (*S. S. Eusebii Hieronymi et Aurelii Augustini Epistolae mutuae*, "Prolegomena," in *Florilegium Patristicum* 22 [1930]: 14), it was probably the author of the Ebionite *Clementine Homilies* who first exegeted this debate as occurring between Paul and Simon Magus, saving Simon Peter's name from embarrassment.

350. *Epistula* 28.3: "For it seems to me that most disastrous consequences must follow upon our believing that anything false is found in the sacred books: that is to say, that the men by whom the Scripture has been given to us, and committed to writing, did put down in these books anything false."

351. Earlier Augustine had written in *De utilitate credendi*, 13: "Believe me, whatever there is in these Scriptures, it is lofty and divine: there is in them altogether truth, and a system of teaching most suited to refresh and renew minds: and clearly so ordered in measure, as that there is no one but may draw thence, what is enough for himself, if only he approach to draw with devotion and piety, as true religion demands."

352. *De mendacio* (A.D. 395). Augustine will later (c. 420) write a book against lying, *Contra Mendacium*. In *On Lying* Augustine debates the question of whether or not it is ever proper to lie. Lies are seen to be any form of "double-mindedness" (3). For God to have one thing in mind and yet signify something different would be to create a falsehood that is contrary to his nature. Augustine argues that dissimulation is always reproved or corrected where found in Scripture. His discussion of the incident between Peter and Paul is in section 8.

353. *Epistula* 40. Here Paul's correction of Peter is not merely a diplomatic ruse. Truth is more important than duty.

354. *Epistula* 83.1.3: "I have learned to yield this respect and honor only to the canonical books of Scripture: of these alone do I most firmly believe that the authors were completely free from error. And if in these writings I am perplexed by anything which appears to me opposed to truth, I do not hesitate to suppose that either the ms. is faulty, or the translator has not caught the meaning of what was said, or I myself have failed to understand it." See *De consensu evangelium* 2.12.28; *De civitate dei*, 21.6.1.

355. Ibid., ii, 6.

356. See Augustine's discussion of examples of apparent falsehood in the Old Testament: Sarah (Gen. 18:15); Jacob (Gen. 27:19); Egyptian midwives (Ex. 1:19–20) in *De mendacio*, 5.

357. *Epistula* 82.2.8–22.

358. Ibid., 2.6.

359. *De mendacio*, 4.43.

360. Wolfson, *Philosophy of the Church*, 29. Wolfson cites *De civitate dei*, 11.3.

361. Ibid., 129–30. Wolfson continues further in his discussion of faith and reason: "From all this it follows that belief and hence also faith, according to Augustine, is an assent not only to rationally undemonstrated teachings of Scripture, but also to rationally demonstrated teachings of Scriptures" (135). See his criticism of the Manichaean use of the Scripture and defense of its full reliability in *Contra Faustum Manichaeum*, 32.19 as cited by Wolfson (136–37); cf. *De civitate dei*, 12.10.2; 18.40.

362. *De mendacio*, 8–9; *De doctrina christiana* II.
363. In the seventeenth century when more editions of Augustine's works were being produced than ever before, this influence was strong, for example, in the thought of the French theologian and philosopher, Antoine Arnauld (1612–94), or the earlier English Calvinist, William Whitaker (1548–95). I owe this observation to John D. Woodbridge. For perceptions of Augustine and his work in the seventeenth century, see the entire edition of *XVIIe siècle* 135 (April/June 1982), entitled "Le siècle de saint Augustin."
364. James Burtchaell, *Catholic Theories of Biblical Inspiration Since 1810: A Review and Critique* (Cambridge: Cambridge University Press, 1969), 1–2. On Augustine's influence, see 110–12, 125.
365. Ibid., 8–44. Burtchaell gives a very detailed history of developments.
366. Loretz traces the background to Vatican II as it touches upon the question of the nature of biblical authority in *The Truth of the Bible*, 71ff.
367. P. Zerafa, "The Limits of Biblical Inerrancy," *Angelicum* 39 (1962): 92–119; quotation is on 92. Examining such limits (literary form, formal object, prophet-hagiographer distinction), Zerafa argues for a close study of specific texts (118), which even then fails to do justice to the plenary sense of the text, manifest in later history or through ecclesial authority.
368. Pierre Benoit, "Les analogies de l'inspiration," in *Sacra Pagina*, ed. J. Coppens et al. (Gembloux: Duculot, 1959), 1:86–99. Benoit argues that information added to the main point of the prophet is not necessarily inspired.
369. Pierre Benoit and Paul Synave, *La prophétie* (Paris: Revue des Jeunes, 1947).
370. This is pointed out by John McKenzie, "The Social Character of Inspiration," *CBQ* 24 (1962): 115–24. See Norbert Lohfink's discussion of this problem, "Uber die Irrtumslosigkeit und die Einheit der Schrift," *Stimmen der Zeit* 174 (1964): 161–81.
371. Zerafa, "The Limits of Biblical Inerrancy," 95. Zerafa cites *de Genesi ad litteram*, 1.18 and 1, 20.
372. Ibid., 103. Zerafa cites Augustine, *De actis rum Felice Manichaeo*, 1.10: "It is enough for men to know about things [the constitution and origin of the world] what they learned at school, for their own use." As Augustine continues, "it is not written in the gospel that the Lord said: 'I shall send you the Paraclete who will teach you about the course of the sun and the moon.' He wanted to form Christians, not mathematicians."
373. Sasse "Sacra Scriptura," 74, 79.
374. Ibid., 80. Sasse writes that we see a clearer attitude toward Scripture in Augustine when he is not involved in polemics. Sasse cites *Confessiones* III, 5; but this is precisely the attitude that led toward his association with the Manichaeans; cf. 7.21.
375. Hans Küng, *Infallible? An Inquiry*, trans. E. Quinn (Garden City, N.J.: Doubleday, 1971), 211. Küng writes: "Finally, it was Augustine particularly, influenced by Hellenistic theories of inspiration, who saw men merely as the instrument of the Holy Spirit: the Spirit alone decides the content and form of the biblical writings, so that the whole Bible is bound to be free from all contradictions, mistakes and errors, or has to be kept free by harmonizing, allegorizing, or mysticizing."
376. Oswald Loretz, *The Truth of the Bible* (New York: Herder and Herder, 1968), 5, 72. According to Loretz, not only were pagan theories of instrumentality important in defining Augustine's attitude, but also he was influenced here as had been Origen by Philo of Alexandria. Loretz cites R. P. C. Hanson, *Allegory and Event* (Richmond: John Knox Press, 1959), 191ff., 368.

377. Ibid., 74–75.
378. Ibid., 5.
379. Strauss, *Schriftgebrauch*, 63.
380. Bruce Vawter, "The Fuller Sense: Some Considerations," *CBQ* 26 (1964): 93. His argument is developed in distinction from the position of A. Bea that the principle effect of instrumentality is inerrancy. Loretz, who cites Vawter, argues that a theory of instrumentality was never defined at Vatican I. Furthermore, Vatican II argued merely that "Scripture is true in a special sense" without using the term *inerrancy*. See Loretz, *The Truth of the Bible*, 7–8.
381. Idem, *Biblical Inspiration* (Philadelphia: Westminster Press, 1972).
382. Ibid., 34. Vawter cites W. Pannenberg, "Was ist Wahrheit?" *Vom Herrengeheimnis der Wahrheit: Festschrift für Heinrich Vogel* (Berlin & Stuttgart: Lettner-Verlag, 1962), 214–39. It is of interest to note the way in which we have now been carried back to our initial question of revelation.
383. Ibid., 35.
384. Jack Rogers and Donald McKim, *The Authority and Interpretation of the Bible: An Historical Approach* (New York: Harper and Row, 1979), 23, 31. At least one reviewer has labeled their work a Nestorian division of that which pertains to God and to man respectively. See Edith Black's review in *New Oxford Review*, (January/February), 1981.
385. Augustine is much more ready to attribute error to a copyist's mistake, our lack of understanding or a mystical meaning of the Spirit, than to the Scripture itself. See *De consensu evangelistarum*, 3.7. 29–31.
386. Beegle, *Scripture, Tradition and Infallibility* (Grand Rapids: Eerdmans, 1973), 138.
387. John D. Woodbridge, *Biblical Authority: A Critique of the Rogers/McKim Proposal* (Grand Rapids: Zondervan, 1982), 41. Woodbridge (esp. 45–46) argues further that he fails to see how some continue to find "mantic" inspiration in Augustine in light of the research of Costello, Kelly, and others.
388. I am aware of and embarrassed by the fact that so little reflection has been given to the understanding of our four areas in this paper as they may be related to the church. The standard Protestant position on this question was given by B. B. Warfield. For Catholicism, see Portalié, *A Guide*, 239. The following statement by Augustine is often cited in this context: *Ego vero evangelio non crederem, nisi me catholicae Ecclesiae commovert auctoritas. Contra epistulam fundamenti*, 5.
389. Johannes Beumer, *L'inspiration de la Sainte Ecriture* (trans. A. Lufoozbe: Historie des dogmas, 5; Paris: du Cerf, 1972), 36. A similar point is made by Strauss (*Schriftgebrauch*, 61–62) in relation to Augustine's controversy with Jerome.
390. *De Genesi ad litteram*, 2.5 as cited by Beumer, ibid., 36.
391. Ibid., Beumer cites *De civitate dei*, 18.38; *De Gen. ad litt.*, 1.19; 2.9, ep. 28.3; *De consensu evang.*, I.35.54.
392. Ibid., Beumer cites *De Gen. ad litt.*, 7.28.42.
393. Ibid., 37. Beumer cites *De Gen. ad litt.*, 2. 9 and *De actis cum Felice Manichaeo* I.10.
394. Ibid., 37. Beumer cites *De civitate dei*, 17.6: "God speaks by a man in the way of men because in speaking thus he is seeking us." Cf. *In Joannis evangelium tractatus*, I.1, and *Confessiones* 7:2.27.

Chapter 3

1. Desiderius Erasmus, *The Collected Works of Erasmus* (trans. R. A. B. Mynors and D. F. S. Thomson; vol. 4, *The Correspondence of Erasmus* [Toronto:

University of Toronto Press, 1977], 34). (Hereafter cited as *CWE*, followed by volume and page numbers, unless otherwise noted.)

2. A. Bludau presents the most complete discussion of Erasmus's controversies in *Die beiden ersten Erasmus-Ausgaben des Neuen Testaments and ihre Gegner* (Freiburg-im-Br., 1902). A recent survey is found in Jerry Bentley, *Humanists and Holy Writ: New Testament Scholarship in the Renaissance* (Princeton, N.J.: Princeton University Press, 1983), 194–213.

3. *CWE* 3, ep. 337.

4. Ibid., 199.

5. *CWE* 5:287.

6. Ibid., 289.

7. Jerry Bentley, "Biblical Philology and Christian Humanism: Lorenzo Valla and Erasmus as Scholars of the Gospels," *Sixteenth Century Journal* 8 (1977): 16. Bentley argues that though Erasmus did have a sense of critical acumen, he was not "a modern textual critic." Aside from a chronological consideration that would make that impossible no matter what Erasmus's ability, it appears Bentley is basically justified in making this distinction, for Erasmus did not possess certain tools and guidelines assumed by critics today. Bentley discusses Erasmus's acumen as a textual critic more fully in *Humanists and Holy Writ*, 137–61.

8. Desiderius Erasmus, *Novum Instrumentu omne, diligenter ab Erasmo Roterodamo recognitum & emendatum . . .* (Basil, 1516), 239.

9. Desiderius Erasmus, *Novum Testamentum ab codem tertio recognitum, Annotationes item ab ipso recognitae . . .* (Basil, 1522), 13–l4. Also see Jerry Bentley. "Erasmus' *Annotationes in Novum Testamentum* and the Textual Criticism of the Gospels," *Archiv für Reformationsgeschichte* 67 (1976): 47.

10. Ibid., 14.

11. *CWE* 5:289–90.

12. *CWE* 3:22 (from ep. 28 to Jerome).

13. *CWE* 5:290.

14. Ibid.

15. *CWE* 5:290–91. While citing this as belonging to the commentary on chapter 3, Eck actually here refers to a comment Erasmus made in regard to chapter 4. Θεραπεύων does not occur until Matthew 4:23, which is the verse to which Erasmus here refers.

16. *CWE* 3:134.

17. *CWE* 6:28.

18. Ibid.

19. Ibid.

20. *CWE* 6:29.

21. See note of *CWE* 5:291.

22. *CWE* 5:291.

23. Most of the standard biographies acknowledge the significance of this relationship, but there is as yet no study that surveys the breadth of the Erasmian corpus. Two shorter pieces are by respectively, John C. Olin ("Erasmus and Saint Jerome," *Thought* 54 [September 1979]: 313–21), and J. Coppens ("Le portrait de Saint Jerome d'aprés Erasme," in *Colloquia Erasmiana Turonensia*, vol. 2 [Paris: Librairie Philosophique J. Vrin, 1972], 821–28).

24. *CWE* 1:308.

25. See note to ep. 396 in P. S. and H. M. Allen, *Opus Epistolarum Des. Erasmi Roterdami* (vol. 2; Oxford: Oxford University Press, 1910).

26. *CWE* 2:26. see also Olin 320.

27. *CWE* 2:94.
28. *CWE* 6:31.
29. Ibid., 33.
30. Ibid.
31. Albert Rabil, *Erasmus and the New Testament: The Mind of a Christian Humanist* (San Antonio, Tex.: Trinity University Press, 1972), 24 n. 68, 116–17.
32. *CWE* 6:33.
33. Ibid., 35.
34. W. Schwarz considers these lineages between Jerome and Erasmus, and Augustine and Luther in depth in *Principles and Problems of Biblical Translation* (Cambridge: Cambridge University Press, 1955), chaps. 5 and 6.
35. Whether they did in fact so connect these facets is impossible to determine.
36. William Whitaker, *A Disputation on Holy Scripture . . .* , ed. William Fitzgerald (Cambridge: CUP, 1849), 37. It would be interesting to know if Whitaker was familiar with Erasmus's reply to Eck.
37. Bentley, *Humanists and Holy Writ*, 204–5. Erasmus "added to his *Apologia* prefaced to the New Testament a passage affirming that the authors of scripture had made no mistakes, that errors crept into Scripture only through inattentiveness of copyists and translators." The fact that Erasmus both received and yielded to this pressure seems indicative of the general mood of the period.
38. *CWE* 6:30.
39. Augustine, *Letters*, trans. W. Parsons, vols. 1–3 (Washington, D.C.: Catholic University of America Press, 1951), epp. 28, 82, 180.
40. In particular, neo-orthodox historiography of the Reformation has repeatedly insisted on drawing a dichotomy between the Word and the words of Scripture, on denying that the theological combatants were interested in Scripture's infallibility. But if Eck's assessment (and Erasmus's sensitivity to it) is anything to go by, the infallibility of Scripture even in details was the "given" of almost all of Western Christendom, a "given" so strongly entrenched that denial of it would provoke outrage.

Chapter 4
1. Stopford A. Brooke, *Theology in the English Poets* (6th ed.; London: C. Kegan Paul & Co., 1880), 69. See also Graham Hough, "Coleridge and the Victorians," *The English Minds*, ed. Hugh Sykes Davies and George Watson (Cambridge: Cambridge University Press, 1964), 175–92.
2. For example, see James S. Cutsinger, "Coleridgean Polarity and Theological Vision," *Harvard Theological Review* 76 (1983): 91–108; Steven Knapp, *Personification and the Sublime: Milton to Coleridge* (Cambridge: Harvard University Press, 1985), 7–50; Martin Roberts, "Coleridge's Philosophical and Theological Thinking and Its Significance For Today," *Religious Studies* 20 (September 1984): 487–96; and L. S. Sharma, *Coleridge: His Contribution to English Criticism* (New Delhi: Arnold-Heinemann Publishers, 1982).
3. "Samuel Taylor Coleridge," *The Oxford Dictionary of the Christian Church*, ed. F. L. Cross (London: Oxford University Press, 1958), 309. For Coleridge's pantheistic tendencies and his ultimate rejection of them see Thomas McFarland, *Coleridge and the Pantheist Tradition* (Oxford: Clarendon, 1969), 107–90, 314–16. For an overview of his relation to German philosophy see John H. Muirhead, *Coleridge as Philosopher* (New York: Macmillan, 1930), 35–96; and G. N. G. Orsini, *Coleridge and German Idealism* (Carbondale, Ill.: Southern Illinois University Press, 1969).

4. This borrowing bordered on plagiarism, but the fact that unorthodox authors were used was probably more offensive than the copying itself. See the introduction by Joseph Henry Green to the second edition of *Confessions of an Inquiring Spirit* (1849) where he struggles to clear Coleridge of the charge of plagiarism from Lessing. (This introduction can be found in the H. StJ. Hart edition of Coleridge's *Confessions* [London: Adam & Charles Black, 1956], 17–33.) See also McFarland, *Pantheist Tradition*, 1–52.

5. "We never know when we shall discover the shadow of Spinoza behind Coleridge's thinking, and it is similarly true with Lessing" (David Pym, *The Religious Thought of Samuel Taylor Coleridge* [Gerrards Cross: Colin Smythe, 1978], 81); see also Basil Willey, *Samuel Taylor Coleridge* (New York: W. W. Norton, 1972), 74–76.

6. On the personal level his addiction to opium and his numerous love affairs would have rendered his judgment suspicious to some.

7. J. S. Mill, *Essay on Coleridge* (1840), cited by Bernard M. G. Reardon, *Religious Thought in the Nineteenth Century* (Cambridge: Cambridge University Press, 1969), 240; and Willey, *Coleridge*, 256. Mill added ". . . the existence of Coleridge will show itself by no slight or ambiguous traces in the coming history of our country; for no one has contributed more to shape the opinions of those among its younger men, who can be said to have opinions at all" (quoted in Hough, "Coleridge and the Victorians," 176).

8. Some examples would be Norman L. Geisler, ed., *Inerrancy* (Grand Rapids: Zondervan, 1980); the entire quarterly issue of *JETS* 25 (1982): 385–506; and John D. Woodbridge, "Is Biblical Inerrancy a Fundamentalist Doctrine?" *Bibliotheca Sacra* 142 (1985): 292–305. The belief "in a uniquely infallible Bible" is one defining characteristic of an "evangelical" Christian according to Nathan O. Hatch, Mark A. Noll, and John D. Woodbridge (*The Gospel in America* [Grand Rapids: Zondervan, 1979], 14. See also Harold Lindsell, *The Battle for the Bible* [Grand Rapids: Zondervan, 1976], 210).

9. The most influential recent attempt to show historically that the church has not consistently affirmed complete biblical infallibility is that of Jack Rogers and Donald McKim, *The Authority and Interpretation of the Bible: An Historical Approach* (San Francisco: Harper & Row, 1979). They argue that the central position of the church has been that the Bible is "infallible" in its teachings on matters of "faith and practice" but not inerrant in issues of fact regarding history, geography, and science. Their thesis is that a belief in factual inerrancy first arose in the thought of the seventeenth-century Swiss theologian Francis Turretin and was most fully developed in the nineteenth-century Princeton Seminary theology of Archibald Alexander, Charles Hodge, and later by A. A. Hodge and B. B. Warfield. See Rogers and McKim, *Authority*, 279–81, 289–90, 333–34. Their views have been extensively challenged by John D. Woodbridge, *Biblical Authority: A Critique of the Rogers/McKim Proposal* (Grand Rapids: Zondervan, 1982). Woodbridge attempts to show that the belief in the factual inerrancy of Scripture has a long tradition and can be seen in prominent Christian theologians in the patristic period, the Reformation, and the centuries following (in authors not connected with Turretin or the Princeton theology). My own opinion is that the analysis of Woodbridge is much more historically accurate and in various places in this paper evidence will be offered to support this.

10. His definition is adapted from that offered by Paul D. Feinburg, "The Meaning of Inerrancy," *Inerrancy*, 294; see also "The Chicago Statement on Biblical Inerrancy," included on pages 493–502. This chapter will *not* deal with the

"original autographs," or the proper "interpretation" (i.e., hermeneutics) involved in this definition.

11. One such attempt is that of Stephen T. Davis, *The Debate about the Bible* (Philadelphia: Westminster, 1977), 23.

12. This explanation loosely follows that offered by the Reformed theologian Louis Berkof in his *Systematic Theology*, and it does not include the very important idea sometimes associated with inspiration of "dictation." A dictation theory holds that the writers of Scripture functioned merely as recording secretaries for the Holy Spirit or as pens in the hand of God. Since there are differences in style, grammar, and patterns of thought in the various books of the Bible, showing the peculiarities of its many human authors, this idea has been rejected by almost everyone familiar with these literary distinctions. It should also be noted that it is possible to hold a view of inspiration (as above) that avoids dictation but preserves inerrancy, but that those who would ascribe to a dictation theory would also affirm inerrancy.

13. "Revelation" in this usage is not equal to Scripture, as many facts of Bible history, geography, etc., would be known from secular sources.

14. Bruce Vawter, *Biblical Inspiration* (Philadelphia: Westminster, 1972), 23.

15. Coleridge repeatedly wrote in support of reading and interpreting the Bible as one would any other book: "I take up this work with the purpose to read it for the first time as I should read any other work—as far at least as I can or dare" (*Confessions*, Hart ed., 41). "But if it be answered, 'Aye! but we must not interpret St. Paul as we may and should interpret any other honest and intelligent writer or speaker,' then, I say, this is the very *petitio principii* of which I complain" (*Confessions*, 49).

16. In a strict sense "higher criticism did not become a live issue in England until the second half of the nineteenth century," but the "way was being prepared by scholars and men of letters" such as Coleridge. S. L. Greenslade, ed., *The Cambridge History of the Bible: The West from the Reformation to the Present Day* (Cambridge: Cambridge University Press, 1963), 280.

17. Protestants generally argued that the Bible alone was "the only sufficient, certain and infallible rule of all-saving knowledge, faith and obedience" (*The Philadelphia Confession of Faith*, 6th ed. [Philadelphia: Baptist Association, 1743]), cited by William E. Nix, "The Doctrine of Inspiration Since the Reformation," *JETS* 25 (1982): 446. The Westminster Confession of Faith (1647) said nearly the same for Presbyterians: "The whole counsel of God, concerning all things necessary for his own glory, man's salvation, faith, and life, is either expressly set down in Scripture, or by good and necessary consequence may be deduced from Scripture: unto which nothing at any time is to be added, whether by new revelations of the Spirit, or traditions of men" (cited by Nix, "Inspiration," 451). The Thirty-nine Articles (1563) were similar in the affirmation that "Holy Scripture containeth all things necessary to salvation" (John H. Leith, *Creeds of the Churches* [rev. ed.; Atlanta: John Knox, 1973], 267). These statements all conflicted with the Roman Catholic doctrine that the unwritten traditions of the church were also authoritative. See the "Decree Concerning the Canonical Scriptures" of the fourth session (1546) of the Council of Trent (Leith, *Creeds*, 401–3). Coleridge accepted the general Protestant view on this point: "As for myself, I agree with [Jeremy] Taylor against the Romanists, that the Bible is for us the only rule of faith" (S. T. Coleridge, *Notes on English Divines*, ed. Derwent Coleridge [London: Bradbury & Evans, 1853], 1:312). Protestants and Catholics also differed in their confidence in the ability of the individual to interpret, understand, and apply Scripture for himself apart from the church.

18. *Catholic Theories of Biblical Inspiration Since 1810: A Review and Critique* (Cambridge: Cambridge University Press, 1969), 1–2. See also Robert Shafer, *Christianity and Naturalism* (New Haven, Conn.: Yale University Press, 1926), 8.

19. Several scholars, who do not themselves favor the inerrancy position, have nevertheless recognized that it was the common view in England at this time: "The Bible was still accepted by nearly all Christians in England as a compendium of infallible oracles, equally inspired and authoritative in all its parts" (Alec R. Vidler, *The Church in an Age of Revolution: 1789 to the Present Day* [Baltimore: Penguin Books, 1961], 80); Coleridge had opposed the Church of England's "almost unanimously held doctrine of the Bible's total verbal inspiration" (Pym, *Religious Thought*, 73); "In the England of 1830–40" the belief "in the 'verbal inspiration' of the biblical writings . . . was both widely held and deeply rooted: so deeply as to be held as a fact and not a doctrine" (Willey, *Coleridge*, 242). Willey explains elsewhere what this "verbal inspiration" meant: "Being inspired in this way 'from cover to cover,' every statement and sentiment it contained, whether historical, scientific, moral or prophetic, and whether expressed in a prosaic or a figurative manner, must be accepted as the undoubted word of God" (*Nineteenth Century Studies: Coleridge to Matthew Arnold* [New York: Columbia University Press, 1949], 39).

20. Cf. J. Robert Barth, *Coleridge and Christian Doctrine* (Cambridge, Mass.: Harvard University Press, 1969), 57–58.

21. Ibid., 58–59. Barth adds that this kind of view "predominated at the time Coleridge was writing his *Confessions*."

22. *Confessions*, 62–63. Even the liberal exegete William Sanday, who himself denied the complete infallibility of the Bible, acknowledged in 1893 that it "was the view commonly held fifty years ago." See his *Inspiration* (London: 1893), 393 (cited in Barth, *Christian Doctrine*, 59).

23. This work was written about 1826 in the "orthodox" interval in his thinking and published posthumously in 1840.

24. On the issue of the reliability of Scripture Socinus said: ". . . sometimes in a minor way a writer has been mistaken about those things that only slightly deal with what we are to believe or do" (*De Auctoriate S. Scripturae*, Cap. I, cited by Woodbridge, *Biblical Authority*, 189 n. 1). Coleridge admitted to being a "Socinian" until 1797. See Willey, *Coleridge*, 42.

25. Spinoza exploited the list of problem texts (relating to Mosaic authorship of the Pentateuch) compiled by the medieval rabbi Aben Ezra (1089–1164) with his own additions regarding other OT books, in an attempt "to destroy complete biblical infallibility" which he recognized was the prevailing view in the seventeenth century (Woodbridge, *Biblical Authority*, 87–88, 191 n. 24).

26. Paradoxically, Simon wrote (in part) to refute Spinoza, but his theory that "Public-Scribes" wrote certain portions of the Pentateuch whose Mosaic authorship had been challenged served merely to anger both Protestants and Catholics. They correctly deduced that this too undermined the reliability of Scripture (see Woodbridge, *Biblical Authority*, 95–96). William Holden influenced Simon by his *Divinae fidei analysis* (1652), where he restricted "not only inerrancy but inspiration itself to the doctrinal matters of Scripture" (Vawter, *Biblical Inspiration*, 134; see also Woodbridge, *Biblical Authority*, 85, 189).

27. Tindal's work *Christianity as Old as the Creation, or the Gospel a Republication of the Religion of Nature* (1730) became the "Bible" of Deism. In it he speaks in passing of "those many mistakes that have crept into the text, whether by accident or design" (336; cited by Herbert Cunliffe-Jones, *Christian*

Theology Since 1600 [London: Gerald Duckworth, 1970], 42). John Toland (1670–1722), another Deist, was even more radical in his *Adeisidaemon.* According to Robert E. Sullivan, Toland "denied that the Old Testament was the word of God the production of His Spirit. Moses had not written the Torah, which was, accordingly, an uncertain authority subject to the errors besetting any human document. . . . The oracles conveyed by the patriarchs and prophets were raptures and dreams, comparable to the hallucinations of other men" (*John Toland and the Deist Controversy* [Cambridge, Mass.: Harvard University Press, 1982], 134, 307 n. 54).

28. Le Clerc was much more radical than Simon, whom he debated in a series of meetings from 1685–87. He conjectured that several whole sections of Scripture were merely historical accounts, perhaps containing moral lessons but not divinely inspired by the Holy Spirit. Simon and Holden had not denied inspiration but rather redefined it to allow occasional errors in areas not related to faith. See Woodbridge, *Biblical Authority,* 96–97.

29. Reimarus was extreme in his denials. He not only attributed errors to the biblical text, but said there was "no book so full of contradictions as this" and the supernatural appearances of God and angels, miracles, etc., were "pure delusion" (*The Goal of Jesus and His Disciples* [Leiden: Brill, 1970], 4–5).

30. Semler was willing to apply literary techniques used on other documents to the Bible. He attempted to distinguish the sacred from the secular while showing a willingness to uphold only the sacred. See Barth, *Christian Doctrine,* 56.

31. Paine's *Age of Reason,* which appeared in two parts in 1794 and 1795, showed a view of Scripture similar to the Deists, Tindal and Toland. He said in it (regarding the New Testament) that nowhere had he found "so many and such glaring absurdities, contradictions, and falsehoods as are in these books" (cited by Pym, *Religious Thought,* 75).

32. Herder tended to deny the divine origin and authority of Scripture by redefining inspiration as an exalted kind of religious enthusiasm inherent more in the writer rather than the writing. See Barth, *Christian Doctrine,* 57; and Timothy Corrigan, *Coleridge, Language, and Criticism* (Athens, Ga.: The University of Georgia Press, 1982), 162.

33. For example, the revised Pietism of Schleiermacher (1768–1834), with its emphasis on feeling as a basis for religion, was noted with interest by Coleridge and may have influenced his concept of sin. See Barth, *Christian Doctrine,* 120; Edward Caldwell Moore, *An Outline of the History of Christian Thought Since Kant* (New York: Charles Scribner's Sons, 1912), 74–89; and Pym, *Religious Thought,* 79. For a general coverage of Coleridge's exposure to German philosophy and biblical criticism see Robert M. Grant, *The Bible in the Church: A Short History of Interpretation* (New York: Macmillan, 1948), 135; and especially Orsini, *German Idealism,* 43–47.

34. Besides Socinus and Spinoza, mentioned above (nn. 25–26), Coleridge was well acquainted with the works of Simon and Semler (Barth, *Christian Doctrine,* 56–57), Le Clerc (S. T. Coleridge, *Coleridge on the Seventeenth Century,* ed. R. F. Brinkley [Durham, N.C.: Duke University Press, 1955], 132), Reimarus (Willey, *Coleridge,* 57, 107), Paine (Pym, *Religious Thought,* 75), and Herder (Orsini, *German Idealism,* 45, 252).

35. Cited in *Lessing's Theological Writings* (London: Adam & Charles Black, 1956),18.

36. Ibid., 20.

37. *On the Proof of the Spirit and the Power* (1777) (cited in *Lessing's Theological Writings,* 55).

38. Ibid., 53.
39. Ibid.
40. Cunliffe-Jones (*Christian Theology*, 46) comments: "Lessing certainly bequeathed to a large section of German Protestant theology in particular a lack of confidence in historical fact."
41. Willey, *Coleridge*, 75–76. Lessing said in a *Rejoinder* (1778) to a critic of his publishing the *Fragments*: "The Resurrection of Christ can be perfectly true, even though the accounts of the Evangelists are contradictory" (cited by F. Andrew Brown, *Gotthold Ephraim Lessing* [New York: Twayne Publishers, 1971], 139).
42. Brown, *Lessing*, 140. See also Leonard P. Wessel, *G. E. Lessing's Theology: A Reinterpretation* (The Hague: Mouton, 1977) 76–78. Lessing said in this context: "In short, the letter is not the spirit and the Bible is not Religion. Consequently, objections to the letter and the Bible are not also objections to the spirit and to religion" (*Lessing's Theological Writings*, 18).
43. *Coleridge*, 76, Stephen Prickett (*Romanticism and Religion: The Tradition of Coleridge and Wordsworth in the Victorian Church* [Cambridge: Cambridge University Press, 1976], 51) also notes that Coleridge generally follows Lessing in viewing a particular verse of Scripture according to the spirit of the whole.
44. Introduction to *Confessions*, Hart ed., 17–18, 21.
45. Ibid., 22.
46. Ibid., 30. In 1799 Coleridge wrote to Josiah Wedgewood from Germany saying he had gathered materials for the purpose of writing a "Life of Lessing" because it "would give me an opportunity of conveying under a better name, than my own will ever be, opinions, which I deem of the highest importance" (*Collected Letters of S. T. Coleridge*, ed. E. L. Griggs [Oxford: Clarendon Press, 1956–59], 283, cited by Willey, *Coleridge*, 75). Although Coleridge never finished this projected biography of Lessing, this furnishes additional evidence that he was steeped in the life and thought of Lessing.
47. It should be noted that on occasion Coleridge took exception to some of the more radical tendencies in Lessing and he certainly did not accept everything Lessing said at face value. At one point, Lessing argues that the early church considered the "rule of faith" and not the Scripture as their foundation. Coleridge writes, "Lessing's logic forsook him here." In the discussion following demonstrating Coleridge's view on the issue, he repeats that Lessing was "mistaken" (cited in Green, introduction to *Confessions*, 27–28).
48. Greenslade, ed., *The Cambridge History of the Bible*, 270, 273. See also K. S. Latourette, *The Nineteenth Century in Europe* (New York: Harper & Brothers, 1959) 2.41–46.
49. Prickett, *Romanticism and Religion*, 66. Coleridge took exception to this theory. For other occasions when Coleridge disagreed with Eichhorn, see Pym, *Religious Thought*, 66–68.
50. Orsini, *German Idealism*, 46.
51. Willey, *Nineteenth Century Studies*, 40.
52. Willey, *Coleridge*, 245. See also James D. Boulger, *Coleridge as Religious Thinker* (New Haven, Conn.: Yale University Press, 1961), 193.
53. Quoted in *Coleridge on the Seventeenth Century*, 153. It should be noted that Coleridge recognized that Eichhorn tended to undermine the reliability of evidence in the Bible for supporting Christianity. Coleridge approved of this, as he stressed the inner validity of Christianity which did not rest on outward evidences.
54. Barth, *Christian Doctrine*, 56 n. 10. Julius Hare, who was a great admirer of Coleridge, recognized this in a preface to his work *The Mission of the Comforter*

(ed. E. H. Plumptre, 1876). Hare said of Coleridge: "his exegetical studies, such as they were, took place at a period when he had little better than the meagre Rationalism of Eichhorn and Bertholdt to help him" (quoted by Pym, *Religious Thought*, 86).

55. Prickett, *Romanticism and Religion*, 67. See also Bernard M. G. Reardon, *From Coleridge to Gore: A Century of Religious Thought in Britain* (London: Longman Group, 1971), 81–82.

56. *Confessions*, 38. A detailed analysis of the place of *Confessions* within the overall religious views of Coleridge is offered in Stephen Happel, *Coleridge's Religious Imagination* (Salzburg: Institut für Anglistik und Amerikanistik Universität Salzburg, 1983), 2:613–48.

57. *Confessions*, 41–42.

58. Ibid., 42.

59. Ibid. He boldly asserted "in the Bible there is more that *finds* me than I have experienced in all other books put together" (*Confessions*, 43). But this still allows for some material in Scripture which does not seem to him to be inspired (and some things in other books which are inspired). This reliance on subjective criteria was similar to the teaching of Lessing.

60. *Confessions*, 43.

61. "I willingly believe the truth of the history, namely, that the Word of the Lord did come to Samuel, to Isaiah, to others; and that the words which gave utterance to the same are faithfully recorded. . . . the faithful recording of the same does not of itself imply, or seem to require, any supernatural working . . ." (*Confessions*, 44).

62. For the possibility of errors in the Bible in nonrevealed matters see S. T. Coleridge, *Notes on English Divines*, ed. Derwent Coleridge (London: Bradbury and Evans, 1853), 1:123–24; and S. T. Coleridge, *Notes, Theological, Political, and Miscellaneous*, ed. Derwent Coleridge (London: Bradbury and Evans, 1853), 328–330.

63. ". . . whatever is referred by the sacred Penmen to a direct communication from God, and . . . where the writer in his own person, and in the character of an historian, relates that the Word of the Lord came unto priest, prophet, chieftain, or other individual—have I not declared that I receive the same with full belief, and admit its inappellable authority?" (*Confessions*, 49).

64. Barth, *Christian Doctrine*, 61–63.

65. *Confessions*, 45, 49–50, 52, 55, 59.

66. Coleridge directed many of his sharpest words against those who implied that the sacred writers were mere "automatons" or "ventriloquists" (*Confessions*, 53).

67. *Confessions*, 54, 66.

68. Ibid., 70.

69. Ibid., 68.

70. Ibid., 75. Further along in this same vein Coleridge said, "the difficulties that still remain" are "few and insignificant."

71. Ibid., 65. He also suggested they were preserved "to make us more grateful" (*Confessions*, 69).

72. Even W. G. T. Shedd, who in general admired Coleridge, recognized a danger to Scripture in his views: "We regard it an error in him . . . that the Canon is not contemplated as a complete whole . . . having a common origin in the Divine Mind . . . as a body of information it is infallibly correct on all subjects . . . even the most unimportant particulars of history, biography, and geography" (Introductory Essay to *The Complete Works of Samuel Taylor Coleridge* [New York: Harper & Brothers, 1868]), 1:57.

73. Chadwick, *The Victorian Church*, 1–39, 97–111; and James R. Moore, *The Post-Darwinian Controversies* (Cambridge: Cambridge University Press, 1979), 193-351. Moore notes that even in 1884 there were many scientists who were willing to sign a petition affirming "it is impossible for the Word of God as written in the book of Nature, and God's Word written in Holy Scripture, to contradict one another, however much they may appear to differ" (83–84).

74. Coleridge stated: "The Bible must be interpreted by its known *objects*, and *ends*, and these were the Moral and spiritual Education of the Human Race" (*Unpublished Letters*, ed. E. L. Griggs [New Haven, Conn.: Yale University Press, 1933], 2:327).

75. While Maurice did not want to be allied with the more liberal tendencies of those he recognized as broad churchmen, he did belong to a group with Carlyle, Hare, Kingsley, etc., "associated with Cambridge" that usually are seen as part of the Broad Church (Charles Richard Sanders, *Coleridge and the Broad Church Movement* [Durham, N.C.: Duke University Press, 1942], 11–15; see also Grant, *Bible*, 136).

76. Willey, *Nineteenth Century Studies*, 64. Arnold read Coleridge's *Confessions* in manuscript form before they were published and commented that the contents were "well fitted to break ground in the approaches to that momentous question which involves in it so great a shock to existing notions . . . but which will end, in spite of fears and clamours of the weak and bigoted, in the higher exalting and more sure establishing of Christian truth" (quoted in Willey, *Coleridge*, 252).

77. Willey, *Nineteenth Century Studies*, 67–68; and Greenslade, ed., *Cambridge History*, 280.

78. *The Miscellaneous Works* (New York: Appleton, 1845),149 (quoted in Sanders, *Broad Church*, 98).

79. Matthew Arnold, *Letters,* 2:23 (1869) (quoted in Willey, *Nineteenth Century Studies*, 264).

80. F. D. Maurice, "Mr. Jeffrey and the *Edinburgh Review*," *Athenaeum* (Jan. 23, 1828) (cited by Sanders, *Broad Church*, 188).

81. Sanders, *Broad Church*, 258. See also Alec R. Vidler, *F. D. Maurice and Company: Nineteenth Century Studies* (London: SCM, 1966), 210–11.

82. Grant, *Bible*, 136–37; and Pym, *Religious Thought*, 92–93. For those who like to speak of "verbal inspiration," Maurice said, they "cannot go further than I should, in calling for a laborious and reverent attention to the words of Scripture" (*Theological Essays* [New York: Harper & Brothers, 1957], 239).

83. Maurice, *Theological Essays*, 236.

84. Ibid., 235.

85. Ibid., 237.

86. Ibid.

87. Ibid., 238–39.

88. Ibid., 239.

89. Ibid., 235.

90. *Coleridge*, 255–56.

91. *History of Interpretation*, 422–24 (cited in Pym, *Religious Thought*, 91–92).

92. E.g., Rogers and McKim, *Authority*, xxii, xxiv n. 13. See John D. Woodbridge, "The Rogers and McKim Proposal in the Balance," *Bibliotheca Sacra* 142 (1985): 102–5 for a review and refutation of this "subthesis" in the Rogers and McKim theory.

Chapter 5

1. Karl Holl, *What Did Luther Understand by Religion?* ed. James L. Adams and Walter F. Bense, trans. W. Meuser and Walter R. Wietzke (Philadelphia: Fortress, 1977 [orig. 1921]), 15.
2. Ibid.
3. Ibid., 6.
4. Ibid., 32.
5. Ibid., 32–33.
6. Ibid., 41.
7. Ibid., 47.
8. Ibid., 109.
9. Ibid., 110.
10. *LW* 36:134. Cf. *WA BR* 2:397, 305, 399; 10^1:728.
11. Karl Holl, "Martin Luther on Luther," in *Interpreters of Luther* (Festschrift Wilhelm Pauck, ed. J. Pelikan [Philadelphia: Fortress, 1968]), 19. Cf. *WA* 23:421.
12. Ibid.
13. Ibid. Cf. *WA BR* 1:73, 352; 2:138; 5:400.
14. *LA* 47:114.
15. Joseph Lortz, "Martin Luther, Grundzüge seiner geistigen Struktur," in *Reformata Reformanda* (*Festgabe* Hubert Jedin, ed. Erwin Iserloh and Konrad Repgen [Münster: Aschendorf, 1965]), 1:215.
16. Ibid.
17. Ibid., 234.
18. Darriel Olivier, *The Trial of Luther*, trans. John Tonkin (St. Louis: Concordia, 1971), 180.
19. Ibid.
20. Ibid., 157.
21. Ibid., 167.
22. John M. Todd, *Luther: A Life* (New York: Crossroad, 1982), xvi.
23. Ibid., xviii.
24. Ibid., 330.
25. E. G. Schwiebert, *Luther and His Times* (St. Louis: Concordia, 1950), 504, 512.
26. Herman Schuster, *Martin Luther Heute* (Stuttgart: Ehrenfried Klotz Verlag, 1958), 38–39.
27. Paul Althaus, "Die Bedeutung der Theologie Luthers für die theologische Arbeit," *Lutherjahrbuch 1961* (Göttingen: Vandenhoeck und Ruprecht, 1961), 13ff.
28. Friedrich Kantzenbach, "Luther Research as a Problem in Comparative Theology," *Lutheran World* 13 (1966): 268.
29. Ibid., 266.
30. Ibid., 267.
31. Ibid., 270–71.
32. James Arne Nestingen, *Martin Luther: His Life and Teachings* (Philadelphia: Fortress, 1982), 5–10.
33. James Atkinson, *Martin Luther and the Birth of Protestantism* (Atlanta: John Knox, 1981 [orig. 1968]), 78. This second edition includes a valuable review of some of the most recent works on Luther, including a section that focuses on Luther's attitude toward the Scripture.
34. Ernst-Wilhelm Kohls, "Die Lutherforschung in deutschen Sprachbereich seits 1970," *Lutherjahrbuch 1977* (Göttingen: Vandenhoeck und Ruprecht, 1977), 28–56.

35. Wilhelm Maurer, *Kirche und Geschichte*, vols. 1, 2 (Göttingen: Vandenhoeck und Ruprecht, 1970). Gerhard Gloege, *Gnade für die Welt: Kritik und Krise des Luthertams* (Göttingen: Vandenhoeck und Ruprecht, 1964). Lennart Pinomaa, *Sieg des Glaubens: Grundlinien der Theologie Luthers* (Göttingen: Vandenhoeck und Ruprecht, 1964). Heinrich Bornkamm, "Erasmus und Luther," *Lutherjahrbuch 1958* (Berlin: Lutherisches Verlagshaus, 1958).
36. Kohls, "Lutherforschung," 55.
37. As in n. 34; see 55–70.
38. Ibid., 71–74.
39. Ibid., 75–88.
40. Ibid., 105–26.
41. So, inter alia, Rudolf Hermann, *Luthers Theologie* (Göttingen: Vandenhoeck und Ruprecht, 1967); August Hasler, *Katholischen Dogmatik* (Munich: Hueber, 1968); Regin Prenter, "Luther Research in Scandinavin Since 1945," *Lutheran World* 13 (1966): 272–83. The latter mentions the work of H. Ostergaard-Nielsen, who says that for Luther the Word meant he understood as the *viva vox evangelii* and not simply be identified with the Scriptures (277).
42. Ernst Bizer, *Fides Ex Auditu* (Neukirchen-Vluyn: Neukirchener Verlag, 1958).
43. *LW* 34:336.
44. Lowell Treen, *How Melanchthan Helped Luther Discover the Gospel* (Fallbrook, Calif.: Verdict, 1980).
45. Ibid., 62, 85.
46. Ibid., 108–9.
47. Ibid., 183.
48. Ibid., 258.
49. Ibid., 264.
50. Uuras Saarnivaara, *Luther Discovers the Gospel* (St. Louis: Concordia, 1951).
51. Schwiebert, *Luther*, 282ff.
52. Atkinson, *Martin Luther*, 76ff.
53. Leif Grane, *Modus Loquendi Theologicus. Luther's Kampf um die Erneuerung der Theologie, 1515–1518* (Leiden: Brill, 1975), 183.
54. A. Skevington Wood, *Captive to the Word* (Grand Rapids: Eerdmans, 1969), 44.
55. Ian Siggins, *Martin Luther's Doctrine of Christ* (New Haven, Conn.: Yale University Press, 1970), 4.
56. Walter Von Loenenich, *Luther's Theologia Crucis* (Munich: Hueher, 1933).
57. Siggins, *Martin Luther's Doctrine*, 9.
58. Roland Bainton, review of Bizer, *JTS* 10 (1959): 191.
59. *LW* 34:337.
60. Gert Haendler, *Luther on Ministerial Office and Congregational Function*, ed. Eric W. Gritsch, trans. Ruth C. Gritsch (Philadelphia: Fortress, 1981), 27.
61. Kurt Aland, *Martin Luther's 95 Theses* (St. Louis: Concordia, 1967), 20.
62. *LW* 40[1].120, 17–25.
63. Mark Edwards, *Luther's Last Battles* (Ithaca, NY: Cornell University Press, 1983).
64. Ibid., 208.
65. Ibid.
66. Ibid., 142.
67. Ibid.
68. Mark Edwards, *Luther and the False Brethren* (Stanford: Stanford University Press, 1975).
69. Ibid., 29; cf. p. 126.
70. Saarnivaara, *Luther*, 26.

71. H. G. Haile, *Luther: An Experiment in Biography* (Garden City, N.Y.: Doubleday, 1980).
72. Ian Siggins, *Luther* (New York: Barnes and Noble, 1972), 187.
73. Scott Hendrix, *Luther and the Papacy* (Philadelphia: Fortress, 1981), 156.
74. Ibid.
75. Gordon Rupp, "John Osborne and the Historical Luther," *ExpTim* 73 (1961–62): 149.
76. Quoted in an article by David E. Anderson, UPI, July 2, 1983.
77. Edwards, *Last Battles*, 208.
78. See esp. my *From Luther to Chemnitz on Scripture and the Word* (Grand Rapids: Eerdmans, 1971), esp. 26–38.
79. See Bernhard Lohse, *Martin Luther: Eine Einführung in sein Leben und sein Werk* (Munich: C. H. Beck, 1981), 163.
80. Wilhelm Maurer, *Kirche und Geschichte: Luther und das evangelische Bekenntnis* (Göttingen: Vandenhoeck und Ruprecht, 1970), 134.
81. Ibid., 136.
82. Ibid., 151.
83. Ibid., 176.
84. Saarnivaara, *Luther*, 124–25.
85. Peter Meinhold, *Luther Heute* (Berlin and Hamburg: Luiherisches Verlagshaus, 1967), 128. Cf. *WA* 50:245.
86. Meinhold, *Luther Heute,* 129.
87. Wood, *Captive*, 93–94.
88. Ibid., 84.
89. Ibid., 123.
90. Ibid., 134.
91. Ibid., 139.
92. Paul Althaus, *The Theology of Luther* (Philadelphia: Fortress, 1966), 50, 86.
93. Cf. Klug, *From Luther to Chemnitz*, 17–25.
94. *SA* 3:8.
95. Nestingen, *Martin Luther*, 28.
96. Ibid., 31.
97. John Loeschen, *Wrestling with Luther* (St. Louis: Concordia, 1976), 62.
98. Ibid., 104.
99. Eric Gritsch, in "Nine and One Half Theses," *Luther und die Theologie der Gegenwart*, ed. Leif Grane and Bernhard Lohse (Göttingen: Vandenhoeck und Ruprecht, 1980), 107–8.
100. Regin Prenter, "Luther als Theologe," ibid., 112, 115.
101. Ibid., 115–22. Roland Bainton shares this view of Prenter, as do many others. Roland Bainton, "The Problem of Authority," *Luther, Erasmus and the Reformation*, ed. John C. Olin (New York: Fordham University Press, 1969), 18.
102. Samuel Preus, in *Luther und die Theologie*, 129–30.
103. Ibid., 133.
104. Regin Prenter, *The Word and the Spirit*, trans. Harris E. Kaasa (Minneapolis: Augsburg, 1965).
105. Ibid., 2–8.
106. Ibid., 11–23.
107. Heinrich Bornkamm, *Das Bleibende Recht Der Reformation* (Hamburg: Furche, 1963).
108. Ibid., 45.
109. Ibid.
110. Heinrich Bornkamm, *Luther's World of Thought* (St. Louis: Concordia, 1958), 7.

111. Ibid., 72.
112. Gerhard Ebeling, *Luther: An Introduction to His Thought*, trans. R. A. Wilson (Philadelphia: Fortress, 1970), 97.
113. Ibid., 104.
114. Philip Watson, *Let God Be God* (Philadelphia: Muhlenberg, 1948), 175.
115. Hermann Sasse, "Luther and the Word of God," in *Accents in Luther's Theology*, ed. H. Kadai (St. Louis: Concordia, 1967), 72; cf. Klug, *From Luther to Chemnitz*, 85.
116. Fred Mauser and Stanley Schnieder, ed., *Interpreting Luther's Legacy* (Minneapolis: Augsburg, 1969).
117. So Ralph Doermann, "Luther's Principles of Biblical Interpretation," ibid., 20.
118. So Theodore Liefeld, "Scripture and Tradition, in Luther and in Our Day," ibid.
119. Ibid., 28.
120. Franz Lau, "Die Theologie Martin Luthers," *Lutherjahrbuch 1963* (Göttingen: Vandenhoeck und Ruprecht, 1963).
121. Sasse, "Luther and the Word of God," 72.
122. Ibid., 83–91.
123. Gordon Rupp, *The Righteousness of God; Luther Studies* (London: Hodder and Stoughton, 1953).
124. Ibid., 15. ET: "Gottes Wort und Luthers Lehr/Wird vergehen nimmermehr."
125. Ibid.; quoted from E. W. Zeeden, *Martin Luther und die Reformation im Urteil des deutschen Luthertums* (Freiburg: Herder, 1950), 100.
126. William Landen, *Martin Luther's Religious Thought* (Mountain View, Calif.: Pacific, 1971), 90ff.
127. Ibid., 96.
128. *LW* 40:212; *WA* 18:117.
129. *LW* 24:93.
130. *LW* 13:235.
131. *LW* 51:391.
132. Hermann Dorries, *Worte und Stunde: Beiträge zum Verständnis Luthers* (Göttingen: Vandenhoeck und Ruprecht, 1970), 3:102.
133. Ibid., 3:176, 399.
134. Grand Rapids: Eerdmans, 1931, 8.
135. Friedrich Beisser, *Claritas Scripturae bei Martin Luthers* (Göttingen: Vandenhoeck und Ruprecht, 1966).
136. Ibid., 33–34; cf. *WA* 18.136.
137. Ibid., 36.
138. Ibid., 51–52.
139. Ibid., 68ff.
140. Ibid., 75–130, passim.
141. Ibid., 131–88, passim.
142. Meinhold, *Luther Heute*, 101.
143. Ibid., 113.
144. Ibid., 121; cf. *WA* 45:522; 50:647.
145. Siggins, *Luther*, 27, 129.
146. Ibid., 162
147. Klug, *From Luther to Chemnitz*, 90–104.
148. Grane, *Modus*, 177.
149. Ibid.
150. Friedrich Gogarten, *Luthers Theologie* (Tübingen: Mohr, 1967), 228ff.
151. Ibid., 232.

152. *Martin Luther's Doctrine*, 10–11.
153. Ibid., 11.
154. Klug, *From Luther to Chemnitz*, 74.
155. *LW* 22:451; see also his *Bondage of the Will* (Parker/Johnston ed.), 66–67, 85, 98, 125, 128; *WA* 18:603–4:619, 653, 655.
156. 59.
157. Hans-Martin Barth, *Der Teufel und Jesus Christus in der Theologie Martin Luthers* (Göttingen: Vandenhoeck und Ruprecht, 1967), 83, 121.
158. Ibid., 81, quoted from *WA* 18:454.
159. Atkinson, *Martin Luther*, 73.
160. Ibid., 82.
161. Ibid., 187–88; cf. *LW* 44:134.
162. Ibid., 198.
163. Schuster, *Martin Luther Heute*, 40; cf. *LW* 36:30.
164. Ibid.
165. Ibid., 41.
166. Ibid., 42.
167. Ibid., 45.
168. Ibid., 47.
169. Ibid., 129.
170. Lohse, *Martin Luther*, 162.
171. Walter Mostert, "Scriptura sacra sui ipsius interpres," *Lutherjahrbuch 1979* (Göttingen: Vandenhoeck und Ruprecht, 1979), 60ff.
172. *LW* 28:268–9.
173. Ibid.
174. A. Skevington Wood, *Luther's Principles of Biblical Interpretation* (London: Tyndale, 1960), 3.
175. Brian Gerrish, "Biblical Authority and the Continental Reformation," *SJT* 10 (1957): 346.
176. Heinrich Bornkamm, *Luther and the Old Testament* (Philadelphia: Fortress. 1969), 262.
177. Kurt Aland, "Luther as Exegete," *ExpTim* 69 (1957): 70.
178. Francis Pieper, *Christian Dogmatics* (St. Louis: Concordia, 1950), 1:278.
179. *LW* 30:107 (Comm. on 1 Peter 3:15).
180. Word, *Captive*, 144.
181. Ibid., 177.
182. Ibid., 59–62.
183. Gerrish, "Biblical Authority," 342.
184. Ibid., 344–48.
185. Gerrish, *Grace and Reason* (Clarendon: Oxford, 1962), 171.
186. Hubert Jedin, ed., *Handbuch der Kirchengeschichte*, contributing editors: Erwin Iserloh, Joseph Glazik, Hubert Jedin (Freiburg: Herder, 1967), 4:22ff.
187. Ibid., 23.
188. Ernst-Wilhelm Kohls, *Luther oder Erasmus* (Basel: Reinhardt, 1972), 1:159.
189. Ibid., 2:184.
190. Karl Holl, "Luther," 25.
191. Ibid.
192. Ibid., 26.
193. Ibid., 30–31.
194. Walther von Loewenich. "Evangelische und Katholische Lutherdeutung der Gegenwart im Dialog," *Lutherjahrbuch 1967* (Göttingen: Vandenhoeck und Ruprecht, 1967), 60–89.

195. Ibid., 88.
196. Ibid., 84.
197. Ibid., 85.
198. Joseph Lortz, *Geschichte der Kirche*, vol. 2 (Münster: Aschendorf, 1964), 68–170.
199. Ibid., 68.
200. Ibid., 70–73.
201. Ibid., 89.
202. Ibid., 93.
203. Ibid., 96
204. Ibid., 122.
205. Joseph Lortz, *The Reformation in Germany*, vol. 2, trans. Ronald Walls (New York: Herder and Herder, 1969).
206. Ibid., 340–41.
207. Ibid., 342–43.
208. Ibid., 347.
209. Ibid., 348.
210. Joseph Lortz, "The Basic Elements of Luther's Intellectual Style," in *Catholic Scholars Dialogue with Luther*, ed. Jared Wicks (Chicago: Loyola University Press, 1970).
211. Ibid., 5, 9.
212. Ibid., 24, 30.
213. Ibid., 22.
214. Erwin Iserloh, "Luther's Christ-Mysticism," ibid, 38–39.
215. D. Hermann Pesch, "Existential and Sapiential Theology," ibid.
216. Ibid., 75.
217. Hermann Pesch, "Twenty Years of Catholic Luther Research," *Lutheran World* 13 (1966).
218. Ibid., 307.
219 Ibid., 309.
220. Ibid., 315.
221. Rupp, *Righteousness*, 27.
222. Ibid., 274. For other criticisms of Lortz, see Friedrich Kantzenbach, "Luther Research," esp. 258; *Lutheran World* 13 (1966), esp. 258; Remigius Bäumer et al., *Martin Luther und der Papst* (Münster: Aschendorf, 1970), esp. 98.
223. Albert von Brandenburg, in *Luther und die Theologie der Gegenwart*, 100.
224. Ibid., 102.
225. Albert von Brandenburg, *Die Zukunft des Martin Luthers* (Münster: Aschendorf, 1977).
226. Ibid., 45–50.
227. Ibid., 50.
228. Harry McSorley, *Luther: Right or Wrong?* (New York: Newman/Minneapolis: Augsburg, 1969).
229. Ibid., 3; emphasis added.
230. Ibid., 7.
231. See esp. Peter Manns, *Lutherforschung Heute: Krise und Aufbruch* (Wiesbaden: Steiner, 1967).
232. Wolfgang Seibel and O. Hermann Pesch, *Luther Heute* (Kevelaer Rheinland: Butzon u. Bercker, 1969).
233. Heinrich Bornkamm, *Luther's World*, 280.
234. Idem., *Luther and the Old Testament*, 190.
235. Althaus, *Theology* 51.

236. *WA TR* 1:674.
237. *WA TR* 5:5677.

Chapter 6

1. Donald Dayton, "The Battle for the Bible Rages On," *TToday* 37 (1980): 79–84. Cf. B. B. Warfield, *The Inspiration and Authority of the Bible* (Philadelphia: Presbyterian & Reformed, 1948), 169.
2. For convenience, I will use "believe" and "accept" synonymously throughout this paper. This is most likely mistaken. See John Perry, "Belief and Acceptance," *Midwest Studies in Philosophy V: Studies in Epistemology*, ed. Peter French, Theodore Vehiling, Jr., and Howard Wettstein (Minneapolis: University of Minnesota Press, 1980), 533–42. Further, I shall use "rationality of inerrancy" for "rationality of the belief that inerrancy is true."
3. Cf. Carl Hempel, *Philosophy of Natural Science* (Englewood Cliffs, N.J.: Prentice-Hall, 1966), 10–18; R. Harre, *The Philosophies of Science* (Oxford: Oxford University Press, 1972), 35–48. For a more technical treatment of induction and its justification, see Wesley Salmon, *The Foundation of Scientific Inference* (Pittsburgh: University of Pittsburgh Press, 1966).
4. See Dewey M. Beegle, *Scripture, Tradition, and Infallibility* (Grand Rapids: Eerdmans, 1973), 15–19, 175ff.
5. Daniel Fuller, *Hermeneutics* (Pasadena: Fuller Theological Seminary, 1974), ix–22.
6. Clark Pinnock, *The Scripture Principle* (San Francisco: Harper & Row, 1984), 59–60. See also p. 76.
7. Timothy Phillips, "The Argument for Inerrancy: An Analysis," *JASA* 31 (1979): 86. See also Pinnock, *Principle*, 231; Robert H. Gundry, *Matthew: A Commentary on His Literary and Theological Art* (Grand Rapids: Eerdmans, 1982), 639.
8. Beegle, *Scripture*, 15–19, 175–79.
9. This seems to be assumed by Robert Gundry. See Robert Gundry, "A Response to 'Methodological Unorthodoxy,'" *JETS* 26 (1983): 95.
10. For an ontological analysis of acts of knowing, see Dallas Willard, *Logic and the Objectivity of Knowledge* (Athens, Ohio: Ohio University Press, 1984).
11. In the article cited above, Timothy Phillips is wrong when he says that foundationalism is the view embraced by all defenders of inerrancy. See Norman Geisler, "Inerrancy and Foundationalism," *BEPS* 3 (1980): 1–5. Even thinkers like Quine, Rorty, and Kuhn admit that there are beliefs closer to the periphery of one's web of belief which receive support from beliefs closer to the core of one's web. See James Cornman, "Foundational versus Nonfoundational Theories of Empirical Justification," *Essays on Knowledge and Justification*, ed. George Pappas and Marshall Swan (Ithaca, N.Y.: Cornell University Press, 1978), 229–52.
12. Alvin Plantinga, "Reason and Belief in God," *Faith in Rationality*, ed. Alvin Plantinga and Nicholas Wolterstorff (Notre Dame, Ind.: University of Notre Dame Press, 1983), 16–93.
13. See Roderick Chisholm, "A Version of Foundationalism," *Midwest Studies in Philosophy V: Studies in Epistemology*, ed. Peter French, Theodore Vehiling, Jr., and Howard Wettstein (Minneapolis: University of Minnesota Press, 1980), 543–64.
14. Plantinga, "Reason," 20–24.
15. See Larry Wright, *Better Reasoning* (New York: Holt, Rinehart, and Winston, 1982), 47–105.
16. Cf. Larry Laudan, *Progress and Its Problems* (Berkeley: University of

California Press, 1977), 155–222; or see Laudan's more recent work, *Science and Values* (Berkeley: University of California Press, 1984). I have argued against conceptual relativism elsewhere: see my "Kuhn's Epistemology: A Paradigm Afloat," *BEPS* (1981): 33–60.

17. I use *"prima facie* justified" in John Pollock's sense. See his *Knowledge and Justification* (Princeton, N.J.: Princeton University Press, 1974), 23–49.

18. Thus, I do not believe the doctrine of inerrancy should be approached by a believer with what Van A. Harvey calls the morality of historical knowledge, namely, methodological skepticism. See Van A. Harvey, *The Historian and the Believer* (New York: Macmillan, 1966).

19. Plantinga, "Reason," 50.

20. See Geisler, "Inerrancy and Foundationalism," for an excellent discussion of this issue.

21. See John Montgomery, "The Theologian's Craft: A Discussion of Theory Formation and Theory Testing in Theology," in *The Suicide of Christian Theology* (Minneapolis: Bethany Fellowship, 1970), 267–313; Arthur Holmes, "Ordinary Language Analysis and Theological Method," *BETS* 11 (1968): 131–38; Norman L. Geisler, "Theological Method and Inerrancy: A Reply to Professor Holmes," *BETS* 11 (1968): 139–46; A. F. Holmes, "Reply to N. L. Geisler," *BETS* 11 (1968): 194–95; Paul Feinberg, "The Meaning of Inerrancy," *Inerrancy*, ed. Norman L. Geisler (Grand Rapids: Zondervan, 1979), 265–304.

22. For a simple introduction to scientific methodology, see V. James Mannoia, *What is Science?* (Lanham, Md.: University Press of America, 1980).

23. Cf. E. D. Hirsh (*Validity is Interpretation* [New Haven, Conn.: Yale University Press, 1967]) for the application of this point to hermeneutics.

24. See W. H. Newton-Smith, *The Rationality of Science* (Boston: Routledge & Kegan Paul, 1981), 19–43.

25. Theory independent facts do, however, exist and they ground the truth of our judgments. See Kevin Mulligan, Peter Simons, and Barry Smith, "Truth Makers," *Philosophy and Phenomenological Research* 44 (1981): 287–321.

26. Laudan, *Progress*, 1–120.

27. See Thomas Kuhn, *The Structure of Scientific Revolutions* (Chicago: University of Chicago Press, 1979); Neal Gillespie, *Charles Darwin and the Problem of Creation* (Chicago: University of Chicago Press, 1979); Stanley L. Jaki, *The Road of Science and the Ways to God* (Chicago: University of Chicago Press, 1978).

28. For a helpful treatment of ad hoc hypotheses in science, see Hempel, *Philosophy*, 22–30.

29. Cf. J. P. Moreland, *Universals, Qualities, and Quality-Instances: A Defense of Realism* (Lanham, Md.: University Press of America, 1985).

30. Warfield, *Inspiration*, 169–75.

31. Roderick Chisholm, *The Problem of Criterion* (Milwaukee, Wis.: Marquette University Press, 1973).

32. See Cornman, "Foundational."

33. See Mas Black, "Reasoning with Loose Concepts," *Dialogue* 2 (1963): 1–12.

Chapter 7

1. Charles H. Kraft, *Christianity in Culture* (Maryknoll, N.Y.: Orbis Books, 1979).

2. Ibid., 18.

3. Ibid., 124.

4. Ibid., 125.

5. Ibid., 12.
6. Ibid., 58.
7. Ibid., 14.
8. Ibid., 7.
9. Ibid., 8.
10. Ibid., 34–35.
11. Ibid., 36.
12. Ibid.
13. Ibid., 193.
14. Ibid., 204.
15. Ibid., 211.
16. Ibid., 33.
17. Ibid., 9.
18. *Religion and the Transformation of Society* (Cambridge: Cambridge University Press, 1971), 5.
19. Ibid., 49.
20. Ibid., 99.
21. Ibid., 50.
22. Ibid., 6.
23. Ibid., 12.
24. Ibid., 52.
25. Ibid.
26. Ibid., 54.
27. Ibid., 57ff.
28. Ibid., 55.
29. Ibid., 56.
30. Ibid., 144.
31. Ibid., 184.
32. Ibid., 115.
33. Ibid., 114.
34. Ibid., 111.
35. Ibid., 115.
36. Ibid., 187.
37. Ibid., 122.
38. Ibid., 120.
39. Ibid., 122.
40. Ibid., 132.
41. Ibid., 215.
42. Ibid., 123.
43. Ibid., 129.
44. Ibid., 116.
45. Ibid., 133.
46. Ibid., 169–70.
47. Ibid., 124–25.
48. Ibid., 126.
49. Ibid., 128.
50. Ibid., 169ff.
51. Ibid., 130.
52. Ibid., 134ff.
53. Ibid., 103.
54. Ibid., 117.
55. Ibid., 118.

56. Ibid.
57. Ibid.
58. Ibid.
59. Ibid., 119.
60. Ibid., 189.
61. Ibid., 184.
62. Ibid., 186.
63. Ibid., 212.
64. Ibid., 256.
65. Ibid., 304.
66. Ibid., 119.
67. Ibid., 173.
68. Ibid., 216.
69. Ibid., 215.
70. Ibid., 211, quoting another.
71. Ibid., 223.
72. Ibid., 197.
73. Ibid., 188.
74. Ibid., 14.
75. Ibid., 15.
76. Ibid., 16.
77. Ibid., 129.
78. Ibid., 213.
79. Ibid., 136.
80. Ibid., 137.
81. Ibid., 138.
82. Ibid., 139.
83. Ibid., 188.
84. Ibid., 137.
85. Ibid., 188.
86. Ibid., 16–17.
87. Ibid., 17.
88. Ibid., 114.
89. Ibid., 103.
90. Ibid., 33, emphasis mine.
91. Ibid., 37.
92. Ibid., 38.
93. Ibid., 133.
94. Ibid., 145.
95. Ibid., 147ff.
96. Ibid., 148.
97. Ibid., 179.
98. Ibid., 180.
99. Ibid., 183.
100. Ibid., 204ff.
101. *Biblical Inspiration* (Philadelphia: Westminster, 1972), 155.
102. Ibid., 212.
103. Ibid., 213.
104. Ibid., 210.
105. Ibid., 224.
106. Ibid., 221.
107. Ibid., 216.

108. Ibid., 187.
109. Ibid., 261ff.
110. Ibid., 263.
111. Ibid., 269.
112. Ibid., 276ff.
113. Ibid., 280.
114. Ibid., 291ff.
115. Ibid., 267.
116. Ibid., 294.
117. Ibid., 296.
118. Ibid., 297.
119. Ibid.
120. Ibid., 297ff.
121. Ibid., 34.
122. Ibid., 29.
123. Ibid., 12.